Nature in the Global South

Paul Greenough and Anna Lowenhaupt Tsing, editors

NATURE IN

THE GLOBAL SOUTH

Environmental Projects in South and Southeast Asia

Duke University Press   Durham & London   2003

© 2003 Duke University Press

All rights reserved

Printed in the United States of America

on acid-free paper ∞

Designed by C. H. Westmoreland

Typeset in Sabon with Twentieth Century display

by Keystone Typesetting, Inc.

Library of Congress Cataloging-in-Publication

Data appear on the last printed page of

this book.

Sponsored by the Southeast Asia Program

of the Social Science Research Council and the

American Council of Learned Societies

CONTENTS

Discursive Environments

for Environmental Discourses

The essays in this volume were gathered in a conference entitled Environmental Discourses and Human Welfare in South and Southeast Asia held in Hilo, Hawaii, in December 1995; they were subsequently revised by the authors, to whom the editors tender their apologies for a substantial delay in publication.[1] One of the several purposes of the Hilo conference was to discuss the unexpected agency of nature, which sometimes rises up against our most careful schemes and plans, and so it is perhaps fitting that from the first many things did not go as we expected. The history of the gathering that produced this particular set of essays is then of some interest in explaining the shape and composition of the volume.

The conference owed its form to the then current organization of the Social Science Research Council (SSRC), New York, which sponsored the conference not only financially but intellectually. At that time, "joint committees" of the American Council of Learned Societies and the Social Science Research Council were organized by world regions; one of the tasks of these committees was to bring together interdisciplinary conferences within and occasionally across regional specialties to explore new scholarly directions. In the spirit of these committees, our conference was planned as a discussion between humanists and social scientists about multiple discourses on environmental issues; we further hoped to make use of the common knowledge of South Asian and Southeast Asian specialists, respectively, at the same time as we began a dialogue across these two regions. Yet none of these things was simple. Humanists and social scientists have been talking to each other for decades, but every newly imagined domain offers a tug-of-war; "environmental discourses" was no exception. The topic, indeed, had first been conceptualized as "environmental narratives," but humanists in the joint committees objected that this conceptualization required specialized disciplinary knowledge that social scientists who came together to talk about the environment would not have. We changed the frame and rewrote the proposal as "environmental discourses"; this time it was the social scientists on the joint committees who objected that discourse was a humanist preoccupation not grounded and hardheaded enough for environmental concerns. We rewrote the proposal again and again and finally slipped by with "environmental discourses and human welfare." Although a conference proposal may never have been rewritten quite so many times, it is a positive testament to the joint committee system that it allowed this long discussion to happen, opening a space of study and reflection that is still new in environmental studies.[2] However carefully crafted, the proposal was far from the end of the line; there was still the conference, which was plagued with technical crises. In consultation with the SSRC staff, we agreed to hold the conference in Hawaii, as it was economically situated among the three locations of most participants: the U.S. mainland, South Asia, and Southeast Asia.[3] Yet as unexpected costs mounted we came under fire for picking a vacation spot instead of a more serious Third World university location. A few weeks before the conference, one participant went into political exile and could not attend; another was confusingly told not to attend by a staff member. To cap off our problems, a partisan struggle in the U.S. Congress led to the shutdown of the entire federal government only a few days before the conference, leaving us without our meeting rooms and lodgings in the federally managed Volcano National Park near Hilo. Last minute arrangements were hectic, and we lost one participant, briefly, who flew to the wrong island. One of two general discussants — who we hoped would craft the frames to hold the conference together — called from the airport to tell us of a family emergency that stopped her from getting on her flight; another participant, said by the hotel management to be resting in his room, turned out to be in a hospital in London. Many papers, which we had asked participants to distribute a month in advance, of course came in at the last minute. In this hectic scene, it was difficult for the organizers to tell exactly what was happening intellectually.

One thing was clear: few of the participants were convinced by the "environmental discourses" framework. Although as organizers we had tried to explain what we meant by the term in the proposal, some participants who mentioned the term in their initial papers wanted it to mean something else. As much as we had insisted that we used the term *discourse* to refer to categorizations with material effects, some participants wanted to use it to refer to insincere political rhetoric. Of those who understood the term in the way we intended, some felt tired of the concept. One, ironically, suggested that it would be more up-to-date to speak of narratives. Others felt hostile to the term, arguing that *environ-*

mental discourses added nothing to the classical sociological concepts of interests, institutions, and ideologies.[4]

The cross-regional conversation was also rather different than what we had imagined. It turned out that, unselfconsciously, we had allowed South Asianists and Southeast Asianists to constitute regions in entirely different ways. The South Asianists were mainly scholars of India, and most were of Indian origin. They immediately fell into detailed conversations and debates involving the history and geography of particular Indian events and locations. In contrast, the Southeast Asianists, largely non–Southeast Asian, worked in four separate countries with markedly different histories; their conversations assumed little prior historical knowledge of the cases they described and instead tended toward comparative and theoretical debate. Regional knowledge meant something so different in each case that the South Asianists were dumbfounded when one participant (Michael R. Dove) not only attempted a cross-regional comparison but also, against all precedent, centered his South Asian case on Pakistan.

In hindsight, we see that the dialogue between South and Southeast Asianists drew from the distinctive legacies of each. Each region, indeed, offers a particular perspective with which to think about what "regions" might mean for scholars. A term like *Southeast Asia* requires one to think about the artificiality — and creative genius — of regionalisms because very few scholars have ever tried to imagine a Southeast Asia disciplined by cultural, political, or historical continuities; regional scholarship has depended instead on picking up theoretically stimulating differences, unexpected parallels, and moments of convergence, syncretism, or collaboration among varied colonial, national, cultural, ethnic, class, and community histories. South Asian studies offers a different perspective for rethinking regionalisms. Scholars from this region have raised questions about the colonial discourses through which ideas about regional "cultures" were elaborated, about the intraregional differences made by subaltern class, caste, religious, gender and ethnic status and about the worldwide spread of diasporic imaginative worlds. To talk comparatively about South and Southeast Asia in the present, then, is to draw on distinct critical legacies. Rather than opening the window on a singular "South and Southeast Asian" region, we have leapt into the middle of ongoing conversations about imagined geographies to find provocative comparisons, transregional similarities, and debates over appropriate and inappropriate matters of scale.[5]

Yet for all this divergence and debate, we did learn something, several somethings, which have gone into the revision of all the essays, making them speak to each other in new and unexpected ways. It would have been impossible to come to these insights without the awkward discussion between humanists and social scientists, the debate over the usefulness of the term *discourse,* and the rockily convened opportunity to speak to each other about connected yet contrasting historical and ethnographic cases. First, we found that landscapes and communities are assembled in changing *environmental projects* in which rhetorics and practices come together in finite moments of politically persuasive and materially effective configuration. Science, state administration, and social movements have played central roles in shaping and reshaping environmental projects. They make forests as well as cities, farms and villages as well as factories and prisons. Second, it is only in examining the *practical enactments* of these environmental projects — the ceremonies of monks, the demonstrations of activists, the timber measurements of foresters, the settling strategies of villagers, the immunizations of health officials — that scholars can appreciate how projects work "on the ground" in every sense. What are called environments, that is, relations between people and nature, get made and remade not so much in the plans but in the process. Third, even where particular rhetorics hold great sway, *environmental terminologies* rarely mean the same things to everyone involved. The political process always involves stretching, debating, revitalizing, and evading prior agreements. As allies break with each other, they dramatize their interests and ideologies as separate; as opponents and interlocutors become allies, they hide their differences in common frames and signs. Hence, stability and agreement may hide flux and contest, and common projects are not necessarily good ones. Fourth, these methodological engagements reveal *distinct periodizations of environmental commitment* in South and Southeast Asia. While no one at the conference would make any claims of homogeneity for the regions, a three-part chronology emerged in an unspoken way to offer a heuristic guide to further conversation. Imagine, then, three eras of environmental engagement: (1) a colonial era of resource management concerned to protect natural resources from human misuse, native or otherwise; (2) a post–World War II developmentalist era of population management and economic growth in which natural resource policy has been secondary to human developmentalist goals; and (3) a postdevelopment "southern environmentalist" mobilization since the 1970s in which values of social justice, on the one hand, and indigenous, romantic, or scientific nature appreciation, on the other, blend to contest top-down developmentalism as well as neocolonial protectionism.

Clearly, none of these environmental commitments ever wielded a hegemonic set of ideas or institutions capable of shutting off debate; no environmental commitment has been snuffed out just because another emerged. The periodization seems useful, however, in framing the debates and challenges present in both South and Southeast Asian studies.

These scholarly agendas inform the essays in this volume. Several discuss how concerns with conservation emerged from colonial interests in observation and administration (Anderson, Zerner, Jeffery and Sundar). Several others describe the environment-making and environment-destroying practices of developmentalist states (Greenough, Peluso, Sivaramakrishnan). Almost half began with the dilemmas of contemporary southern environmentalism; in particular, they investigate villagers' points of view (Gold, Darlington) and show the divergent agendas that divide some villagers and the activists who claim to advocate for them (Baviskar). One surveys a campaign raised initially by a forest-dwelling people against loggers that in time spiraled out to include numerous sites of support around the world (Brosius). Two others offer provocative and very broad historical and regional overviews (Dove, Tsing).

One contribution of reading these chapters together is in showing environmentalist goals, rhetorics, and dreams in relation to the challenge of "sustainable development" they are often pitted against. Whether sustainable development will go down in history as an expansion of authoritarian developmentalism or a movement for local empowerment and environmental survival is yet to be seen. The outcome is not predetermined, and these essays suggest numerous alternative points of possibility in an always unequal struggle.

Readers will appreciate the authors' scholarly thoroughness and detailed grasp of local and regional environmental issues. In publishing the collection, however, we also have the ambition to show a nonacademic audience how readily expert studies of the environment dovetail with broad political concerns for human welfare. A sense of possible welfare improvements in South and Southeast Asia is the unspoken "conditionality" that gives these chapters their heft. To highlight these possibilities we have labored in the introduction over the scenario of a fantasied Museum of Human Welfare. While this is an effort to frame, as if through the lens of a settled history, the major themes that agitated environmentalists at the end of the twentieth century, we expect that readers will focus on the themes rather than the fantasy frame. In any case, it is premature to talk about building a Museum of Human Welfare; not only are too many of the issues raised in the essays left unresolved, but human welfare itself is a discursively moving target that may look very different fifty or seventy-five years hence.

1 Four other scholars — Suman Sahai, Ravi Rajan, Philip Hirsch, and Ramachandra Guha — were very active participants in the Hilo conference, and
their rich empirical knowledge and abundant insights made a strong impression. Alas, their contributions have not been included as essays in
Nature in the Global South. The historian Richard Grove, who fell ill as
the participants were winging their way to Hawaii, was a much missed
presence there and here.

2 Many colleagues worked on writing and rewriting the conference proposal. Jane Atkinson, Ann Gold, Vicente Rafael, Ravi Rajan, Toby Volkman, and Charles Zerner were all key contributors to the process.

3 We wish to thank David Lelyveld who during 1995 was the responsible
South and Southeast Asia program officer at SSRC; Lelyveld was a model
of tact and skill and greatly contributed to the conference's success.

4 Nonetheless, *environmental discourses* was clearly in the air in the mid-
1990s; at least ten serious studies or collections employing the term in the
title or subtitle have appeared since 1995: Renn, Webler, and Wiedemann
1995; Hajer 1995; Dupuis and Vandergeest 1995; Milton 1996; Dryzek
1997; Harre, Brockmeier, and Muhlhausler 1998; Darier 1999; Benton
and Short 1999, 2000; Coppola and Karis 2000.

5 A recent development is a new interdisciplinary journal, *Bridges: Berkeley
Research Journal on South and Southeast Asia,* founded in 2002, which is
committed to dialogue between the fields of South and Southeast Asian
studies. We interpret its appearance to the dissatisfaction with existing
regional divisions of thought and labor.

Paul Greenough and Anna Lowenhaupt Tsing

INTRODUCTION

UPSTAIRS IN THE MUSEUM

It is late morning a century in the future. You are between flights and striding toward a grandly built edifice, the Museum of Human Welfare. The renowned museum, its wings forming a huge compass rose, sits on the site of a former prison in Port Blair, green capital of the Andaman Islands, a favorite stopover on the Kamchatka to Capetown shuttle. Unlike other museums, the Museum of Human Welfare displays no objects; instead, its halls are filled with HoloVue™ screens that conjure up historical ensembles — recordings of archived voices, images and texts in many media. Accompanying these vivid holographic displays is an interpretive narrative that retells past struggles to protect bodily health and longevity, to shield face-to-face comradeship from all scaling up exercises, and to stabilize the biodiversity that has arisen from evolution rather than genetic engineering. In the museum's central foyer, there are young men and women, docents, one of whom sits with you and relates the events leading up to the passage of the Universal Declaration of Responsible Interconnections in the year 2057. This was the famous global compact that made it a criminal act for governments, public corporations, or private institutions to exert claims over natural or social resources without first assessing and publishing the probable impacts on nature and human welfare. *Impact* was defined broadly to include not only the immediate destructive effects on natural and social systems but the subtler stresses at three and four removes that would eventually wither the most fragile ecosystem and the most obscure tribe. Before 2057, mistaken policies based on opaque slogans of progress, growth, development, and nation building had destroyed whole ecologies and communities. Hence the reality-defining and world-making effects of national, developmental, and corporate rhetorics came under the closest scrutiny. In the decade after 2057, a period when the global economy skidded badly, thousands of anthropologists, rhetoricians, critical theorists, historians, and ecologists were sent into the world as observers and listeners. As a result of their researches — which involved speaking with a million peasants, forest dwellers, artists, politicians, industrialists, journalists, and many others and assembling a huge archive of documents, testimonies, scientific studies, and off-air transcripts (all of which are now stored in the museum's lower level) — the shadowy links and levers that have always connected discursive practices to power and interest were demystified. Researchers homed in on particularly tragic episodes in which discourses and policies promising wealth, security, and long life in fact initiated a downward cycle of pain, poverty, and insecurity. The ensuing investigative reports (known as Butterfly Bulletins because of a distinctive logo on the researchers' caps) were then taught in schools everywhere in accord with provisions in the Declaration of Responsible Interconnections. This giant investigative and educational effort, which continued to find new objects of concern, continues at a lessened pace down to the present day.

If you stand before one of the museum's HoloVue™ screens and utter a string of precise terms — for example, *Chicago, urban wage workers, political economy, mid–nineteenth century* or *Amazon basin, indigenous peoples, human rights, late twentieth century* — a holo narrator springs forward like a genie to guide you through these poor, working, and marginalized people's struggles during the most distressing eras of the past. But if you are uncertain about how to begin, the narrator senses your hesitation and discreetly prompts you with some well-known categories and locations — for example, *landless laborers, Bangladesh; rubber tappers, Belize;* or *charcoal makers, Mozambique.* Having made a choice, you can then command "Close up!" or "Interpret!" which slows down the flow of information and lets you interrogate terms, concepts, technologies, and institutions that once shaped action and affected survival. Giving finer-grained commands such as "Historicize!" or "Deconstruct!" will elicit even greater detail, frequently in the form of contending voices; these disputants sound remarkably like scholars wrangling in academic seminars. On the contrary, repeatedly uttering the commands "Step back! Summarize!" will cause the narration to retreat from the local to the regional, hemispheric, and then global levels until our whirling planet is observed from the widest perspective. At this scale, the history of the long struggle to preserve the biosphere and secure human welfare turns noticeably melancholy.

A peculiarity of the museum is that the clarity and detail of the exhibits taper off as visitors' inquiries approach the present day. Now and then one hears hesitation in a narrative. It appears that there is a backlog; while the museum's capacity for storage and display is almost limitless, human effort is still required to select, interpret, and dramatize the raw data and archived images. Another peculiarity is that the spoken account accompanying each exhibit subtly alters its emphasis according to a visitor's age, gender, and social class, so that when different visitors ask about the same topic they will sometimes come away with contradictory memories about what was highlighted. Nonetheless, such is the poignancy of these narratives that few who spend any time in the museum emerge unmoved.

Now, oriented, forewarned, and sure of your own interests, you approach a vacant HoloVue™ screen and give your first commands: "South and Southeast Asia, environmental struggles, late twentieth century. Close up! Interpret!" As the screen swirls and the narrator approaches to begin a response, you interrupt with even more specific concerns: "Why did environmental struggles come to prominence in South and Southeast Asia in the late twentieth century? Against what previous social and environmental programs did they argue? How did mid-twentieth-century natural resource management affect human welfare?" The narrator nods and begins:

"After World War II, colonialism was discredited in South and Southeast Asia. The common international program for economic and political coordination in the newly emerging postcolonial nations was called 'development,' a seductive concept that suggested a well-known path of transformation to a destined maturity. Development plans from the 1950s through the 1980s drew heavily on colonial era natural resource management projects even as they opposed the idea of colonialism. More so than under colonial science and administration, natural resources were placed at the center of the new nations' political ambitions. It was the hope for rapid advancement through the exploitation of resources, tied to cultural and technological modernization, that produced the national dream of 'development.'

"Under the sway of the development dream, new nations became the appropriate managers of natural resources. As had been the case under colonialism, resource use was imagined from the perspective of international elites, not local residents. Elements of nature — forests, soil, minerals, water — were defined as 'natural resources' only if they were of use as raw materials for industry; they would be managed rationally by national bureaucrats to produce industrial growth. In this framework, local residents were mostly sidelined or criminalized, while ecological regeneration was ignored. Thus, the development dream set in motion the linked challenges of environmental integrity and social justice for local resource users by destroying ecologies and communities with an equal vigor."

"But wait," you protest. "Weren't those postcolonial blunders corrected in the 1990s by 'sustainable development'?" The narrator continues:

"By the 1990s it became clear that development programs had rarely resulted in human well-being and that deep concern about the environment was justified. The critics of development became an organized force everywhere, and environmental movements grew up worldwide. Some groups were mostly concerned about the survival of cherished plants and animals, while others focused attention on difficult human living conditions. Despite their differences, they agreed that environmental destruction for the sake of economic growth, or for the sake of the nation, was not a good idea. In this context, corporations and states quickly learned to use the language of environmental preservation to justify their projects. One crowning piece of rhetoric welded *sustainability* to *development:* that is, the advocates of development promised that it would henceforth be responsible and not lead to permanent and irreplaceable human and environmental destruction. Without binding common standards for 'destruction,' however, *sustainable development,* too, often meant that states and corporations continued with their same old practices while claiming to be anxiously thinking about people and the environment. In other cases, 'sustainable development' led to new departures but not necessarily good ones. For example, exotic tree plantations with few local uses and fewer ecological benefits were substituted for natural forests. While the rhetoric of sustainable development sometimes brought national resource managers into productive dialogue with environmentalists, more frequently it meant that national resource managers could dismiss social and environmental groups by claiming that governments and corporations were already addressing the problems. By the turn of the twenty-first century, the balance sheet on sustainable development suggested a giant fraud."

So, you ask, "Who were the environmentalists you mention in South and Southeast Asia? How significant were twentieth-century southern environmental movements?" The response is as follows:

"In the 1960s and 1970s, environmentalism was mainly known as a social movement of the North; when it reached the South, it usually took a limited form, favoring northern conservation priorities — 'saving' tigers, 'rescuing' elephants, 'protecting' biodiversity, and so on. In the 1980s and 1990s, however, southern environmental movements blossomed and began to articulate a new agenda. In some places, villagers organized themselves to resist the enforcement of national and international development plans. This rural mobilization often took place in concert with the efforts of new national and international antidevelopment organizations and green campaigns. Middle-class professionals and students were prominent in the national environmental movements in many southern nations. Some of these movements were particularly concerned with urban environmental problems; others paid more attention to rural people's subsistence needs. At the core of these national movements there were often nongovernmental organizations (NGOs) that were linked regionally or internationally, forming wider networks of financial aid, political resolve and information sharing. For their concerns to be listened to and to be seen as legitimate, however, all national environmental movements crucially required some degree of collaboration with community spokespeople.

"One kind of rural struggle that became very important in this period involved 'tribal,' 'indigenous,' and 'traditional' peoples. While it was possible until late into the twentieth century for some of these marginalized peoples to live their lives far away from state development projects, and thus to retain a good deal of their cultural and political autonomy, their isolation ended in the 1980s and 1990s when state agencies and corporations pushed their projects to the farthest edges and deepest interiors of their territories. Too often this 'development' authorized the theft of marginal peoples' lands and resources and forced them to bow to repressive state demands. What changed in the last decade of the twentieth century was that effective resistance became possible as local communities linked themselves to national and international allies. These wider movements championed the causes of displaced and expropriated marginal groups, and together with local leaders they articulated demands for 'indigenous rights' as well as social and environmental justice. In this context, marginal and tribal people's struggles were sometimes linked to poor farmers' struggles and past national populisms to reframe democratic politics.

"Another type of environmentalism that grew in force in the 1980s and 1990s was called *global environmentalism*. Although there was considerable struggle over this term, it most often referred to the environmental politics of internationally recognized politicians, resource managers, and scientists. These international leaders and experts imagined themselves to be in charge of worldwide environmental management programs — for example, slowing global warming, rain forest logging, or the harvesting of marine resources. Northern conservation scientists were usually enthusiastic about these positions, but many southern environmentalists opposed global environmentalism, seeing in it an extension of colonial management science practices."

You ask, "Were the South and Southeast Asian regions sites of unusual social and environmental activism? Was there something special in these areas that gave rise to fervent environmentalist activity?"

At this, the narrator peers out and searches your face and those of your companions before answering. "Hard questions! The unselfconscious way in which you use the terms *region* and *area,* though, is a problem. Let me explain. After World War II, the United States became a leader in higher education. One scholarly framework introduced at this time divided the world into a handful of geographic regions ('areas'), through which, it was believed, scholars in all disciplines could better explain political and cultural dilemmas. Terms such as *South Asia, Middle East,* and *Southeast Asia* were formulated in this scholarly moment, while an older terminology — *Indies, Levant, Tropics* — simply faded away. There quickly grew up around the new terminology interdisciplinary practices and institutions that made each region seem unique, and what had been self-conscious geographic innovations in the 1950s came to feel like real, substantive differences by the 1970s. Regional or area geography meanwhile spilled out of universities into government and the media and then into everyday conversation.

"To be sure, dividing scholarship according to an 'area studies' framework was highly productive and unleashed much creative work. Yet toward the end of the twentieth century some scholars began to feel constrained; they formulated cross-regional and transarea research questions that brought into doubt the logic of regionalism itself. Southeast Asia was a particularly good part of the world in which to rethink this logic because few scholars had seriously proposed that it possessed an enduring essence or was disciplined from within by shared cultural principles or distinctive social practices. It was apparent to most observers that a region that claimed to group the Philippines with Thailand or Cambodia with Indonesia was merely nominal. Scholarly attempts to identify common cultural themes, as well as borrowings, convergences, and moments of shared trajectory, refreshed a field known mainly for the disparateness of national and cultural studies. South Asia, on the other hand, presented a more formidable illusion of regional unity; serious efforts *had* been made to describe its enduring practices, deep essences, and social continuities. Yet by the late twentieth century scholars revealed how the premise of deep and broad social and cultural continuities had masked intraregional differences according to class, caste, religious, and ethnic status; further, they clarified the role of colonialism in shaping these essentializing discourses to produce civil order and governmentality.

"By the end of the twentieth century, then, many South and Southeast Asian scholars no longer felt impelled to play the regional game; they were determined instead to find an appropriate geographic scale for each research issue. Although we still use the terms *South Asia* and *Southeast Asia* in the museum, we do so with skepticism, knowing that words and concepts reveal certain realities while blinding us to others.

"Now—to answer your question about the origins of environmental activism—by the 1980s, nongovernmental organizations blossomed across both South and Southeast Asia to address linked problems of environmental preservation and social justice. These organizations were diverse, yet they participated through telecommunications and face-to-face meetings in loosely linked conversations that were stimulated by international campaigns and conferences. Organizations such as the World Rainforest Movement worked to create ties between key South and Southeast Asian activists, while exemplary grassroots movements, such as the North Indian Chipko struggle and the Save the Narmada River Movement, inspired attention throughout southern Asia. By the 1990s, the voices of prominent South and Southeast Asian environmentalists and their movements had become globally influential, pressing for 'southern' strategies that differed sharply from those found in the north. Scholarly research contextualized these movements in regional politics and culture, assessed and criticized their accomplishments, and brought them to new arenas and audiences. In fact, scholarship and activism proceeded in relation to each other, both making human welfare a key issue in assessing environmental policies and setting the stage for twenty-first-century concerns.

"Take for example, the scholarly reinterpretation of colonial forest conservation, which remade southern Asian landscapes in the nineteenth and early twentieth centuries. Colonial foresters turned the forest into a new kind of natural object, altering its composition at will and re-generating timber needed for imperial expansion. Yet they did so by removing and regulating forest-dwelling peoples and changing forever the state's relationships with local populations. Research on forestry in the 1980s and 1990s was influential in demonstrating that colonial con-servation has to be considered simultaneously a form of applied science, an expression of political authority, and a pitiless attack on marginal peoples' subsistence — insights that became the basis of activism.

"Similarly, research on the role of the 'science' behind conservation, not only under colonialism but under the new national governments, was illuminating. For instance, transnational economics and state policy combined in the mid–twentieth century to forge the powerful prescrip-tion called development as the international cure-all for postcolonial nations. At this time, scholars across the political spectrum were deeply involved in making development work; only at the end of the 1980s did they become critical of the project as a whole. An early turning point was research on the effects of the 'Green Revolution' in South and Southeast Asia. (The Green Revolution was the 1970s rural campaign that had pushed farmers to grow high-yielding, genetically engineered crops that required big inputs of chemical fertilizers and pesticides.) Social science was quick to discover the human and environmental disadvantages of raising these crops, which were implicated with concentrating wealth and landholding among the rich, and foisting unemployment, pesticide poisoning, and landlessness on the poor. When policymakers proved deaf to their criticisms, many scholars became alienated from the development agenda. Their research then exposed the often callous design of development programs and the ways in which development led directly to social and environmental destruction.

"Finally, as researchers turned away from the always deferred advent of universal development they began to emphasize the enormous physical and social diversity throughout southern Asia. Indeed, late-twentieth-century South and Southeast Asia included mixed tropical rain forests shaped by generations of tribal forager-cultivators; capital-rich and biodiversity-poor plantations; capital-poor and biodiversity-rich peasant farms; and great, sprawling, pollution-heavy cities. This diversity of landscapes was paralleled by a similar diversity of social-historical landscapes: multiple colonizations by nearly every great world power; adherents of nearly every world religion (and some of the more circumscribed ones); livelihood commitments of every stripe and scale, from peasant tenancies to transnational firms; and political cultures both tolerant and bigoted, practical and utopian, nationalist, universalist, ethnic, sectarian, and pluralist. The significance of this demonstration of diversity was that it subverted national or transnational efforts to apply uniform solutions in every setting or to claim that the wants of a few leading social groups were characteristic of the needs of vast majorities. Scholarship made at least some of the old politics and management games harder to play!"

With this last remark, the narrator nods his head emphatically.

"We've never thought about these issues quite this way," you cry. "Thanks!"

If you take the museum's back staircase and descend three flights, you'll come to a door marked "Staff Access Only." Slip inside, and you find yourself standing in the Auxiliary Museum Collection, a vast space where all manner of currently underused artifacts, documents, and information is stored. The first thing you see is a long bank of desktop computers and other data storage devices surrounded by vast numbers of slipcased books shelved along the outer walls and hundreds of cabinets whose wide roll-out drawers are filled with old-style printed newspapers, maps, and atlases. As your eyes adjust to the dim light, you become aware of a towering glass and metal structure in the center of the great room; this is StorIt™ the automatic storage system, which holds humankind's largest collection of historical and ethnographic records. Ever since the StorIt™ system was installed nearly twenty years ago, museum staff members rarely consult the Auxiliary Collection. On those occasions when a record or book is needed, a dozen robots whir up and down, back and forth, plucking out the required items; later they will return them to their appropriate places.

Go ahead and wander about — the robots won't stop you — and you'll find that other users have snuck into the Auxiliary Collection, just as you have. They're outfitted rather unusually, though. Here's what looks like an eighteenth-century colonial surgeon, his smock stained red-brown, puffing on a Meerschaum pipe; there's an Amazonian shaman with lip plugs of bone and paint on his face. In short order, you'll also see a gray-haired lady birdwatcher wearing sensible shoes and peering through binoculars; a bearded professor meditating cross-legged on the floor; a white-robed marabout in sunglasses clicking prayer beads; and more than a few North American computer nerds, pale-skinned and squinting through thick glasses. What an odd bunch — completely silent as they intently examine books, maps, computers, and paper records. After observing for a while, you realize that their costumes are constantly changing, adding or losing layers of clothing, color, and decoration as they work. Intrigued, you approach what appears to be an elderly Buddhist nun, who turns away and disappears among the cabinets. You follow and make an unexpected discovery: behind the StorIt™ tower there's a cubbyhole with a rice cooker steaming on top of a computer terminal and a cutting board with freshly minced chives. Quilts and extra clothes are piled neatly under the desk. Somebody is living here!

Then it hits you: these strange and unauthorized shape-shifters are the true devotees of the Museum of Human Welfare's vast collection.

They're intellectual freebooters who study the archived records with passion and persistence. They regard old documents and images not just as sources of knowledge but as sources of power. Whether we call them sorcerers, scholars, or petty scientists, they work against the grain to make and remake themselves through their reading, noting, and comparing. See that young man there, sitting across from us with his thick-soled sandals, rough garments, and wild eyes? Don't be surprised if he exactly resembles an Indian environmental activist — he's immersed himself in reading about the 1990s people's movement to save the Narmada River from destructive dams. And look over there at that handsome native hunter with his woven bamboo cap and colored loincloth; he's made himself that way by studying the records of the nomadic Malaysian Penan. These shape-shifting basement folk are eager to relive historical roles, and although they are irregulars they have plenty of insight, integrity, and even influence. Let's see what they are reading.

Ever since the Universal Declaration of Responsible Interconnections, it's been easy to find out what anyone is reading or viewing in the museum's archives. You just click on the "TrakIt"™ icon, and the computer traces the chosen person's viewing history. Take, for example, that orange-robed and shaven-headed Buddhist lay nun three seats down, the one with the wire-rimmed glasses. She's reading about the late-twentieth-century environmental movements in Thailand that brought together poor and marginal rural people with middle-class urban activists. The documents she's viewing now show activist monks discussing the importance of "radical conservatism" in mobilizing villagers to fight for the right to manage their own forests. Just before this, though, she was studying how the Thai state tried to co-opt the middle class into supporting its political and economic agendas for class formation and control. It's clear to her that environmental rhetorics were important tools used by Thai military and state bureaucrats to exert control over late-twentieth-century villagers. Upstairs, in the attractively organized museum exhibits, the staff would know how to represent her insight in an uplifting narrative: the "environmental monks" must ultimately win because they represent the "people," while the bureaucrats must fail because they are liars and scoundrels. But the basement scholars and sorcerers aren't satisfied with simple dualities: reading back and forth between oppositional movements and repressive state development programs, the nun has made notes on a pad beside her terminal. At the top, she has printed and then underlined "Bad Compromises?" while below she has written the following.

1. Monks learn development discourse and adapt it — twist it — for villagers' uses.
2. Elites learn environmental movement rhetoric but deploy it for repressive ends.
3. Discourse and counterdiscourse, each mimics and defaces the other; environments and human welfare concerns are made in this juxtaposition.

As the nun-reader has noted, it is the *interplay* of discourse and counter-discourse that produces environments and human welfare concerns, and, relying on this insight, she conjures herself again and again as she works through the old records. Maybe you think her heartless or cynical in admitting that the productive effects of discourse are used by both repressive governments and oppositional movements, but it is clear from her renunciant's garb that she's taken sides. Still, she's pasted on her terminal a boldly lettered challenge: "YOU THINK I HAVE NO STAN-DARDS BECAUSE I REFUSE TO NATURALIZE YOUR COMPROMISES."

And what about the computer user sitting across the aisle, that man with a balding head, white shirt, and the slightly bulging belly of a civil servant? What's *he* researching? His reading credits show him pursuing late-nineteenth- and early-twentieth-century forestry in India, military hygiene in the Philippines, and Indonesian natural history. "DREAMS, STANDARDS, AND PRACTICES," he has scribbled on a slightly oily nap-kin. "HOW DO THEY GET WRAPPED TOGETHER TO BECOME PROJ-ECTS?" The term *projects* is underlined three times. This sorcerer, too, has gained insights into the making of environments and the foreground-ing of social welfare concerns, which both emerge from the grinding of scientific knowledge and state power. He's added, "EFFECTIVE KNOWL-EDGE REQUIRES EFFECTIVE POWER; PRACTICAL POWER REQUIRES PRACTICAL KNOWLEDGE." There's another regularity that he's found striking: for every late-twentieth-century project on his reading list, there's an early-nineteenth-century analogue. The demon of difference, the specter of comparison, drives his eyes back and forth between the colonial and postcolonial records. Rereading each account from the per-spective of the other, he finds that nineteenth-century projects are still with us at the turn of the twenty-first century but not necessarily in ways their colonial designers intended. For example, national forestry in post-colonial India discovered new economic products and markets, but the independent Indian state never relaxed the controls that had kept vil-lagers in doubt for a century about their rights to gather fuel and minor forest products. Another example: in the Netherlands East Indies, a unified field of science called "natural history" around 1900 had fractured to become Indonesian "conservation biology" and "indigenous knowledge" by 2000. Could these latter two, so completely at odds, share any premise except their common discursive history? Our civil servant-scholar has found that by conjuring with tools of divergence and convergence, of interweaving and interruption, history's agency has brought to life both social facts and natural landscapes. Having had these insights, what are his moral commitments? He, like many scholars, is less resolved than the nun-reader and finds much to admire and much to deplore in both the Dutch and Indonesian periods.

You will say that these basement readers are minor players, and perhaps you are right. They excel at exploring the historical interplay of power and knowledge, but this only stirs the archival dust. The world seems hardly affected. But there's a secret process at work here that not everyone understands. If we reveal it, you can hardly pass it on, being an intruder in the museum archives yourself. So we may as well confess it: these reader-scholar-conjurors are not just reading the museum's documents and viewing its old artifacts. *They're changing them, sometimes little by little and sometimes in great scene-shifting blocs, just as they are changing themselves.* When you stroll in the museum upstairs and listen to the narrators' appalling tales of past injustice or view exhibits that document some thrilling triumph for humankind, the evidence has already been tampered with. Yes! The transparency that narrators and museum exhibits promise is alluring but almost always false because the sorcerers and scholars below have been tampering with the original records. Worse, to the extent that they are good at what they do, you can't tell the difference between the original and reconstituted records. Once documents are read, the history based on them is never the same. We are all stuck with distorted and revisited records, yet these are all the evidence we have.

PERSPECTIVAL KNOWLEDGE

Through the fantasy of a Museum of Human Welfare we have tried to imagine a state of human-environmental relations in which nature isn't solely a resource for corporations and state bureaucracies and livelihood struggles actually meet human needs and protect nonhuman life forms. Some such imagining is required if we are to mobilize against the elite development that grinds down the poor and the rural, against majoritarian ploys that squeeze out minorities, and against a myopic growth ethic that dooms "junk" species to extinction. While action and intervention depend on usable knowledge of the sort so abundantly present in the museum's upstairs exhibits, the figure of the museum's basement archive is meant to suggest the ambiguities and complexities of knowledge making. Indeed, there will always be tension between the effective truths of committed action and the ironies and dilemmas of perspectival knowledge; this tension appears as a contrast between confident narrators who intone the saga of progressive well-being and more hesitant sorcerer-scholars who toil for insights that are at best contradictory and often less than conclusive. This same tension and its resulting ambiguity crop up regularly in environmental studies of South and Southeast Asia, including the dozen essays that follow.

Scholarship that thematizes social justice and human welfare requires an awareness of the *perspectival nature of knowledge*. For one thing, it's difficult to separate subaltern interest and agency from the ideologies that subalterns and their agents endorse. While ideology is sometimes a self-conscious "cover-up" deployed to advance someone's or some group's interests, ideology also creates interests and points to possible modes of action through which to realize them. In this view, ideology is a positive force because its categories and frames create the ability to understand the world and act on it; this intelligibility effect is characteristic of discourse to which ideology is an analytic cousin. The needy and aggrieved peasants, proletarians, and tribals who populate the essays below, and threatened tropical and near tropical species and the spaces where they subsist, are themselves creations of historical frames like those that allowed the authors to even think of advocating for them. Furthermore, the authors cannot tell their stories without using recognizable genres of narration and analysis, and these genres implicate us all in legacies of story-telling, in established ways of making distinctions, and in conventions for attracting an audience. The regular result of the interplay between ideology, narration, and analysis, on the one hand, and historical experience, on the other, is knowledge of the world that is partial and positioned — what we call perspectival knowledge. Following Michel Foucault, the basement sorcerers see that power and knowledge are inextricable and realize that power makes both domination and resistance possible. They historicize the agency of subaltern as well as elite actors, placing it in a comparative context in order to reveal its gaps and transformations, thereby helping to explain how social action is imagined, planned, and practiced. Aware of the limitations of their craft, we see them practicing scholarship as it must be practiced at the turn of the twenty-first century — skittishly, reflexively, diffidently.

Of course, there are critics who complain that undue attention to ideology, power, narrative, context, and genre makes it impossible to revise the historical record and that scholarship is about to dissolve into a cacophony of ironic and incoherent perspectives. They also fear that thinking openly about the practice of knowledge making inhibits interventions on behalf of those who have been oppressed or marginalized. Our position is that the tension between an awareness of perspectival knowledge and committed political intervention is necessary and contributes to better scholarship and, sometimes, to better political practice. True, the analyses and interventions that arise at the edge of this tension can never be fully self-assured, but perhaps diffidence is advantageous; to the extent that perspectival studies are attentive to their own positioned stances, they remain wary of efforts to remake the world in one general rush toward "development" or "progress." There has been enough of that. Instead, perspectival studies commend careful listening for abuses of modern, progressive frames, and they show that commitments to justice, diversity, and well-being are historically specific and must be regularly stretched, transformed, and challenged if they are to be of any use in making a livable world.

Despite the premise of a global transformation in human welfare and environmental integrity by the year 2057, we actually write at a moment when most development policy refuses serious consideration of the environment and most environmental policy refuses any consideration of the well-being of local residents. Scholars, policymakers, and activists thus need to continue to focus attention on and enlarge the overlap between environmental concerns and concerns for social justice and human welfare. Throughout this volume, the authors suggest new vocabularies and frameworks that can help us to see desired social and natural objects in a shared light. In some cases, this involves moving beyond a blinkered conservation biology that views each nonhuman species in its own autonomous evolutionary space outside of human histories; in other cases, it requires moving beyond a narrow development sociology that imagines only the welfare of human beings, using nonhuman species as their always available and willing servants.

Two concepts that will be useful in pursuing a twenty-first-century scholarly and activist agenda are *the making of landscapes* and *the coherence of projects*. Landscape refers to the organization of land and nature at the scale of human experience. It is both the scene visualized by a human eye and the landform itself as it is lived in by particular eyewitnessing humans. The term *landscape* emerges from two legacies. Artists paint landscapes by making pictorial depictions of natural scenes; planners, builders, farmers, and urban and rural residents use and transform landscapes by making fields, roads, waterways, houses, forests, parks, and waste places. It is precisely because of this double heritage that the term has become so useful. In this volume, *landscape* refers both to the material form (human and nonhuman features) of the land and to the aesthetic standards and legacies through which people observe and know it.

Because landscapes are simultaneously social and natural, to make landscape a unit of scholarly analysis is to track the conjoined making of nature and culture. The essays in this volume attune readers to both the social and natural elements of landscapes by presenting historical episodes — exhibits if you will — that contain human and nonhuman elements. Implicitly the essays argue that we can only understand these social/natural landscapes through positioned knowledges that have developed in practical routines. Several essays focus on landscapes that are seen as particularly rural, even "wild," and are most likely to be confused with the "raw materials," "reserves," or "resources" that allegedly lie outside of human fashioning and historicity. Other essays describe alternative ways of seeing landscapes in which social histories can be represented as natural histories, and vice versa. While most environmental scholarship stretches analytic frameworks in the social sciences and history to encompass landscape making, it usually ends up reaffirming these frameworks. Instead, this volume questions the frameworks themselves. What are these strange things: "management," "advocacy," "science"? Several essays explore the cultural logics of hegemonic frames as they come to life in the materiality of landscape-making projects.

Projects are relatively tight clusters of ideas and practices that appear as particular historical undertakings; they are often dreams made concrete and are most identifiable in relation to their practical arrangements. Like "culture" and "discourse," "project" is a concept that allows scholars to investigate social life without taking its common-sense assumptions for granted. Some examples of projects discussed in this volume are natural history, conservation campaigns, and colonial forestry. In comparison with culture and discourse, though, projects are temporally limited and sputter to an end; a prime example of an exhausted project is colonialism itself. Projects, like Foucauldian discourses, show us frames of understanding in relation to social worlds, yet the analysis of a project begins with the concreteness of an undertaking rather than with an abstract field of meaning. Projects are organized through cultural frameworks, yet any single culture includes many divergent projects and several cultures can participate in the same global project. Unlike the concept of culture, a project is not constrained by the ethnic identification or physical location of its adherents. For example, in investigating projects of landscape making, the contributors to this volume stay close to the historical record while refusing to naturalize cultural frameworks. Several essays concern the rational or religious management of what are considered "wild" species and places and are thus particularly vivid examples of nature-making projects. Other chapters are saturated with struggles over justice and survival for humans and nonhumans. These struggles make and remake the landscape for the social projects of particular coalitions of claimants, some of whom flourish, others of whom fail.

Most scholarly work at the border between history and the social sciences emphasizes the power of projects, and thus their successes, which they link to the grand building blocks of historical studies. For example, some scholars point us toward cultures, which are represented as coherent wholes; others speak of seamless, hegemonic discourses. We are even offered epistemes and epochs (such as tradition and modernity, globalization, or the successive accumulation regimes of capitalism). These imagined eras, cultures, and discourses are useful signposts with which to see big, often unrecognized historical regularities. However, they have the effect of overemphasizing the power of the projects, which never fully accomplish the work their framers set out for them. It is in this context that this volume turns to *unfinished and awkward projects* in their historical context. The tentative, contested, and uncoordinated aspects of landscape-making projects illustrate how regularly expert and managerial efforts are incomplete in their realization. It is in their bumblings, their failures, and their reformulations that projects show us the most about the contingencies of landscape history.

Project is a contaminated term; that is, while it can be applied in many times and places, its most egregious association is with the management of late colonial and postcolonial modernity. Many twentieth-century projects came into being as dream threads in the improvement-oriented plans and planning processes of modernization; reckless haste and overbearing confidence were the key characteristics of their implementation. By refusing the commonsense status of modernization, a focus on state-managerial projects both indexes dreams of modernity and allows us to stretch our analysis around, into, and beyond them. In the harsh light of the outcomes engendered, new scholarly questions about these projects stand out. Can we show the life forms and landforms that projects caused to flourish *and* their exclusions? Can we show *both* the material solidity of these projects, their success in landscape formation, and at the same time their historical fragility?

The volume addresses these challenges with four approaches. First, the chapters work against the taken for granted status of dominant projects of science and state making by showing their historical and cultural *specificity.* They drain ineluctability from the term *natural,* and they question the inevitability of its human and nonhuman arrangements. Where is this place called the Tropics? What constitutes "health"? Who are the peasants? What is property? The essays thus refocus our attention on both the subjects and the objects of environmental scholarship.

Second, the essays take a close look at how *agency* is formed. Agency is much valued in the scholarship and popular culture of the early twenty-first century, but few have paid attention to how someone or something comes to be an agent. History isn't made through willpower or attitude alone; only some kinds of agency make a difference. Just what practices and meanings create "foresters," "environmentalists," or "villagers" in particular times and places? And how did practices and meanings emerge as significant in making history?

Third, the chapters attend to the making of *scale.* Landscape-making projects necessarily conjure particular scales, from the "locality" of community making to the global scale of imperial dreams. Most analysts have been unselfconscious about their claims concerning these scales. The essays here ask how scales at multiple levels are formed, how they coexist, and how they alternately reinforce and interrupt each other. Regionality is also an important theme across the essays, and several explore the regional scale of the tropical.

Fourth, the chapters pay special attention to the self-conscious efforts called *mobilizations* or *campaigns,* whether by state agencies or grassroots movements. Mobilizations require bringing adherents in. In the process, the initial cause is continually diverted and changed. Disparate allies are thrown together, fighting for divergent causes. Answers to the questions "Who will become an ally?" and "Who is the enemy?" cannot be predetermined. By attracting new supporters to a cause, mobilizations extend the cultural logics of landscape-building projects to new domains and in the process spoil and transform them. Hence awkward and uneasy alliances are a necessary feature of the mobilizations, contributing to their success. They can also, of course, contribute to their failures.

The essays in this volume focus on two domains where awkward alliances, with all their idiosyncrasies, are particularly obvious: state formation and the formation of social movements. The authors document state resource managers who extend the logic of bureaucratic administration into new domains. Yet this extension is never simple because the contingent encounters that make extension possible — between bureaucrats and villagers or foresters and trees — deform state mechanics and give rise to new dreams and debates. Social movements are similarly shaped by their contingencies. For example, alliances between outside activists and villagers have been the crux of environmental movements oriented toward social justice in rural South and Southeast Asia. Yet these alliances are strained. Villagers and urban-based environmentalists often want different things, and any common agenda must be creative and at best tentative. The history of collaborations, whether smothering or vitalizing, moves analysis beyond the endorsement or criticism of environmental movements to show how they do and don't work.

A SHORT SYNOPSIS

We have divided the volume into two parts to clarify the agenda outlined above. The essays in part 1 locate and analyze knowledges and practices through which social/natural landscapes in South and Southeast Asia are created, maintained, and transformed. They focus on science, administration, and livelihood, as these both create lenses for seeing nature and provide new architectures for landscape formation and restoration. The essays in part 2 trace campaigns and mobilizations intended to produce livable environments; they draw our attention to the good and bad compromises that have been necessary to produce these campaigns.

The first five chapters develop a historical view of the scales, logics, and agents that have shaped social/natural landscapes. An initial subset of chapters traces the formation of "tropical" landscape knowledges — the frameworks that made South and Southeast Asian landscapes knowable to the naturalists, doctors, foresters, and colonial administrators who explored the area in the nineteenth and twentieth centuries. Warwick Anderson shows how the category of the Tropics was formed with a particular political and cultural specificity in the early-twentieth-century Philippines. "Climate," Anderson comments, "is, after all, an abstraction"; climatic regions such as the Tropics were recognized by politically charged deployments of colonial science. The Tropics, he argues, was a trope for the difficulties and possible limits of colonial expansion; it was the zone that made civilization, and the white man, sweat. Furthermore, it was a mutable sign. In the early-twentieth-century Philippines, the

Tropics was redefined as a zone not so much of nature's power as of technoscience's prowess.

Charles Zerner's chapter also foregrounds shifts between nineteenth- and twentieth-century scientific views of the Southeast Asian landscape. Nineteenth-century European naturalists, Zerner argues, recognized the hustle and bustle of markets *within* Indonesian natural landscapes as well as in the trade that brought their products to Europe. In contrast, twentieth-century conservationists segregated sacred nature and market-driven culture, demanding cordoned-off reserves in which nature could operate free from human influence. It has been the genius of Indonesian activists to use and revise conservationist tropes to include local communities in their claims for the reserves that environmentalists might struggle to make real. Yet even their portrayals do not incorporate the landscape-making practices and knowledge of local residents.

Roger Jeffery, Nandini Sundar, and their colleagues reverse the moment of surprise to show continuities even where there seems to have been an enormous shift in science and policy. Colonial forest policy in India separated "major" forest products — favored timber species — from "minor" ones, that is, everything else people used in the forest. In recent years, nontimber forest products have become increasingly important in forest policy, as forest administrators have become attuned to their importance in forest biodiversity and in state-mandated community participation in forestry management. Yet, whether they are considered major or minor, nontimber forest products cannot be managed outside of the complex and varied systems of customary access rights through which these products are known and claimed. Despite enormous changes in forestry rhetorics, this nexus of rules, rights, and concessions remains the basis through which forests and local people interact in making landscapes.

A second subset of essays in part 1 examines in detail the making of rural landscapes through the interwoven effects of conceptual frames and administrative practices. (Jeffery and Sundar's chapter contributes to this effort.) Michael R. Dove's ambitious comparison of rural landscapes in South and Southeast Asia foregrounds, in particular, precolonial histories of language use, politics, and settlement in each area. He tracks the process in which precolonial states in South Asia constructed and reconstructed "jungle" — first inside and then outside civilization. In a somewhat parallel process, he argues, states in Southeast Asia drew back from recognizing the livability of the forest, in which fields and forest rotate, replacing this with a sharp nature/culture divide. These histories prove suggestive in contextualizing later regional convergences as well as divergences in thinking about, and making, forested landscapes.

Anna Tsing's chapter returns to colonial and postcolonial transformations in rural landscaping. Beginning with the curious dichotomy in contemporary environmentalism between the distinct kinds of conservation imagined in relation to "peasants" and "tribes," she explores the history of allegorical and administrative commitments that have given a consistent look to peasants, and peasant landscapes, in Southeast Asia. In progressive mid-twentieth-century politics, peasants represented basic human livelihood concerns unmediated by distorting ideologies. In contrast, Tsing shows how shifting colonial, nationalist, and populist commitments created the figurative peasant and stimulated practices for making landscapes and communities that kept this figure in place.

Ann Grodzins Gold's richly ethnographic study of people's stories of the landscape in a village in contemporary Rajasthan turns us to local landscapes—and the making of a "local" scale. The Indian villagers Gold studied differentiate "foreign" trees pressed on them by the state from vegetation they consider local; they recall histories of the introduction of foreign vegetation and the ways in which it has transformed nature and society in the village. The landscape is discussed in relation to changing political conditions for making a living after royal forest reserves suddenly became accessible but overgrazed terrain. These changes provoke a sense of ambivalence, as the "moral ecology" of the local landscape is portrayed as having been invaded by foreign social/natural benefits and ills. Through this ambivalence, villagers imagine locality.

The second part of the volume takes these insights about the making of rurality, science, scale, and local knowledge into examinations of environmental campaigns. The emphasis here is on the complexity with which these campaigns shape social and natural histories. They may mix contradictory goals, they may miscommunicate with allies, they may use terrifying disciplines to mount high-sounding rhetorics, and they may advocate overwhelmingly hopeless causes.

The importance of the state in setting agendas for making rural landscapes is explored in the first set of chapters in this section. Paul Greenough compares two 1970s Indian state campaigns to manage species diversity: the campaign to save the tiger and the campaign to eradicate the smallpox virus. The landscapes in question lay in forest reserves (realm of the tiger) and in the human body (realm of the virus). Despite the fact that the rhetoric of each campaign stressed benefits for humanity and nature, both campaigns turned to a similar set of coercive tactics, involving the containment and resettlement of villagers. Each campaign was as much an exercise in governance as in health or nature preservation, and the pattern of scattered subaltern voices shows that the local understanding of this fact was total.

Nancy Lee Peluso pursues the logics of state governance tactics to show how even oppositional movements for community rights may adopt state logics in reenvisioning rural landscapes. She argues that the colonial and postcolonial national states in Indonesia have adopted territorial approaches to controlling rural areas. They have mapped, demarcated, reserved, and administered rural territories. In recent years, both environmentalist NGOs and villagers in Kalimantan have picked up on these territorial strategies in making claims to resources. Thus, NGOs have mapped villages to claim local rights; villagers have planted trees to claim areas within the village sectors (as well as areas within nature reserves) as property. State logics shape both organized and everyday attempts to recoup access rights from the state.

K. Sivaramakrishnan shows concretely, in historical detail, how a rural landscape is made through a state agenda. In late-nineteenth-century Bengal, forestry was professionalized in the hands of scientific foresters. Forestry became a new mode of governance at a moment of development of the colonial state, "when political consolidation converged with technocratic assertion." In the early twentieth century, the forest landscape of Bengal was transformed under this regime, as foresters developed a practical knowledge of both landscape and land administration. It is Sivaramakrishnan's insights to show how the routine practices of foresters — demarcation, inventory, reservation, regeneration — led not to the automatic reproduction of a master plan of European forest science but to debate among foresters and active revisions of their working plans as landscape making became practically localized.

The chapters by Greenough, Peluso, and Sivaramakrishnan offer a glimpse of the kind of compromises through which all environmental mobilizations are formed. Greenough, in particular, suggests the bad compromises of state management of environmental causes; Peluso and Sivaramakrishnan are more ambivalent about the advantages and limitations of state logics. The issue of bad compromises and "uneasy alliances" is even more explicit in the final chapters. These explore the collaborations through which environmental mobilizations articulate their causes, reach out to allies around the nation and the world, and make claims over social/natural landscapes and communities. Some of these alliances are deadly, some are promising, some seem truly unexpected and creative, and some seem calculating and manipulative. The authors manage to explore some of the most available types of collaborations that arise when we try to think through the connections between environmentalism and social justice in South and Southeast Asia: north-south alliances, urban-rural alliances, middle class–peasant alliances, and religious-secular alliances. Each of these is problematic, yet without them no one could ever build a movement around both environmentalism and social justice. The chapters document the fact that collaboration is no guarantee of either wisdom or success and are alternately hopeful and critical of the efforts they study.

Amita Baviskar analyzes the coalition between activists and tribal people that emerged out of the more than a decade long campaign (which still continues) to "save" the Narmada River. The antidam campaign was broadened through this coalition to fight for local rights to forest land through a new organization, the Organization for the Consciousness of Workers and Peasants. Tribal people worked with activists to hold on to the forests and fields they had claimed through customary rights; together they found an issue of joint concern for tribal livelihood, on the one hand, and activist models of sustainable development on the other. Yet activists and tribal people do not always see eye to eye. Tribal people have been increasingly attracted to the identity politics of tribal leaders who have struggled to claim a share of regional government. Activists maintain their commitments to environmental sustainability even when tribal people offer other developmental models. And neither tribal leaders nor activists consider the plight of tribal migrant workers, who have been left out of all current mobilization concerns.

J. Peter Brosius also analyzes the relationship between activists and tribal people; his case is the international campaign on behalf of the Penan of Sarawak, Malaysia, and their tropical rain forests. In other publications, Brosius has discussed the representations of "primitives" and "nature" that held the attention of northern activists, even as they were irrelevant or damaging in the Malaysian context; here he asks how the campaign changed over time in response to criticisms of and responses to these representations. Thus, when the Malaysian government responded to the Penan campaign by labeling it "eco-imperialism," northern activists became more sensitive to the criticisms of their Malaysian allies. By investigating the "biography" of the campaign, Brosius shows how strategies of representation and action shift over time in relation to dialogue among both partners and opponents.

Susan M. Darlington's chapter is also concerned with an environmental campaign. She offers an ethnographic account of how monks and villagers in rural Thailand have worked together to build a community forest. Phrakhru Pitak is an "ecology monk" who returned to his home village to mobilize community sentiment around protecting the forest. Drawing from "radical conservative" ideas among Thai monks and building on the eclectic folk religious sentiments of villagers, many of whom moved to the area rather recently, he has created a community rite of "tree ordination" to mark the sacredness of the community forest. Darlington's analysis nicely shows how environmental mobilization remakes landscapes and communities through a creative mixture of national, local, Buddhist, animist, environmentalist, developmentalist, and on-the-spot practical ideas, rites, and routines. Her chapter returns the volume to themes of the making of scales; of the construction of rural landscapes; and of the adoption, refusal, and reformulation of state, scientific, and otherwise official doctrines and practices of landscape making.

PART 1

Scales, Logics, and Agents

Tropical Knowledges

Warwick Anderson

THE NATURES OF CULTURE

Environment and Race in the Colonial Tropics

"The main army of science moves to the conquest of new worlds slowly and surely, nor ever cedes an inch of the territory gained," wrote T. H. Huxley in 1890 (1894; clxxxi). But in the early twentieth century the tropics were still not scientifically subdued, even if the imperial powers had formally taken possession of most of the region. The Tropics had been defined cartographically as lying between Cancer and Capricorn, meteorologically as a region of continuous heat and humidity (the latter not readily measured until the 1890s), and botanically as lying within the "palm line." In the early twentieth century, medical scientists attempted a further physiological and racial enclosure of the Torrid Zone, proposing that it was the region where a representative of the white race would feel uncomfortable and displaced. The founders of modern geography drew a "white race climograph" that delimited this tropical region. Into the twentieth century, then, tropical nature resisted easy categorization, but to Europeans and North Americans it generally conveyed an image — both attractive and repellant — of luxuriance, excess, and danger.

Raymond Williams has suggested that what is often being argued in the idea of nature is the idea of man (Williams 1981; Horigan 1988). In trying to define nature, colonial scientists were at the same time structuring (and restructuring) the relations of humans — whether local or alien — to the environment and one another. The bounding and typing of tropical space through tropes of mimesis and comparison thus produced definite types of racialized and gendered bodies (Duncan and Ley 1993, 39–56). Accredited knowledge of tropical nature provided a code for the proper inhabiting and managing of the region. One might even say that a discourse on equatorial environments brought the tropical colonized and alien colonialist into being. In particular, the regular declension of *tropical, wild,* and *dangerous* allowed the expression of a necessarily ambivalent and assailable environmental difference that worked well both corporeally and socially. These "tropicalisms" shaped masculinist European and North American self-perceptions (civilizing, containing, controlling) even as they provided opportunities for disciplining tropical bodies and botany (luxuriant, wasteful, extravagant, grotesque). But in the early twentieth century, as colonial scientists increasingly emphasized the actual plasticity of the Tropics as an environmental and racial site, we find the elaboration of a sociospatial discourse of tropical development — a new frontier — that promotes the "modernization" of a natural difference that was artfully, if incompletely, constructed during the previous century.

This essay examines late-nineteenth- and early-twentieth-century efforts to render the colonial Tropics scientifically legible. Although I intend to sketch the general development of late-nineteenth-century tropical expertise, my focus is on scientific debates over environmental difference in the Philippines under Spanish control and, after 1898, under U.S. domination. While Ken de Bevoise and others have recently demonstrated the force of arguments that treat tropical nature as a historical actor, I am not so concerned with the study of the environment's "autonomous place in history" (Cronon 1990, 1122; de Bevoise 1995; Crosby 1986). Rather, I want to reconstruct the material and discursive productions of natural boundaries, typologies, and hierarchies. In Paul Carter's words, I am interested chiefly in "the spatial fantasies through which a culture declares its presence" (1989, xxii). Our places in the world have been framed and ordered as much through this deployment of geographical metaphor as through any irruption of unmediated ecological agency (Demeritt 1994; Duncan and Ley 1993, 1–24). Here I pay attention to the development of scientific vocabularies for assigning environmental and human difference.

My work thus supplements Richard Grove's extensive analysis (1995) of the metaphors and images Europeans invoked to describe and manage their colonial possessions before 1860. Like Grove, I emphasize the perceptions of the naturalist and scientist on the colonial "periphery" (which thus becomes, for both Grove and myself, central). But unlike Grove I find these local experts sloughing off their environmental determinism and working toward ideas that imply greater cultural autonomy and mobility over the surface of the globe. What I am describing, in general terms, is a decline in the nineteenth-century preoccupation with the environmental shaping of racial types and the development instead of the idea of humans as independent agents whose impact on the environment, however destructive, will have only a minimal effect on their own mental and physical well-being. By the early twentieth century, the "Hippocratic agenda" — what David Livingstone has called an "ethnic moral topography"[1] — is a dead letter in medicine and anthropology (though perhaps still finding a few eager recipients in geography and historical studies). In other words, while Grove has described the elaboration of theories of man as a natural agent subject to what he has wrought, here I trace the emergence of the scientific assumption that civilized man is a natural agent who can evade, through technocratic expertise, the consequences of his actions (Glacken 1967). In a sense, then, I am trying to identify the point at which biomedical science ceases to be an environmental discourse in the Asian Tropics and becomes primarily a discourse on social citizenship.

CLIMATIC TYPOLOGIES, ENVIRONMENTAL DETERMINISM, AND TEMPORAL ORDER

In 1985, Karl L. Hutterer suggested that there was "no such thing as tropical ecology; rather, there is only ecology in the tropics." It was difficult to provide a precise account of tropical environments and their ecology, as "tropical regions contain the most diverse and complex ecosystems in the world." And yet he could not entirely forsake the notion that there was something distinctive about a tropical environment: "certain fundamental biotic or nonbiotic conditions . . . (such as levels of light radiation, temperature, humidity, soils, flora and fauna)" must define tropical nature — and yet it was not easy to specify them. Nevertheless, he attempted to provide a compendium of environmental difference. Geographically, the Tropics was a sector of the globe between Capricorn and Cancer, but these latitudinal limits "delineate the distribution of tropical environments only in the crudest of terms." Hutterer then reproduced a century or more of conventional tropical description: the region was sunny, hot, wet, and the equatorial flora was "one of the richest and most luxuriant." But he also used terms that would have sounded odd even fifty years earlier: the environment was remarkably diverse, complex, and fragile. It was so diverse, indeed, that it had become evident that "we are not dealing with a single environmental type but rather a broad range" (1985, 58, 59, 60). While vestiges of typological thinking remained, policing the conventional boundaries of the tropical had become less important than finding out what went on within them.

But a hundred years earlier Alfred Russel Wallace, a British champion of natural selection, had described the "wonderful uniformity" of the Tropics, the "monotony of nature" between Cancer and Capricorn. The climate he experienced in the Malay archipelago was "essentially the same": sunny, hot, and wet. As a result, the vegetation — far from appearing fragile—"overshadows and almost seems to oppress the earth." It was "luxuriant" and "abundant," indeed, a "vast treasure-house, which is as yet but very partially explored." Wallace was convinced that further scientific exploration would identify and make available an inexhaustible trove of commodities for civilized man. "There are probably a large number of kinds of timber which will some day be found to be well-adapted to the special requirements of the arts and sciences," and many products of the forests were "already more useful to civilized man than to the indigenous inhabitants" (Wallace [1878] 1891, 217, 240, 246, 245; McKinney 1972; Camerini 1994). Wallace and other natural historians in the late nineteenth century did not doubt that the Tropics was a distinctive region, a climatic zone, a type of flora and fauna, an inexhaustible source of wealth, and a condition of life—and it could be appraised and exploited scientifically.

Observation of the usefulness of biology, medicine, and other technical discourses for European and North American imperialism has become a historiographic commonplace (Godlewska and Smith 1995; Fanon 1978; MacLeod and Lewis 1988; Arnold 1989). But the sciences were not only "tools of empire" in a narrowly instrumental sense; they also helped to shape the meaning and significance of European expansion. Expert knowledge frequently gave geographical and racial form to distant possessions. To a trained readership, the apparently dispassionate and abstract languages of science—an especially plausible genre toward the end of the nineteenth century—seemed capable of capturing mimetically the places and peoples of the empire. Through fieldwork and subsequent elite analysis, these representational sites could be bounded and filled out. They were, in a sense, collected and then displayed in miniature (Pratt 1992). A new representational site—the Tropics, for example—might then be compared to a European frame of reference or master plan, providing grounds for a hierarchical classification of one sort or another. The precise character of the typology and hierarchy varied enormously during the nineteenth century, but the underlying logic of essential structure and natural order remained compelling in scientifically literate circles.

The argument for climatic zones has a long history in Europe. Until early modern times, climates were arrayed and ranked simply according to latitude: if the equatorial zone was more torrid, it was because it was more exposed to the sun. But during the eighteenth century studies of the distribution of pressure, wind, and temperature postulated an atmospheric circulation that did not map precisely onto lines of latitude. Over the next hundred years, the spread of observation stations through the expansionist European empires produced masses of new meteorological information. In 1817, Alexander von Humboldt published the first isotherm chart, onto which botanists and zoologists proceeded to map an increasing muster of plants and animals. "The curves of the isothermal lines," declared Humboldt, "correspond with the limits which are seldom passed by certain species of plants and of animals that do not wander far from their fixed habitation." Furthermore, it appeared that the "luxuriant zone of the tropics offers the strongest resistance to . . . changes in the natural distribution of vegetable forms" (1850–58, 2:347).[2] The climatic boundaries sketched by Humboldt's successors would become ever more distinct, though never incontrovertibly so. Whether a tropical region was best defined by parallels of latitude, vegetation (the "palm line," for instance), isotherms, or humidity, remained open to dispute, but no one doubted that it did indeed exist.[3]

By the last decade of the nineteenth century, the earlier, more general classifications of climate became fragmented as concepts of global circulation grew more complex: climatic regions began proliferating into smaller and smaller subspecies. Although most scientists sought to identify secure categories in nature, no one could agree on just what they should measure if they were to define such entities. Climate is, after all, an abstraction and not readily identified at any given moment. Botanists could classify and survey "characteristic" vegetation, but its distribution was never uniform, even under the same climatic conditions. Meteorologists could measure temperature and precipitation, but at which point did these statistics become unequivocally tropical?

All the same, few commentators on southern Asia failed to describe the climate as distinctively tropical. When Sir John Bowring, the governor of Hong Kong, visited the Philippines in the 1850s, he found the archipelago typically torrid, with constant "oppressive" heat combined with wet and dry seasons. The islands were "visited by the usual calamities gathered by the wild elements round that line which is deemed the girdle of the world." Elaborating on the gendered conceit, he was struck by "the awful serenity and magnificent beauty of their primeval forests, so seldom penetrated, and in their recesses hitherto inaccessible to the foot of man." As he thrust onward, Sir John felt "as if vegetation reveled in undisturbed and uncontrolled luxuriance." Such alluring tropical nature would prove "inexhaustible through countless generations" (1859, 74, 85, 86).[4] Other foreign encounters, while often less explicitly venereal, confirmed the image of exuberance and excess. Fedor Jagor, a German ethnologist traveling in the Philippines a few years after Bowring, thought the islands a "lotus-eating Utopia" in which the "hospitality of nature" dissolved European cultural baggage to the extent that "one would gladly dispense with all clothing save a sun hat and a pair of shoes." The *dolce far niente,* he concluded, "only blossoms under the shade of palm trees" ([1873] 1965, 29, 34, 29). Tropical nature was luxuriant and verdant, overflowing any distancing analytic framework; it verged on the grotesque.

When Ramon Reyes Lala, an *ilustrado* expelled by the Spanish and living in New York, wrote an account extolling the new U.S. possessions, he described the "great wealth" of Philippine plant life, the "richness and abundance" of fruits, the "lush tropical forests," and the "luxuriance and beauty" of the vegetation. The islands were a "botanist's paradise" presenting the "appearance of a virgin wilderness." Here was a "spectacle of beauty seldom excelled." He assured his American readers that "there are thousands of square miles of dense forest within which the foot of the white man has rarely ever set; thousands perhaps upon which none but the natives have ever gazed; costly woods, whose value can be reckoned only in millions of dollars" (1898, 151, 155). Evidently the virgin woods were available to American masculine enterprise.

It would be wrong to imagine that culture has been erased from these accounts of tropical nature. Jagor thought that the natives of the Philippines presented "an interesting study of a type of mankind existing in the easiest natural conditions": they were a people who had homologously "sunk into a disordered and uncultivated state." Even the long-term Spanish residents had become "uneducated, improvident, and extravagant" ([1873] 1965, 27, 264, 24). Wallace observed that the Malay race had failed to develop its economy to European levels because the profligacy and ease of tropical nature had exerted no selection pressure on it ([1878] 1891, 310). Even Reyes Lala thought that the "go-ahead American spirit" was needed to sharpen Filipino sensitivities: "what is now confusedly enjoyed and but vaguely beheld in nature will . . . become simple, clear, sympathetic, and clearly formulated to their apprehension" (1898, 156). Americans were only too willing to agree. According to Fred W. Atkinson, the first U.S. superintendent of education in the Philippines, the "high and uniform temperature which the thermometer reaches throughout the year is the chief reason which . . . produces in the natives the laziness and inertia which characterizes them" (1905, 127). Americans were the tough products of a more stringent environment. Examples of such cultural disparagement could be multiplied indefinitely: they reiterate the assumption that an overnurturing Mother Nature had allowed her human charges to stay louche, irresolute, and primitive. Thus, the Malay race represented an earlier, and clearly inferior, level of physical development and cultural sophistication.[5]

This environmental determinism took other forms in medical theory. The principle that a race was best fitted to resist the diseases of its ancestral realm — and, as a corollary, was especially susceptible to ailments encountered in a foreign land — was a remarkably resilient element in nineteenth-century biomedical understandings of disease susceptibility. Such standard assumptions of natural immunity pervade the Philippine medical record (Anderson 1996). Accordingly, Filipinos generally should resist "tropical diseases" unless they had become particularly reckless and depraved — after all, the race was supposed to have a long process of adaptation on its side. Spanish colonialists were perhaps more susceptible to the diseases deemed peculiar to hot countries, although many medical experts argued that their southern race, to some degree, was preadapted to tropical disease environments. The North American type, however, would be uniquely vulnerable to alien pathogens in the Philippines. It did not much matter whether one believed that a beneficent God had placed each race in its correct surroundings or that a long process of evolution (Lamarckian or Darwinian) had gradually fitted the races to their local ecology. Nor did changes in etiological reasoning disturb these abiding anxieties about racial dislocation: as long as disease was geographically distributed, its actual cause — miasma or microbe — was insignificant. The problem was that the natural order, structured through racial and environmental typologies, had been transgressed. A European in the Tropics was matter out of place: degeneration to local standards was the likely consequence (Douglas 1976; Stallybrass and White 1986).[6] Medicine thus introduced a paradox into European colonialism: the Tropics finally had become available to white dominion, yet they were still no place for a white man. It was, of course, a paradox that called for considerable investments in environmental and medical research: racial mobility had been configured as a great experiment, and so it should be conducted as such (Anderson [1994] 1995).

Benjamin Kidd, the American social Darwinist, was one of the more influential writers on this tropical dilemma. Taking 30 degrees north and 30 degrees south to embrace the tropical zone, Kidd observed that this region, so rich in commodities, was still existing in "a state of anarchy, or of primitive savagery" (1898, 8, 15). He lamented that "in dealing with the *natural* inhabitants of the tropics we are dealing with peoples who represent the same stage in the history of the race that the child does in the history of the development of the individual." They could not govern themselves. Nor could higher order whites continue to administer these possessions in situ. "In climatic conditions which are a burden to him; in the midst of races in a different and lower stage of development; divorced from the influences which have produced him, from the moral and political environment from which he sprung, the white man . . . tends himself to sink slowly to the level around him." Indeed, Kidd did not doubt that "in the tropics the white man lives and works only as a diver lives and works under water" (50–52, 54).[7] Therefore, the Tropics must be administered from abroad, as a trust for a civilization that could not prosper in moist heat.

For most nineteenth-century natural historians and medical scientists, the climatic zones that they had abstracted, and the ideal types with which they populated them, each had suggested a secure rank in the natural order. The evolutionary theories of Kidd and others further temporalized this spatial order. The "Tropics" were not only luxuriant but primeval; native races were as primitive as they were uncultivated. Geographical difference was thus read as temporal or developmental difference (Fabian 1983).[8] According to Kidd, it was futile to attempt "to reverse by any effort within human range the long, slow process of evolution which has produced such a profound dividing line between the inhabitant of the tropics and those of the temperate regions (1898: 30)."[9] Kidd remained a pessimist, but to many other, more optimistic policymakers it was a slow process of development that appealed as the more logical and compelling solution to this spatialization of time, for the activity of differentiation had implied the possibility of eventual integration. An advance, on European terms, might yet occur. But how could such a process of dispossession and synchonization be achieved, especially since in the early twentieth century a further physiological enclosure of the Tropics—a reinscribing of its boundaries—was taking place?

DEVELOPING THE TROPICS

Not content with climate descriptions derived from measures of temperature and precipitation, the eminent British physiologist Leonard Hill had devised a wet katathermometer, an object that he thought would function like a human body yet provide a simple measurement of comfort (Hill, Griffith, and Flack 1916, 183). A simulation was achieved by registering the temperature of the mercury as it was affected by the cooling of a wet linen jacket. The katathermometer thus indicated the cooling power of a locality: below certain values northern European workers and industrialists were known to feel uncomfortably hot. It proved to be immensely popular, even though the method was time consuming and tedious (a week's investigation of conditions in the examination hall of the King Edward VII College of Medicine at Singapore sorely tried the tempers of the staff). Other investigators found Hill's method too reductive. They tried instead to derive empirical relationships from a statistical study of the white body's actual behavior under various combinations of meteorological variables. Thus, Houghten in the United States elaborated an "effective" temperature scheme based on the experience of well-dressed white males. Subjects were placed in a room with one set of atmospheric conditions and then moved to another room with different atmospheric conditions; they were then asked whether the room felt warmer or cooler. It was found that an atmosphere with a dry bulb temperature of 78°F, a wet bulb temperature of 62°F and a wind velocity of 200 feet per minute gave the lads the same feeling of warmth as a still, saturated atmosphere at 68°F. So the effective temperature of the first atmosphere was deemed to be 68°F (Houghten and Yagloglou 1923, 163; Vernon 1926, 392). This effective temperature was then used to give an index of the habitability of different regions for the white race. The Tropics were the region in which the white organism felt uncomfortably hot.[10]

But would this signal lack of white racial comfort in the Tropics really be enough to provoke a breakdown of civilization? Certainly, on first exposure to the Philippines, many North Americans imagined themselves to be degenerating physically, mentally, and morally. Examples are legion. Hubert Howe Bancroft thought that "for a time and with care the several races may live anywhere on the globe . . . [but] the white man cannot live and labor permanently in the tropics." As a result, "we may give ownership but not the occupation of the tropics to the white race" ([1899] 1912, 403, 430). The irascible Col. Charles E. Woodruff, M.D., knew from personal experience that tropical colonization was fundamentally a biological process. Citing Morel and Kidd, Woodruff declared that "the instrument for the extinction of men in unnatural climates is degeneration in its modern sense, and it is brought about in the tropics by nervous exhaustion." In a hot climate, nature favored the least active: "low tropical savages are the fittest for their environment, and the strenuous white man is the unfit." Biology insisted, therefore, that imperialism must be based on "commensalism," not colonization (1909, 239–41, 257, 274).[11]

Ellsworth Huntington's work marks perhaps the high tide of climatic determinism. In 1915, he proposed a "climatic hypothesis of civiliza-tion" as the basis for the "new science of geography" (1915, v).[12] Hun-tington argued that "human character as expressed in civilization" (v) could be mapped onto physical and organic phenomena in order to determine the relations of man and his environment. It was a truism that "the nature of a people's culture, like the flavor of a fruit, depends pri-marily upon racial inheritance which can be changed only by the slow processes of biological variation and selection" (1). But it seemed to Huntington—a staunch environmentalist—that the role of climate in the selection of race culture had been understated. (He did admit that it had been "generally agreed that the native races within the tropics are dull in thought and slow in action" [35]). From his analysis of the rec-ords of hundreds of white American males, Huntington found that "mental activity reaches a maximum when the outside temperature aver-ages 38 degrees, that is, when there are mild frosts at night" (8). From these data, he drew a map showing how human energy was distributed throughout the world. It was, in effect, a physiological projection of the white male body onto the whole of the globe. The Tropics were redefined as an "unstimulating environment" (38) where it would be impossible to sustain "European and American energy, initiative, persistence, and other qualities upon which we so much pride ourselves" (41). Not sur-prisingly, England, Northern Europe, New Zealand, and the Pacific coast of the United States had ideal climates for civilization; the chief defect of California was that it was "too uniformly stimulating," a factor in generating "nervous disorders" (134); and the level of white energy in Australia was generally dismally low. "Man," according to Huntington, was "much more closely dependent upon nature than he has realized" (298). He concluded piously that "if we can conquer climate, the whole world will become stronger and nobler" (294), but he dismissed any hope for progress in the Tropics. The climatic impediment to white civili-zation was simply too great in the Torrid Zone.

But many of Huntington's medical contemporaries had become far less pessimistic over the past two decades. Longer tropical experience and new laboratory research in Manila and other centers of colonial science had been reducing the salience of climate in explanations of systemic physical disease. Americans felt no more uncomfortable in the Philippines than they might in Washington, D.C., during the summer months — except that along the equator there was no seasonal relief. But even if they could not conjure up snow, as a stratum of American institu-tions and personnel was deposited over the archipelago after 1898, the new colonialists felt ever more secure and in control of the land and its people. Americans in the civil government, most of them young and many from elite universities, were fashioning for themselves identities as toughened, scientific, interventionist progressives. They set about analyzing and transforming the tropical environment, particularly through the work of the Bureaus of Forestry and Agriculture, and as they did so tropical nature seemed ever more amenable to domination (Worcester 1914, 2:846–60).[13]

Colonial administrators soon became convinced that the new tropical frontier could be managed effectively with many of the techniques that had so successfully domesticated the American West. Most of the American military officers in the islands, and many of the civilian officials, already had taken part in the closing of the western continental frontier. For them, Manifest Destiny simply had stretched across the Pacific.[14] "It is destiny that the world shall be rescued from its natural wilderness and savage men," wrote Sen. Albert J. Beveridge, a leading expansionist. "It is possible for us to govern them as we govern Indian tribes," declared W. H. Taft, governor of the islands and later president of the United States (Beveridge [1900] 1908, 128; Taft 1902, 1:329).[15] The debilitating, wild Tropics had come to resemble the manageable Wild West. And with the disarming and the further disciplining of this new "frontier" landscape its effects on the new geographical agents came to appear ever more trivial. Certainly, many alien administrators, doctors, and scientists still came down with "tropical" afflictions, both physical and mental, but generally these ailments seemed more readily avoided and less devastating than at first feared.

They even seemed less intrinsically "tropical." The Manila experts in the Bureau of Science and the Bureau of Health, all of them full of enthusiasm for the new laboratory medicine, soon came to believe that illness would not arise solely from a mismatch of racial constitution and alien environment. Since the 1890s, in the control of malaria, hookworm, and even dysentery, medical officers everywhere in the colonial world had been more likely to concentrate on limiting the transmission of the recently discovered microbial causes of these ailments. Few colonial physicians still claimed that tropical diseases derived from the harsh and unrelenting climate: they were identifying germs for each of the local diseases and tracing the pathogens through the region's human and insect populations. The control of personal conduct and social interaction, whether internalized or imposed, seemed to offer a new prospect for limiting disease transmission. Hygienic stipulations now promised to insulate vulnerable whites from the animatedly pathogenic physical and social environment. The sources of tropical danger had shifted from the ubiquitous depleting climate to the insidious "native customs and habits" that seemed constantly to replenish the region's reservoirs of microbial pathology. The local races had thus been brought from the anthropological museum (where they were both an anachronistic curiosity and an object lesson) into the biomedical present (where they became a somatic danger). Medical time was being removed from natural history.[16]

During this period, new theories of heredity seemed to imply that these primitive and pathogenic tropical race cultures might be capable of modification over many generations of colonial governance. It seemed more likely than ever that constant discipline and correct training might slowly inculcate in natives (and lower class whites) a sense of self-control and self-possession. Just as tropical races (and poor whites) were recognized as disease dealing, so were they deemed disinfectable. I have described elsewhere how the expansion of the repertoire of disease control to include regulation of the personal and domestic hygiene of local inhabitants sanctioned, as never before in the colonial Tropics, reformation of everyday life and personal knowledge.[17] My point here is that by invoking parasites and "apparently healthy" native carriers as agents of tropical disease and discounting the impact of a climate that was less readily disciplined the new tropical medicine held out the possibility that expert social intervention might yet naturalize a northern "civility" in the Tropics. If separated from its environmental moorings, race culture might gradually be modified through the inheritance of traits acquired through early education. Both aliens and natives thus could resist or overcome their environment.

The control of native customs and habits promised to render unnecessary the earlier expansive colonial efforts to segregate Europeans and natives (Swanson 1977; Curtin 1985; Cell 1986).[18] When it took place, racial segregation generally could be justified using older environmental notions of disease causation: native towns produced more filth and noxious emanations and therefore should be located far from European habitations. But now cause and prevention would focus more on the native body itself and its movement through space, especially through European privatized space. Mobile, disease-dealing native bodies would be identified and isolated or retrained. The whole race did not require a separate location, just its own bounded "natural" setting. Differentiation and assimilation, not segregation, became the main tendencies of colonial public health in the twentieth century. In settler societies, segregation might still seem worthwhile on economic, political, or aesthetic grounds, but the scientific framework for such an investment had become very shaky indeed (Wright 1987).

It might be said that the old environmental determinism was shading into a laboratory-sanctioned possibilism.[19] The new laboratory science thus promised to resolve the apparent medical paradox of tropical colonialism that had been so artfully constructed over the previous century: modern bacteriological and physiological research indicated that with uncompromising surveillance and discipline of subordinate alien and native populations the white man's burden would be lightened and perhaps might eventually be carried by all—whites and "developed" natives alike. With this general mobilization, on strict medical terms, of all incipient (or prodromal) citizens, the Tropics had come to resemble a mere subdivision of Manifest Destiny.

For a few more decades, mental deterioration remained the last bastion of tropical pessimism, cited by some authorities (usually British) until the 1930s as an obstacle to implanting white or whitelike civilization. But the more scientifically minded and progressive American colonial officials were quick to discount these localist theories. William S. Washburn, the chairman of the Philippine civil service board and also a medical doctor, was one of many who endorsed the belief that social infractions caused more breakdowns than the supposedly "enervating" climate ever did. To maintain the mental health of aliens (and, less certainly, of natives), all that was required were "regular habits, the leading of a temperate life, and the absence of indulgence in excesses." Washburn approvingly quoted Maj. Gen. Leonard Wood, the governor of Moro Province and formerly a Rough Rider: "A moral life, with plenty of hard work, will be found to counteract in most cases the so-called demoralizing effects of the Philippine climate" (Washburn 1905, 513, 515). Medical officers in the Tropics increasingly were convinced that relentless supervision and regulation of personal and domestic hygiene—with a particular emphasis for whites on manly restraint and strenuous exertion—promised to prevent local pathology, mental or physical. (Colonialists thus tried, more optimistically than ever before, to build up for themselves an ascetic culture that promoted self-contained masculine virtues.) With attention paid to the rules of personal, domestic, and public hygiene and with the careful regulation of social life, the "acclimization" of the white male would become unnecessary and the transformation of natives into citizens possible, if endlessly deferred (Anderson 1998). By the late 1930s, Huntington's exclusionist arguments sounded decidedly nonphysiological: by then, medical scientists in the colonies had, they thought, established that a more or less white civilization could be projected onto the globe at any point and not degenerate. Through an iatrocratic colonialism, the representative of civilization (still conventionally white but sometimes "colored") could at last transcend the tropical environment.

Scientific tropical narratives in this period seem to mute the late-nineteenth-century rhetoric of sublime nature and to substitute for it a rhetoric of the technoscientific sublime.[20] In place of Alfred Russel Wallace's awe of the immense jungles, we find Leonard Hill's trembling before the electric fan.[21] For Wallace, in the rain forest there had been "a weird gloom and a solemn silence, which combine to produce a sense of the vast — the primeval — almost of the infinite. It is a world in which man seems an intruder, and where he feels overwhelmed by the contemplation of the ever-acting forces which, from the simple elements of the atmosphere, build up the great mass of vegetation" ([1878] 1891, 268–69). A European intruder in the forest during the 1870s would notice a "vastness, a solemnity, a gloom, a sense of solitude and of human insignificance, which for a time overwhelm him" (268–69). There was a sense of danger mixed with splendor. And, according to Reyes Lala, "tropical scenery cannot be pictured in words . . . it must be seen to be comprehended" (1898, 153). (Rarely, if ever, is tropical nature presented during this period in terms of the picturesque.) But in the early twentieth century tropical nature is exhaustively described — even overcome and diminished — in geographical and medical texts, making space for the eventual production of a touristic tropical chic. It is the irresistible technical force of modern colonialism — better cooling, refrigeration, "physiological" housing, railways, the telegraph — that stuns the new generation of scientists, exciting wonder and trepidation.[22]

CONCLUSION: NARCISSISM AND VOYEURISM

When touring the Philippine archipelago in 1909, Gov.-Gen. W. Cameron Forbes reflected on his difficulties in understanding the territory: "There is a fascination about unknown uninhabited islands off in these tropic seas. I feel, however, the lack of scientific knowledge. I'd like in these cases really to add something to the scientific knowledge, and want to bring with me experts on fish, trees, and birds, that I may be able to learn what the significance of these places be."[23] But the experts whose tutoring he required had remained behind in the Manila bureaus. It was there that the "microscope supplanted the sword, the martial spirit gave place to the research habit" (Heiser 1906, 245–47).[24] The government laboratories in the capital had become centers for this concentrated scientific activity. Even though fieldwork had not yet brought the whole of the archipelago into the laboratories' orbit, the results of the local scientific investigation of medical and agricultural problems were impressive. In 1909, the director of the Bureau of Science, Paul C. Freer, could proudly announce to a new class of medical students that "In Manila we now have a scientific library which gives access to all the recent literature, laboratories which subject the existing diseases to the search light of exact investigation and which give certain means of diagnosis and accurate statistics, hospitals in which careful studies can be carried on, medical associations which bring us into contact with the members of the profession in contiguous countries, and a journal by means of which the results of the work accomplished may be placed in the hands of our colleagues throughout the world" (1909, 72). So great were these opportunities that a number of "ambitious and well-trained investigators" had come to the islands from the University of Michigan, the Johns Hopkins University, and the University of California, Berkeley, to transform the conventional understanding of the Tropics.

While I have focused here on the Philippines, a similar pattern was repeated throughout Asia, in part as a result of the rise of the United States to international power and the diffusion of its colonial administrative practices and theories of nation building through the International Health Board of the Rockefeller Foundation. Gradually, the equatorial region was reconfigured from a place hostile to civilization to a place that a relatively autonomous white civilization could transform, "modernize," and exploit.[25] The tropical environment was no longer deemed a major impediment to global citizenship; what was left was an accessible, and generally innocuous, resource for northern industry — in a sense, the new frontier ready for development.[26] It may still have felt uncomfortable, but even in its wildest reaches it was no longer lethal, nor would it necessarily exhaust civilization. Climate and vegetation had been reduced, disarmed, and exonerated; "nature" appeared ever less determinate and implacable. Instead, the local race cultures were identified as the chief threat to alien corporeal security and peace of mind, although their menace, too, seemed ever more reformable, even if a clean bill of health was always to be retracted when sought. It could be said that everyone, regardless of race, was deemed capable of becoming an alien and therefore potentially a citizen (although in practice older hierarchical notions of race still informed the estimates of this achievement, if not the theories of capacity). In the laboratories and in the field, "tropical nature" and "tropical culture" had been reframed as separable and then brought into a global economy together.

But this summary perhaps rather too neatly disguises the underlying ambivalence of these narratives of tropical nature. The need for transcendence and dominance was always mixed with a desire for intimacy, even in the more reductionist and distanced scientific texts. Gillian Rose has suggested that the geographical gaze is "torn between two conflicting impulses: on the one hand, a narcissistic identification with what it sees and through which it constitutes its identity; and on the other a voyeuristic distance from what it sees as Other to it" (1993, 103). There was a longing for reunion with tropical plenitude, luxuriance, and nurturance and at the same time a fear of incorporation with an overnurturing, consuming topography. Cameron Forbes was fascinated with tropical nature and wanted to understand his place in it, but he also needed to distance himself through an investigative, controlling, voyeuristic gaze. It is from these intersections of voyeurism and narcissism, of transcendence and identification, of knowledge and pleasure, that modern observers continue to view the landmarks of culture and nature in southern Asia.

NOTES

1   By Hippocratic agenda, Livingstone means the neo-Hippocratic notion that "climate has stamped its indelible mark on racial constitution, not just physiologically, but psychologically and morally" (1994, 140).

2   This style of collecting masses of physiographic data has been called Humboldtian science by Susan Faye Cannon (1978); see also Anderson 1992.

3   The development of climatic typologies runs in tandem, of course, with the elaboration of racial typologies in this period (see Stepan 1982; and Fredrickson 1987).

4   Interestingly, earlier visitors do not seem particularly interested in describing and classifying the region (see Martinez de Zuñiga 1873 [1893] and MacMicking 1967).

5   A few visitors remarked on the more noble or martial character of many hill tribes, which had presumably evolved in a more temperate environment.

6   For a discussion of this medical poetics of space, see Anderson 1995a.

7   Kidd's emphasis.

8   "Geopolitics," Fabian writes, "has its ideological foundation in chronopolitics" (1983, 144).

9   For an even more pessimistic account, see Pearson 1893.

10 Thus, Griffith Taylor went about constructing white race "climographs"

and "isoiketes" to delimit the physiological Tropics in northern Australia (see Taylor 1916, 1918, 1923). Taylor founded the geography department at Sydney University and after 1928 was a professor of geography at the University of Toronto and the University of Chicago (see Sanderson 1988; and Christie 1994).

11 Sadly, Woodruff himself had recently been repatriated from the Philippines with "tropical neurasthenia" (see Anderson 1997).

12 For more elaborate charts of the distribution of climatic energy, see Huntington's *Character of Races as Influenced by Physical Environment, Natural Selection, and Historical Development* (1924). Huntington was a professor of geography at Yale University (see Livingstone 1994).

13 As Michael R. Dove points out in this volume, concepts of "nature" to some extent coevolve with nature.

14 It is significant that the Bureau of Insular Affairs was initially organized within the War Department along the lines of the Bureau of Indian Affairs (see Drinnon 1980). Perhaps the more apposite analogy would have been with the conquest of the U.S. Southwest (see Limerick 1987; and Horsman 1981).

15 On American continental "wilderness" as a counterpoint to European identity, see Cosgrove 1995, 27–41. More generally, on the late-nineteenth-century "cult of wilderness," see Nash 1982; and Cronon 1996, 69–90.

16 I use the term *biomedical present* to echo James Clifford's *ethnographic present,* as described in Clifford 1987. Of course, this time travel is also space travel (see Fabian 1983).

17 See Anderson [1994] 1995, 1995a, 1996.

18 My argument here is basically an extension of Cell's remarks (1986) on the evanescent medical justification of segregation.

19 This anticipates P. Vidal de la Blache's argument (1926) that nature does not dictate but sets limits.

20 This is a rhetorical sublime (in the sense that it enters language definitionally), not a Kantian metaphysics of the unpresentable. It is a colonial displacement of the sublimated (and therefore dehistoricized) spectacle of national empowerment that Rob Wilson describes (1991, 1992; also see Nye 1994). Cronon notes that with the earlier taming of the West the wilderness "sublime in effect became domesticated" (1996, 75).

21 "The electric fan has revolutionized the condition for civilian work in the tropics" (Hill 1914, 325). Hill was the professor of physiology at the University of London.

22 One could argue that in our own time technoscience increasingly has been desublimated and nature resublimated in environmental narratives. For an effective example, see Broad with Cavanagh 1993.

23 W. Cameron Forbes, "Journal," Sept. 23, 1909, vol. 3, p. 303, fMS Am 1365, W. C. Forbes Papers, Houghton Library, Harvard University. Forbes, a friend of William James, later endowed the first chair of tropical medicine at Harvard.

24 Heiser was the director of health in the islands and later the Director for the East of the International Health Board of the Rockefeller Foundation.

25 See also K. Sivaramakrishnan's account in this volume of the emergence of

a "development regime" for colonial scientific forestry in Bengal during this period. For an analysis of the return (or, rather, the amplification) in the late twentieth century of conservationist counternarratives predicated on environmental determinism, see Zerner, this volume. Environmental determinism of a nostalgic sort perhaps more specifically explains the salience of "tribes" (and the absence of citizens or even minority groups) in global environmental narratives during the 1990s (see Tsing, this volume).

26 Frederick Jackson Turner presented his address on the significance of the frontier in American history in 1893. In 1924, he declared: "I prefer to believe that man is greater than the dangers that menace him; that education and science are powerful forces to change these tendencies and to produce a rational solution of the problems of life on a shrinking planet" ([1924] 1932, 234). In the same address, he noted the shift of American attention to Asia and the Pacific. See also Coleman 1966, 22–49.

Charles Zerner

DIVIDING LINES

Nature, Culture, and Commerce in

Indonesia's Aru Islands, 1856–1997

Debate on the consequences of linking varieties of free market capitalism and its green market cousins to the fate of nature and local communities has intensified within the past decade, including critical thought about the boundaries and interconnections between markets, nature, society, and space (Appadurai 1996a; Gupta and Ferguson 1997; Malkki 1992).[1] This essay explores the ways in which conceptions of nature, markets, and culture have been organized, valorized, deployed, enforced, and resisted in a variety of contexts, including conservation legislation and projects, governmental and nongovernmental commentaries and programs, and natural history texts and travel narratives on nature in Aru, an Indonesian island near the coast of Irian Jaya in Southeast Maluku Province.

I argue that nineteenth-century images of market-nature-culture relations in Aru were representations of a productive, positive nexus of overlapping territories and mutual imbrication: a rich yet blurred, naturally productive space without sharp cleavages, defined borders, or zones. For mid- and late-nineteenth-century observers in Aru, naturally productive marketplaces and commercially productive nature were entwined features of the natural world. The market was part of a vibrant economy in nature's productions, drawing them to it and stimulating exchange, dispersal, intercourse, and connections to remote worlds and consumers.

In section I of this essay, I track the narratives and descriptions of Alfred Russel Wallace, a natural scientist and contemporary of Darwin, focusing on his articulations of species (nonhuman and human), race, the market, and their intersections. Wallace possessed a vision in which markets, natural landscapes and species, and human cultures intersect and interact. In his writings, he fashioned an image of the market as a site through which cultural and natural productions are concentrated and funneled to distant locales and remote, consuming publics. The space of the nature-culture-market nexus, is, for this mid-nineteenth-century observer and collector, one of fantastic spectacle, productivity, performance, and display.

Wallace's attempts to map the distribution of the "races" of man form part of his grand project to understand relationships between geology, geographical distribution, and the history of evolutionary development. But his descriptions of Aurese and English nature, society, and market relations also implicate perspectives on comparative political economy, justice, and society.[2] Wallace's legacy is richly ambiguous and has been appropriated by advocates of pure biodiversity conservation as well as social and environmental activists seeking to reinstate concerns for society, culture, justice, and political economy within the global and Indonesian environmental movements.[3]

By the 1980s and 1990s, I argue in section II, many Indonesian as well as global conservationists' images of nature, culture, and the market were no longer contained within this singular conceptual space. Rather, nature and the market were conceptualized as distinct zones marked by cartographic boundaries and in some cases criminal sanctions against movement across the borders. Nature conservation, as seen in plans, debates, and discussions about managing the Aru Tenggara Marine Reserve, was a legal regime excluding all but the most disinterested scientific human activity. In an era characterized by political-economic segregation of populations and resources, with separate methods for controlling each, I argue that distinct spatial and legal spheres of pure nature are cordoned off as if they constituted separate "nature plantations," while economically productive zones of nature are cordoned off in areas of controlled production, including timber concessions and offshore maricultural concessions for pearl oysters.[4] Nature, in the conservationist plans and projects of the 1980s, had become a spatially and ontologically separate zone, an exclusive precinct. By reviewing the history of the Aru Tenggara Marine Reserve, a marine conservation zone in Southeast Aru, I follow oscillations in the ways in which nature, culture, and the market are conceptually and cartographically zoned, enforced, and resisted. The writings on Aru of David Quammen, a distinguished contemporary nature traveler, are also examined. I argue that Quammen's assumptions about the fate of intact, pure patches of nature, a nature not yet scarred by the marks of an axe or chainsaw, embody, in literary form, similar assumptions and normative conceptions of a separate zone of nature, a world isolated from markets, livelihoods, and cultural history, including practices affecting landscapes.

In section III, I argue that in the 1990s social and environmental non-governmental organizations (NGOs) began to tactically capitalize on the existence of global and national "green spaces" in order to organize politically. At this time, I argue, they forged and disseminated, in stories, films, videotapes, booklets, museum exhibitions, and other forms of environmental publicity, a kind of nature-culture fusion. This new articulation was a nature-culture zone, a richly imagined territory in which the customs of local peoples were seen as integral to conservation and environmental management. Nongovernmental groups, in attempting to right the injustices of an oppressive political economy underwritten by a national government that splits exclusive nature zones and productive market zones, sought to replace dichotomous conceptions and schemes for separate natural and economic zones with a synthetic nature-culture space. Rather than the nature "plantations" of conservationist imaginings and programs — and exclusive, extractivist, economic development zones under state, parastatal, or private sector control — nongovernmental organizations proposed community-managed nature-culture zones in which nature is cultured and the wild may be locally managed, equitably harvested, and rightfully claimed by communities. The nature-culture *imaginaire* is a space of justice, culture, and nature.

As the prime example of the nature-culture imaginaire, I analyze the "Portrait of Defeated Peoples," (Portrait hereafter) an extraordinary document embodying one of the creative turns in the history of environmental discourses on Aru produced in the 1990s.[5] Portrait and related documents constitute reactions against the exclusive, dichotomous zoning of nature, economy, and society and an exclusive focus on biodiversity. They attempt to place local human communities at the center of the environmental canvas. Portrait turns away from conceptualizations of "nature" produced by naturalists and conservationists and the "economy" as constructed by state economic planners, constructing instead images of small-scale human communities that effectively manage, even merge, with their natural environments. Focusing on the history of an oppressive Indonesian political economy based on the extraction of marine and terrestrial natural resources, Portrait deploys images of local communities intended to redress centuries of coercive economic relationships on Aru, in particular, and throughout the Maluku Islands more generally.

If the lens of nineteenth-century naturalists and twentieth-century international conservationists was a green one, peripheralizing the presence of human communities in shaping and maintaining the environment, Portrait sees the landscape through the red eye of conflict and the unequal powers of economic actors. In the sites where naturalists discovered and collected, with a turn of their butterfly net, or, more recently, captured in photographs and nature writing extraordinary natural species and scenes, nongovernmental activists are discovering distinctive cultural communities that are specieslike. But these attempts at the conceptual remapping of nature, culture, and the economy are more accurately perceived as efforts to organize and mobilize around an emerging, animating version of space and territory in a newly fashioned conceptual zone we might call "nature-culture."[6]

I. TRAVELING TO ARU
WITH ALFRED RUSSEL WALLACE

It was during the rainy season in December 1856, that Alfred Russell Wallace hauled his mosquito nets, guns, collecting boxes, and specimen pins onboard a Bugis prau, setting sail atop a seventy-ton vessel "shaped something like a Chinese junk" for the islands that are one of the two sources of birds of paradise. In drawing his readership into this remote region, Wallace crafts an environmental image of the Aru Islands as an outback environmental cornucopia linked to distant European markets: "These islands are quite out of the track of all European trade, and are inhabited by only black mop-headed savages, who yet contribute to the luxurious tastes of the most civilized races. Pearls, mother-of-pearl, and tortoise shell, find their way to Europe, while edible birds' nests and "tripang" or sea-slug are obtained by shiploads for the gastronomic enjoyment of the Chinese. . . . The trade to these islands has existed from very early times, and it is from them that Birds of Paradise, of the two kinds known to Lineas, were first brought" ([1869] 1983, 309).

For Wallace, who had been navigating throughout the archipelagic world of Southeast Asia, a visit to the Aru archipelago represented a journey to the outermost periphery of the Malay world to collect and categorize species and develop his understanding of evolutionary history. Ensconced in his little thatched hut on deck, while the gales blew outside, Wallace contemplated the possibility of capturing the fauna and flora of Aru in terms that were breathlessly romantic: "Even by Macassar people themselves, the voyage to the Aru Islands is looked upon as a rather wild and romantic expedition, full of novel sights and strange adventures. He who has made it is looked up to as an authority, and it remains with many the unachieved ambition of their lives. I myself had hoped rather than expected ever to reach this 'Ultima Thule' of the East" ([1869] 1983, 309).

Species are the centerpiece of Wallace's observations, while landscapes are situated as geomorphological backdrops, stages for dramas of collection, preparation, and theoretical ruminations. Schemas for the classification and description of local peoples, cultural practices, and languages are, for Wallace, regarded in much the same way as are species of birds and plants. They are exotic, specieslike beings linked through historical and geographical connections, which are to be deciphered on the basis of comparative biological, cultural, and geographic analysis.

Naturally productive marketplaces and commercially productive beauty repeatedly appear throughout Wallace's representations of nature, culture, and markets in Aru. Productive natural beauty, epitomized in the appearance, structures, and performances of the bird of paradise, is parallel to the productions of native cultures — exotic, specific, and worthy of intensely detailed description and historical reflection.

On the eighth of January, Wallace landed at Dobo, the seasonally active trading settlement on the windward side of the Aru Islands.[7] One day after his arrival, he was tramping about the swampy ground behind a village, scoping out the prospects for collecting in his "first trial of the new promised land" and capturing as many "productions of nature" as he could in his butterfly net. On capturing the king bird of paradise (*Paradisea regia*), Wallace writes as follows.

The greater part of its plumage was of an intense cinnabar red with a gloss as of spun glass. On the head the feathers became short and velvety, and shaded into orange.... Merely in arrangement of colors and texture of plumage this little bird was a gem of the first water; yet these comprised only half its strange beauty. Springing from each side of the breast and ordinarily lying concealed under the wings, were ... plumes which can be raised at the will of the bird, and spread out into a pair of elegant fans when the wings are elevated.... These two ornaments, the breast fans and the spiral tipped tail wires, are altogether unique, not occurring on any other species of the eight thousand birds that are known to exist on earth, and, combined with the most exquisite beauty of plumage, render this one of the most perfectly lovely of the many lovely productions of nature. ([1869] 1983, 339)

The image of nature as a master craftsperson is suggested in Wallace's last reflections on his journey to Aru: "In such a country, and among such a people, are found these wonderful productions of Nature, the Birds of Paradise, whose exquisite beauty of form and colour and strange developments of plumage are calculated to excite the wonder and admiration of the most civilized and the most intellectual of mankind, and to furnish inexhaustible materials for study to the naturalist, and for speculation to the philosopher" (439).

Although Wallace's images of naturally productive marketplaces and commercially productive natural beauty link images of productivity and markets in the same spaces, Wallace also sketches a complementary and darker construction of the market, manufacture, and the consequences of an inequitable capitalist economy in England: "Our vast manufacturing system, our gigantic commerce, our crowded towns and cities, support and continually renew a mass of human misery and crime *absolutely* greater than existed before. They create and maintain in lifelong labour an ever increasing army, whose lot is the more hard to bear by contrast with the pleasures, the comforts, and the luxury which they can see everywhere around them, but which they can never hope to enjoy; and who, in this respect, are worse off than the savage in the midst of his tribe" ([1869] 1983, 457). Wallace praises nature as the supreme factory, the ceaseless artificer. As an impassioned political economist, he critiques the effects of an untrammeled market and state-backed systems of private property rights that permit the social barbarism of eviction and enclosure. His mode is comparative, comparing specieslike societal forms and the qualities of justice in Aru with mid-nineteenth-century rural England: "We permit absolute possession of the soil of our country, with no legal rights of existence on the soil to the vast majority who do not possess it. A great landholder may legally convert his whole property into a forest or a hunting-ground, and expel every human being who has hitherto lived on it. In a thickly-populated country like England, where every acre has its owner and its occupier, this is a power of legally destroying his fellow creatures; and that such a power should exist, and be exercised by individuals . . . indicates that . . . we are still in a state of barbarism" (458).

At first reading, Wallace's descriptions of racial and ethnic differences in Kei and Aru suggest that he also mapped human beings within the world of the biological. The antic behavior of the Kei islanders onboard Wallace's ship, described as "forty black, naked, mop-headed savages . . . intoxicated with joy and excitement," prompts a discussion of the physical, moral, and behavioral differences between two kinds of human beings, the Malay and the Papuans. For Wallace, the shape of nutmeg pigeon beaks and the brilliant hues of local beetles' caparaces, the coloration of human skin or the varieties of nose shapes, form part of the normal landscape of observed biological variation among species. His physical descriptions suggest specieslike racial and moral differences between the men of his crew, whom he calls Malay, and the inhabitants of Aru, whom he classifies as Papuans.[8] In his words, "The sooty blackness of the skin, the mop-like head of frizzly hair, and most important of all, the marked form of countenance . . . the Malay face is of the Mongolian type, broad and somewhat flat" ([1869] 1983, 319).

But Wallace's cultural and biological descriptions of the "races" of the Malay archipelago are more than a rote repetition of nineteenth-century condescension toward brown-skinned peoples and backward places. Although Wallace's summation of the physical and moral characteristics of the "races" of the Malay archipelago begins by drawing boundary lines around cultural groups, as if race, biology, and culture were all congruent and followed biologic and geographic logic, it culminates in a discourse that reverses the valorization of European culture and the lowly "savage," demoting the former and elevating the latter. A classic description of racial and cultural types ends as a biting critique of the European courts, law, and societal indifference to poverty and general human welfare.

> I have lived with communities of savages in South America and in the East, who have no laws or law courts but the public opinion of the village freely expressed. . . . In such a community, all are nearly equal. There are none of those wide distinctions, of education and ignorance, wealth and poverty, master and servant, which are the product of our civilization; there is none of that wide-spread division of labour, which, while it increases wealth, produces also conflicting interests; there is not that severe competition and struggle for existence, or for wealth, which the dense population of civilized countries inevitably creates. . . . We shall never, as regards the whole community, attain to any real or important superiority over the better class of savages. . . . This is the lesson I have been taught by my observations of uncivilized man. ([1869] 1983, 456–57)

After a sojourn in Aru's hinterland to search for new specimens, Wallace returned to Dobo in early March. His descriptions of Dobo as a site of natural productivity, markets, racial mixtures, and cultures is a paean of praise for the complexity, richness, and cultural polyphony of urban life and for the civilizing virtues of commerce. Dobo is rendered as a site of sartorial, linguistic, and even musical plurality in which the flowing robes of the Bugis hadji and the braids and trousers of Chinese traders, as well as piles of pearl oysters and sea cucumbers, are signs of concentrated vitality and civilized society: "In the morning and evening spruce Chinamen stroll about or chat at each other's doors, in blue trousers, white jacket, and a queue into which red silk is plaited till it reaches almost to their heels. An old Bugis hadji regularly takes an evening stroll in all the dignity of flowing green silk robe and gay turban, followed by two small boys carrying his sirih and betel boxes" ([1869] 1983, 335). Wallace's Dobo is an outback metropolis, a polylingual, multicultural gathering of races and cultures from Maluku, Sulawesi, Java, and Papua. For Wallace, Dobo is an instance of civilization and cosmopolitan life in the most remote circumstances.

> I dare say there are now near five hundred people in Dobo of various races, all met in this remote corner of the East, as they express it, "to look for their fortune;" to get money in any way they can. They are most of them people who have the very worst reputation for honesty as well as every other form of morality — Chinese, Bugis, Ceramese, and half-caste Javanese, with a sprinkling of half-wild Papuans from Timor, Babber, and other islands — yet all goes on as yet very quietly. This motley, ignorant, bloodthirsty, thievish population live here without the shadow of a government, with no police, no courts, and no lawyers; yet they do not cut each other's throats; do not plunder each other day and night; do not fall into the anarchy such a state of things might be supposed to lead. It is all very extraordinary! It puts strange thoughts into one's head about the mountain-load of government under which people exist in Europe. (335–36)

This orderly, tolerant, peaceful state of affairs in a potentially fractious, multiethnic settlement, a place with the potential for feuding and disputing, is attributed to the civilizing effects of commerce. In his rhapsody, the processes of world trade are linked to a wise restraint among the formerly "ferocious" Bugis and "wild" Babberese. In a passage notable for its nineteenth-century enthusiasm for the virtues of commercial society, Wallace writes that "Here we may behold in its simplest form the genius of Commerce at the work of Civilization. Trade is the magic that keeps all at peace, and unites these discordant elements into a well-behaved community. All are traders, and all know that peace and order are essential to successful trade, and thus a public opinion is created which puts down all lawlessness" (336). For Wallace, the Dobo marketplace is the site that draws natural productions and productive regional as well as local cultures together.

Wallace's critique of the political economy of England, the disastrous social effects of the enclosure movement, and the cost of creating laboring classes for the productive system also situates him as a political economist and natural scientist concerned with justice, economics, and the rights of the poor as well as the mysteries of natural history and species variation.

But there were limits on Wallace's capacity to articulate the nature of Aruese political economy. Although he waxed eloquent on the civilizing virtues of international commerce, as well as the ravages of an unregulated commerce on the livelihoods and lands of the English poor, he remained ignorant of the historically long term, hidden violence of an unregulated extractive economy on the Aruese villagers, especially women, and Aruese environments. Reports of colonial officials testified to the widespread brutality and asymmetric power relations between Bugis traders and Aruese divers. In 1824, Lieutenant Colonel Kolff, in the employ of the Dutch East India Company, observed that Aruese pearl divers on the Backshore, "have been considerable sufferers from not having the protection of the Dutch authorities, as the Bughis and Macassars, who come here to trade, are great extortioners, and appeared more in the light of plunderers than of friendly traders" (1840, 177). Colonial reports were "rife with descriptions of conflicts that broke out between traders and Backshore peoples over debts. . . . [To]gether with repeated mentions of confrontations among the islanders themselves over access to sites of collection, these descriptions evoke an especially violent image of the history of trade in Aru" (Spyer 1997, 4). During the 1880s and in 1917, the Backshore was swept by an indigenization movement, characterized by the Dutch as a "rebellion" led by "zealots," "rogues," and "agitators." The rebels sought "to rid the islands of international commerce and its concomitant civilization: the Buginese, Makassarese, and Chinese traders, the Dutch colonial administration" (6). Resistance to outsiders' domination over local markets, environments, and labor, as well as the project of indigenization, are themes that would return to center stage more than a century later in the form of NGO projects and analyses.[9]

II. POLICING THE STATE OF NATURE:
THE SOUTHEAST ARU MARINE RESERVE

The second section of this essay follows environmental texts about nature, culture, and the market in the Southeast Maluku Islands in the 1980s and 1990s. I argue that many of the descriptions of nature in recent conservationist and nature writers' accounts presuppose a relatively rigid split between the spaces of nature, culture, and the market.[10] What is striking in these texts is the cordoning off of natural areas: beauty must now have its own scheduled and policed locations. Similarly, economic zones are no longer interspersed and intertwined with natural productivity, recently renamed as "biological diversity" or "biodiversity." Nature has become a special precinct, a zone that should be protected from the market and livelihood-linked activities by the power of legal texts and enforcement procedures. Extracting, collecting, harvesting, and responding to the currents of global, national, and regional markets are now outlawed within "nature." The lively, overlapping fecundity of naturally productive places and commercially productive nature described by Wallace is absent. And the classification, appreciation, collection, and circulation of exotic Aruese nature shift to a preoccupation with a new conservationist mission: the preservation and protection of endangered species within larger territories or "threatened habitats."[11] The conceptual space in which nature is imagined has become conceptually thin at the same time that nature's territory has expanded. Nature is now scheduled and mapped as a "reserve."

THE ARU TENGGARA MARINE NATURE RESERVE

In 1991, a marine reserve was created in Southeast Aru based on the principle of strict separation between nature, economic activity, and culture. In the discussion below, I examine the texts of the 1991 Indonesian legislation establishing the Aru reserve; a newsletter article published in a European community bulletin in 1994; a booklet jointly prepared in 1994 by the Indonesian branch of the World Wide Fund for Nature (WWF) and the Indonesian Department of Nature Conservation (PHPA); and the activities of an IUCN project that supported the Aru reserve. This discussion is followed by a review of recent enforcement activities and resistance to the reserve restrictions and illegal trawling in 1997.

My discussion of the Indonesian legislation emphasizes the exclusive way in which boundaries are drawn around "natural" areas and other separate areas for economic activity. Discussion of the European newsletter item on Aru, as well as the WWF-PHPA booklet on the Aru reserve, highlights the international links, through finances, media, and project support, to Indonesian management of the reserve. Analysis of the IUCN support for legal enforcement, through raids on commercial operations and local resistance to enforcement activities, demonstrates that the Aru reserve is more than a series of lines and policy pronouncements about a strict nature reserve. Rather, it has become an object of development and a zone of contestation at the local, national, and international levels. As a contested zone, the strict boundaries and rules laid down in the 1991 legislation are sites of resistance, enforcement, and political mobilization.

In Indonesia, a strictly managed nature reserve (*cagar alam*) has the highest level of conservation protection accorded to lands or seas under governmental protection. Nature is reserved in the strictest sense of the word. Severe restrictions are placed on the kinds of permissible human activities that may be conducted within its boundaries, including research and species propagation projects. Pursuit of livelihood-related activities is prohibited.

In 1991, a ministerial decision by the Indonesian minister of forestry established a region of sea, islands, and marine creatures in Southeast Aru as a strict reserve. With a line inscribed on a government map, the decision temporarily established the boundaries of the Aru Tenggara Marine Reserve, an international "target area" (see below) of 114,000 hectares:[12] As described in the decision, the "Temporary boundaries of this area and their surroundings within the Southeast Maluku Islands are drawn with purple ink on a map accompanying this Decision, while the exact boundaries will be determined later in the field" (Surat Keputusan Menteri Kehutanan Republik Indonesia 1991, 2). In 1994, both the WWF and the PHPA produced a booklet and began discussing joint projects based on this strict separation of nature, culture, and markets in Aru. In this publication, the Aru reserve is described as if it were an underused, almost uninhabited area in which only nonhuman creatures are in need of protection: "The Marine Nature Reserve, as part of the Southeast Aru Islands is comprised of 5 little islands including Enu, Mar, Karang, Jeh and Jeudin. These above mentioned islands are not inhabited in continuous fashion by inhabitants. Only during particular periods do several sailors take shelter or overnight on an island for a few days" (WWF/PHPA 1994, 1). Within the boundaries of the "strict conservation zone," three kinds of ecological landscapes in need of protection are identified, including coral reefs, mangrove forests, and sea grass meadows; within these zones, several species of turtle as well as mother-of-pearl and dugong are mentioned (2). Anyone discovered in the act of changing the "integrity" or "intactness" (3) of the environment within these boundaries or anyone who exploits natural resources within the reserve is liable to criminal and civil penalties, including up to ten years in jail and substantial fines (3).

In the ministerial decision that mandated the establishment of the Aru Tenggara Marine Reserve, the livelihoods and historic presence of local fishing and farming communities are not even mentioned. In the magic circle of prose that established this reserve, crocodiles, dugongs, turtles, mother-of-pearl, and the king bird of paradise are established as the fully entitled citizens of this state of nature. The reserve is divided into regions on the basis of "ecosystem types," whose purpose is to advance "knowledge, education and culture" (Surat Keputusan Menteri Kehutanan Republik Indonesia [Decisional Letter of the Minister of Forests, Republic of Indonesia] 1991, 3). By drawing a line on a sketch map issued with the decision and stipulating the natural inhabitants, the ministerial letter obliterates the historic connections of local peoples to this region; their dependence on the mother-of-pearl beds, which they have harvested for centuries; and their claims to community-defined territories.[13] The state's security role in controlling nature and human behavior within the reserve is clear: the "Government must conduct routine patrols . . . for the security of the Nature Sanctuary" (13). The environmental texts construct and authorize images of the Aru reserve environment as a kind of *terra nullius* inhabited only by nonpermanent communities with little consciousness of the marine environment or how to use it.

Although enforcement during the early years was minimal, the Aru reserve soon began to receive attention and funding from European sources. In 1994, the *European Union Newsletter* announced the formation of "target areas" for its environmental projects. Aru, among other sites in Southeast Asia, was selected as a target for European Union environmental projects due to its "extremely interesting flora and fauna" and large tracts of pristine rain forest and mangroves (Van der Wal 1994). The item zeros in on two target islands just south of Workai Island, on Aru's Backshore, which are described as containing nature of "internationally recognized importance." Global interest and financial support for the Aru reserve has underwritten enforcement of a strictly dichotomous zoning of nature.[14]

With the support of international funding from the IUCN Marine Turtle Project, which promoted the study of turtle populations in Southeast Asia, raids on illegal turtle holding pens were conducted and the pens destroyed in 1997.[15] The turtle capture operations included destruction of illegal pens built by nonlocal Bugis and Butonese fishermen operating in Aru reserve waters. These outsiders pay fees to local customary leaders in exchange for permission to capture turtles within the reserve boundary (Persoon et al. 1996). Villages claiming customary jurisdiction over the waters and islands located within the reserve boundaries customarily receive money or other goods from ships that anchor in their areas or extract natural resources there. These community-managed territories, or *petuanan,* and the revenues derived from regulating access to them have been invalidated by the Aru Tengarra Marine Reserve. Local leaders are incensed that their legal institutions, and revenues derived from their operation, are no longer recognized.

Responses to the imposition of the Aru Tenggara Marine Reserve are not limited to "the weapons of the weak" (Scott 1985). Southeast Aru is the site of Indonesia's largest naval operations base. In 1997, observers in Southeast Aru reported that shrimp trawlers illegally operating within the reserve boundaries were being escorted by large naval vessels (Victor Dundee, personal communications, June 1997). State support for regulation of the Aru reserve is highly selective and favors the interests of large-scale fisheries operations with international connections.[16] Local fishermen inhabiting the Southeast tip of Aru and adjacent islands are intimidated and prevented from fishing or diving for pearls within the reserve boundaries. But they are not afraid to protest the state-sanctioned shrimping operations in portions of the reserve under community customary claims. In the spring of 1997, a trawler that had been operating within the reserve boundaries set anchor in a harbor near an Aruese coastal village. The trawler was surrounded that night by village craft, and its crew was told to abandon the ship. After the crew left, the ship was burned and sunk (Dundee, personal communication).

The conservation mission in Southeast Aru amplifies and extends earlier nature descriptions that focus on species by seeking larger spaces as target areas for conservation. The education program proposed by WWF-Indonesia for the Aru reserve endorses a green *mission civilatrice* in which reeducation of local peoples is critical. Reeducation, sometimes called "environmental awareness" programs, may be as culturally interventionist and socially oppressive as restrictive zoning and police powers: they suggest a superior knowledge about the "nature of nature" and proper social relations to it that needs to be disseminated to ignorant peoples. Hitipeuw et al. (1994), for example, recommend using the good offices of a local pastor in Aru as a personal and institutional means of supporting the global biodiversity conservation mission in its local incarnation: "Among others, Pastor Yopi is ready to support our conservation work and spread the word in the islands. Through trade and transmigration Islam is expanding and now church and mosque are often side to side. This holy place is also a good place to pass-on the message" (5). The "message," apparently, is the global gospel of conservation, which should be passed on through the good offices of local churches and mosques. In the 1991 government text recognizing the reserve, the map of legality and transgression in space and society was redrawn and former subsistence activities were criminalized.[17] Forms of expertise, scientific and international, are deployed to determine and rationalize the values, purposes, priorities, and strategies for intervention in particular environmental sites. The 1991 ministerial decision incorporates elements of a topographic map, a map of morality and criminality, a development intervention, and a constitution.

However, the history of the Aru Marine Reserve is not as darkly monochrome as this analysis of legislation, booklets, and news items might suggest. The rigidly dichotomous zoning of the Aru reserve has provoked at least some nongovernmental activists and academics to attempt creative interpretations of customary resource management practices, customs, livelihood patterns, and knowledge.[18] As early as 1979, when the Aru area was first surveyed and a foreign consultant proposed the reserve, some attention was paid to the needs of local peoples.[19] The plethora of plans, consultancy documents, and proposals produced since 1979 embodies the tensions between the primary goal of protecting and preserving the biota and an occasional emphasis on recognizing community needs, participation, and rights. In 1989, Djohani, a WWF-Indonesia marine conservation expert, opposed the existence of a strict marine reserve and urged that "In practice, the area [Aru reserve] be managed and zoned for multiple use," including "traditional use zones for local fishermen" (1989, 6).[20]

The analyses and recommendations of a team of international and Indonesian experts visiting the Aru reserve in 1994 encapsulated many of the tensions and contradictions between an exclusively dichotomous view of nature and a more ambiguous, complicated image in which nature, culture, and the market are mutually imbricated. While the group clearly and unequivocally recommended that the "status of the reserve should be changed to a Marine Park," permitting traditional uses in some areas (Hitipeuw et al. 1994, 18), they also constructed a vision of local communities as ignorant or empty vessels that need to be targeted, bombarded with information, and missionized.[21] In 1997, at least one visit by a conservation education unit was met with laughter and irritation when members of the unit proposed that families cease fishing and farm unsuitable portions of scrubland to provide food and income (Osseweijer, personal communication, 9 May 1997).

While the 1994 team of experts recognized the customary boundaries and claims of two local communities to portions of the waters and resources contained within the strict reserve boundaries, it failed to discover how utterly different the nature and boundaries of the natural world were, as imagined by local communities, from the imagined world of tropical biodiversity and habitat the team was attempting to map and protect.[22] A single recommendation is emblematic of the failure to take local mappings of nature — conceptual and topographic — into account. The team suggested that "Changing the reserve boundaries from an ellipse into a rectangle, will allow the coordinates to be easily transferred on navigational maps" (Hitipeuw et al. 1994, 18). Rather than exploring complex Aruese mappings of nature, including local knowledge of the region, as well as the history of resource extraction in these waters, the team set its sights on rationalizing coordinates into a universal Euclidean space in cartographic language easily recognized by the navy.[23]

By 1997, the WWF had designed a program and allocated funds for the Aru Tenggara Marine Reserve, and other international funding organizations seemed to be interested in supporting enforcement and development of this site. Although there is some mention of local peoples' participation, little thought is given in the proposals to the actual implementation of this idea. Most significantly, the concept of the traditional use zones, allowing particular forms of natural resource exploitation, is no longer mentioned (Persoon et al., in press). The proposal to integrate culture and livelihood into the same space as "nature" had dropped out of the picture.

"The Song of the Dodo": Traveling to Aru with David Quammen

In "The Song of the Dodo: Island Biogeography in an Age of Extinctions" David Quammen (1995) undertakes a metaphoric and material voyage to Aru, retracing Wallace's journey to bear witness to the state of nature. Aru's remaining forests, including the inland haunts of the bird of paradise, are the promised lands of island biogeography in an age of extinction. Quammen's quest is to assess the state of nature in Aru, where the forests and birds of paradise are seen to represent synecdochically the fates of biologically rich yet imperiled islands throughout the world.

I present Quammen's discussion of Aru because it is a learned, highly popular, accessible, and influential vision of the state of nature. Rather than legislating and enforcing a normative vision of nature as a pure precinct of otherness, untouched by history and culture, it embodies this vision in the form of a first-person narrative. Quammen's "Song of the Dodo" is an impassioned argument for "getting back to the wrong nature" in William Cronon's poignant phrase (1995). Quammen's nature is conceptualized as a series of broken fragments, a nature that has been violated by the ax, a market in natural commodities, and peoples' behaviors. I argue that Quammen's quest is based on the same fundamental presuppositions as those that underlie the Aru reserve legislation: nature, culture, and markets are conceived as separate realms.[24]

Quammen's journey is one informed by encyclopedic knowledge and passion but also by an underlying romanticism and nostalgia for a state of nature that may never have existed. His vision of nature is that of a fallen realm, a zone of the world that may once have existed in a state of uninterrupted integrity, that has now been ruptured by global market forces and human history. All that remains of this former world are fragments. Can wild, untouched nature, intact and unfragmented, continue to exist in Aru? How fares the Kingbird of paradise and greater bird of paradise in their remote habitat? "If time is hope, there's still hope," Quammen muses (1995), and, we might add, still time to trope. Aru is a landscape in which mankind is potentially redeemable and nature is relatively untouched.

From the moment Quammen arrives in Aru's harbor in Dobo, the opposition between productive markets and intact, innocent nature is prefigured. Quammen wanders to the door of a warehouse, where he finds, "shuffling from doorway to doorway," the creole figure of Mr. Gaite, a Christian "half-Papuan," a guide to the interior of the islands. Mr. Gaite traffics surreptitiously in a trade in living birds of paradise. Stored in a "shadowy room lit only by narrow shafts of sun," near a "lurid color print of the crucified Christ" (1995, 618), the bird is caged in a dark corner and covered with a mat. When Mr. Gaite lifts the mat, Quammen discovers a male *Paradisaea apoda* in full breeding plumage and looking "like a crow dressed for coronation" (618). The following conversation ensues.

> "So pretty," I mutter inanely.
> "More pretty if you look at it in nature, ya," says Mr. Gaite. He seems suddenly ambivalent: proud of this magnificent creature but slightly embarrassed to reveal that he's dealing in contraband birds.
> "Ya," I agree. Ya, more pretty in nature. Are there others still living where this bird comes from? (618)

Quammen suggests that Mr. Gaite, the quintessential commercial "operator" shuttling between cultures, is embarrassed by his consciousness of wrongdoing. But how does Quammen know this? Perhaps Gaite is merely a knowledgeable broker who can read his client, who can recognize a learned ecojournalist who prefers his birds uncaged and wild when he sees one. For Quammen, Mr. Gaite's assurances that there are "lots of good forest over there on the main cluster [of Aru Islands]" is not to be trusted. The natural world, imagined as a pure zone of biogeography separate from human cultures and pursuits, is in peril: "But who knows what 'lots' or 'good' may mean to a gentleman who works in a warehouse in Dobo. How much has been cut for timber? How much has been cleared and burned for settlements, gardens, copra plantations, mining operations, and cattle? How badly has the remainder been fragmented?" (1995, 619).[25]

For his journey to the interior of Aru, Quammen locates and hires a seaworthy boat and crew. Mr. Samuel, "a serious Moluccan man with a Chinese wife . . . who speaks not a word of English" (1995, 619), captains the boat through the narrow seawater channels that course between Aru's islands, leading Quammen to a village not far from a portion of forest where the birds perform their famously raucous display behavior known as *lekking*.[26]

As they sail past a small settlement, "nameless on my map and nameless on Wallace's" (and therefore nameless?), Quammen notices a small rooster-shaped weather vane perched atop the steeple of a church. "Dutch missionaries prefer the rooster icon to a cross," he observes. "Less literal, less gruesome, it's intended to symbolize the clarion cock-a-doodle of God's call. To me at that moment it suggests nothing so much as *P. apoda*, the greater bird of paradise, raising its plumes in lubricious display" (1995, 622–23). On land at last, under a starry sky, Quammen conducts a pidgin Indonesian negotiation with Peter, "an eminent hunter," who will lead him before dawn to the site of the bird of paradise's lekking tree. Peter hunts birds of paradise as well as other feathered prey. At three in the morning, Quammen makes one final condition of his quest clear: "Clumsily, I say: Peter, *mengerti saya mau lihat cenderawasih, tidak mau memburu cenderawasih, ya?* Peter does understand, doesn't he, that I want to *see* birds of paradise but I don't want to *hunt* them? Ya ya ya, I'm assured. *'Tidak memburu,'* no hunting. He understands" (624). As the dawn breaks and Quammen bushwhacks up a hilly limestone terrain, he "savors" the landscape and begins to realize that he has reached the place of his dreams and that the bird of paradise's habitat is fairly intact. The landscape that Quammen describes is apparently in a state of biological grace, spared from destruction. It is "good mature tropical rainforest . . . graced with epiphytes in the limb crotches, lewd fungi on the deadfalls, dangling lianas, a thick canopy and a fair number of great trees with buttress roots like the blades on a giant ship's propeller" (625). Although this is a landscape that has "known the machete and maybe the axe, passingly," Quammen pronounces it "innocent of the chainsaw," for the "sad, dire things that have happened elsewhere, in so many parts of the world — biological imperialism, massive habitat destruction, fragmentation, inbreeding depression . . . ecosystem decay, trophic cascades, extinction, extinction, extinction — haven't yet happened here" (625). At dawn, as a "chorus of squawking" becomes audible in the trees above his head, signifying the approach of the greater bird of paradise's display, another kind of innocence, or possibly redemption, is suggested. Johnny, the Chinese-Moluccan son of Mr. Samuel, may also have been graced with the realization that it is not necessary to hunt to appreciate the natural world: " 'Meester,' Johnny alerts me. Here in the depth of the forest, he's still wearing his 'COOL AS ICE' cap. But now even he seems thrilled. *'Sudah, suara cenderaswasih!'* Already, he says, it's the song of the cenderawasih," the bird of paradise (625). In the apparent enthusiasm of the native "other," Quammen seems to be witnessing a conversion, at least for a moment, to the recent faith of biodiversity and habitat conservation. Quammen, not unlike the authors of the Aru reserve legislation and numerous reports on how to manage the reserve, seems to believe that there is a singular form of intact nature that must be preserved; that this nature is and should be protected from culture, custom, and market forces; and that local people must be converted to the historically particular form of nature reverence that Quammen believes to be not only scientifically true, but morally unimpeachable, and universally applicable: a conversion in the wilderness.

THE INVENTION OF NATURE-CULTURE

Portrait of Defeated Peoples

At roughly the same time as green lines of demarcation and prohibition were being drawn about the Aru Tenggara Marine Reserve in the early 1990s and conservationists were retracing Wallace's journey, reorienting his natural history of Aru in the service of the conservationist agendas of the late twentieth century, nongovernmental social and environmental groups were inventing a new space, a synthetic, politically potent form of "nature-culture," which they injected into the political, legal, and environmentalist debates on regional, national, and local stages.[27] Their invention or discovery of a nature-culture sphere simultaneously redescribed Moluccan terrain as it pressed for rewriting the agenda for action.[28] Activists who had witnessed and experienced repressive national politics at the political center in Java, carried their lessons from the center to the Aru Backshore and relatively remote islands throughout the Southeast Maluku. On these remote sites, they began to produce a new kind of political space in which local communities' cultural practices, customary law, and nature management were inseparable from nature itself. To protect nature, they argued, it was necessary to recognize and respect local legal and cultural practices and structures.

To create the grounds for this new terrain and socioenvironmental program, at least some activists sought to recuperate descriptions of the Maluku Islands in ways that injected politics, culture, and the economy into nature. In the early 1990s a team of NGO activists conducting action-oriented research in the Maluku Islands had this to say about the overabundance of biologically focused descriptions of Aru:

> Already too much has been written about Aru, but much too little is known about the 'people' of Aru. The problem is that among the researchers or explorers that came to this cluster of islands, almost all of them were more drawn to their natural enchantments. The classic work of Wallace alone finished almost hundreds of pages only to talk in detail about the plants and creatures. . . . As a result, discussions about Aru up through this day are almost always about insects, birds, reptiles, mammals, forest, mangroves, coral, shark, tuna, turtles, pearls and the like (Ukru et al. 1993, 119).

The eloquent polemic of Ukru and his colleagues, "Portrait of Defeated Peoples: Cases of Marginalization of the Indigenous Inhabitants of the Maluku Islands" (Portrait hereafter), crystallizes the nature-culture imaginaire, placing local communities and the political economy of natural resource control firmly on center stage. Portrait's Moluccan landscape is, in many places, a ravaged natural region inscribed with the power of an oppressive, extractive economy of historic dimensions. In the Maluku of Portrait, a clove tree in Ternate, one of the original centers of clove cultivation, is not a mute object of global biodiversity conservation missions. Rather, it is an animated witness testifying to the vagaries of history, power, and hegemony in an extractive economy. Portrait relates that "In the center of Ternate, at a height of 300 centimeters, the Cengke Apo [clove tree of Apo] is a still living witness to the long history of the Maluku as the most important trade center of the world. Cloves and nutmeg were, to the Arab, Chinese, and subsequently the European traders the most exotic tropical plant, the reason they crossed vast oceans to see them and to control them. . . . The Cengke Apo is a natural monument to the struggle for hegemonic power over that economy which later became an arena for European military and political hegemony in Southeast Asia" (2–3).

If an ancient tree bears witness to the historic contestation for control of these remote islands and their natural products, an airplane trip reveals the scars of an environmental devastation that is still in progress. The authors narrate the results of Indonesia's natural resource exploitation and development program "Look East in an imaginary tour: "If you take a plane at 10,000 feet altitude, each person will witness that there is not even one island that remains without the red lines that intricately criss-cross and intersect: the roads for transporting wood (the logging roads!) [in English]. And, on the sea and forest land which have begun to be opened, the summary of a long story about humankind and its inhabitants, presenting a narrative which is different: subjection, condemnation, marginalization that was systematically carried out" (Ukru et al. 1993, 1). In this devastated landscape, the authors describe Southeast Maluku as they imagine it appears to contemporary speculators and investors.[29] What appears "before the eyes" of the "*neuva conquestadores*" of the late 1990s is a richly endowed natural landscape that can be plundered because it is still perceived as a "terra nullius," an uninhabited landscape:[30] "The people who ravenously search for profit can only see the extended tropical forest, crowded with volcanoes and expanses of wide seas that are rich in natural resources. If there were people living in these island clusters on the edge of the Pacific Ocean, they pay almost no attention to them at all. The same as those who came before them in past centuries, these *nueva conquestadores* consider themselves to be opening up *la terra nueva,* without any inhabitants and which, therefore, can be plundered until it is exhausted" (4). The authors reveal to the reader a portrait of the contemporary Moluccan environment that focuses on indigenous cultures and the consequences of a globally linked extractive economy that has dominated some Aruese cultures for centuries.

> Possibly many Indonesians or even Moluccans up to now did not know that throughout the marine and coastal areas of Aru there are in operation off the Aru coast not less than 28 diving and pearl culture business which add to the glow of metropolitan sign: hundreds of European, American, Australian, Japanese, Korean, and Taiwanese workers swarm . . . [to] the Aru islands [unclear phrase]. Pearl is only one [of the objects of investment]. Coral crocodiles, deer, sea turtles, and most especially the feathers of the yellow bird [the indigenous inhabitants' term for the bird of paradise] have become basic commodities in the centers of the fashion world that drove aristocratic women wild in Paris, Rome, and London. (124)

Dobo, the city through which commerce in Aruese natural resources has historically flowed, is described as a portal of corruption, "A Metropolis at the End of the World" in which speech itself is deflected and subverted by the "smear of money":

> Aru has become a "dollar area" (*daerah dollar*) far in advance of other areas in Maluku, and in the East Indonesian region it was valued by development planning experts in Jakarta. . . . The smear of money that overflows in Aru now makes it difficult for indigenous Jarjui people as well as outsiders to

speak of anything other than the topics of "business" and "money." It will not surprise [you] that Aru has become a region of modern industrial extraction, with complete infrastructure and also excesses that simultaneously glitter as signs of its cosmopolitanism: Aru at this moment is the biggest prostitution zone in Maluku. . . . Newspapers published in Ambon even have mentioned Dobo as the "City of Prostitution." (124–126)

If an oppressive political economy imposed from the outside by a variety of strangers is responsible for environmental and social inequities in Aru, then the authors' mission is to find and describe the features of an original, uncorrupted, indigenous Aruese nature-culture and to reinstate this culture in its rightful place within the political and cultural economy of contemporary Indonesia. The creative genius of Portrait is to fashion a vision of Aurese culture, including law, ritual, language, and resource management practices, that is inseparable from and indispensable to nature.

A search "in the field" for the remainders of Aruese culture, however, proved frustrating for Ukru and his colleagues, the team of researchers sent to Aru in 1992.

Who are Aru people actually? Those who consider themselves authentic people of these islands refer to themselves as "Jarjui" people. . . . But, where are they from? Rarely is even one authentic Jarjui person himself able to explain [his origins]. Peoples' legends, which were recorded during the field observation, only made the lack of clarity more obvious. . . . In reality, all the inhabitants of the Aru Islands at this time are a hodgepodge of several ethnicities that are unique. Original Jarjui people — in the true sense [that they] have not yet experienced mixing [their] blood with strangers [arrivals: *pendatang*] — can be said to be an ethnic minority in the land of their own ancestors. (Ukru et al. 1993, 121)

Portrait found it difficult to locate the imagined nation of indigenous Jarjui people intact, untouched, and uncorrupted by the invasions of desire, capital, goods, and the political-economic inequities that have characterized life in the Aru Islands for several centuries. For the authors of Portrait, the everyday lives of indigenous Aruese are dominated by outsiders who have subverted indigenous conceptions of the natural environment. In a section of their manuscript entitled "Lost within [Their] Minds," the authors relate the story of a Chinese cargo ship that sunk in the vicinity of Aru. The cargo, escaping from the foundering ship's hold, transformed itself into Aruese nature in all its bewildering marine varieties.[31] The authors of Portrait assert that this story is a fiction disseminated by outsider-traders, metropolitan middlemen seeking to confuse indigenous Aruese about their true relationship to the environment: "Jarjui people in the coming days will be increasingly surrounded on their ancestral land, which has been transformed into one modern 'metropolis' zone in the truest sense. Their natural way of thinking has for a long time been subjected to a legend that 'misleads,' and now their daily life has begun to be subjected to large-scale, systematic actions that do not cast even one eye on their existence" (128). The authors contend that internal colonization of an indigenous, natural "way of thinking" is paralleled by the historic colonization of Aruese lands and resources.[32] Since the Indonesian government's announcement of the Look East development policy (Marlessy 1991), the marine and forest resources of local communities have once again been subjected to invasion, recolonization, and neocolonial enclosure: "Traditional divers in many districts of Aru nowadays have begun to complain because the pearl harvest, over time, is losing in competition with the number of businesses owned by immigrants, who use modern technological equipment. This disquiet increasingly surfaces when they are faced with the fact that these businesses have begun to parcel the marine districts along the whole length of the coast of Aru Island and they are forbidden to dive to search for pearl shell within the boundaries of the poles [indicating] the marine realm that was parceled out" (Ukru et al. 1993, 127).

In Portrait, Aru is a landscape of natural devastation and cultural confusion and domination. Aru's original cultural and natural integrity has been compromised and irrevocably mongrelized by centuries of forced involvement in the currents of world trade. Aru is a site of forgotten origins, of confusion about who really owns local environments and the natural resources they contain.[33] People's minds as well as the natural landscape have been colonized and subjugated.

Barely thirty miles from the west coast of Aru lie the islands of Kei and to the southwest the islands of Tanimbar Kei. For the authors of Portrait, these islands are Aru's ideal twins, the unsullied political and cultural counterparts to the compromised, mongrelized history of Aru. To conjure up the nature of these cultures and cultural landscapes, the authors deploy what they describe as the original names of these places, the names still used by local inhabitants to refer to these islands: Evav (Kei) and Atnabar Evav (Tanimbar Kei), a term that suggests the appearance of an original, authentic landscape of traditional cultures and the sounds of local languages. Evav and Atnabar Evav are elements of a countermap that reorganizes local claims and names of the landscape of Southeast Maluku.[34] Evav and Atnabar Evav are produced as spaces of natural landscape and cultural geography that are still "whole" and uncorrupted. The system of customary law that the authors discover, moreover, is based on two principles: "responsibility to respect local nature," and "local peoples' livelihoods."

If Aru is constructed by these authors as a site of confusion and obscurity, a zone sullied by the "smear" of money and global markets, then Tanimbar Kei is presented as a site of cultural and legal clarity. In this relatively "intact" site, customary law is described as unified, codified, understood by everyone, and obeyed everywhere. It underwrites a "harmonious" relationship with the natural environment. Tanimbar Kei is seen as a site of integrated, unified cultural communities situated in a spectacular and uncorrupted natural landscape. It is a world epitomized as "The Last Testing Stone of Tradition" in which cultural and institutional forms produce social and environmental harmony. In this extraordinary landscape, Portrait establishes links between nature, customary law, and livelihood.[35] The authors find in Tanimbar Kei a landscape "which retains almost the entire indigenous panorama of Evav in forms that are still whole" (Ukru et al. 1993, 117). The peoples of Tanimbar Kei "or the People of Atnabar Evav are the last testing stone of the continuation of the social order of customary society and authentic tradition in Southeast Maluku" (118). Counter to the "monolithic" and "centralized" prohibitions of Indonesian national law, the authors of Portrait find in Evav a form of indigenous environmental customary law, known as *sasi,* that is "still intact."[36]

Tanimbarese "nature-culture" is presented as an alternative cultural, political, and environmental vision for the future of these islands and their peoples. The authors suggest that

> if the negative effects of primordialism from the traditional Evav social structure (the caste system) can be eliminated, along with examples of this kind, by the Evav peoples themselves . . . then their law and indigenous customary institutions will provide an interesting alternative for resuscitating the strength of efforts to conserve the environment, local autonomy, the system of communal choice, and collective life with, most importantly, the basis of their own cultural identity and integrity . . . it is not impossible that they will appear as a genuine [in English] alternative to the tendency toward global hegemony at this time. (Ukru et al. 1993, 118)

By finding, in the cultural and institutional landscapes of Tanimbar, and especially in Tanimbar Kei, the existence of vibrant, complex, and unsullied indigenous cultural forms, customary laws, environmental management institutions, and religious practices, the authors of Portrait are able to project onto the future of Southeast Maluku a visionary cultural and political geography. In the spaces of that landscape, greater autonomy, cultural difference, local legal authority, and indigenous environmental management institutions function as antidotes, perhaps idealized, to the excesses and injustices of a highly centralized and mercilessly extractive national political and economic culture.[37]

As Indonesian activists and organizations continue to develop the imaginary of nature-culture, it remains to be seen whether this discourse — as program, institution, and a way of organizing people, practices, and conceptions — will continue to serve as an animating, emancipatory discourse for political organizing, networking, and mobilization. It is too early to tell whether in its strategic linkages and engagement with international conservation and development agencies, for example, these progressive programs will be engulfed or ensnared by the sustainable development and green marketing programs that are increasingly commonplace and problematic (Schroeder 1997; Crush 1995b).

During the mid-1990s, emerging projects in Southeast and Central Maluku sponsored by bilateral aid agencies and foundations deployed ideas of "sustainable yield," "resource management plans," "monitoring," and "assessment." These conceptions constitute part of the family of rationalistic methodologies, surveillance and social control mechanisms, and technocratic tools of global development and bureaucratic apparatus (Ferguson 1994; Escobar 1995a, 1995b). At the same time, these "community-based resource management" projects hold forth the promise of promoting justice; increasing local political autonomy and community economic and cultural rights; and, not the least important, continuing a critique of the political center, its devastating cultural politics and political economy.[38]

IV. ZONING NATURE'S FUTURE IN ARU: REFLECTIONS

In this essay, I have shown how ideas of the market, nature, and culture were mutually imbricated in mid- and late-nineteenth-century visions of Aru in the work of Alfred Russel Wallace. Naturally productive marketplaces and commercially productive nature were features of the world. Productive markets stimulated the concentration, exchange, and dispersion of nature's varied productions. By the late twentieth century, in the legislation and reports concerning the Aru Tenggara Marine Reserve as well as in the travel writing of at least one gifted global nature writer, David Quammen, I show how conceptions of nature, culture, and the market were split conceptually, spatially, and legally into exclusive domains. Nature, culture, and the economy were organized as separate spheres, each with its own scheduled, mapped, and policed locations. The market, as a zone of pure economic development linked to natural resource extraction, was separated into its own locations as well: state sanctioned and mapped spheres of intensive economic development, including cordoned-off zones of mariculture and trawling, as well as timber concessions were codified and cadastralized, leased, rented, and, often without the consent of local communities, exploited.

In the early 1990s, and largely in response to the political, legal, and cultural marginalization of communities living in Southeast Aru during the Suharto era, Indonesian activists and nongovernmental groups began to forge their own counter-category of "nature-culture," a sphere in which local communities and cultures became linked to effective conservation and management of environments prized by national nature lovers as well as international scientific communities, environmental organizations, and other global social welfare and human rights institutions. The effort to resuscitate, and in a sense make visible, the rights, practices, and cultures of marginalized communities involved linking the destinies of local communities, including their economic and social rights as citizens, to their management of nature-culture and their "possession" of distinct, intact, indigenous cultural forms. This move was, and continues to be, a creative attempt to perform a kind of high-wire rhetorical acrobatics, hitching the fate of local communities to the power of nature conservation publics, programs, discourses, and funding at the national and international levels and to an ambiguously pluralistic legal system (Fitzpatrick 1997; Burns 1989).[39] Whether the choice to mobilize around the "nature-culture" imaginaire is ultimately an enabling move, increasing recognition of the rights and plights of citizens in remote Aru, or is fraught with a variety of new problems is an open question. Indeed, after the ouster in 1998 of Suharto, Indonesia's strongman ruler, many questions remain including the very possibility of democratic politics and institutions.

ACKNOWLEDGMENTS

I gratefully acknowledge the Rockefeller Brothers Fund and the Rainforest Alliance for supporting the research for and preparation of this essay. I am indebted to Patricia Spyer for her generosity in sharing many sources, as well as insights, on the political economy of Aru and the cultural complexities and implications of trade in the Aru Backshore. Frances Gouda skillfully translated Dutch texts. Gerard Persoon generously provided useful source materials of his own (Persoon et al. 1996) on the history of the Aru reserve. Discussions with

Warwick Anderson and Ravi Rajan helped me to clarify and reconceptualize this essay. Toby Volkman provided special input through our discussions and her critical review of this essay at several stages in its preparation. J. Peter Brosius and Anna Tsing encouraged these explorations. Anna Tsing's imaginative comments on early versions of this essay significantly contributed to the organization and argument presented here. I gratefully acknowledge the technical assistance of Eric Holst, Hilary Roberts, Kristen Ohlsson, and Ina F. Chaudhury. All the usual disclaimers apply.

NOTES

1   See Hvalkof 2000; Watts 1991, 2000; Peet and Watts 1993; Schroeder and Neumann 1995; McAfee 1997; Dove 1993a, 1994; Zerner 1999, 2000; Luke 1997; and Karliner 1997 for several critical accounts of markets and market-linked conservation.

2   Wallace's impassioned cultural critique and comparison contrast sharply with the aestheticized, apolitical visions of landscape produced by Henry Forbes, a Scottish nobleman who wrote during the high Victorian era. Forbes, a naturalist-traveler who followed Wallace's historic trajectory through an area now known as the Southeast Maluku Islands during the 1870s and 1880s, produced several works of travel writing, taxonomy, and nature observations (1885).

3   Warwick Anderson drew my attention to the richly ambiguous nature of Wallace's conceptions of the natural landscape and its links to culture. See his essay in this volume.

4   See Guha's analysis (1989) of "Southern" and "Northern" perspectives on nature conservation and livelihood.

5   These discourses are produced collectively by Indonesian nongovernmental social-activist groups, including Baileo Maluku, Sejati, and Hualopu, as well as individual authors (Rahail 1993, 1995).

6   See Harley 1988, 1989; and Wood 1992 for analyses of maps as political and cultural representations.

7   Dobo is located on Wammer Island, a small body of land separated by a narrow strait from the main islands of the Aru cluster, Wokam, Kobror, and Trangan. The east coast of Aru, known as the Backshore, includes the islands of Barakai, Workai, Jin, Karang, and Enu, among others. These remote Backshore communities have provided the labor to extract birds nests, sea cucumbers, and Aru's famed pearl shell for more than three centuries. Birds of paradise were caught in the forested interior of Wokam and Kobror. In the eighteenth, and increasingly by the nineteenth, centuries, hundreds of sailing boats would arrive in Dobo to bargain for this diverse collection of natural products and visit the Backshore to bargain for pearl shell.

8   See, for example, his attempts to map, conceptually and topographically, the characteristics and geographic distribution of races in the Malay Archipelago (Wallace [1869] 1983, 446–58).

9   In 1892, the rebels, sailing in an armada of eighty-five local vessels and

armed only with "kris, bows, and arrows and pick axes," launched an attack against Dobo and its traders, risking decimation by highly armed Dutch mercenary troops and steamships. On the Backshore, the rebels attacked and killed Bugis and Sino-Indonesian traders. Vastly outarmed and outnumbered, the rebellion was quickly put down with a scorched earth policy of burning the "rebel" villages to the ground, capturing key leaders, and confiscating valued ritual objects, including brass gongs and Indian elephant tusks. See Spyer 1995b for a more detailed account. For a sense of the intensity of the indigenous opposition to trade and its representatives, as well as the disparity between local opposition and the colonial response, see Koloniaal Verslaag 1893. I am indebted to Patricia Spyer, who generously provided this reference, and to Frances Gouda, who translated this text with élan.

10   Anna Tsing's perceptions of this shift have materially contributed to this line of argument.

11   The shift from the collection of tropical specimens for Western European museums to attempts to preserve whole regions of tropical habitat in situ may represent a historical shift from the perception of the Tropics as exotic, dangerous, and overwhelming to visions of a region that is domesticable, a vast commercial landscape or an exotic garden of global biodiversity, as Warwick Anderson speculates in this volume.

12   Attempts to define and map conservation zones in the Aru Backshore did not begin in 1991 or 1994. See the report of the Forestry Department (Departemen Kehutanan 1989). See also the work of Compost (1980), who made a survey of the area and strongly recommended the establishment of an extensive reserve area that would include turtle-nesting areas, dugong-populated seas, and the nearby island of Baun, where birds of paradise live. The Indonesian delegation at an IUCN National Parks Symposium in Bali announced the the establishment of a 250,000 hectare reserve, which was followed by a UNDP-FAO-sponsored National Park Development Project study recommending the establishment of a 250,000 hectare reserve (Persoon, de Longh, and Wenno 1996, 16). With the sole exception of Compost's 1980 study, however, and a 1989 report by Djohani, a WWF program officer, none of these studies deal with the potential conflicts that might be caused by claiming national jurisdiction over waters historically controlled by local communities.

13   By claiming they do not have a "continuous" presence on the islands, the Aru reserve is able to restrict the presence of people. Only "permanent, continuous occupation" and utilization of natural environments constitute presumptive evidence of an ownership claim. See Dove 1983 for an analysis of similar Indonesian governmental discourses on mobile swidden agriculturalists in Indonesian forests. Spyer notes that "Bemunese also frequent a number of small islands lying to the east and southeast of Barakai: Koltoba, Marjinjin, Jaudeng, and Je. While members of the *fam* and households with coconut plantations on these islands may spend several weeks there . . . producing coconut oil and copra, other villagers without plantations also frequent them during the off seasons to exploit the riches of the shallows off their coasts" (1992, 42).

14 See Botkin 1990; Zimmerer 1994; and Zimmerer and Young 1998 for critical, historical analyses of ecological theory and its links to the kind of dichotomous zoning described here. For an analysis of recent cases of repressive, dichotomously organized, globally funded nature zoning, see Zerner 1994a and b.

15 Persoon, de Longh, and Wenno (1996) report that the demolition of the pens belonging to Krei village on Solea Island and Longarapara village on Kelapa Island occurred within the reserve boundaries. Turtles captured by nonlocal fishermen are stored prior to shipment to Bali where they will be slaughtered for use in Balinese ritual ceremonies. Critics of the trade in turtles maintain that they are killed for the benefit of foreign tourists who desire exotic foods linked to unusual rituals.

16 See Lowe 2000 for an analysis of links between the Indonesian military, regional government, and foreign fishing fleets involved in the cyanide-based extraction of Napolean (humphead) wrasse (a large, multicolored reef fish) in Indonesia's Togean Islands to supply the live fish markets in Hong Kong and Singapore.

17 See Peluso 1992, 1993; and Neumann 1992 for accounts of the social consequences of restrictive zoning in conservation and environmental management in Indonesia and Tanzania, respectively. See Grove (1995) for a comprehensive review of the global history of conservation ideologies and their various social implications. See also MacKenzie 1988, 1990, on the politics of conservation and imperialism in Africa.

18 In the 1990s, Aru, the Kei Islands, and many of the more famous Central Maluku islands, became focal points for an emerging social and environmental imaginaire. It is an imaginaire in which progressive social schemes and green dreams are aligned but in tension and sometimes in contradiction; it is a space in which local needs and visions of a just regional political economy meet with the trajectories of internationally funded conservation missions, intersecting in multiple configurations. These are attempts to heal the wounds of an oppressive political economy, to imagine a new national cultural politics, and to save portions of a natural world believed to be increasingly fragmented. On nongovernmental activities and interpretations of community in Central Maluku, see Zerner (1994a, 1994b, 2003a; von Benda-Beckmann et al 1992).

19 In 1979, Compost proposed the creation of a reserve that would permit sustainable utilization of some species of turtle as well as *teripang* (sea cucumber) by local peoples for livelihood purposes. Compost also recommended reforming the Japanese natural pearl farms, based on harvesting viable specimens from the wild, so that sustainable yields could be obtained and local people involved in training and pearl cultivation efforts (1980, 43).

20 One of the more striking aspects of the liberalization schemes for the Aru reserve is the degree to which they have been funded by international, particularly Dutch, environmental and social organizations. The historical and cultural links between earlier Dutch colonial efforts to recognize the status of customary law and to map *adat* (customary law) regions, on the

one hand, and the attempts of contemporary Indonesian nongovernmental groups, on the other, to effect similar changes is also noteworthy. See Zerner 1994a.

21 On targeting local communities, Hitipeuw et al. (1994) state that "an 'information receiver' is needed within each target village." They then suggest a process of education that sounds a bit like forced feeding: "To achieve this, motivated persons should be selected from the different villages, to participate in brief training sessions" (17). The intersections of development, military (pacification), and conservation mission discourses and praxis are a fertile ground awaiting further exploration.

22 The group made several discoveries. One was that practically no one living in the Backshore villages adjacent to the reserve knew it existed: "most people were neither aware of the boundaries of the area, nor of the legal status of the area . . . excluding all human activity" (ibid., 15). Moreover, "the function of a marine reserve in general, and more precisely of the SE Aru marine reserve, was not at all clear for any of the target groups" (15). Finally, the group learned that the restrictions on turtle hunting were "not a major concern of the local Aruese" (13). These assertions contrast sharply with the more recent reports of Persoon et al. (1996) and several observers of the local situation in Southeast Aru. For attempts to articulate culturally idiosyncratic constructions of nature, see Brenneis (2003); Tsing (2003); Zerner (2003a, 2003b); Brody 1981; and Spyer 1995b.

23 See Spyer 1995a, 1995b, 1995c, 1999.

24 This is also a quest based on the assumption that there is a simple transparency to the idea of nature: that *the* nature that Quammen seeks to preserve is a universally understood and accepted idea. For a sense of the social and political histories of the idea of nature, see Williams 1980, 67.

25 On the limits of Quammen's assertion that we now live in a "world in pieces," from an ecologist's perspective, see Boucher's review of Quammen: "This is actually an ancient, Manichean view of the world, with everything being either God's country or the Devil's deep blue sea. . . . It has nevertheless been the basis of most conservation efforts — declare a reserve and put a fence around it and make sure that this island at least will not be invaded by the forces of civilization" (1996, 31).

26 The choice of Aruese rain forests as emblems of pure, remaining fragments of unsullied habitat may be problematic. According to Persoon, de Longh, and Wenno (1996), many of the southern islands of the Aru archipelago are characterized by woody and grassland savannah rather than tropical rain forest (2). The forests through which Quammen traveled may have been secondary forests, that is to say, forests that have been culturally shaped by decades, possibly centuries, of rotational swidden agriculture (4).

27 On NGO aspirations for community-based resource co-management in the Moluccan region see Yayasan HUALOPU 1996. See also Buchori 1995; and Retraubun 1996.

28 See Escobar 1995a, 1995b, for speculations on emerging forms of political activism that link nature and indigenous cultures in creative syntheses.

29 See Marlessy 1991 for a critical overview of the political economy of Indonesian fisheries.

30 Wallace, for whom the social and economic devastation of the enclosure movement in England was both anathema and an emblem of the uncontrolled forces of capitalism, would have immediately grasped the significance of the processes that Ukru and his colleagues describe. For example, compare their description to Wallace's vitriolic perceptions of enclosure in the English countryside.

> This all-embracing system of land-robbery, for which nothing is too great or too small; which has absorbed meadow and forest, moor and mountain, which has appropriated most of our rivers and lakes and the fish that live in them; making the agriculturalist pay for his seaweed manure and the fisherman for his bate of shell-fish; which has desolated whole counties to replace men by sheep or cattle, and has destroyed fields and cottages to make a wilderness for deer and grouse; which has stolen the commons and filched the roadside wastes; which has driven the labouring poor into the cities, and thus been the chief cause of the misery, disease, and the early death of thousands . . . it is the advocates of this inhuman system who, when a partial restitution of their unholy gains is proposed, are the loudest in their cries of "robbery"! (quoted in Marchant 1916, 381)

31 The story of the ship is recited as follows.

> Once upon a time, Aru's natural resources came from a large trading ship from China that sunk in the area mentioned above at some particular moment in the old days. Ancient porcelain plates from China carried by this trading ship became the Aruese pearl shells that are rather well known and expensive. The hull of the ship itself became sharks and giant turtles whose fins and shells were very valuable. The large oars became schools of tuna. The rigging, the sail masts and beams, and the torn fragments of sailcloth transformed themselves and became fish schools of other kinds. Food supplies on the boat shape-shifted and became sea cucumber, sea grasses, and several other kinds of coastal biota. Even the beautiful birds, especially the yellow birds, which were carried by the trading ship from the Papuan mainland, flew away from the ship as it began to founder and then became the inhabitants of the Aru jungle. Consequently, all Jarjui people believe that the natural wealth of their ancestral lands originated from outside and is not originally from Aru. (Ukru et al. 1993, 126)

32 For a contrast to this account of internal colonization of an already existing indigenous point of view, a pure autochthony, see Spyer 1995b. In analyzing how the "undersea imaginaire" of Aruese divers is constructed, Spyer excavates local constructions of history, trade, and the undersea world in which the agency of local Aurese is recognized. She proposes that Aruese configuration of the marine world may be seen as "an open-ended kaleidoscope that refracts, fragments, reassembles, and illuminates aspects of the commercial, gendered, and interethnic encounters and exchanges" (Spyer 1995b: 33).

33 On the high degree of linguistic variation among Aruese languages alone, see the work of Hughes (1987, cited in Persoon, de Longh, and Wenno 1996), who distinguishes twelve distinct languages within the Aru family.

34 See Paluso 1995 for an excellent analysis of countermapping strategies in Kalimantan.

35 Constructing this link has been an integral part of nongovernmental strategy in arguing the case for cultural and legal autonomy in other parts of Maluku (Zerner 1994a, 1994b, 2003a) and, in a larger context, in indigenous rights movements throughout Indonesia (Talbott and Lynch 1995). In publications produced by the media savvy Sejati Institute, the guiding principles of customary law have been subdivided into more particular prohibitions and regulations in a process of codification and rationalization. Indonesian regional and national organizations, supported in part by a variety of global conservation and environmental groups, have increasingly promoted these activities.

36 To Portrait's description of integrated and perfectly functioning environmental control systems compare Kolff's descriptions of the exhaustion of the pearl beds in 1824: "Among the chief villages on Vorkay, are Old and New Affara, Longa, Uri and Goor, before the last of which lies a great pearl bank. The natives informed me that it was exhausted, and that they had not fished it for two years" (1840, 177). The periodic boom and bust of local resource manias, including the desire for birds of paradise, pearls, sea cucumbers, and, most recently, shark's fins, has been characteristic of resource extraction throughout Southeast Maluku. Spyer (1992) asserts that before the eighteenth century Aruese fishermen did not know how to dive for pearls. For accounts of contemporary extractive economies and community-management of marine resources in the Kei Islands, see Thorburn 2000, 2001.

37 In the fall of 1991, the small, forested island now known as Yamdena Island (Timor Laut) attained international notoriety when skirmishes erupted between local communities claiming ancestral rights to local forests and watersheds and protesting central government support of timber concessions that ignored local claims to territory and resources (see the newspaper and newsletter coverage in *Skephi*, 1992; *Jakarta Post*, 1992; *Setiakawan*, January–June 1992; and *Down to Earth*, 17 June 1992, 28 February 1996).

38 The reader is reminded that this essay was drafted in 1996, two years before the fall of the military-based Suharto government. See Brosius et al. (in press) for a fuller discussion of the complexities and problems of the community-based resource management movement and its engagement with the international development apparatus. See also Malkki 1992; and Pieterse, Nederveen, and Parekh 1992 on cultural and ethnic essentialization and territorialization.

39 Stuart Hall's (1996) concept of articulation as "speaking for" and "linking" is a useful description of the rhetorical techniques I am describing. See Li 2000; Tsing 1999; and Zerner 1994a, 2003a, for examples of Indonesian communities and nongovernmental organizations attempting to

create new articulations that provide increased political leverage, access to funding, or opportunities for fashioning political alliances across former boundaries. See Keck 1995 for a description of how a labor movement operating among Brazilian rubber tappers gained transnational and national political leverage through articulation as an environmental struggle. For a broader view of the strategies of issue framing and the politics of articulation by transnational nongovernmental groups, see Keck and Sikkink 1998.

Roger Jeffery and Nandini Sundar,

with Abha Mishra, Neeraj Peter, and Pradeep J. Tharakan

A MOVE FROM MINOR TO MAJOR

Competing Discourses of Nontimber

Forest Products in India

A common story about the origin of *mahua* begins with a raja feasting his subjects. This version from Dumiripada, Koraput District, Orissa, was related to Elwin by Bondos: "After they [the Bondo and Gadaba subjects] had finished eating they sat around with full bellies and could think of nothing to say. Mahaprabhu came there and said, 'What is the matter? Why are you so dull?' They replied, 'There is no fire in us.' Mahaprabhu then showed them how to make rice-beer and how to distil spirit from the mahua flowers, and from that day there has been laughter and dancing in the world" (Elwin [1949] 1991, 338). If this sweet creamy flower (*Bassia latifolia*), gathered at the beginning of summer by entire villages across Central India from Gujarat to Orissa, brought laughter into the life of Adivasis, it brought wealth into the hands of traders. To Adivasis, mahua has meant food in the monsoon months when grain is scarce, oil in the days when kerosene was unknown or unaffordable, firewood, fencing, timber, and of course liquor. But drinking mahua liquor was not confined to Adivasis alone. Only in the early twentieth century did Parsi drinkers in South Gujarat turn to foreign liquor. As the British centralized distilleries and leased them out to Parsis and others, they extinguished famous indigenous brands of mahua.[1] Its illicit distillation symbolized popular resistance to state encroachments on customary usage.[2] In Bastar, the trade in mahua and other nontimber forest products (NTFPS) is the most important part of local cash income for villagers, and many traders have relatively rapidly made their fortunes from mahua.[3] Thakurs from eastern Uttar Pradesh (UP) and Marwaris have settled in large numbers in South Bastar in the past few decades; the trade in mahua and *galla dhanda* (other NTFPS) has allowed them to grow from small, itinerant traders trying to sell inferior cloth and miscellaneous goods to Adivasis to great merchants who own fleets of trucks and whose presence dominates the markets and daily lives of forest villages (Sundar 1997). For the postcolonial state of Madhya Pradesh (MP), mahua is also a substantial revenue earner, in 1979–80 generating about Rs 3 million or 3.4 percent of Forest Department revenue (Madhya Pradesh Forest Department 1981). The wealth of the forest can turn individuals from small-scale to wealthy traders, make or break political careers, and build or destroy lives.

The Indian state is currently changing the terms under which forest-dependent people in villages all across India can access all kinds of forest produce, mahua included, through the introduction of "joint forest management" (JFM), which creates local-level arrangements between villagers and the forest departments of the state governments. Villagers are helped to form forest protection committees that enter into agreements with the local forest department to protect a particular patch of (state-owned) forest land in return for a share of the benefits accruing from that patch—both intermediate benefits like grasses and other NTFPs and the final timber harvest. Since 1990, when the government of India directed the state forest departments to involve local people in the management of degraded forests, almost all states have passed resolutions to implement JFM. Donor agencies assimilated the concept into their funding programs: in 1996, nearly a third of the total outlay of Rs 17.6 billion (about U.S. $500 million) coming into the country from fourteen large, externally aided forestry sector projects was earmarked for the development of "participation." A new local government policy for "scheduled" areas has gone further and given ownership rights to minor forest products to village communities.[4]

Sponsors of this change in policy have argued that cooperation, reward, and negotiation will replace relationships between the state and forest-dependent peoples characterized by conflict, punishment, and evasion. The new policy is expected to reverse the process of deforestation, protect biodiversity, meet local subsistence needs, and contribute to sustainable development in forest areas. In this essay, we explore some of the competing ways of understanding NTFPs that underpin the new policy and the stakes of the different actors involved.

CONTESTED MEANINGS

Elsewhere we have traced in some detail different ways of characterizing JFM, each associated with different genealogies linking key events that led to JFM and stressing different aspects of it as the core or essential elements (Sundar et al. 2001, chap. 1). Different actors prioritize different goals (biodiversity, economic benefits to the local population, reforestation, empowerment, and democratic renewal, for example). Village committees often contain competing visions of future paths, with those who look for cash returns preferring different management strategies from those who want to protect grazing or firewood collection. Multiple views of JFM have been described as a strength, allowing different social interests to find sufficient common ground to allow JFM to act as an intermediate path (Sushil Saigal et al. 1996), but they can also cause conflict.

We can unpack the different meanings of JFM by looking in more detail at the assumptions made about rights to nontimber forest products. The emphasis on NTFP in JFM arises for several reasons. In most states, villagers generally have much better access to NTFPs than they have to timber. Offering villagers an increase in NTFPs as a part of JFM agreements does not normally require any change in the legal rules or existing balance of power. Second, timber products take a long time (forty years in the case of teak) to come to maturity. Third, the degraded lands that are given for JFM may never be capable of supporting good marketable timber, whereas even the most degraded patch is probably capable of providing some NTFPs — fuel wood, grasses, and so on.

Many "minor" forest products in India have multiple uses in domestic consumption, manufacturing, and so on. These uses are set within a world of rights and concessions, ownership and access, which have been the subject of dispute and negotiation throughout recorded history. Access to forests and forest products has been differentially structured for different groups of people (the state, monopoly traders, villagers, men, and women) through the colonial and postcolonial periods. The conflicts over *nistār,* a term commonly in use in the erstwhile Central Provinces (including Sambalpur in Orissa) to refer to local user rights in forests for domestic use (fuel wood, grazing and minor forest products), exemplify this particularly well. We examine the assumptions underlying nistār policies, by considering mahua (both flowers and seeds), a common item that is crucial to the subsistence and cash income of many forest-based communities in Central India. The historical material is taken from a variety of published reports on nistār and forest rights in Orissa and the Central Provinces.[5] It represents one aspect of our research on responses to forest policy initiatives and the negotiation of joint forest management arrangements in Dewas District, MP, and Sambalpur District, Orissa.

The term *minor forest produce* contains within it the entire history of "scientific forestry" in India and highlights the predominantly timber- and revenue-oriented development of the forest departments. The distinction between major and minor forest products is cross-cut by the distinction between plantation and nonplantation products. Some varieties of timber (such as teak) can be raised in plantations, whereas others (especially *sal*) have not adapted to plantations; some NTFPs can be raised in plantations, whereas others are collected only from standing mixed forests. Nonetheless, in many other respects a series of implicit dichotomies can be drawn between major and minor products. Major products involve a small number of (mostly) large items, which take a relatively long time to regenerate and have high unit values relative to their labor input. Their presence or absence in an area is easy for outsiders to assess. Minor products typically involve the reverse characteristics, requiring the gathering of large numbers of small items on a yearly, seasonal, or more frequent cycle, with large labor inputs depending on intimate knowledge of specific local forest environments.

Coined in the colonial period, the term *major forest products* included those that could be profitably exported, mainly timber, fuel wood, and charcoal (Prasad 1994, 81–91). Minor forest products initially referred to those that had largely local uses. They included a mind-boggling variety of items — animal products such as hides, horns, silk cocoons, ivory, bamboo, and about three thousand plant species, even by official definition, including canes, drugs, spices, fibers, flosses, grasses, gums, resins and oleoresins, lac, tans, dyes, vegetable oils and oil seeds, leaves, minor minerals (such as mica, lime, and shells), and edible items (Maithani 1994). Gradually, as these products gained in commercial importance, the distinctions between major and minor items became increasingly untenable and the term *minor forest product* rapidly became a misnomer. In the Fourth World Forestry Congress held at Dehra Dun in 1954, there was a move to call minor forest products "economic forest products other than wood." The term was abandoned as being too unwieldy, however, and over the years has come to be replaced with "nonwood forest products" or "nontimber forest products" (Rajan 1994, 8). Yet organizational memory within the Forest Department lingers, and foresters routinely refer to these items as minor forest products (as, from time to time, does the Ministry of Environment and Forests).[6]

Increasingly, NTFPs have been sources of revenue for the state, especially since timber supplies have decreased. Estimates suggest that of the aggregate annual employment in forest activities, 80 percent is provided by NTFPs (Bennett 1991). The share of exports of NTFPs in total exports from India was about 12 to 15 percent on average between 1960–61 and 1990–91, and the share of forest product exports was 56.5 to 75 percent during the same period (Shiva 1993).

Village categorizations of NTFPs collected during our research in Sambalpur emphasize subsistence items — roots, fruits, leaves, mushrooms, and so on. In contrast, the official lists of products that earn revenue for the Forest Department concentrate on items that are inputs into other manufactured products and form part of a commercial chain. The villagers' lists tend to shorten as products become unavailable, while the number of revenue-earning items on the list provided by the Forest Department has increased dramatically, from nineteen items of NTFP in 1904–5 to sixty-five in 1979–80. Yet, the two lists are not entirely at cross purposes and not entirely opposed as subsistence versus market. Forest dwellers have long been integrated into the market economy through the trade in forest products, and it is this interface that we need to study further — the conflicts and the cooperation that come into play at the point where the trader or the state purchaser meets the forest products collector and its effect on the sustainability of the forest itself.

Historically, the label minor forest product illustrates the material efficacy of certain discourses over others. Under the banner of scientific forestry, forests were managed for timber or major forest products at the expense of a diversity of minor ones. By terming certain species and products minor, colonial forest management practices affected their future regeneration and sustainability. For example, multispecies forests have been transformed into pure stands and the "health" of a forest has been defined in terms of tree stems rather than canopy cover and density of undergrowth. Thus, plantation practices include close planting of saplings so as to force plants to grow higher to catch sunlight and in the process acquire cleaner boles. The entire science of forest management is based on thinning the bushier trees and ensuring straight boles.

The standard definition of *normal forest* taught to all forestry students brings out clearly, first, the emphasis on timber/stems and, second, the objective of sustained commercial yield: "A normal forest is an ideal forest which serves as a standard with which to compare an actual forest so as to bring out the latter's deficiencies for sustained yield management. It is a forest which for a given site or given object of management is ideally constructed as regards growing stock, age class distribution and increment and from which the annual or periodic removal of produce equal to the increment can be continued indefinitely without endangering future yields" (Mathur 1968).

Although in a narrow technical sense this includes minor forest products, the main object of forest management has usually been timber and everything else has been incidental or minor. Although in some "backward" areas such as Bastar there are working circles (sections of forest land) designated for "Adivasi upliftment," which concentrate on income-generating NTFPs, historically the emphasis has been on production forestry and working circles have been divided accordingly. The existence of different working circles, each potentially with a selective emphasis on certain species, helped to establish the importance of minor forest products for their revenue function, but the forest itself is still hierarchically understood.

Contrast this to the situation described by Savyasaachi in an article based on field research among Kharias in the Simlipal tiger reserve in Orissa. According to the Kharia index of forest health, the state of the forest is determined by the abundance of honey available, which implies "a high canopy, having grown through a three-four story structure of a forest; a dense undergrowth, a rich diversity of flowering plants providing an important source of nectar" (Savyasaachi 1994, 34). This relatively holistic model is antithetical to the commercial emphasis on only certain specific species. However, in many cases rising commercial demand has also induced a change in forest dwellers' attitudes toward forest products, leading to collusion in the overexploitation of certain species. Thus, the Kharias find themselves collecting honey before the proper time, and collecting it from shorter trees, as all the sal is being cut down. Both of these situations have accelerated the deterioration of the forest, as understood by forest officials and the Kharias alike (32–33).

To summarize thus far, the term *minor forest product* was an outcome of the Forest Department's original preoccupation with timber or major forest products (initially to fulfill the need for railways, shipbuilding, etc.) and its predominantly revenue orientation (which was met by the commercial demand for timber) since the colonial period. As commercial demand for these products developed, they began to achieve a more respectable status in the hierarchies developed by forest administrations. Yet even this elevation in nomenclature and the consequent attention given to these forest products have not changed the basic state orientation toward forest management, which prior to the forest policy of 1988 was still largely oriented toward forest management for particular (commercially valuable) species rather than biodiversity in general. In the following section, we explore the way in which access to minor forest products was structured in the colonial and postcolonial periods, affecting different classes of people in different ways.

RIGHTS OR CONCESSIONS?

Although the state (in various ways) attempted to define the access of villagers to forest products as "concessions," villagers were often able to negotiate these into de facto (and sometimes de jure) rights of access and use, known as nistār in the Central Provinces and parts of Orissa.[7] Although it is possible with hindsight to create a structured and systematic account of a coherent colonial discourse on who held what rights to forest resources, at the end of the colonial period different individuals and groups even within one province had varying rights and obligations. Conflicts were a recurring element in people-state relations in Madhya Pradesh and Orissa, leading to several changes in nistār policy throughout colonial rule. With respect to the commercialization of forestry, British policy was internally contradictory: on the one hand, colonial administrators were keen to promote capitalist penetration by encouraging the marketing of NTFPs on a national or international scale; on the other, they attempted to protect the rights of many of the groups dependent on forest products.[8] Conflicts over nistār intensified in the 1930s and 1940s. The considerable local and regional variations gave rise to the dissatisfaction of one or another agent in the system, and the demands of many of the residents of Indian princely states in Orissa and MP were taken up by Praja Mandals as part of the nationalist movement. These conflicts gave rise to official enquiries and reports in Bengal, Orissa, and the Central Provinces written by officials deputed to try to make the system more uniform (Bengal Forest Committee 1939; Kamath 1941; Ramadhiyani 1941).

The Kamath report of 1941 attempts a precise delineation of different categories of persons, uses, and lands and provides a fascinating insight into the official discourse on minor forest products in the Central Provinces at the end of the colonial period.[9] Kamath's main problematic was to answer a question: on what basis, who has what rights to which forest products on what lands? Reading somewhat against this analysis, we can see how he classifies the bureaucratic or political "problem" posed by breakdowns in social order as a result of conflicts over these rights at the time he was writing and why he proposed the solution he did.

Kamath says that villagers defined *nistār* as follows: "the actual right of user; an item or items of jungle produce required (for example, *Nistār lane gaye the*); the bona fide domestic use (for example, *Nistār ke waste laye hain*)" (Kamath 1941, 34).[10] Nistār included grass for thatching, fencing material, creepers, roots, barks, leaves, fuel, and wood for agricultural implements, the erection and repair of houses, and other bona fide agricultural uses (Kamath 1941). This does not, however, entirely specify the answer to the question of what kinds of access villagers had to nistār — free or after paying some form of compensation to the "owner" — nor of what use was made of forest resources that fell outside the definition of *nistār*. The nistār rules were developed in conjunction with the reservation of the marketing of certain forest products, so they also had implications for cultivators who grew those products on their own land.

The forest and the field had coexisted in precolonial times as well, of course, generating interests that at times conflicted and at others complemented each other (Rangarajan 1994, 149–51). While emphasizing forests as spaces beyond the reach of settled agricultural empires, the frontiers of fealty in Mughal and Vijayanagar times, and consequently inviting military expeditions, several scholars have also emphasized the contribution of the forest to state finances and political stability. Chetan Singh, for instance, notes that in the early days of the Mughal empire income from pastoral products (*ghi* or "clarified butter") was quite significant and only as the agricultural base expanded did land revenue come to be the mainstay of the empire. But interaction between pastoralists and farmers and fluctuations between the lands they respectively used (forests and fields) continued to be the norm, with one being converted into the other (Singh 1995, 33–35; see also Guha 1999a).

The trade in minor forest products symbolized an interface of mutual interaction between forest dwellers and settled agriculturists. Describing India in the eighteenth century, Bayly writes: "The tribesmen and nomads furnished the settled with beeswax, honey, spices, carriage, milk and soldiers. The settled provided the fringes with money, cloth and grain" (1988, 31). Banjaras, itinerant traders, and Gossains, Hindu ascetics and mercenaries, were instrumental in carrying out this trade (Bayly 1983, 29).

How far colonialism marked a watershed has come under some debate, with precolonial state controls over forests coming to light — for example, certain jungles were maintained for strategic reasons or for the exclusive hunting grounds of rulers, and local rulers reserved to themselves the right to certain valuable species. The Marathas also set up plantations for shipbuilding and revenue (Grove 1993, 321; Rangarajan

1994). But as Rangarajan (1994, 152) points out, these did not amount to a complete system of forest management. In the colonial period, in contrast, most aspects of forest management, including conservation, were subordinated to the paramount need for timber to feed the process of shipbuilding and railway expansion. In the process, local rights of usage were controlled, and access to minor forest produce was no exception. In their overview of the debates over the Forest Act of 1878, Gadgil and Guha note that the "annexationist" position, which sought to vest all ownership and control over noncultivated lands in the state, attempted to justify this by reference to practices in precolonial states (1992, 118–21, 136–39). The ostensible recovery of the state's "customary" rights, which were then reduced and recorded as law, was in most cases, however, a legal fiction masking the right of conquest (124–34; for a more comprehensive view of the debate, see Pathak 1999).

The threefold distinction between prohibited (reserved), partially prohibited (protected), and open (village or nistāri) forests, enshrined in the Forest Act of 1878, has been well documented (Gadgil and Guha 1992, 134). In protected forests, duties on NTFPs were elaborated and extended under colonial rule. Between 1866 and 1890, they took four different forms in the Central Provinces: "the *kham* system; the system of leasing forests for *nistār;* the system of summary settlements; and the commutation system" (Prasad 1994, 113–16).

Under the kham system, the villagers collectively paid nistār dues to the state through the headman, while under the system of leasing forests, contractors were given monopolies on the extraction of forest products on payment of a fixed sum to the government. Contractors then "sold" the products to the villagers. In practice, the peasants themselves performed the actual work of extraction, effectively becoming wage laborers in addition to having to pay for their nistār needs. Both of these systems proved disadvantageous to the state since it lost both revenue and control over the forests. Under the system of commutation dues, which seems to have been the dominant form across the Central Provinces, households paid a fee in return for the right to take forest products for domestic consumption. Summarizing the position regarding grazing and nistār in the Central Provinces estates (or large *zamindaris*), a position similar to that which prevailed in the princely states, Kamath notes that people's access to forests in the pre-colonial or early colonial period was generally unrestricted except for certain species of timber.[11] The practice of charging commutation dues was generally initiated in court of wards estates (i.e., those that came under direct British management generally due to the minority of a ruler or his so-called gross ineptitude) as a source of additional revenue, the justification being that these estates were generally in debt.

But Kamath's report paints an extraordinarily complex picture of how the state intervened to qualify and distribute rights to nistār. The legal definition of types of land was basic. Kamath distinguishes between land in the princely states and British India (which could be further divided into land owned by the government, land settled under the *malguzari* system (or *khalsa* land), and land settled as zamindari land).[12] Only then could Kamath distinguish clearly the land to which his report related (only to trees and forest products on land in the zamindari areas) and then classify the land further into village forests and wasteland *mahals* (land far from villages that was owned by *zamindars* but not cultivated). Because all of these types of land could be mixed together in a patchwork, rights could vary dramatically even within a few miles and in a single local agro-ecological zone.

Kamath divides forest products into "large timber," grazing, and nistār, although he acknowledges that nistār rights require the maintenance of "large timber" so as to produce an environment in which nistār products could flourish. Types of people are distinguished, partly on the basis of their occupations (middle peasants vs. tenants vs. laborers vs. village nonagricultural classes) and partly on the basis of residence. Thus, in some villages residents had rights to grazing or nistār on the lands of other villages; elsewhere, rights were restricted to those tenants who paid more than a specified minimum rent. Under successive land settlements, (from the 1860s to the 1930s), obligations to provide labor in return for rights to nistār were in some cases commuted into dues and progressively refined.

Distinctions drawn between agricultural and nonagricultural or commercial classes of people were used to explain or justify a host of taxes and cesses, which differentiated between subsistence needs and access to commercial inputs. For example, "occupational nistār" was levied on shopkeepers and artisans for forest products used. When the Forest Rates in Indore State were revised in 1912, the shoemakers of Neemuch were charged twelve annas for a cartload of first-class fuel wood, while agriculturalists paid six annas. Also, with respect to grazing, agricultural cattle (i.e., those used for cultivation) were distinguished from nonagricultural cattle (those that met the household needs of the noncultivating laborers and artisans and those that were kept for commercial purposes). In addition, other restrictions were introduced on types of trees cut, areas in which nistār was allowed, and so on (Kamath 1941, 27–32). Finally, the collection of minor forest products from certain classes of trees was increasingly taxed, whether on zamindari or state-owned forest or private land, but needless to say this situation varied considerably as well (27–32).

Mahua (described by Kamath as "the nistār fruit par excellence") presents a complicated case, being both an item of domestic consumption and an important item of sale. Forcing tenants to sell to a lessee appointed by the government or zamindar was common, but in many places the right to collect mahua was also taxed. This tax was either in cash or kind, either a lump sum for the whole village (as in Dondi-Lohara) or the obligation to give the zamindar (or his appointed lessee) a certain portion of the amount picked (as in Kamatha). In some estates, the flowers and fruit from mahua trees were divided equally among all the households in a village, regardless of whose holding the tree was in, indicating (as Kamath notes) the importance of the tree to rural economies. In their statements to Kamath, landless laborers expressed their desire to retain this custom; not surprisingly, tenants who had a large number of mahua trees wanted exclusive rights. But virtually all agriculturists wanted the right to sell the products from trees in their holdings to anyone they liked (Kamath 1941, 78–79).

Thus, the possibility of profit was crucial to Kamath's underlying model of rights and development. For example, in his proposal to divide people into agricultural and nonagricultural categories, "grazing is to be free for all cattle of agriculturalists, instead of for all agricultural cattle" (1941, 91). The purpose of this restriction was to reduce the number of excess cattle and to make grazing more expensive for all cattle kept by people who "are engaged in selling milk and milk products or in selling cattle *as a profession*" (97, italics in original) — in other words, people who trade in animals or animal products rather than those who keep animals to help them cultivate the land or to feed or clothe their own family directly. Similarly, when he writes of the needs of village artisans for jungle products Kamath is very clear.

> The fuel which a blacksmith wants to feed his forge with is not a domestic necessity, but what might be called an occupational or professional necessity. He is not entitled to have it free. No objection can therefore be taken to commutation dues of this kind. The next question is whether they should be subject to any control by the State. Control of some sort appears necessary only in two cases —
>
> (a) where the artisan is an indispensable element in the life of the village; and
> (b) where the industry carried on deserves encouragement by the State, but might languish and die if overtaxed by the zamindar. (114–15)

Here and elsewhere Kamath contrasts the moral rights to subsistence with the lack of rights to marketable products. He presents nistār as entirely in the realm of moral claims for subsistence: "the general principle is that nistār is free only when it is required for carrying on a day-to-day existence and not what is required on the occasion of a rare, though inevitable, event [in this case, a marriage]" (1941, 115). For forest peoples proper, he employs something akin to a Chayanovian model: aware of class differences between households, he does not see these differences as allowing for the accumulation of surplus. His focus is on the fact that households of different sizes and landholdings will need access to differing amounts of subsistence products from the forests, whether it be grazing for plow animals or mahud for alcohol. Economic relationships based on the market are almost all presented as resulting from relationships with outsiders, or those brought in from outside, who are the ones likely to profit from the exchange.

Kamath presumes that forest people are incapable of handling such relationships satisfactorily. He discusses the loss of large timber in the nineteenth century, blaming petty zamindars who were unable to negotiate a good market price for their timber. He claims that the unrest of the late 1930s was generated by the increasing indebtedness of the zamindars and their consequent need for new sources of revenue, which led them to remove rights previously enjoyed by other forest-dependent people (1941, 32). Kamath defines his own role as one of protecting the "ignorant and backward in wild and remote areas" from unreasonable demands by absentee zamindars bent on transforming feudal relationships into cash ones. The move to the law of supply and demand was both undesirable and inevitable (101). The problems for his analysis posed by those forest dwellers who were part of the market economy — cattle breeders and milk sellers or migrant grazers — and by the subsistence interests of those involved in the market, are glossed over.

Kamath presents the state as holding the ring between the competing claims of zamindars, tenants, outsiders, and state officials, but he recognizes that the state has its limitations. In the nineteenth and early twentieth centuries, according to his presentation, the state was unable to enforce the rules that it drew up for forest management. It could not implement the surveillance necessary to know if the rules were being followed; it could not control the activities of zamindars; it did not have enough professional advisers to carry out its own prescriptions in favor of scientific forest management; and, through the rules it passed, it made forest people vulnerable to harassment by forest guards through false accusations and arrests.

Agricultural laborers and landless tenants (known as *thaluas*) were the worst hit in this situation. They had to pay for both grazing and nistār at nonagricultural or commercial rates, which were often double the agricultural rates. In Pagara zamindari, the definition of *thaluas* was enlarged to include marginal tenants who paid less than Rs 2 in rent, another case of the more marginal farmers being most affected (Kamath 1941, 58). Commutation dues also varied between areas set aside for nistār and the "zamindari reserves," commercial rates being charged for the latter. The attempt to limit or strictly define these nistāri areas formed an important part of the struggle between peasants and landlords or the colonial administration itself. Landlords sometimes (e.g., in Bhadra zamindari) appropriated reserves carved out of village forests, while in others, even in the allotted nistār areas, villagers were allowed to remove nistār only once a year and then in the presence of a forest guard. In another zamindari, Kamtha, "whole village communities have to join together and take on lease at an auction what areas are necessary for them for ordinary *nistār*. As the lease is given to the highest bidder, they have also to provide the middleman's profit, where it goes to a professional *thekedar*" (62).

Petty controls were inevitably intensified by the variety of legal restrictions. Forest guards and others invaded peasant homes in the hope of catching out illegal nistār removals: "Complaints have been made that structures have at times been demolished. A single pole brought from the jungle if cut in two or more parts while building the house or *kotha* is counted as two or more as the case may be and penalties are levied, and sometimes the 'excess quantity' is also seized" (Kamath 1941, 70). Kamath's conclusion is worth quoting here in full. He observes that

the grazing and *nistār* "customs" are frequently breaches of the old rights, which the tenants have been unable to maintain. . . . This does not of course mean that the conditions of the 1860s must be or can be reproduced today. That is frankly impossible. For we cannot possibly ignore the changes that have taken place since then — the expansion of cultivation, the decline in the area of forest and waste, the increase in numbers both human and bovine — all of which must alter the grazing and *nistār* position. But at the same time, it would be well to bear in mind that the tenantry has lost all along the line in the matter of grazing and *nistār* rights.

The tenantry obviously was unlikely to suffer this without protest. Major rebellions in Bastar in 1910, and the forest *satyagrahas* (civil disobedience movements) of 1930, are examples of direct opposition; at other times, peasants used the "weapons of the weak": poaching, illicit grazing, and taking whatever products they needed (Baker 1984; Scott 1985; Sundar 1997). In 1929–34, the number of forest offenses in the Central Provinces and Berar as a whole amounted to 22,258; following the onset of the depression, they increased to 27,137 in 1934–39. More than half of this amount in each case was for illicit grazing and the removal of NTFPs (Grigson [1944] 1993, 340). Since forest guards and zamindars alike preferred to avoid the courts if possible, these figures almost certainly heavily understate the extent and significance of disputes over NTFPs in this period.

MAJOR MONOPOLIES ON MINOR FOREST PRODUCTS (1900–1947)

Not all of the encounters between the state and peasants were of a confrontational nature. Nothing reveals this more clearly than the marketing of minor forest products. The terms of trade were often structured against peasants by granting lessees monopsony rights, and there was inevitably scope for conflict there, but there was also an element of mutuality involved.

A distinction generally existed between those items of nistār deemed to have only domestic uses and those with commercial value such as *harra* (*Terminalia chebula*), mahua (*Madhuca latifolia*), or *chironji* (*Buchanania lanzan*). With the exception of mahua, in much of Orissa and the Central Provinces collection for domestic consumption of these commercially valuable items was free, but any amount beyond that had to be sold to a monopsonist appointed by the state or zamindar (Orissa Forest Enquiry Committee 1959, 47; Kamath 1941, 77). People had to accept whatever rates they were offered, not only for products collected from the forest but for any plants cultivated on their own land. As Ramadhiyani noted, such arrangements effectively turned cultivators and collectors alike into laborers on a meager wage — if indeed the full price was actually paid (1941, 35). An additional problem was one of nonstandard measures: in Pagara zamindari, peasants complained that the measure used was three times the normal one, thus reducing their wages threefold (Kamath 1941). Prices of some NTFPs, particularly harra, were linked to prices in the London market, and the state experimented with different collection methods, depending on its perception of profitability and future preservation. In Bastar, a duty was initially charged per maund of harra. In 1906, the forest administration organized the trade themselves, advancing money to peasants for the collection of harra and buying it from them. As prices of harra fell during World War I, the state decided to grant long-term leases to merchants (Sundar 1997).

The escalating global demand for certain items of NTFP in the early twentieth century also led to a new kind of symbiosis among the state, capitalist firms, and forest dwellers. Tracing the penetration of capitalism in the Central Provinces from the second half of the nineteenth to the mid–twentieth century, Archana Prasad uses lac as an example to show how this occurred. Local artisans (bangle and toy makers) used lac; forest dwellers collected it and marketed it to them. In the second half of the nineteenth century, there was a growing export demand from America, England, and Germany: lac was used in gun factories, as an insulating varnish, as a preservative for wood, and so on (Prasad 1994, 123–25). Contracting with large firms for collection solved the problem of reconciling the government's interest in revenue with efficient extraction. The end result was that "The imperial government benefited either way. It got royalty from the firm which got the contract for trading in lac and it levied taxes on lac collection by individuals. Though it preferred to give the lac collecting contract to the firms, the forest communities possessed the required knowledge for breeding lac cocoons and were experts at the labour processes involved. In the second half of the nineteenth century they were to be used by the Colonial government for the departmental control of lac" (90).

Prasad concludes that this new development had a differential effect on collectors and local artisans. The former benefited from the new labor opportunities, particularly in the wake of other restrictions on their gathering and cultivation activities, but the artisans lost the source of their raw material, as the lac was diverted to the international market. In the process, local links between artisans and forest dwellers were broken (Prasad 1994, 128).[13] Because the legality of tree ownership changed and zamindari was abolished, the relative benefits of NTFP trade shifted for different classes of people.[14] The practice of granting monopolies for the purchase of NTFPs is still a feature of forest policy in one form or another, however, despite repeated objections.

NISTĀR IN THE POST COLONIAL PERIOD (1947–95): MADHYA PRADESH AND ORISSA

The nistār situation changed after the merger of the former princely states, the abolition of the zamindari system, and a new land revenue code (in 1959). In MP, the new post-Independence government promised to honor existing nistār rights as recorded in the village *wajib-ul-arz* and appointed nistār officers to assess people's nistār requirements.[15] The responsibility for nistār was given to the revenue department. However, lack of experience led to the formation of nistār zones that did not match actual availability; this in turn led to an increase in "offenses" as pass holders took their nistār from nonspecified areas or reserved forests (Madhya Pradesh Forest and Nistar Products Committee 1959, 23–25). In 1949, nistār forests were converted into protected forests and transferred to the Forest Department (133–35).

In 1957, the MP government issued a revised Nistār Forest Policy in which forests closest to villages were to be managed to meet nistār requirements. In response to complaints about the existing policies — including the nonavailability of materials, wide variations in the value of concessions granted in different regions, and a flawed method of distribution — twenty coupes (forest sections) were earmarked in each zone to satisfy nistār requirements. Other changes included reducing the number of contractors working these coupes in favor of departmental employees and working through the collector and a chain of village heads and village *panchayats* to issue permits. Nistār holders were charged half the commercial rates of royalty for material gathered from reserved forests, while rates in protected forests (which included the erstwhile nistāri forests) continued on the existing nominal terms plus the cost of felling (Madhya Pradesh Forest and Nistar Products Committee 1959, 133–35). For a while, the system of commutation continued in some parts of MP, for example, in Vindhya Pradesh (Rewa and surrounding regions), while in others (e.g., Mahakoshal), it was abolished by 1959 (108).

In 1957, the value of nistār concessions was estimated to be more than Rs 2.5 million per year (Madhya Pradesh Forest and Nistar Products Committee 1959, 135). The *nistār* facility, which following Independence was unique to Madhya Pradesh, extended to all villages, not just those bordering nistār forests. By 1992, there were 2,496 nistār and 725 commercial depots where products were sold (Khare 1993, 15). In 1995, there were five different categories of nistār: free (for minor forest products), concessional (for timber poles at 50 percent of royalty rates and fuel wood and bamboo at 5 percent of market rates), occupational (for basket makers, *beedi* frame manufacturers, and so on), commercial (for bamboo and timber at 80 percent of royalty rates for villages not covered under concessional nistār), and finally consumer (for timber up to half a cubic meter for commercial fuel wood depots) (Singh 1993, 9–10). In his study of forest products marketing in MP, however, Khare estimated that the rates charged to various categories of nistār holders have increased rapidly in recent years and are fast approaching the rates charged to commercial or industrial houses. For instance, rates on nistāri bamboo rose from 25 paise per piece in 1985 to Rs 1 per piece in 1992. The average gross revenue per notional tonne for the entire state from nistāri bamboo (including that supplied to occupational groups) was Rs 559.88 per notional tonne, while for Orient paper mills the figure came to Rs 550 per notional tonne. On the other hand, the supply of bamboo met only 1.5 percent of the demand, while the supply of fuel wood met about 10 percent of the demand. The gap between demand and supply, Khare points out, led to several abuses of the system, giving forest officials arbitrary powers and leading to the sale of nistāri materials on the open market (1993, 14–16).

Following several studies in preparation for a World Bank Forestry project launched in October 1995, the MP Forest Department decided to eliminate the nistār system in April 1996. Villages engaged in protection are now given royalty-free nistār in return for their efforts; all others are charged commercial rates, in keeping with the philosophy of joint forest management in which rights are associated with responsibility for protection.[16] In practice, despite all the legal arrangements regarding depots, villages that abut forests continue to supply their nistār requirements directly.

In Orissa after Independence, the Madras Forest Act of 1882 affected the southern districts of Ganjam and Koraput and parts of Phulbani District, and the Indian Forest Act of 1927 applied to the rest of the state. The former princely areas also had different rules. But, despite the variation in rules, overall the practice was broadly similar. In the reserved forests, or "A" reserves, the only concession was the free removal of NTFP, while there were expanded rights in the protected forest, or "B" reserves, rights to take reserved species at concessional rates, free grazing and removal of NTFP, and so on. Village residents were charged a nistār cess or commutation dues, usually assessed on the basis of annual land revenue paid; once a cess was paid there was usually no restriction on the amount of products extracted. According to the Orissa Forest Enquiry Committee of 1959, this led to gross denudation of nistāri areas, and the nonavailability of products in turn led to a demand for the abolition of cesses. The committee estimated that the state lost more than Rs 60,000 annually from the supply of concessional nistār (Orissa Forest Enquiry Committee 1959, 26–28). It recommended the abolition of the cess and, among other things, the allotment of forest patches (B class, protected or village forests) to villages within a ten-kilometer radius, with distribution to be determined by village panchayats or special committees ap-

pointed for the purpose. Where there were no such forests, it recommended converting a portion of the A reserves into B forests to meet
villagers' demands (48–52). In a note of dissent, P. K. Deo, Member of
Parliament, argued that to abolish nistār cesses and charge a uniform
rate across the state, for adivasis and traders alike, would be a "gross
betrayal." The blame for forest denudation, he pointed out, should not
be attributed to villagers' exercise of nistār rights but to the inadequacy
of the Forest Department (2–3).

Thus, nistār policy in both Orissa and Madhya Pradesh has been subject to conflicting pressures both from villagers who see changes in the
policy and the increase in rates as encroachments on their customary
rights and from forest officers who view villagers' overuse of nistār as the
main problem.

> In Madhya Pradesh, discussions with field officers indicate that throughout
> the last two decades two processes led to fast deforestation. One, arising out
> of political populism, to allow people to harvest in an unsustainable manner
> more and more in the name of Nistār, and the other pressure on officers to
> contribute more to revenues. . . . Ironically, before an election, according to
> these officers, it was common for a Minister to order that the forest be
> opened for *nistāri* for both tribals and non tribals without penalty. But after
> the election, the same Minister was likely to demand more revenue from the
> same forest. (Saxena 1993, 2–3)

CONCLUSION

The multiplicity of rules, rights, and concessions described by Kamath
and Ramadhiyani remain important today for two reasons. First, there is
still a crazy patchwork of customary practices, many of them unre-
corded, that surface in times of dispute. Grazing at certain times of the
year or collecting certain kinds of NTFP from a particular forest may be
allowed, but the same behavior by different people, at different times of
the year, or in relation to other NTFPs may generate bitter disputes. Thus,
JFM agreements are not introduced in an uncharted sea but are super-
imposed (often by people unaware of the existing patterns of rights) on
complex patterns. Villagers themselves differentiate between different interests when they manage their JFM forest patches. In Lapanga, Orissa,
for example, the forests are managed for timber for house repairs and
firewood but not for *tendu* leaves, so the poor who depend on this
particular NTFP are forced to go elsewhere. In general, men and women
of different castes and classes are differentially dependent on NTFPs and

have different kinds of access to them. In Dewas, MP, only Nals collect NTFPs, and so they have an interest in helping the Forest Guard to catch offenders. In Panchmahals, Gujarat, only Naiks (low-status adivasis) collect a particular gum, and they do not collect tendu leaves. Similarly, in Haryana, low-status Banjara women process grass into rope, but Gujjar women refuse to do such work (Sarin 1996b, 9).

Second, the government still structures people's access differently, though not along the old lines. No doubt, deciding competing claims is part of the government's raison d'être, but in India, despite the occasional radical rhetoric, propertied classes have benefited from most such decisions (Bardhan 1984). Joint forest management is one more mechanism through which the government is intervening to differentiate between populations. Thus, villagers living near high forest enjoy different rights from those living near degraded patches, and within small areas JFM agreements have often generated new disputes within and between villages (Sundar et al. 2001). In some cases, women have argued that the only change is that the guards who stop them from collecting fuel and fodder in neighboring forests are now men from their own villages rather than Forest Department employees.

Instead of contrasting categories, then, we need keep in mind the source of variation among forest-dependent people. Furthermore, the presumed hostility between the values of those relying on NTFPs and those who want to use major or minor forest products for commercial purposes must also be questioned. *Down to Earth* (30 November 1995) reported an interview with the headman of a Madia Gond adivasi village in Gadchiroli District, Maharashtra. He was asked how the government policy that gives forest lands to the paper industry for captive plantations will affect him. After stating his opposition to such a venture, he responded as follows.

> If the industry wants wood, they can buy it from us. But they will have to ask us. We will decide whether we will sell at all, and if so, on what terms.
>
> *So you are against industry?*
>
> No, we are very much for industry. But we have to ask who benefits from industry. Are they for the people, that is *adivasis* like us? Or are the *adivasis* fodder for industry?

By starting from the differential power and economic interest among the groups involved in JFM, we can see that it does not resolve all the issues such differentials generate. Supporters of JFM often assume (wrongly) that subsistence is the appropriate use for NTFPs. By critiquing commercialization yet failing to propose an alternative, such JFM agreements threaten to leave forest dwellers on the margins. To expect a single policy like JFM to solve questions of availability, access, and equity in forest products as well as preserving biodiversity is perhaps to invite not only disappointment but an enhancement of the conflicts it was supposed to reduce.[17]

NOTES

1 Hardiman (1985, 181, 190, 192) notes that mahua liquor is mentioned in the *Vishnudharma Sutra* (ca. A.D. 100–300).
2 Hardiman writes of illicit distillation in early-twentieth-century Gujarat that "Among the poor and landless no stigma was attached to breaking the law in this manner; rather it was considered admirable to thus outwit the Parsi and the police" (ibid., 192).
3 A study by D. N. Tewari in 1981, quoted by Arvind Khare, found that on average households earn Rs 1,500 out of a total income of Rs 1,750 from the sale of NTFPs (Khare 1993, 17).
4 Provisions of the Panchayats (Extension to the Scheduled Areas) Act, 1996.
5 Sambalpur was part of the Central Provinces until 1912, when it was merged with the province of Bihar and Orissa.
6 See, for example, the letter of the secretary, Department of Environment, Forests, and Wildlife, 1 June 1990, reprinted in Poffenberger 1990.
7 There are close similarities with *mafikat* (literally, "free cutting") in Gujarat.
8 For similar arguments with respect to agriculture, see Dirks 1992b; and Washbrook 1981.
9 We are grateful to Dr. Crispin Bates for drawing our attention to, and providing a copy of, the Kamath report.
10 These phrases can be translated as "gone to get nistār" and "brought for nistār."
11 Commutation dues and differential rates for agriculturists and commercial users prevailed in zamindari areas, the princely states, and British India.
12 Zamindars had higher status than malguzars, had certain powers concerning law and order, and could not (in principle) divide their holdings nor alienate them to others, whereas malguzars were not controlled in the same way. Zamindari estates might also be taken over and managed by the state if they fell into debt or maladministration. Furthermore, malguzars had no right to the income from their forests, whereas zamindars did.
13 However, Prasad cautions against generalizing this trend to all products, using the case of silk and iron ore to show that the penetration of capitalist firms had very different effects on different categories of artisans.
14 See Gold 1999b for a discussion of the effects of zamindari abolition on forest cover in parts of Rajasthan.
15 The wajib-ul-arz contained a specification of village "customary relations

and mutual obligations" on zamindari estates when they were first settled by the British (Kamath 1941, 162). Village "customs" were listed, but there was some doubt as to whether these had the force of law unless this was explicitly stated (Baden-Powell [1892] 1972, 2:482–83; Kamath 1941, 161).

16 A. K. Khare, Chatrapati Singh, N. C. Saxena, and others have recommended an additional relaxation of the rules for felling trees on private lands. Khare has advocated that nistār rights for fuel wood should be allowed to continue, however (1993, 16).

17 How JFM may exacerbate intra- and intervillage conflicts among forest-dependent peoples is discussed in Sivaramakrishnan 1996b. See also Sarin 1996a, 1996b; Sundar et al. 2001; and Hobley and Wollenberg 1996.

Rural Landscaping

Michael R. Dove

FOREST DISCOURSES

IN SOUTH AND SOUTHEAST ASIA

A Comparison with Global Discourses

The West has a special relation to the forest, and deforestation.
— Giles Deleuze and Félix Guattari

Discourses that articulate the place of the local in the global are nothing new. Past examples might articulate a southern land to a northern one in monarchic terms (colonial India as "the jewel in the crown"), religious terms (Jerusalem as "the Holy Land"), or mercantile terms ("the mines of Madrid").[1] Over the past several decades, in conjunction with the popularization of holistic planetary images (Ingold 1993; Sachs 1994), a discourse of global articulation has emerged that is based on a new dimension, the environment and its transformation. The emergence of this discourse has gone hand in hand with the rise of enormous interest in the role in the global ecosystem of forests and forest loss, especially in the Tropics. Efforts by global environmentalists to mobilize interest in addressing the causes of tropical deforestation have led to the development of conceptually and politically powerful metaphors. A characteristic example is the reference to tropical forests as "the lungs of the world."[2]

This reference can be read as a straightforward representation of the great efficiency of the tropical forests in maintaining the earth's atmosphere through carbon dioxide absorption (Dixon et al. 1994; Houghton and Skole 1990). It also can be read as a pragmatic effort to persuade a global audience to take an interest in a regional matter by representing it in global terms. From another perspective, however, the global lungs image is clearly problematic. For example, although tropical forests are especially efficient in absorbing carbon dioxide, all forests perform this function; so why are the tropical forests alone being constructed as the global lungs? The asymmetry inherent in this image is made more apparent if we replace *lungs* with some other body part, such as *muscle* (referring to tropical less developed countries as the muscles of the globe while the northern developed nations are, e.g., the global brain). I will suggest here that one way to better understand the use of such images in global environmental discourse is by looking more closely at local discourses.

THE CRITIQUE OF GLOBAL ENVIRONMENTAL DISCOURSE

The emergence of a global environmental discourse almost immediately generated debate about what constitutes proper versus improper representation of the global environment, in particular what role Western cultural, economic, and political biases implicitly play in these representations. A starting point for a number of critiques was the dubious validity of the premise of linear, cumulative environmental degradation in less developed countries exemplified by McCann's (1997) critique of representations of deforestation in Ethiopia by leading Western environmentalists.[3] A number of critics have questioned the emphasis on forests and forest loss in global discourses.[4] Deleuze and Guattari (1987) attribute this emphasis to the reliance of Western symbolic thought on the image of the tree as opposed to the rhizome.[5] Perhaps more tenable than this essentializing, cultural explanation is the political explanation of Buttel (1992, 19), who famously characterized the emphasis on forests as "forest fundamentalism." Buttel argued that the overweening focus of global environmentalists on tropical forests not only deflects attention from the ecotypes in which most tropical peoples live (i.e., agricultural, grassy, or bushy landscapes), but it also deflects attention from problematic ecotypes and uses in the nontropical, industrialized countries. The self-privileging aspect of the emphasis by northern environmentalists on southern forests has been noted by a number of critics in both the North and the South. The latter are exemplified by Malaysia's Prime Minister Mahathir, who gained prominence by deflecting northern attacks on his country's rapid deforestation with questions about historic deforestation in the critics' own countries as well as their role in perpetuating a global economic order that, according to him, does not support resource conservation in the less developed countries.[6]

Another major turn taken in the development of this global environmental discourse has involved counterposing a local discourse to it. Building on earlier ethnographic studies of local environmental relations, there have been a number of recent attempts to ask not what forests mean to environmentalists in the industrialized nations but what they mean to local peoples in the less developed countries that are the focus of deforestation fears.[7] These attempts include, for example, Bird-

David's (1990) analysis of the metaphoric equation of forest with grand-parent among the Nayaka of South India, Fairhead and Leach's (1995, 63) analysis of "single forest" as a metaphor of political solidarity for the Kissi of Guinea, and the analyses of Rival (1993) and Mosko (1987) of the forest as a mirror for social structure among the Huaorani of the Amazon and the Mbuti of Zaire, respectively. There have also been some self-conscious efforts to denaturalize the global environmentalist discourse by identifying explicitly divergent local discourses. An example is Richards's (1992) study, in which he contrasts the environmentalist premise that people protect the forest with the premise of the Mende of Sierra Leone that it is, rather, the forest that protects people.[8] More pointed yet are studies that purport to reveal local dislike of forests and cultural support for deforestation such as those by Bloch (1995) on the Zafimaniry of Madagascar and by McCann (1997) on the Gera and Ankober of Ethiopia.[9] These studies are part of a wider body of work that critiques the global environmentalist vision of indigenous forest communities in less developed countries as "primitive conservationists" (e.g., Diamond 1986; Ellen 1986; Redford 1991). Misuse of ethnography in the environmentalists' representation of primitive conservation has been specifically critiqued by Brosius (1997a).

The reliance in these studies of local environmental discourses on our own conceptual conventions (Dove 1998a; Greenough and Tsing 1994, 96) and the emphasis on counterposing the local to the global has led, perhaps inevitably, to some eliding of the internal differentiation and dynamics of the local. As a result, our understanding of such discourses is still in its infancy (Greenough and Tsing 1994, 95). We are ill prepared as yet to either interpret local, colloquial environmental discourses or assess their implications for our global discourses. For example, in con-temporary Pakistan people who live beyond the bounds of society are commonly referred to as *jungli log*, "junglelike people," and in Indonesia the latex-producing, forest-bound smallholdings of indigenous peoples are commonly and derisively referred to *hutan karet* or "rubber jungles." Analysis of these colloquial, local discourses suggests that they may be relevant to our understanding of global forest discourses.

THIS STUDY

I will employ a historic, "genealogical" approach (Foucault 1973) to the study of these forest discourses. I also will take a comparative approach, comparing local and global environmental discourses and comparing local discourses from two different parts of Asia. Recent examples of such comparative analyses include Brosius 1997a; Conklin and Graham 1995; Turner 1991; and — especially apposite here — O'Connor's (1995) analysis of agriculture and society in Southeast Asia and Zerner's (1994a) analysis of local and global discourses of conservation in eastern Indonesia.[10]

My comparative data are drawn from research in both Indonesia (focusing on Borneo and Java) and Pakistan (focusing on the *barani,* or "rainfed," tracts of the Punjab and the Northwest Frontier Province). Reynolds (1995, 429, 432), in a recent review, notes that comparisons of the two regions are surprisingly rare, although they share many aspects of cultural history. The cultural-ecological congruence between the two regions is well expressed by the fact that the folk analogy that the relationship between a king and his people is like the relationship between a tiger and a forest (in that the former both "live off" of the latter) is common to both regions (Moertono 1981, 22). On the other hand, Day's (1994, 181–84, 194) comparative analysis of environmental representations in temple carvings in the regions shows that the apparent similarities disguise equally profound differences.

Indeed, the cultural ecologies of the two regions are far from identical, and in some respects they are even antithetical. To give but one example, the current forest cover of Pakistan amounts to less than 4 percent of the country's land area, whereas in Indonesia this figure is 48 percent.[11] The difference between the figures is a function of both biophysical and social factors: the historic vegetation of most of Pakistan is tropical thorn forest, whereas in most of western Indonesia it is tropical lowland evergreen rain forest (Champion, Seth, and Khattak 1965, 111; Whitmore 1975). Whereas state formations responsible for massive engineering of the environment extend back just over one millennium in Indonesia, they extend back four and a half millennia (to pre-Aryan, Indus civilizations) in Pakistan (Allchin and Allchin 1988). The greater time depth of intensive land use in South Asia, in what is perhaps inherently a more fragile physical environment, has been associated with longer-term alteration of this environment.

This study will focus on describing and comparing two particular forest histories and discourses, one from Pakistan and a second from Indonesia. I will suggest that both discourses share an emphasis on environmental change, linkage of this change to changes in social identity, and contested and subjective interpretation of both changes. Comparison of the two Asian environmental discourses to the global environmental discourse suggests that the global discourse shares most of the elements of the local Asian ones, differing only in a more self-conscious assertion of objectivity.

TWO ASIAN FOREST DISCOURSES

The origin of this study lay in my observation of some curious linguistic data pertaining to forests in both South and Southeast Asia. In the latter case, I observed that in different parts of Indonesia seemingly related pairs of terms were used to mean "house" and "village," on the one hand, and "field" and "forest" on the other. In South Asia, I observed that the contemporary term for "wild forest" has roots in an ancient term for "tamed savanna." Both sets of data opened up to me the possibility of an inquiry into local visions of the historical relationship between society and forests.

South Asia

The term *jungli,* cited earlier, comes from the Anglo-Indian term *jungle,* which is based on the Urdu term *jangal* (Yule and Burnell [1886] 1903, 470).[12] *Jangal,* in turn, originally derives from the Sanskrit term *jangala* but with an interesting change in meaning. Whereas *jangala* originally meant "arid, sparingly grown with trees and plants" (Monier-Williams 1899, 417), *jangal* today means "a wood, a forest, jungle" (*Urdu-English Dictionary* 1977, 265). The change in meaning can be summed up by comparing the symbol of the *jangala,* the Indian antelope (*Antilope cervicapra*), with the symbol of the *jangal,* the dacoit or outlaw. The ability of the antelope to live on the land was the ancient definition of *jangala,* of land that was suitable for Aryan settlement and the propagation of Brahmanic culture and religion (Zimmermann 1987, 61), whereas the ability of dacoits to escape capture in the riverine forests of contemporary Pakistan is a symbol of the limitations and boundaries of contemporary society.[13]

As characterized in the Vedic texts produced by the ancient Aryan invaders of the subcontinent (e.g., the Rgveda [Griffith 1973], the Arthasastra [Kangle (1969) 1988], and the Laws of Manu [Buhler (1886) 1964]), the jangala was open bush or savanna (Zimmermann 1987). It was arid country but healthy for humans and also crops, provided that river or well water was available. It was concentrated in the west, in the central plains of the Indus Valley, in that portion of the subcontinent today called the Panjab in both Pakistan and India. Above all, it was ritually "pure." The jangala was not created by natural forces alone, however. In the absence of human intervention, the climate of this part of the subcontinent tends to produce a low thorn forest, not an open savanna (Champion, Seth, and Khattak 1965, 111). The savanna represented what happened to the thorn forest when it was modified by the livestock and fire of the pastoral Aryan peoples (see Allchin 1963, 170–71; and Zimmermann 1987, 18, 44). In other words, the jangala represented what happened when the thorn forest was partially cleared and then prevented from fully reconstituting itself. The jangala is a "depanperate" vegetative cover, therefore, maintained through periodic disturbance by people and animals (Champion, Seth, and Khattak 1965, 27–28, 3833–40; Spate and Learmonth 1976, 73–74; Whyte 1968, 167, 173, 174, 188). The role of anthropogenic fire in this process is reflected in Vedic beliefs about fire: in the *Rgveda*, for example, hymns associate the fire god Agni with cattle and fodder grasses in a context of renewal (Griffith 1973, 45, 541, 639). This analysis of the anthropogenic characteristics of jangala is supported by ancient tenurial codes, which granted rights based on clearing grasses but revoked them if the clearing was not repeated within a given amount of time (Ghoshal [1929] 1973, 108; Zimmermann 1987, 14).

Since Vedic times, the jangala has been succeeded by jangal. The vegetative and geographic referents of the latter term differ considerably from the former: it typically refers not to open savanna but to a bloc of closed forest, and it typically is found not in a central but a marginal location such as in hills or seasonal flood plains. A major shift in symbolic referents also took place between jangala and jangal: the latter is typically wild, as was the former, but it also is beyond civilization, whereas the former was not. Whereas pastures and fields once lay within the jangala, they do not lie within today's jangal. Jangala was the place where the Aryan felt most "at home"; jangal is the place where contemporary rural people "feel fear." Whereas jangala encompassed Aryan civilization, jangal is excluded from contemporary society. As a result, the wild and the domesticated, nature and culture, are much farther apart on the contemporary landscape than they were on the ancient one. Whereas the principal divide on the contemporary landscape is between nature and culture, the principal divide on the ancient landscape lay between civilization and barbarism — with the former subsuming *both* nature and culture. The differences between the two cultural geographies are summarized in Figure 1.

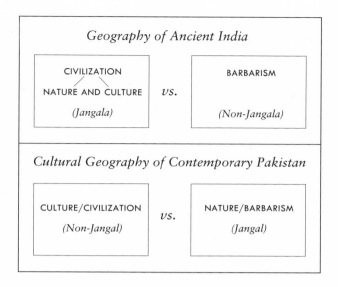

Figure 1. Ancient *Jangala* vs. Contemporary *Jangal*

Central polities as well as local communities, have been involved in the social construction of both jangala and jangal, as can be seen in ancient state prescriptions regarding where the Aryans should live. Thus, the Vedic *Laws of Manu* states "Let him [the king] take up residence in a *jangala* place" (Zimmermann 1987, 39). The implication that the jangala was a natural environment waiting for the Aryans to come along and settle it, as opposed to an anthropogenic environment that they had to create, reflects a historic conflation of the categories of nature and culture. The role of the contemporary state in resource management, on the other hand, contributes to not a narrowing but a widening of the distinction between nature and culture. For example, the Pakistan Forest Service traditionally considered all small farmers to be inveterate tree haters who posed a constant threat to state forests and were incapable of on-farm tree cultivation (Dove 1992b). This reflected the government's view of a chasm between forests and people, between nature and culture.

Linguistic data from my Southeast Asian project reflect similar changes in the physical and conceptual landscape, but in this case what is involved is the historic conflation of the meaning of multiple terms.

Linguistic Evidence In a prescient but now overlooked essay written forty years ago, Harley H. Bartlett (1962, 274) observed that there is an interesting pattern of variation in the meaning of the common Malayo-Polynesian term *uma*. He states that in some societies it means "agricultural field" (which he thinks was its original meaning), whereas in others it means "house" or "field and house."[14] This same pattern can be seen in contemporary Indonesia and Malaysia. For example, *rumah* means "house" in Indonesian and Malay, and *humah, omah,* and *umah* similarly mean "house, home" in Javanese (Echols and Shadily 1992, 468; Horne 1974, 411, 685; Prawiroatmodjo [1957] 1981, 1: 653; Wilkinson 1959, 2: 987–88), but in Malay *uma/huma* means "dry field," and in the Ibanic dialects of Borneo *umai* means "(swidden) field" (Richards 1981, 410–11; Wilkinson 1959, 1:414, 2:1263). An analogous series involves the term, *kampung.* In common Indonesian, Javanese, and Malay, *kampung/kampong* means "village" or "(urban) quarter" (Echols and Shadily 1963, 163; Horne 1974, 254; Wilkinson 1959, 1:503), but in Ibanic dialects *kampong* means "primary forest" (Richards 1981, 137) and in Simpang Dayak *kampong* has the intermediate meaning of "former village site/fruit grove."[15]

Of most interest is the fact that there is cross cutting *covariation* between the two afore-mentioned patterns:

Indonesian/Malay	Ibanic Languages
rumah/kampung	*umai/kampung*
"house/village"	"field/forest"

The terms for house and village tend to occur together, as do the terms for field and forest. Thus, the paired terms *rumah/kampung* mean "house/village" in Indonesian/Malay, whereas the paired terms *umai/kampung* mean "field/forest" in Iban. The one pair appears to map onto the other.[16] Whereas the various uses of *kampung* appear to be cognate, *rumah* and *umai* in fact are not. In Proto-Austronesian, *rumah* (house) and *umai/huma* (field) actually have different linguistic etymologies (Blust 1984, 220–21, 235; Blust 1987; Dempwolff 1937, 3:61, 70).[17] The uses cited above therefore represent conflated "folk etymologies." Fox (1973, 350–51), following Turner (1967, 286), says that such "fictitious etymology" is an important means of integrating systems of classification.

The classificatory system involved here — with its association between "house" and "village" on the one hand and "field" and "forest" on the other — addresses the most basic relations of social production and reproduction. The elements in each of the terminological pairs, *rumah/kampung* (house/village) and *umai/kampung* (field/forest), are related through dialectical processes of ecological transformation. Fields are cut out of, but ultimately return to, the forest in upland systems of swidden agriculture.[18] In a similar fashion, households are created by, but ultimately dissolve into, the village in the lowland peasant societies of Indonesia and Malaysia. In short, both the household and the swidden field have a similar, ephemeral character within a wider cycle of creation and destruction. In Indo-Malay cultural-ecological history, thus, the relationship between the household and the village is like the relationship of the field to the forest:

field : forest : : household : village

This analogy — field is to forest as household is to village — maps onto the two most widespread, historic modes of economic production and social reproduction in Southeast Asia: forest fallow shifting cultivation, in which fields are termed swiddens, and permanent cultivation, typically irrigated agriculture, in which the fields are called pond fields.[19] The fundamental difference between these two modes of production is a reversal in valuation of the factors of production. The swidden system is characterized by scarce labor and abundant land, and so returns to the former are maximized, whereas the pond field system is characterized by abundant labor and scarce land, and so returns to the latter are maximized (Dove 1985). Thus, the pond field system exploits labor and the swidden system exploits forested land.[20] This fundamental difference in the productive base of society is reflected in the folk saying, cited earlier, that "the relation of a king to his people is like the relation of a tiger to a forest." Pond field societies in fact are based more on the exploitation of human capital, "the people," whereas swidden societies are based more on the exploitation of natural capital, "the forest." This difference between the two structures of production and reproduction has come to be reflected in Indo-Malay language and thought in the "fictitious etymological" relationship between *field/forest* on the one hand, and *house/village* on the other.

Cultural and Political Valorization The difference between the swidden and pond field systems in scarce factors of production, and in whether returns to land or labor are maximized, is associated with a series of differences in cultural values. Labor and people are more highly valued in swidden societies, whereas land is more highly valued in pond field societies. Similarly, the value placed in pond field societies on getting the maximum yield out of each square meter of land is not shared by swidden societies; nor do the pond field societies value the swidden farmer's ability to satisfy basic subsistence requirements with a limited amount of labor, thus freeing labor for tasks such as gathering of forest products or production of export commodities.

The opposing cultural valuations of swidden versus pond field systems play out within a wider framework of historical, political, and geographic relations. Swidden versus pond field cultivation is a fundamental point of distinction in the history as well as the geography of Southeast Asia. Swidden agriculture can be practiced, and once was practiced, all over the Southeast Asian landscape. However, state development, which was concentrated in the lowlands and promoted the development of pond fields for ease of extraction and control (see Scott 1998, 282, on the "fugitive" swidden fields and peoples of the uplands), over time relegated swidden agriculture to the margins of governance, meaning the hills and mountains. Flight beyond the reach of the state, one of the most important historic mechanisms of peasant resistance to state oppression, also contributed to this pattern (Dove 1985). By the twentieth century, throughout Southeast Asia pond fields and swiddens had become identified in hegemonic national discourses with, respectively, lowlands versus uplands, contemporary versus archaic technologies, and central civilization versus peripheral barbarism (Burling 1965; Dove 1985). This pattern of valorization is reflected in the development within the region of cultural myths of lowland societies settling the uplands, whereas the reverse was often the case (Reid 1997). The fact that the extractive economy that supported the state was generally more suited to pond field than swidden cultivation, and that swidden cultivation mostly came to characterize areas at the limits of, if not beyond, state control, exerted a powerful influence on the topographical norms of the state. Southeast Asian states have characteristically demonstrated a strong bias in favor of pond fields and their open lowland landscape, on the one hand, and against swiddens and their upland forested landscape on the other (Dove 1985).[21] This bias is not without its complexities, however.

During the era of precolonial kingdoms of Java, for example, state hostility toward forest-based society and economy was tempered by recognition of the important role that the forest wilderness played in opposition to the civilized central state. This recognition can be seen in the fights staged between tigers and buffaloes — the symbols of the forest and the royal kingdom, respectively — at coronations in the Javanese courts (Wessing 1992).[22] The fact that the fights were often "rigged" so that the tiger would lose is important, but the fact that the tiger was allowed to fight at all is also significant. This linkage to the forest is also reflected in the use of the "tiger in the forest" as a metaphor for the proper relationship between a king and his people. The historical Javanese states saw the forest as a distinct realm, therefore, but one that operated on principles somewhat similar to their own and one whose existence was important to their own (see Burling 1965, 6; Leach 1960).[23] This valorization of a landscape containing forested as well as non-forested areas was reproduced on a smaller scale in the idealization of an agricultural system that included both intensive (pond fields) and extensive (swiddens).[24] Christie writes (1991, 32) that "The oldest term to be applied to Javanese settlements in the legal literature is *wanua*. . . . This territory appears to have been large, based perhaps upon the territorial requirements of mixed agricultural systems including swiddens. The formulas in the charters relating to *wanua* land include such phrases as, 'the forests, swidden fields, and rivers, in the valleys and on the hills,' 'their valleys and mountains . . . their *sawah* [pond fields] and orchards,' 'their *sawah*, dry rice fields, marshes and orchards,' and others in the same vein." On an even smaller scale, it is likely that both individual Javanese communities and many of their constituent households historically, as well as today, based their agricultural strategies on the simultaneous exploitation of a "portfolio" of different resource bases that formerly included lowland pond fields and upland swiddens.

The linkage of the two ecotypes continued throughout colonial and postcolonial rule in Indonesia, but its ideological support did not. Perhaps the most famous example of the linkage during the Dutch era was the system of tobacco cultivation in Deli, Sumatra.[25] The tobacco growers utilized the dynamics of the local swidden cycle to provide them with planting sites cleared of forest, and after their tobacco had exhausted the soil they relied on the dynamics of the swidden forest fallow to reforest their sites (Geertz 1963, 106–11; Pelzer 1957). By insinuating their crop into the local swidden cycle, therefore, they wrested an economic and ecological "subsidy" from this cycle. A number of other important export crops were similarly subsidized by swidden agriculture. Notwithstanding this fact, the colonial Dutch customarily referred to swidden agriculture as *roofbouw*, "exhaustive or robber agriculture" (Jansonius 1950, 1245). The term *robber* reflected the Dutch belief that this system of agriculture flourished only at the cost of "robbing" the environment of an above average amount of resources. By implication, the pond field–based cultivation of rice or export crops that the Dutch favored did not involve any robbery of this sort. The Dutch did not accept, therefore, the fact that swidden cultivation based on scarce labor and abundant land was just as legitimate a system of production as pond field cultivation, based on scarce land and abundant labor. The Dutch denied, that is, the swidden and pond field trade-off between land and labor. By using the term *robber* to characterize swidden agriculture, the Dutch were in effect saying that if swiddens performed as well as pond fields it was only through "cheating." The fact that the Dutch themselves relied on this cheating in systems such as the cultivation of Deli tobacco did not dissuade them from what was thus a heavily ironic characterization.

This depreciation of a resource use system by a society that was all the while profiting from it continued into the postcolonial era. The production of many of Indonesia's most important export commodity crops continues to be linked to swidden agriculture: these crops are cultivated by smallholders to meet market needs while swidden crops are cultivated to meet subsistence needs. Policymakers have resolutely ignored this linkage, however, and they have continued the tradition of state vilification of swidden agriculture. Indeed, until the 1990s, swidden agriculture was commonly not even acknowledged in national government circles as a system of agriculture, and often swidden forest fallows are still perceived as "abandoned" land if not, indeed, as "natural" forest.

SIMILARITIES AND DIFFERENCES IN THE TWO ASIAN DISCOURSES

The agro-ecological typologies that lie at the heart of the South and Southeast Asian discourses discussed here are idealized cultural constructs, but they also have great local value and thus importance. The fact that the typological boundaries are frequently crossed or otherwise violated is less significant than the fact that the cultural constructs invest all such crossings with special meaning. The interpretive power of these constructs is such that outside observers have also employed them to make sense of these regions: witness the prominence of the swidden–pond field dichotomy in the classic analyses of mainland and insular Southeast Asia by Burling (1965) and Geertz (1963), respectively.

Social and Environmental Change

One of the most obvious similarities between the South and Southeast Asian discourses is that they both concern change, specifically change in nature-culture relations. In both regions, a major historic transformation occurred in the terms of negotiation between nature and culture: in the South Asian case, the civilization-encompassing jangala became the civilization-excluding jangal; and in the Southeast Asian case the dialectic between field and forest was replaced (in some places) by a dialectic between household and village. The local representations of these transformations remind us that forest discourses — and the human environment relations that produce them — did not begin with contemporary, northern environmentalism, nor with the colonial era. Greenough and Tsing (1994, 98) and Rangan (1995), among others, have pointed out that the "standard environmental narrative" developed in recent years by intellectuals and activists in South Asia, which posits the colonial era disturbance of a previously unchanging and undegraded environment, is not in keeping with the historical facts. It is certainly not in keeping with the historical discourse of jungle described here.

The two regional discourses link changes in environment with changes in society, including changes in the way society thinks about the environment. Greenough and Tsing (1994, 95) write that "Knowledge of the environment . . . is socially constructed in environmental practices."[26] As practices change, so too does both nature and its conceptualization change. In both regions, indeed, the conception of nature has changed as relations between society and the environment have changed (see Dove 1998a; and Kirch 1994). In South Asia, cultural views of the jungle changed from positive to negative as the predominance of jungle in the landscape waned, and in Southeast Asia cultural valorization of a field-forest dialectic shifted to a household-village dialectic as the forest cover (and thus the forest-field cycle) similarly waned. The conception of nature in these two cases has thus "coevolved" with nature (Dove 1992a).

This coevolution affected more than just society's concept of the environment, however, for both regional discourses treat the nature-culture dialectic as a contest with winners and losers — as was indeed historically the case. Thus, the ancient Aryan populations of the subcontinent pushed the non-Aryans out of the jangala regions into the wetter, less healthy, heavily forested regions (of the Ganges Plain), the *anupa* (Zimmermann 1987). In contemporary Pakistan, society pushes those who do not belong to it, such as dacoits, into the jangal, the contemporary equivalent of the anupa. Similarly, the enemies of the historic Javanese kingdoms fled into the forests (Dove 1985), whereas in contemporary Indonesia the federal government forcibly moves tribal peoples out of forests (in a program called Resetelmen Penduduk, "Population Resettlement") to render them more susceptible to state control and the forests more available for exploitation by state elites. In the South and Southeast Asian discourses, therefore, environmental transformation is not sociologically neutral; it is all about power and identity and, inevitably, changes in power and identity.[27] Indeed, it is precisely the possibility of such change that gives environmental transformation the great cultural significance that it holds in the two discourses.

Contest and Agency

The question of who or what is the agent of environmental transformations is salient and contested in the two discourses.[28] This contest is expressed, in part, in differing perceptions of the mechanisms of deforestation and reforestation. An example can be drawn from my Pakistan project, which involved an effort by the Forest Department of the Northwest Frontier Province to fence and reforest a barren hillside (Dove 1992a). This effort was based on the planting of seedlings of an indigenous tree, *Acacia modesta*. One of the biggest constraints that the seedlings faced was competition from spontaneously occurring "weeds," to the suppression of which the Forest Department was devoting considerable resources. Researchers from my own project discovered, however, that many of the so-called weeds were also *Acacia modesta,* which proliferated naturally on the hillside as soon as it was fenced and browsing by local goat herds ceased. Thus, the Forest Service was simultaneously planting and uprooting the same species of tree. The two actions were differentiated solely by the question of agency: the planted *Acacia* required the agency of the Forest Service and were thus supported, whereas the naturally occurring *Acacia* did not require its agency and so were combated.[29]

A second example, from Indonesia, involves the *hutan tanaman industri* (HTI) or "industrial tree plantation," which enjoyed great official support during the 1990s as a response to deforestation (and has also been supported by an extensive public relations campaign on "Green Indonesia" financed by the major logging companies). The basic logic of the HTI, that the best way to respond to deforestation is by planting trees, is based on two disputed premises. The first is that the forest itself lacks "agency," that the felled trees must be replaced using human agency if the forest is to be restored. Ecologists take issue with this premise, arguing that it overlooks the fact that all of the natural environmental forces in Indonesia are predisposed toward generating tree growth, that it is only human agency that retards this, and thus that it is human factors that must be addressed to reverse deforestation. The second disputed premise of the HTI is that it is a sociologically neutral, purely technological intervention. In fact, it is much more than that: the act of planting itself has profound implications for proprietary rights to the forest, decisively tipping the balance between indigenous rights holders and the external elites that control the timber companies. For this reason, many of the the tribal people of Kalimantan say that they fear the HTI far more than the *hak pengusahaan hutan* (HPH), or "forest concession," which concentrates on the extraction of the natural timber and then departs.[30] Indeed, the HTI has been used by elites in Kalimantan as a vehicle for appropriating indigenous resource rights.

A third and final example, also from Indonesia, involves the common sword grass *Imperata cylindrica* (Dove 1986). *Imperata* is disparaged by state scientists and policymakers and has long been the subject of eradication and afforestation programs. These programs are premised on the belief that *Imperata* is a terminal, vegetative edaphic climax that can only be altered by means of state agency. Research on the role of *Imperata* in local human ecologies offers a different perspective on the grass, however, suggesting that it typically constitutes a rather tenuous fire climax species that is maintained (i.e., is blocked from spontaneous succession toward afforestation) by means of periodic, intentional burning by local communities, which value it for fodder and ground cover. From the local perspective, therefore, *Imperata* is the product of a fine balance between the agency of nature and the agency of the local community. The state denies these latter claims for agency, however, thereby increasing the conceptual space for its own managerial and proprietary authority while decreasing that of the local community.[31]

These three examples all reflect similar contests over the issue of agency in environmental transformations. Community-level discourses in South and Southeast Asia tend to locate agency either in nature or in the dialectical relationship between nature and culture. In contrast, national-level discourses tend to locate this agency in the state. The two points of view can be distinguished by asking whether a temporary cessation of human intervention in the environment will lead to restoration or further degradation of that environment. In both South and Southeast Asia, a premise of state discourses is that not forebearance but active intervention by the state is a prerequisite for restoration (e.g., reforestation) under such circumstances.

Exceptions to this state denial of local social and natural agency are revealing. An example is India's Joint Forest Management program (Malhotra 1993; Poffenberger 1994), which stands out as one of just a handful of instances, out of hundreds of attempts over the past half century in South and Southeast Asia alone, in which a reforestation program has achieved any meaningful measure of success.[32] The key to the program is a written agreement between a local community and the government's Forest Department in which it is agreed that if the community helps to protect a proximate tract of forest the department will share with it the resources and income from that forest. Reviews of this program demonstrate that when such agreements are effectively implemented forests that had been degraded to the point of barren ground can often begin to return to a healthy state remarkably quickly and *often without any further input by either foresters or villagers.* That is, cessation of the misuse that is brought about by conflicts between the community and the Forest Department over what uses are to be permitted itself suffices to restore the resource. The key to this restoration is prior identification of agency, both the agency responsible for the degradation of the forest (community-state conflict) and the agency responsible for its restoration (unfettered natural dynamics). The potentially great rewards of consensus on agency show how powerful are the institutional forces that prevent these rewards from being realized. The most important of these forces may be the fact that (in both regions) the self-conception of the state depends in part on environmental intervention.[33]

The contest over agency is reflected in the two terms with which this study began: *jungli log* and *jungle rubber.* Whereas the latter term differentiates trees, the former differentiates people; whereas use of the latter signifies the importance to society of distinguishing between commodities that are more wild as opposed to cultured, use of the former signifies the importance of distinguishing between people who are more wild versus cultured. In fact, there are few if any true "forest peoples" in the South Asian regions where *jungli log* is used, and there is little true jungle rubber coming to market anymore in Southeast Asia: the smallholder rubber to which this term is applied is economically more important and almost as cultured as the product of the parastatal estates with which it competes (Dove 1993b). The terminology used in both cases is thus ironic, which reflects its inherently political character.[34] The ironic

118   Michael R. Dove

invocation of nature supports the state project of allocating agency to itself in both regions while denying it to local communities.

DISCUSSION AND CONCLUSION

This analysis of two South and Southeast Asian forest discourses places the global discourse of deforestation in an interesting perspective. Counterintuitively, perhaps, a comparison between the local and global discourses reveals more similarities than dissimilarities. First, and most obviously, both the local and the global discourses invoke powerful images of change. The South and Southeast Asian discourses discussed here emphasize the transformation of forested and uncivilized landscapes into deforested and civilized ones, and the global discourse emphasizes the transformation of pristine natural landscapes into degraded cultural ones.

Further, both the local and global discourses are concerned with change in not just the environment but society — including the way in which society conceives of the environment. The global perception of tropical forests as the "lungs of the earth" is associated with perceived global deforestation just as much as the perception of the forest as a refuge of barbarism is associated with perceptions of the receding forest frontier in Asia. In both cases too, perceived changes in the environment — past, present, and threatened — are associated with perceived changes in identity. Just as the local oppositions of jungle and civilization or swidden and pond field entail a fundamental distinction between self and other, so, too, does the global opposition of temperate and tropical zones (Tsing 1993, x).

Because of the perceived impact of such change on society as well as environment, its interpretation is politically charged. This is reflected in the elision, in both the local and global discourses, of environmental history. Just as the cultural-ecological origins of contemporary society are obfuscated in the South and Southeast Asian discourses, so, too, in the global discourse of tropical deforestation is there an absence of references to, for example, the cycles of deforestation-afforestation that the industrialized countries once experienced themselves (Mathers 1992; Panayotou 1994).[35] Particularly obscured in both cases is the issue of agency, referring to control over positive change and responsibility for negative change. The agency of afforestation is obfuscated and contested in the Asian and global discourses, the latter being exemplified by the northern environmentalists' charge that Malaysian elites are destroying the country's forests and the Malaysian government's countercharge that the real culprit is the northern-dominated global economic order (Thompson 1993).

Subjective interpretation of environmental change is a central feature of the global as well as the local discourses. Indeed, it could be said that this is what both discourses are all about. The global discourse of deforestation is no less political, rhetorical, or idealized than the Asian forest discourses. The global discourse, based on a binary opposition of deforestation and afforestation, is just as essentialized as the Asian discourses, which are based on oppositions of swidden and pond field or jungle and civilization. Nor is the global discourse any more reflexive in this regard than the local discourses: both represent themselves as objective, notwithstanding their subjectivity. The global discourse is, if anything, more guilty in this regard due to its sometimes unwarranted privileging of scientific rhetoric and its assumption of a self-conscious premise of objectivity.

Given these structural similarities between local and global discourses, we would expect to find intellectual cross-linkages between them, and we do. For a number of years now scholars have been documenting the intellectual and political relations between local and global discourses (Dove et al. 2003; Tsing 1993, 13). Examples include studies of the way in which valorization of indigeneity at the global level has reversed its value in local discourses (Jackson 1995; Zerner 1994a) as well as studies of the way in which accounts — often essentialized and romanticized — of traditional community-level resource use have empowered national- and international-level discourses (Brosius 1997a; McIntosh 1994; Rangan 1992).[36] Further comparisons of local and global environmental discourses and examinations of the relations between them should be a fruitful area of study.

ACKNOWLEDGMENTS

Research in Indonesia was initially carried out between 1974 and 1976 with support from the National Science Foundation (Grant no. GS–42605) and with sponsorship from the Indonesian Academy of Science (LIPI). Additional data were gathered during six years of subsequent work in Indonesia between 1979 and 1985, with support from the Rockefeller and Ford Foundations and the East-West Center and with sponsorship by Gadjah Mada University. A recent series of field trips to Indonesia, beginning in 1992, was supported by the Ford Foundation, the United Nations Development Program, and the John D. and Catherine T. MacArthur Foundation, with sponsorship by Padjadjaran University and the Indonesian Central Planning Ministry (BAPPENAS). Research in Pakistan was carried out between 1985 and 1989, with support from the Foresty Planning and Development Project, jointly funded by the government of Pakistan and the U.S. Agency for International Development, under the direction of the inspector general of forests and under contract to the Winrock International Institute for Agricultural Development. The author is grateful to Carol Carpenter, James J. Fox, Paul Greenough, and Anna Tsing for comments on earlier drafts. The author alone is responsible for the analysis presented here.

NOTES

1 I follow Greenough and Tsing (1994, 95) in defining *discourse* as "both ways of speaking and clusters of non-verbal practices, as these create and maintain distinctions and identities."
2 I am indebted to Carol Carpenter for drawing my attention to this point. In a related vein, the well-being of tropical forest inhabitants has been likened to the well-being of the "miner's canary" (Durning 1992, 48–49).
3 Cf. the contributions by Blaikie (1985), Guthman (1997), Ives and Messerli (1989), Metz (1989), and Thompson, Warburton, and Hatley (1986) to a seminal debate about assumptions of deforestation and erosion in the Himalaya.
4 Scholars of Southeast Asia, for example, have noted how the emphasis on deforestation marginalizes considerations of human needs (e.g., Bryant, Rigg, and Stott 1993, 101; Falkus 1990, 75–76).
5 See Bouquet's (1995) review of historical Western uses of the tree as an organizing symbol and the collection of anthropological analyses of tree symbolism edited by Rival (1998).
6 See Dove 1998b for an analysis of Mahathir's famous response to an English schoolboy's criticism of Malaysian deforestation.
7 Less common have been attempts to contrast the views of local and extra-local scholars. See the comparison by Grove, Damodaran, and Sangwan (1998b, 11) of the focus of U.S. researchers on land use change in South Asia with the focus on resistance and discourse of South Asian scholars.
8 For other critiques of the environmentalist premise of "saving," see Haraway 1992; Ingold 1993; and Sachs 1994.
9 See Dove 1985 on the historic cultural valorization of clearing versus preserving forest in Java.
10 What are termed global and local discourses in this essay to some extent represent discourses from North America and Europe, on the one hand, and discourses from South and Southeast Asia on the other.
11 Recent data on forest cover in Pakistan and Indonesia are taken from, respectively, ⟨http//www.wcmc.org.uk/forest/data/cdrom2/csetabs.htm#Table1⟩ and ⟨http//www.wcmc.org.uk/forest/data/cdrom2/instabs.htm#Table1⟩.
12 This sections draws on Dove 1992a.
13 See Cronon 1991, 213–18, for a similar analysis of the relationship be-

tween the bison and Native American society. See Ludden 1996 for an analysis of changing agrarian oppositions in Tamil Society.

14 See Adimihardja's (1992) observation among the Kasepuhan of West Java that they "interpret the word *huma* (field) as *imah* (home)."

15 Kristianus Atok, personal communication. Similarly the term *dusun* means "orchard" in some parts of Borneo (Evans [1923] 1970, 2) and "village" in others.

16 In some cases this mapping involves a reversal of meaning: thus, *reuma* and *kampung* mean "forest and village" in West Java (Adimihardja 1992, 45), whereas *rumah* and *kampung* mean "village and forest" among the Iban (Richards 1981, 137, 312).

17 I am grateful to James J. Fox for drawing this to my attention.

18 This ecological cycle of rebirth may be reflected in the genealogical cycle in Javanese mythology wherein the mother of the forest spirit *kala* is said to be *uma* — another cognate for *swidden* (Carpenter 1987).

19 This dichotomy of swidden and pond field has been criticized however, for ignoring hybrids of the two as well as the existence of additional subsistence systems such as the home garden (Padoch, Harwell and Susanto 1998).

20 Kirch (1994, 161) maintains, however, that in parts of historic Polynesia pond field cultivation was less labor intensive than dryland swidden cultivation.

21 See Hutterer (1985, 64), who writes that "Populations engaging in permanent field agriculture have essentially 'locked themselves out of the forest' conceptually. This fact is quite easily demonstrated by the mythological conceptualization among such societies that the forest is dangerous and fearful, and by their practical reluctance to enter the jungle (e.g., Lombard 1974)."

22 Other evidence includes the historic practice of keeping at court representatives of Java's autochthonous peoples (e.g., the *Gadjah, Kumang*, and *Ladja*).

23 Compare the ambivalence between village and bush among the Dogon of Mali (van Beek and Banga 1992).

24 See Foley's (1987, 68–69; cited in Wessing 1992, 297) description of the idealized early Javanese landscape. "This is a kingdom with mountains behind, wet rice fields to the right, dry fields to the left, and a great port in front."

25 A similar system of swidden tobacco cultivation was practiced in colonial North Borneo (John and Jackson 1973, cited in Doolittle 1999).

26 See Nyerges 1994 on the "ecology of practice."

27 See Rangan 1995 and Bloch 1995 on varying interpretations of environmental change according to local political and ethnic affiliations, respectively.

28 The subject of indigenous agency is drawing increasing attention from historians of the region (Reynolds 1995, 432).

29 Robbins (1998) similarly notes that in India state afforestation introduces not just species but environmental meanings and priorities. See

Bryant 1996 on colonial Burma and Sivaramakrishnan 1998 on contemporary India.

30 Institute of Dayakology Research and Development, Pontianak, Indonesia, personal communication.

31 Fairhead and Leach (1995) have argued that state misreading of grassland-forest succession in West Africa as forest-grassland succession serves the same function of privileging the state.

32 Some scholars (e.g., Sivaramakrishnan 1998) argue that, notwithstanding this measure of success in vegetative terms, the Joint Forest Management program can still be criticized as the latest stage in a history of state redefinition of community, control, and resource expertise that dates back to colonial times and beyond.

33 State assertion of agency in this context is remarkably unaffected by politics. Thus the governments of Indonesia and Vietnam have labeled forest-dwelling swidden peoples "communists" and "feudal [right-wing] revisionists" respectively, but both labels really meant "junglees." The state policies pursued in the two cases are remarkably similar.

34 It is precisely where these terms would have the most relevance that they are not used. For example, the governments of Indonesia and Malaysia call their respective forest-dwelling tribal populations not "forest peoples" but *suku terasing,* "the foreign people," and *orang asli,* "the original people."

35 The industrialized countries also were responsible, of course, for some (but not all) of the colonial era deforestation in the countries where this is now seen as a problem. See Said's (1978, 226) reference to a line in one of Kipling's poems, which reads, "Now, this is the road that the White Men tread, When they go to clean a land."

36 See Grove's (1995) study of the linkages between contemporary global environmentalism and colonial environmental discourses.

Anna Lowenhaupt Tsing

AGRARIAN ALLEGORY AND GLOBAL FUTURES

"[O]nly two forces are essentially national and the bearers of the future: the proletariat and the peasants," wrote political theorist Antonio Gramsci early in the last century (1968, 51). Workers and peasants formed the basic categories for thinking about politics in the twentieth century. Yet both have disappeared from public discussion in the twenty-first century. They are unnamed — but they everywhere inform policy and scholarship. The tropes through which we know them have seeped into well-known "facts" about urban and rural social life, respectively. They show up as statistics, anecdotes, and truisms; they are glossed as "social realities." Yet these realities are shaped by the questions we pose and the story lines we offer. Peasants and workers are allegorical figures whose stories are still with us. This essay considers the formative allegories of the peasant. To make peasant stories clearer, I throw them up against the recently refurbished allegory of the tribe.

Throughout the global South, two kinds of rural allegories shape administrative policies, academic programs, and advocate agendas as well as the goals and schemes of the rural people with whom administrators, academics, and advocates work: peasant allegories and tribal allegories. International considerations of conservation, development, and equity take us again and again to imagined rural scenes of peasants or tribes. I use the terms *peasant* and *tribe* loosely to refer to traditions of thinking about the rural South, whether as a place of often poor, disadvantaged, and rebellious farmers ("peasants") or culturally rich and politically distinct communities ("tribes"). My subject here is not the terms or the people they describe but the images, narratives, assumptions, frameworks, and conventions of knowing, helping, or ruling that have made these imagined rural scenes so internationally powerful. In environmentalist circles, tribes have guided plans to link the preservation of biological and cultural diversity; peasants are instead invoked to consider environmental equity. The divergence between tribal and peasant agendas is often wide; the environmentalist programs just mentioned are often deeply at odds with each other, refusing each other's agendas as outside what each imagines to be good politics. Yet these agendas may be aimed at the same people.

Consider two men I know who live in the Meratus Mountains of South Kalimantan, Indonesia, Rintas and Isan.[1] Both are articulate, ambitious, and recognized leaders in their respective communities of shifting cultivators and rain forest foragers. Yet their dreams of leadership and global future differ.

Since becoming village head, Rintas has busied himself building fences and registering farmland. Before Rintas became headman, no one had fences or land claims recognized by the state; he wants to change that. He hopes to make his villagers rural citizens in the eyes of the government. To achieve that goal, he is willing to domesticate village ceremonies, sedentarize traditionally shifting housing plans, and follow national development dictates of appropriate rural customs, including the divide between claimed field and unclaimed forest. He has a dream — perhaps a fantasy but no less realizable for it.

That dream has also influenced Isan's village, where a cluster of permanent housing reflects government standards for rural life. Yet Isan is taking a different route; as a village elder, he is working with a regional environmentalist group to claim the forest, promote ecotourism, and protect village rights to "indigenous" resource management. He too has a dream, and to achieve that goal he is willing to exoticize village ceremony, show off jungle knowledge, map village forest claims, and revive customs that might count as local.

As a kind of shorthand, one might call Rintas's dream of settled farms, laws, and taxes a peasant fantasy and Isan's dream of forests managed by indigenous knowledge a tribal fantasy. Neither dream is strictly local; both involve engagements with powerful outsiders and ideas that have circulated, in varied forms, around the globe. Neither dream is based on a neutral, objective description of a Meratus village; both require reimagining and remaking the village to bring the dream to life. Both demonstrate the importance of "agrarian allegory" in shaping contemporary situations and histories.

Some of the most promising moves of "southern" environmental politics involve mixing up these story lines. Southeast Asian environmental movements use tribal and peasant allegories in a creative, eclectic manner to further their mobilizations. One of the most exciting features of the social-justice-oriented wings of the national environmental movements in Indonesia, Malaysia, and the Philippines is their interest in people who have never before been included in national populisms — people once considered too marginal, too culturally different, or too uninformed about national political standards. These are the allegorical tribes: upland peoples, rain forest peoples, non-Christians in the Philip-

pines, and non-Muslims in Malaysia. In these environmental movements, they are mixed into the same discussions as poor rural populations long at the heart of national debate, that is, peasants. Whereas
Indonesian populism once addressed only the Javanese, environmentalists have brought in Dayaks from Kalimantan and Papuans from Irian.
The Malaysian environmental movement considers the dilemmas of
nomadic Penan as well as Malay farmers. The Philippine environmental
movement brings upland Bukidnon and Magindanao into national political discussions that once led mainly to Central Luzon tenant farmers.
These inclusions create a difference from earlier progressive and nationalist movements, which focused on a much narrower "peasant"
story about the rural populace.[2]

National attention does not solve the problems of urban-rural hierarchy or mean that urban organizers have a full understanding of rural
problems (see Baviskar, this volume). However, it is an important development and one that bodes well for the new discussions of national
democracy that these movements are trying to engender. By mixing up
and combining tribal and peasant storytelling, those identified as tribes
and peasants are included in the same publicity; the allegories rub off
constructively. Tribes are brought into peasant populist concerns with
land rights and social justice. Peasants gain through tribal claims to
indigenous knowledge and customary forest management. By juxtapos-
ing the rhetoric associated with tribes, on the one hand, and peasants, on
the other, a new political opening is created for national dialogue about
the conditions of the countryside.

Scholars have not been so well inclined toward creative confusion
of tribal and peasant story lines. Instead of looking at the ways in
which stories shape institutions, landscapes, and lives, scholars have
been stalled in trying to separate true stories from false ones. Listening to
academic talk, one gains the impression that tribal stories are insincere
fantasies while the peasant condition is real. Although I can understand
how this divide developed, it is not helpful; it leads to both political and
intellectual dead ends. How did scholars get here? Two progressive
agendas have run backward into each other. Cultural anthropologists
and postcolonial literary critics criticize ideas of tribal cultural difference
as false exoticization.[3] Peasant studies scholars demystify elite ideologies
by uncovering the people's truth.[4] At first glance, then, the tribes are false
and the peasants true. Yet to divide liars from truth tellers banishes
questions of representation, meaning, and narrative from our consideration. A better frame put tribes and peasants on an equal footing as

categories that have shaped not just scholarship but landscape making administrative policies, political and economic strategies, and rural lives.

To address the formative role of allegory in shaping global to local environmental projects requires that we pay attention to specific histories. In this essay, I trace the formation of the figure of the peasant in Indonesia, Malaysia, and the Philippines. Tribal stories will be my concern mainly as a reminder of the specificity and limits of peasant stories. In particular, I examine the making of an image of rural landscape as the site of poverty, national identity, and class struggle. In the figure of the farmer or landless laborer situated in this landscape, scholars have found a teller of important truths, truths that challenge internationally dominant political-economic dogma by showing the underside of hierarchy, exploitation, militarization, state governance, technical expertise, and capital expansion. Ideologically charged claims of homogenizing globalization make this subaltern knowledge ever more important for anyone concerned about the world today.[5] Yet it gains its ability to tell politically important truths from a history of "peasanting" the landscape, that is, shaping it in relation to peasant allegories. The figure of the peasant gains its political charge within the institutionalization of a set of landscape-making commitments, ranging from colonial administrative projects through nationalist and development-oriented remakings of the rural populace.

The allegorical construction of the peasantry is an important question around the world, yet Southeast Asia is a particularly rich location with which to begin a discussion. First, although Southeast Asia has often been described in the classical terms of peasant stories, tribal motifs are also conspicuous; this combination makes the peasant theme important, as it also shows its limits. In contrast, in East Asia peasant stories so dominate understandings of the countryside that it is impossible to imagine history except as stories of peasants and elites. A further contrast would be with Africa, where the idea of the tribe has dominated. Given the resentment of many educated Africans of the concept of the tribe, I cannot imagine a positive role for tribal allegories in African environmentalism. This kind of pejorative connotation is not so fully hegemonic in Southeast Asia, where tribal stories offer villagers the possibilities of cultural autonomy as well as the stigma of backwardness. In the Philippines, for example, upland leaders in the 1980s demanded that their people be called tribes not "minorities." In Southeast Asia, both tribal and peasant allegories are available as resources for environmentalist mobilizations.

Second, the difference dividing those imagined as tribal and those imagined as peasants has never been institutionally fixed; as these categories shift, their allegorical features emerge most clearly. Southeast Asia never experienced the massive waves of European and African immigration that in Latin America created a special category of indigenous people, imagined as tribes, divided across racial, cultural, linguistic, and civilizational lines from white settlers, former slaves, and "settled" farmers imagined as peasants. In Southeast Asia, unlike India, tribal is not a legal identity separated from the caste-organized majority and adherent to persons even out of their native environment. Instead, the division between tribal and peasant is oriented toward the organization of landscapes and communities. Every student of the area begins by learning distinctions between the upland and lowland Philippines, East and West Malaysia, and outer and inner Indonesia; these rule-of-thumb divides guide descriptions of the countryside in tribal versus peasant stories. The historical fragility of these distinctions draws attention to the formative role of agrarian allegory in designing landscapes and communities in Southeast Asia.

Yet, third, Southeast Asia is far from a homogeneous place, and many of the scholarly arguments for considering it a region at all have to do with attention to its diversity. The landscape of Indonesia, Malaysia, and the Philippines is both too big an area to consider and too small; my goal is not to present a definitive history but to open doors to new ways of thinking. Furthermore, Southeast Asian studies is privileged with a number of "classic" ethnographic and historical descriptions of rural life, each of which has opened influential theoretical paths in the social sciences. In each section of my account, I analyze one of these to illustrate the promise and challenge of rethinking peasant narratives.

This essay explores the development of the allegorical figure of the peasant as a source of politically challenging truths. These truths are not just those articulated by the peasant but also those learned by scholars, advocates, and policymakers through their contact with peasants. I argue that this truth-telling ability arises from a specific history of politicization and landscape construction in insular Southeast Asia. Indigenous elites developed distinctive ideals concerning productive landscapes and loyal communities that centered on wet rice cultivation. Colonial administrators were influenced by these ideals and both redesigned and extended them to fit their notions of administratable rural populations. The "core peasant" groups and locations around which they were most active in turn became models of peasantness for the imagination of colonial control. Core peasant models were reproduced in new places, and

128 Anna Lowenhaupt Tsing

other kinds of rural communities and landscapes were politically marginalized, criminalized, or redesigned. Rural political administration centered around core peasants and their landscapes.

The new nations that developed out of these colonial territories took on this political privileging of core peasant communities and landscapes; with national independence, these groups became the rural representatives of the nation. In this role, these core peasant groups and landscapes also became the main targets of development interventions, political mobilizations, and internal security alerts. Yet in the process their construction as core peasants was forgotten; rather than peasants, they were described as economic, political, or demographic masses. They became the allegorical source of the nation's Everyman.

Peasant studies scholarship intervened in this formless social description to point to the structural features of core peasant life even in the midst of nationalism and development. Stratification suddenly became clear again. As peasants, these poor rural Everymen had something new to say, often something acutely critical of the flabby indifference of elite views. Yet peasant studies inherited the nationalist Everyman naturalization of core peasants, and the particularity of the social construction of these subaltern political critics was often forgotten. In arguing for a newly critical attention to the history of peasant storytelling in both scholarship and administration, I hope to clear the space for more flexibile tellings, as these might include more kinds of people and rural stories. In a moment in which political ecologists, social ecologists, and other kinds of environment and social justice theorists appropriately draw from the heritage of peasant studies in order to think through agrarian dilemmas, we need to use this heritage as richly as possible.[6]

With this guidebook in hand, I invite the reader on a tour across a regional historical terrain too large for any one scholar to know in proper detail. The archives on core peasants are huge and daunting; my vantage point is not encyclopedic but rather the unaccustomed eyes of a scholar of "marginal" people left out of these archives. Let my mistakes be sources for a continuing conversation on these issues.

When Europeans first traveled to Southeast Asia, they found a variety of interlocked social forms: inland kingdoms supported by irrigated rice; coastal kingdoms taxing trade routes; seagoing "pirates" and traders; coastal, lowland, and upland villages; shifting cultivators on isolated plots; traveling collectors of sea and forest products; and more. The Europeans recognized only the kingdoms as political actors, and they negotiated trade, fought battles, and extracted territory through treaties with them. Looking back through the archives, scholars have described these kingdoms as mandalas, galactic polities, theater states, and segmentary states in order to show their distinctiveness (Reynolds forthcoming). In these kinds of states, rural producers are peripheral participants and audience members in state-making rituals; inside and outside of state ideals, they endorse "little tradition" versions of elite ideologies (Scott 1977). And, while many rural producers found themselves within the magnetic pull of lordly power, there was mobility from one sovereign's domain to another as well as much room on the periphery of every sovereignty. While pockets of irrigated rice cultivation — with their settled and often dependent cultivators — were present, more of the landscape was farmed by means of shifting cultivation, which was difficult for rulers to tax and control (Dove 1985). Forests were vast. Mobility was common. Routes of travel and trade were well developed.

When Europeans did come to transform rural landscapes and communities to fit their standards of administration, they of necessity worked with Southeast Asian elites as well as less elite community members in bringing new kinds of political economies into being. Landscape and community change involved hybrid projects in which Southeast Asian elites, community members, and European administrators all had their own stakes. Yet only some of these hybrid projects became models of colonial rural administration. Colonial rule allowed these models to proliferate as administrators introduced them to new areas. A new form of politicization embraced those rural communities and landscapes in which colonial administrators wanted most to produce model-like conditions. It is this colonial remaking of peasant politics and culture that characterizes what I identify as the "core peasantry." Its making forms the first stop on my tour.

PEASANT FANTASIES 1: READINGS

For some time past the Rulers of the Federated Malay States and their Advisers have been caused grave anxiety by the fact that their Malay subjects deluded by visions of present but transitory wealth have been divesting themselves of their homestead and family lands to any one willing to pay in cash for them. Blinded by the radiance of the inducement offered, entranced by the visions of lethean pleasures conjured up they fail to realize that for those elusory [sic] pleasures they are surrendering and sacrificing the happiness of a life-time. Thus a race of yeoman-peasantry aforetime happy and prosperous incapable from the very nature of their country and genus of supporting themselves in any other country find too late that they have become homeless wanderers in their own land. The Rulers of the Federated Malay States and their Advisers conclusively feel that unless a better judgment is exercised on their behalf the result will be extinction of the Malay yeoman-peasantry. — Preamble to the 1912 draft legislation of the Malay Reservations Enactment

Despite the pleasures of stumbling through extraordinary colonial peasant-fictions, such as the one just quoted, a reinterpretation of primary sources is beyond the scope of this essay. Instead, my argument about the making of Southeast Asian peasants is formed from reading several separate bodies of historical interpretation at the same time. First, I draw on the work of many authors who tell of incidents of "traditionalization," "feudalization," "involution," "reservation," and even "peasantization" (see, e.g., Geertz 1963; Kahn 1980; Ong 1987; Lim 1977; and Stivens 1983).[7] In various times and places, we learn, Southeast Asian farmers have been the objects of military, commercial, and administrative policies that tie them to particular plots of land, encourage them to farm it using family-organized labor, specify crops and technologies, disallow entrepreneurship and mobility, and bind them in particular relations to elites. This rich and exciting literature works self-consciously against ideologically charged assumptions that peasant "tradition" is the initial given now dissolving to make way for the new and "modern." The literature shows that state policies and economic programs can have a variety of cultural, political, and economic influences on rural people, including those that make them seem more "traditional" than they were before.

My contribution is to draw attention to the repetitive patterning of these state interventions. Most of the literature portrays colonial administrators and military and commercial elites as creating rational, sensible, economic — that is, not culturally marked — plans to fit their current interests. Administrators are shown reorganizing rural society to gain more income, form self-serving local alliances, or ensure rice supplies for their own uses. If they aim to segregate commercial and subsistence interests by keeping rural cultivators out of commerce, it is suggested that this is the most rational response to their own economic predicaments. Rural cultivators may experience these schemes in "cultural" ways; administrative schemes, however, are not described as in themselves culturally shaped. This formulation promotes assumptions that local peasant cultural peculiarities stand in contrast to globally circulating cosmopolitan rationalities. If instead we ask about the discursive shape of colonial plans, we can get a better sense of the local and global interactions in which both centers and peripheries, city and country, and global North and South are formed.

To identify the elements of state and commercial agrarian programs during the colonial era, I turn to another kind of historical analysis, that which has examined knowledge production about rural areas. In particular, there is an important literature on the misrepresentation of the Asian village in scholarly and policy-oriented writing. Jan Breman (1988) has shown how Asian villages have been portrayed as closed, homogeneous, static, and subsistence oriented; he argues that this seriously misreads the historical record in both precolonial and colonial Asia (see also Kemp 1988; and Dove 1985, 1992b). From this literature, one can begin to see how the images through which peasants are discussed and ruled have been forged by discursively shaped desires.

> The village community has been identified as the social foundation of the peasant economy in Asia. The literature on the subject has long focused on a closed corporate formation that depends on small-scale production to meet its own subsistence needs. With few variations of the standard pattern, this system is said to have been repeated *ad infinitum* throughout most of Asia and to have reproduced itself in the course of many centuries with little if any change. . . . The image of the ancien régime that thus came about dates from reports written in the early decades of the nineteenth century by men who were in charge of colonial policies and faced with the task of devising an administrative system for the Asian colonies (Breman 1988, 1).

These systemic misreadings point to the fact that colonial writers and administrators had their own ideas about the countryside. They helped to remake the peasant landscape according to these preconceptions. Colonial administration in rural areas was often fragile. Just to do their jobs well, administrators tried to make the kinds of peasant communities they thought they could understand and control. Their remakings, of course, could only be effective to the extent that they found some common cause with local community leaders as well as indigenous elites. Certain areas seemed more worth controlling and understanding than others. Those areas that formed the locus of colonial attention were appreciated as *models* to the extent that they evoked administrators' own ideas about rural landscapes. These then informed projects for knowing and administering other areas.

The advantage of seeing the peasant landscape in relation to the models through which it was administered and understood is not to ignore variation and the indigenous agency of Southeast Asian villagers.[8] One can, however, pay attention to the historical dynamics of proliferation:

how and when did images, rules, and practices drawn from certain areas become blueprints for other areas? One can also ask about exclusions: what groups and areas never made it inside the ring of peasant fantasy?

One reason why the colonial interpretations and transformations that created these models have not been obvious to scholars is that those who describe nineteenth-century peasant landscapes find them traditional. But we cannot take this quality for granted. "Tradition" was a central characteristic through which the peasantry was known in Europe in the nineteenth century, and this influenced colonial perceptions in Southeast Asia. With tradition as the definitional quality of peasants, it made sense for observers to see the peasant landscapes made by colonialism as original and authentic. The sleight of hand was imperceptible. Colonial administrators looked at the countryside and saw the peasants of their imagination or at least peasants who were slipping away, would-be peasants, or peasants in some distress. By the early twentieth century, colonial programs had put these perceptions into place in administratively important segments of the Asian countryside. Furthermore, they were so naturalized that it rarely occurred to anyone to question their traditional nature.

A third literature must inform my argument: discussions of the nineteenth-century European images and debates about the countryside that informed colonial administrators. Thus, I take a detour to Europe on my way to the colonial landscape of Java.

PEASANT FANTASIES 2: IN EUROPE

> during my travels, which tend to create illusions . . . I kept coming across the same rural architecture as in the Lorraine countryside of my boyhood: the same clustered villages, the same open farming, the same cornfields, the same triennial rotation, the same images. — Fernando Braudel

By the nineteenth century in Europe, the peasant landscape was already a scene constituted by memory and nostalgia. This characteristic of peasant landscapes is still with us. Thus, Braudel describes the European countryside as an illusive, memory-driven scene of the repetition of boyhood. This is not his point. He is telling real rural history. But the peasant landscape engulfs his intention. As tradition in a modern world, it can only be the past escaping, distorted and reconstituted through the lens of memory. If the definitional problem in representing a tribe is its dependence on the spectacle and performance of cultural difference (are the tribal Tasaday of the Philippines real or are they actors?), the definitional problem in representing a peasant landscape is its dependence on the frailties of memory to reconstruct the continuity of the tradition that gives it shape. This memory project itself, however, has a limited scope and time depth. It was formed in nineteenth-century Europe. Just as rural areas are undergoing profoundly "modernizing" transformations, they come to be refigured as always repetitive and never fully realized repositories of tradition. It is this slipping away village that was carried to Asia by colonial observers and administrators. Since it is always described from a moment of displacement, it is impossible to find the original village on which these "not quite" models were made.

European ideas about peasant landscapes refer to issues that emerged in varied times and places. Two imagined scenes of peasant life were particularly important in nineteenth-century European discussions and debates. One located the peasantry in a paradox of rebellious but conservative backwardness; the other saw the making of cultural value in the folk. These themes overlapped and traveled across many sites of state policy, popular mobilization, and intellectual reflection. However, it seems useful to think about them in relation to their focused references to France and Germany, respectively.

The nineteenth-century integration of the French peasantry into a trajectory of national development provided many of the images of peasants that have entered discussions of peasants as exemplars of tradition in a modernizing world. This is a culturally specific way of imagining peasants. It depends on notions of peasants as both dependent and different. They are key subjects of the state, but they are hard to understand, even irrational. Their tradition creates a paradox (Dewald and Vardi 1998): on the one hand, it is a form of conservatism that supports the status quo; on the other, it is given to unruly behavior, from rudeness to outright rebellion.

In the eighteenth century, a cosmopolitan culture developed in France that characterized rural cultivators as alien to the ideals of Enlightenment philosophy and bourgeois economics that were thought to characterize the advance of civilization. Peasants were cut off from the "progress" of cosmopolitan social life; their customs thus seemed exotic and archaic, even savage (Lehning 1995). Whether idealized as noble or condemned as brutes, peasants were different. To the extent that cosmopolitan trajectories became identified as French (and sometimes they appeared as universal), "peasants" and "Frenchmen" became oppositional categories.

By the nineteenth century, enormous efforts were advanced to bring rural communities into the French national trajectory, that is, to turn these imagined non-French peasants into citizens of a unified nation. Peasant tradition came to seem full of paradox. Peasants were key objects of state reform and regulation. Their tradition made them difficult to control, not only because it involved local, unregulated customs but because it recalled an earlier history of rebellion. And yet when peasants did revolt they sometimes fought for the return of previous regimes of power rather than for the modern social transformations to which the urban bourgeoisie, as well as emergent working class leaders, were increasingly committed. This was certainly how many social commentators understood the Revolutions of 1848. They saw peasants opposing reformers and proletarians and supporting earlier hierarchies and rights. Social commentary on the events of 1848 was particularly influential in allowing cosmopolitan Europeans to label peasants "conservative" (see, e.g., Marx 1972).[9]

This image of the conservative, backward-looking peasantry was important to administrators in Southeast Asia. In the midst of fierce anti-colonial struggles, they began to imagine peasants as possible supporters of the colonial regime. Conflict was caused, it seemed, by civilizational differences such as the intransigence of Islam. In contrast, the rebelliousness of conservative peasants would mainly be of a traditional variety and thus possible to control. Particularly when and where they imagined a peasantry that would support colonial rule, they instituted reforms that they hoped would promote the stability and commitment to land that were seen as basic features of peasant conservatism.

The peasants they ruled in Southeast Asia were especially easy to imagine as traditional because of European notions of the backwardness of Asia as a continent. In the nineteenth century, "Asia" became the site of oriental despotism and static, feudal customs (e.g., Shanin 1990, 6). Even the European peasantry began to look Asian to the extent that it was characterized as static and traditional. In socialist debates about the Russian peasantry in the late nineteenth century, Russian peasants were often described as Asian, as opposed to Russian workers. To socialist theorist Plekhanov, for example, peasants "represented Asia, the East, and humanity's past," while workers "represented Europe, the West and humanity's future" (289). It seems likely that such discussions of the Asian stamp on the European peasant both drew on and disguised the growing European impress on the Asian peasant under colonial rule.

Meanwhile, another story about peasants had become important. In reaction to the hegemony of French "civilization" in Europe, Germans were forming a national consciousness that depended on peasants as its central creators of value and continuity. German intellectuals and nationalist spokesmen worked to uncover the folk cultures that, they argued, spoke to a separate German way of life that reached back into prehistory. This way of life was exemplified by peasant traditions, which could be at the heart of nation building. As one social commentator put it, "The peasant is the future of the German nation; he constantly refreshes and rejuvenates the life of our people" (Wilhelm Riehl, quoted in Rosener 1994, 2). A new branch of study, *Volkskunde,* generalized these sentiments to argue for the examination of peasant life in order to find the cultural inheritance of the nation (Farr 1986). Historical linguistics and folklore took off as branches of study devoted to learning more about the folk, their values, and their history.

Colonial administrators in Southeast Asia drew from this conversation both to imagine the peasantry as objects of reflection and to romanticize the institutions and values of the village. Colonial administrators sometimes saw rural life as taking place in politically autonomous village "republics" with strong communal traditions. The nostalgia through which administrators observed rural life is indebted to these European developments. With the independence of Southeast Asian nations, German nationalist ideas about peasants came to have an even greater impact on *national* discussions of peasants. All over Southeast Asia, peasants became the soul of the nation. That motif informs a later portion in my story. Here I am concerned with colonial fantasies of peasant tradition, as these encouraged administrators' attempts to tap the paradox of conservative but rebellious backwardness and to best use the heritage of communal values.

These were conversations that crisscrossed Europe. It is also true that colonial administrators were influenced by ideas about agrarian landscapes from their own national and imperial trajectories.[10] Thus, the Spanish, who began their colonization of the Philippines in the sixteenth century, were informed by an earlier vision of a rural domain in which Christianization was the key goal of subjugation and rule. Spanish administrators gathered scattered Philippine settlements under the sound of church bells. In contrast, Northern European empire builders, such as those from England and the Netherlands, imagined their colonial acquisitions in relation to their trajectories of mercantalism and economic "progress." The English had rid themselves of most of their peasants by the eighteenth century; rural life, however, remained a site for nostalgia and the imagination of simple pleasures and contentments. This nostalgia informed colonial policy in the nineteenth century. The Netherlands, known for the early economic specialization of its countryside and the development of commerce, presented another story of advancement (de

Vries 1974). Even during the Netherlands' nineteenth-century economic decline, the Dutch imagined themselves in relation to their past commercial power, and Dutch farmers were portrayed as dynamic entrepreneurs, just like the "calculating merchants in Amsterdam" (Gouda 1995, 126).[11] At the same time, the Dutch also engaged in utopian "rural romance" (see Stoler forthcoming). Dutch administrators mixed expectations of progress and tradition in their colonial projects, which were further figured through a fantasy of Asian feudalism.

To explore colonial fantasies and impositions further, I turn to Southeast Asia. One place has become particularly well known in relation to both foreign and indigenous elite nostalgia for traditional culture and the premodern mass of its peasants. It is the place that John Pemberton (1994) insightfully tied to its quotation marks: "Java."

PEASANT FANTASIES 3: THE MAKING OF CORE PEASANTRIES

> This scene of swarming humans in a worn and often ravaged ecological setting could not be more different from the Java of the early nineteenth century. Then, the island was a thickly wooded, lightly populated place.
> — R.E. Elson

In Java, the Dutch worked up a complex, hybrid fantasy of feudalism. In the eighteenth century, the fantasy centered on the construction of a hybrid nobility, seen as Asian in its pomp, opulence, and status hierarchy but European enough in its political and personal ties to Dutch centers of commerce and power. Jean Taylor describes the mestizo culture of eighteenth-century Batavia, where visitors from Europe found the Dutch officials so immersed in hierarchical dress codes, mixed race family cultures, and aristocratic expectations of personal service that they were culturally unrecognizable (1983). John Pemberton describes the transformation of Javanese aristocrats as rulers surrounded by Dutch supervision and deprived of political power learned to focus on self-absorbed ceremony (1994).

Only in the nineteenth century did the Dutch begin to imagine peasants as a key site for social reflection and intervention.[12] As the quotation that opens this section suggests, Java was not densely populated at this time; rural settlement was concentrated in fertile valleys and lowland plains, interspersed with mountains, forests, swamps, and unfarmed land. Some historians suggest that rice was not yet the principal food for a large portion of the Javanese; the great spread of irrigated rice fields was yet to come (Pelzer 1945, 75). This was not, then, the core peasant Java whose images come to us today.

Although they were not everywhere hegemonic, Javanese rulers had their own peasant fantasies. For the inland precolonial kingdoms of central and east Java, wet rice cultivation was the essential feature of subject populations. As Michael Dove has argued, Javanese kingdoms created an "agro-ecological mythology" that featured *sawah* (wet rice cultivation) as the proper agricultural system for the support of the kingdom and for inclusion in its realm of protection, taxation, and sovereignty (1985). In tenth-century Java, for example, rulers offered grants of land to temple-based groups, offering them the king's protection in exchange for turning the land into sawah (Vickers 1986; Christie 1991). One tenth-century inscription offers a grant of land for "it to become *sawah,* to stop being a fearsome place" (Vickers 1986, 156). Beyond the sawah, according to the rulers' logic, bandits lurked and unsettled conditions prevailed; the king offered protection for trade, water control, and fertility-enhancing rituals. Sawah became part of an elite aesthetic of nature in which the king's presence could be felt in the ordered landscape (Day 1994). Thus, sawah cultivation was a key feature of a model of "peasant making" in which rural people could be settled within the hierarchical vision of the kingdom. When Dutch administrators set out to control, reform, and profit from rural areas, they were very much influenced by these models of indigenous elites. At the same time, the imagined tradition of these models allowed the Dutch to unselfconsciously import European concerns about peasantries.[13]

Three features of the peasant condition seem particularly important in the ways in which colonial schemes aimed to transform the landscape. First, the colonial regime tried to *stabilize* peasant villages, making them units of territory and administration. Second, the regime worked hard to guarantee the *governability* of peasants, that is, either their docility or the "customary" (i.e., self-limiting) character of their rebellions. Third, colonial officials helped make the Javanese countryside a place of *tradition* and imagined continuity with the ancient past — in contrast to the dynamic forces of Dutch capitalism. In contrast, precolonial rural Javanese moved around a lot, carried arms and fought wars for their patrons, and were no more tied to the past than anyone else.[14] Taken together, these three features go a long way toward defining the political culture of the peasant in the nineteenth-century European imagination. In giving the rural populace these characteristics, the colonial administration can be said to have made Javanese farmers into colonial core peasants.

Dutch colonial administrators in the nineteenth century did not have homogeneous attitudes toward the Javanese countryside. Debates raged between liberals and conservatives about the best way to rule the colony (van den Muijzenberg and Wolters 1988). Liberals believed that free enterprise would stimulate economic development; administrators must free rural cultivators from the burdens of feudal hierarchy to allow this. Conservatives trusted more fully in the power of the state and worked together with social elites to stimulate production. In discussing Java, the two factions argued particularly about the nature of traditional land tenure. Liberals claimed that individual private landholding was a Javanese tradition, while conservatives saw communal village land tenure as the traditional norm (Boomgaard 1989). Together they forged a discursive frame in which peasants were the political and economic basis of Javanese colonial society. Furthermore, those groups that would count as peasants had special characteristics: they were wet rice cultivators and lived in settled, production-oriented villages. The state had a responsibility to control and advance these peasants. The goal of Dutch rural administration in Java was to increase the stability of the countryside by making the wet rice village a more stable and productive unit.

Nineteenth-century Dutch conservative ideas about the countryside were particularly influenced by German rural historians, who provided models of communal peasant villages at the base of human evolutionary processes (van den Muijzenberg and Wolters 1988). In contrast, Dutch liberal ideas in Java were influenced by the short period of English rule at the beginning of the nineteenth century (1811–15). Lieutenant Governor Stamford Raffles, in the liberal tradition, aimed to free rural people from the corrupt extortions of the feudal hierarchy by eliminating middlemen between the colonial state and the village. He made the village the base of his system of taxation and empowered village heads as agents of the colonial state.[15] From this period on, both liberal and conservative administrators regarded the village as the basic unit of colonial administration. Village governance was thought to be the best way to administer a large mass of people with few European personnel and limited funds. This scheme worked even more productively for the Dutch under the Cultivation System, which was put into place in 1830 and lasted until 1870.

Under the Cultivation System, rural cultivators were forced to produce export crops for the European market as well as to feed themselves. Through this program, Governor-General van den Bosch turned administration toward the conservative perspective: peasant cultivation could only be stimulated by the direct pressure of the state, working together with local elites. Peasant labor was made available for colonial projects by drawing on indigenous hierarchies, with their expectations of labor exactions. Scholars are still debating the economic implications of the program, such as whether it led to economic stagnation or progress. However, all agree that program administrators worked hard to create new kinds of Javanese villages. The rural landscape was transformed.

A number of kinds of changes are especially relevant to peasant making. First, the plan of villages was regulated and regularized. Dutch officials disapproved of the disorder of Javanese settlement.[16] In the opinion of the first director of cultivations "the village should be shaped as a square, with two or four entrances, and protected by a hedge or moat or stone wall, and able to be securely closed off at night" (Elson 1994, 156). Dispersed hamlets were centralized. "What the Dutch wanted was a permanent, tightly defined community of people" (156). Despite obstacles to the establishment of these ideal peasant villages, changes were made, and by the beginning of the twentieth century, the historian tells us, Javanese villages were surrounded by hedges (157).

Second, village leaders were empowered and transformed into local administrators, and in the process the social structure of the village was given a new concreteness. Villages became communal political units from the perspective of higher authorities; at the same time, they formed new, less flexible divisions in their internal structure.[17] Meanwhile, the administration portrayed the village as "a small independent republic with an aristocratic form of rule" (resident of Cirebon, 1846, quoted in Elson 1994, 158).

Third, the colonial police force was developed to curb rural mobility and insubordination. In the colonial eye, it was never appropriate for peasants to be armed. Mobility was interpreted as banditry or tax evasion; thus, mobility was insubordination. Insubordination was seen as customary unrest rather than war (e.g., Kartodirdjo 1973). Javanese rulers who led rural rebellions were portrayed as "religious" or "millennial" figures who lacked the power to make war or revolution; thus, whether obedient or troublesome, peasants were always traditional.

Fourth, the administration courted Javanese aristocrats in order to maintain control over village labor.[18] Support of this aristocracy strengthened ideas that the village institutions that were being promoted were the people's very own. As Governor-General Van den Bosch wrote in 1831, "we must not interfere with [the people's] domestic or religious institutions, we must protect them against all mistreatment, and administer them as much as possible according to their own notions" (quoted in Elson 1994, 180). The peasants they created were, of course, traditional.

The Cultivation System came to an end in 1870, but the new liberal changes that were put in place at that time only confirmed the traditionalism of the newly formed core peasant landscape. The Agrarian Law of 1870 divided land into unalienable native lands and fully salable private lands; "natives" were, more than ever, defined as static, subsistence cultivators in contrast to European entrepreneurs. This ushered in the period in which, as Clifford Geertz (1963) argues, the Javanese peasant economy became stultified and "involuted." It is probably unnecessary to review the arguments for peasant stagnation under what Geertz calls the Corporate Plantation System. However, it is useful to recall that the Javanese rural population increased enormously and new rice lands became harder and harder to come by. New models of colonial and scientific forest management further segregated forests and fields (Peluso 1992). By the early twentieth century, the Javanese countryside had become the model for Boeke's influential general theory of the segregated "dual economies" that separate the static native peasantry and the entrepreneurial colonizer (1953). The characteristic dilemmas that we imagine in peasant landscapes and villages were firmly in place and quite able to form models for other areas.

The core peasant model, by its definition as remembered tradition, is transferable; it is always part of a chain of proliferation. In the Netherlands Indies, it was transferred and transferred. Thommy Svensson writes about one of the earlier transfers from Central and East Java to the western part of the island (1990). In the 1850s and 1860s, he writes, the colonial administration sponsored a forced "sawahization" of the Sundanese Priangan area. Before this, various kinds of agriculture, including both irrigated and shifting cultivation of rice, had been juxtaposed and combined. The colonial administration organized corvée labor teams to build the wet rice fields that could stabilize and increase the population as they also gave new landholding rights to local collaborationist elites. After 1870, the administration also forced people into village communities designed on a Central and East Javanese model. It was from these forms of local organization, then, that Sundanese peasant dilemmas developed. This process was repeated in other areas in the Netherlands Indies.

Perhaps the most complete proliferation fantasy involving Javanese peasant landscapes was reached in agricultural colonization, or "transmigration," projects, which beginning in the early twentieth century created Javanese villages on other Indonesian islands. Transmigration, which has continued through the present, aims to relieve the population pressure of Java as it brings progress to areas seen as underpopulated and undeveloped. Writing on the eve of Indonesian independence, Karl Pelzer complained that "through all the discussion of agricultural colonization in the Indies runs the thought that the ultimate aim should be to create villages and communities in the Outer Islands that would be exact duplicates of those in Java" (1945, 230). Perhaps the Javanese peasant, he thought, could progress. Yet he thought that Javanization would still bring important benefits to the Outer Islands through the formation of peasant landscapes: "Under the stimulus of the Javanese example, indigenous peoples who heretofore have practiced shifting cultivation [will] change over to permanent cultivation" (231). He even waxed elagiac: "Land that in the past was either entirely uncultivated or used only occasionally by a hunter, gatherer, or shifting cultivator, is fundamentally transformed. The forest disappears, and in its place, as far as the eye can see stretch irrigated rice fields, interspersed here and there with villages set among gardens and groves of fruit trees" (231). The fantasy landscape stretches out as far as the eye can see — and as far as the administration can rule.

The themes I have collected here are commonplace in the literature on nineteenth- and early-twentieth-century Java, but my attention to peasant fictions and fantasies adds a slightly different emphasis to well-known histories. Thus, one might reread Clifford Geertz's classic *Agricultural Involution* (1963), ignoring for a moment controversies over class, population, and sugar ecology, to focus on the consequences and exclusions of peasant making. Two of the least contested assumptions of the book become problematic and interesting in this light: why are sawah (wet rice cultivation) and swidden (shifting cultivation) thought to be different "systems" and why did Java become the heartland of Indonesian national history?

Geertz begins his discussion of the history of rural Indonesia with the contrast between sawah and swidden, and many of us grew up with this contrast as our introduction to Southeast Asian studies. There were two kinds of peoples and places: lowlands and uplands, inner and outer, peasants and tribes mixed with plantations and smallholder entrepreneurs. Yet many Southeast Asians are to this day involved in agricultural endeavors that mix irrigated fields and swiddens and other things as well. How did this particular contrast come to seem so central and systematic? What if the Malays of coastal Sarawak, described by Tom Harrisson (1970) as having one of the more eclectic economies I can imagine, had become the icons of Southeast Asian livelihood? Sarawak did not have a peasant-making administration. The Brookes loved tribal difference, armed the Iban, and never discouraged shifting cultivation. In the Netherlands Indies, in contrast, sawah was made the center, the inner circle. Agricultural eclecticism was outlawed and erased from Java;

rather than the system guiding its own requirements, shifting cultivation, as the "robber economy," was criminalized and driven to the margins of colonial rule (Pelzer 1945). In Geertz's text, too, swidden moves to the margins. After the swidden landscape is introduced as an ecosystem, swiddeners disappear from history. Plantation workers and rural entrepreneurs fill their Outer Island spaces. There is no room for a tribal landscape in these stories of development and nation building. Indeed, the systematicity attributed to swidden does not operate to structure the history of the Outer Islands; the swidden landscape is replaced with other agricultural arrangements. It is only sawah that holds its systemic nature as a guide to social and natural history. Some people and landscapes become marginal; others take center stage. And the center is the replicating rural landscape of the colonial imagination. Might the integrity and autonomy of the sawah ecosystem themselves form claims within this proliferation-driven political culture?

That Javanese peasants are at the center of modern Indonesian history seems so obvious that it is hardly worth raising. Certainly, demographic and political factors privilege the Javanese in the national story. But what about the requirements of national stories themselves? "Indonesia's future hinges on the fate of the Javanese peasantry," writes Gillian Hart (1986, 1). The sentence appears to need no explanation.[19] After all, the majority of Indonesians are Javanese peasants. But numbers never speak for themselves; if majorities translated into priorities, we would see a lot more women, peasant and otherwise, in our historical narratives. Could it be that the very peasant-like-ness of the Javanese, in the international imagination, privileged their participation in the story of the nation? But this question takes me beyond the colonial era.

By the early twentieth century, colonial projects in the Southeast Asian countryside were firmly in place, and the challenge of making rulable landscapes turned in new directions. Rather than needing to differentiate peasants from tribes, it was the differentiation of peasants and their own landscapes that became the new challenge. Reconceived as resources, landscapes could be exploited with or without their peasantries; reconceived as populations, peasants could be moved or rearranged without fundamental disruption. Early-twentieth-century colonial racializations and census enumerations helped form populations; resource management bureaucracies took over the surveillance of their landscapes. This is the separation that led us to the international knowledge that populations destroy resources. And, indeed, under the conditions the framework helps to form, they do. Clearly, there is a lot to say

about this, but here I track only the post–World War II transformation
of core peasantries.

NATIONAL DEVELOPMENT 1: FROM PEASANTS TO POPULATIONS

> The beginning of wisdom in an approach to any situation is the accumulation of facts. . . . The general picture of poverty and backwardness is delineated in specific figures. — Socorro Espiritu and Chester Hunt

Espiritu and Hunt's *Social Foundations of Community Development,* from which I have just quoted, formed part of an international effort to provide the facts and figures required to launch the new Southeast Asian nations that emerged after World War II on the best trajectories of development and nation building. The new nations faced dilemmas that differed from those of their colonial predecessors. The colonial model of dualism, that is, the necessary separation of native subsistence and colonial entrepreneurship, had been repudiated; instead, the new nation-states entered an international scene increasingly committed to a language of development, modernization, and life improvement for all. Yet this vision was to be realized on the landscapes inherited from the past. In this section, I argue that colonial core peasantries came to occupy the center of national imaginings of the future at the same time as those who studied and described them increasingly forgot, and erased, the conditions of their formation as core peasantries. Erasure of the embeddedness of these cultivators in a historically forged natural landscape was key to this project. Social science played a significant role in reimagining the countryside as a space of national development. In order to do so, it documented typicality and recast core peasantries as national populations. Meanwhile, core peasant landscapes became national resources.

Core peasant landscapes were fertile valleys for conceptualizing the intersection of nation building and international development. Their inhabitants were imagined as those who needed the most international help, because of their poverty and traditionalism, and who were its most appropriate beneficiaries as citizen representatives. Their fields became domains of underdeveloped national riches. During the 1950s and 1960s, it was taken for granted that development should have a national shape, that it involved empowering and enriching national elites as its first goal, and that particular pockets of national citizenry needed to be appeased, if not mobilized, to represent national and international development rip-offs as people-oriented programs. The core peasant land-scapes created by colonial programs proved to be the ideal location for the advancement of these visions.

First, core peasants were already defined as proper subjects and objects of administration; despite a change in the goals of the administration they were still objects of state rule and thus, too, the proper subjects of its national aspirations. Malayan history illustrates this well, for Indians and Chinese were never proper political subjects in the view of the colonial administration, in part because they were not seen as peasants, even when they lived in the countryside. This barred them from presenting themselves as proper political subjects of the new Malayan nation. In contrast, Malays had been actively crafted into peasants, and through this status they were ready to become national citizens and *bumiputera,* "sons of the soil." The fact that many of these citizens had recently immigrated from other parts of Southeast Asia did not mar their indigenous status because they were, after all, "Malays" — the race the British imagined as "yeoman-peasants."

Second, the abilities of core peasants to mobilize and make trouble were respected by colonial administrations, and they passed this respect to the new nation-states. The new states learned from colonial models of governance, which charted the possibilities of core peasant appeasement and rebellion. Yet the terms of governance had shifted. No one was sure of the future anymore; if the great colonial powers could be toppled, anything could happen. "Peasant revolutions" — in China, Vietnam, and Cuba — were increasingly shaking the world. Rural leaders and movements that once would have been dismissed as traditional seemed now to be the possible creators of modern political futures. Furthermore, rural mobilizations for national causes were in some instances very important for the establishment or maintenance of the new national regimes. They also threatened these regimes. In this context, the new states and their international backers equated "popular" movements and core peasant activities; unlike the annoying but not seriously undermining rebellions of noncore ethnic groups, core peasant mobilizations were seen as coming from inside the nation, with the potential of either strengthening it or tearing it apart. Core peasants became privileged political actors on the horns of this ambivalence.

Third, the agricultural works of core peasants, which had already been designed for ease of control and intervention, became arenas for national resource development. The strategies of property stabilization and agricultural intensification that had created colonially approved farms were reversed. In places where colonial governments had cordoned off native lands, national governments universalized property laws and made all lands available for resource development. Where colonial governments had demanded labor intensification, national governments turned the miracle of technological intensification on these same sites, demonstrating the national potential for modernization. If peasants lost their land and livelihood in the process, this was irrelevant to resource development.

Fourth, the density of core peasant populations privileged them within rhetorics of national representation; core peasants were the masses of the populist-conceived nation. If every individual deserves an opportunity to advance, the most populous groups deserve the most opportunities. Core peasants were numerous, even crowded. But there was an ambivalence there: if a big population means a healthy polity, it also signifies the problem of using up national resources and reproducing poverty. The privilege of core peasants, in demography as in political action, was formed in the development nation's desire to control them, even as it gave them special benefits.

The research and policies that emerged from this ambivalence about demography illustrate the ways in which peasants, once so carefully constructed, stopped being recognized as peasants. In the formation of peasant landscapes, colonial administrations worked hard to increase their populations. One of the most explicit goals of the British on the Malay Peninsula in the late nineteenth century was to increase the Malay population (Lim 1977, 16). To promote population increase, they encouraged immigration, newly stable ties to land and village sites, and the extension and exclusivity of permanent-field subsistence cultivation. The logic of increasing core populations is not altogether lacking in more recent policy (Ong 1990), but it was particularly in the population *limitation* programs that emerged as part of the international development apparatus that peasants were enumerated, amassed, and removed, textually, from their histories.[20] Reproduction was portrayed as an issue of conglomerate statistics, on the one hand, and individual contraceptive decision making on the other; there was no room for the specificity of core peasant landscapes. Yet the histories of population-increase programs in the making of these landscapes provided the hidden parameters in which masses and individuals were to be counted and controlled. Thus, the characteristics of core peasantries were both disguised and universalized as the natural features of any national rural populace.

Rural Southeast Asia from the 1950s through the 1970s was the site of relentless data gathering in this spirit. Descriptions of villages, portrayed as nationally "typical," piled up. No one but the most dedicated tribalist anthropologist studied noncore groups; instead, energy turned to national rural representatives. What these studies have in common is their self-assurance about the need for sound, neutral, and objective information. The international experts are at their most invisible; many do not feel the need to even argue theory. The call to describe rural life is enough. It is assumed that we agree on the importance of modernization and development, the problem of poverty, and the disadvantages of tradition. Within this agreement, we need the figures and charts that tell us which interventions have a comparative advantage. Through these numbers and equations, which portray rural people in the internationally rarefied space outside of dynamic cultures, struggles, and histories, national citizens could be made. And, while it seems right to feel outraged over development social science, which after so many thoughtful interventions (basic needs, peasant resistance, culture, class, world systems theory, conservation, indigenous knowledge, and much more) is to this day supported in unrecanted nonreflexiveness by powerful institutions all over the world, it is probably worth trying to remember that at least at one time it may have accompanied a sense of hope, of international advancement without the chains of imagined cultural difference, and of national accomplishment and pride.

Development funds made possible the flow of benefits to core peasants. In some areas, a limited amount of land reform was tried; more commonly, "new lands" were cleared and offered to core peasants as settlers. In Malaysia, Federal Land Development Authority (FELDA) schemes resettled Malay peasants on tree crop estates; in Indonesia, Javanese transmigration continued to form peasant villages across the archipelago; and in the Philippines tenant farmers from Luzon colonized lands in Mindanao, Mindoro, and other islands. No one cared about the people who lived in those lands before they were "opened" for core peasants. In some situations, direct payments also have come into core peasant villages as political patronage. In Malaysia, for example, Malay village adherents of the ruling party receive patronage benefits (Scott 1985). As with the opening of new lands, the goal is not to dismantle village inequalities but to create alliances between core peasants and national elites and to appease core peasants just enough to prevent their mobilization against the state.

This strategy of building national loyalty among the core peasantry, imagined as the residents of an amorphous "countryside," shaped international policy, including U.S. foreign policy. To consider this issue, I turn to the Philippines. The U.S. colonial administration in the Philippines developed a rhetoric of nation-building farmers that influenced post–World War II national development, both in the Philippines and around the world. Farmer protagonists of the story of the nation could emerge out of colonial core peasantries, turn toward the future, and employ their massive solidity to build democratic nations. As subjects and objects of the nation, they form characters in stories in which national autonomy and neocolonial international development are inextricably intertwined.

NATIONAL DEVELOPMENT 2: FARMERS AND FRONTIERS

> I think that the real intent of land reform is to create free men, men who own the land they till, men who will lay down their lives in defense of their birthright because that birthright is, at last, theirs. I think that the bedrock purpose of land-reform is the creation of a nation that will endure.
> — Conrado Estrella

Of all the colonial rulers in Southeast Asia, the one least interested in restoring a fantasy of lost feudalism was probably the United States. When the United States fought its way into colonial authority in the Philippines at the turn of the century, it took charge of a good deal of Spanish-instituted core peasant landscape. The Spaniards had tried to force their scattered Filipino subjects to abandon shifting cultivation and settle in centralized villages. By handing out these stabilized villages and fields as feudal landholdings, by strengthening the position of leading families, and, rather later, by allowing commercially oriented Chinese mestizos to enter the landholding ruling circle, the colonial administration also managed to create densely populated pockets of tenancy and sharecropping. The Americans, like their Spanish predecessors, considered these pockets to be central to the problem of colonial governance. Like the Spanish, they saw working together with the landholding elite as they key to successful rule. However, they distinguished themselves from their predecessors by means of an ideological project in which colonialism was cast as a training program in democratic nation building. In this project, the core peasant, the Tagalog *tao,* was the "common man." The symbolic valence of core peasants thus needed to be changed; no longer imagined as traditional subjects of feudalism, they were asked to become carriers of democratic national loyalties.

In this guise, core peasants became *tenant farmers,* and overcoming their tenancy was seen as a major challenge of Philippine democratic development. This "problem" of tenant farmers occupied a good deal of the attention of the U.S. colonial administration. The personalistic ties between tenant and landlord were decried as backward, oppressive, and undemocratic. The farmer, it was argued, needed his own land if he was to develop a commitment to the planned nation-state. Yet it was impossible to displace the landholding elite because its members were the key collaborators in U.S. rule.

One compromise was the "opening of new lands," particularly in Mindanao. Mindanao was "the frontier." Never mind the fact that Muslims and upland, "non-Christian" peoples already lived there; like Native Americans on the U.S. frontier, they were not imagined as possible national citizens.[21] Core peasants moving from Luzon were to be "homesteaders," advancing the pending national project. Village settlement was depicted as archaic and unnecessary due to the new possibilities of frontier settlement (Pelzer 1945, 110–12). The language of relocation thus contrasted sharply with the Javanese resettlement projects designed around the same time in the Netherlands Indies. Whereas Javanese peasants were sent to replicate their traditional village landscape in new territories, Luzon farmers became the new democratic and forward-looking pioneers of the pseudonational frontier. The project self-consciously recapitulated U.S. stories of the development of the nation: first the escape from traditional Europe and then the spread from east-coast hierarchies into the wild but democratic frontier. This is the process, or so the story is told, that built the American national character. The colonial administration impressed this story on Filipinos in order to build the kind of national project U.S. administrators could imagine.

Pioneer settlement in Mindanao probably worked better as an aid to adminstrators' storytelling than it did as a means of addressing dissatisfaction in core peasant areas. Indeed, very few Luzon farmers moved to Mindanao during this period. Furthermore, core peasants ended up developing more effective means of organization. When the United States lost the Philippines to Japan during World War II, Central Luzon farmers formed the anti-Japanese Hukbalahap movement. With the return of the U.S. administration, the Huks became the object of massive military suppression. But this suppression, directed at entire peasant communities, only raised the stakes and popularized agrarian rebellion. This was the countryside that the U.S. handed over to the new Philippine nation on the best national birthday of 1946, July 4.

The Philippine national administration closely followed U.S. guidance. It continued to practice military repression in the Luzon countryside; at the same time, it worked to develop a program to appease the demands of the Luzon farmers. It was at this early point, then, that land reform entered the agenda of Philippine nation building. The story of the fate of land reform proposals in the late 1940s and early 1950s illustrates the emergence of the core peasant, in his guise as the ordinary farmer, as both a privileged player at the center of national stories and an object of focused concern about social control.

Directly after World War II, U.S. foreign policy was rather enthusiastic about land reform. Frightened by revolutionary mobilizing in China, the United States was ready to appease peasants: land reform, advocates believed, could make the difference between a developing nation's swing toward communism or the free world. American advisers thought they had achieved some success in dismantling oppositional power structures and preventing left-wing swings in Japan, Korea, and Taiwan by promoting land reform (Putzel 1992). In the Philippines, too, U.S. advisers suggested agrarian reform. American army troops disseminated land reform promises, and the Economic Development Corps offered Huks and potential Huks pioneer settlement in Mindanao (Olson 1974, 80–81). In 1950, the Foster-Quirino Agreement tied U.S. reform supervision to foreign aid. A U.S. land reform adviser issued a report in 1952 offering a strong endorsement for the elimination of tenancy: "Relief from the oppressive burden of *caciquism* [feudal landlordism] has been too long sought—and too long denied. . . . Tenants demand correction of the basic inequities which characterize the agrarian pattern. . . . it is apparent that, until remedied, the land tenure system stands as an obstacle thwarting all efforts of the United States to develop a stable and democratic economy" (Hardie Report, quoted in Monk 1996, 182–83).

Philippine oligarchs did not support the U.S. position, which was shaped by New Deal liberals, and President Quirino called U.S. land reform advocacy a "national insult" (Putzel 1992, 91). Yet the U.S. position sparked a debate among Philippine politicians in which land reform "liberals" were pitted against landholding "conservatives." The latter argued that economic progress required government support of free enterprise and private property; agrarian reform should boost productivity but not redistribute land.[22] With U.S. liberal support, Ramon Magsaysay ran for president on a serious land reform platform—and won. The agrarian reform agenda had proved popular among voters. Yet was the United States really willing to attack its elite landholder allies? No one had a chance to find out because by the time Magsaysay assumed the presidency in 1954 the mood in Washington had changed. Land reform advocates from the United States were recalled from their posts in the Philippines; their replacements offered much less support for liberal programs. Besides, the success of the military campaign against the Huks (led, ironically enough, by Magsaysay himself in an earlier job as secretary of national defense) meant that the Huks were no longer considered a major security threat (Olson 1974, 84). The bill Magsaysay was able to put together and push through the Philippine Congress ended up privileging landlords. The size of landholdings to be expropriated was so large that practically no landowners were affected; even huge estates could only be redistributed if a majority of the tenants petitioned for expropriation (Putzel 1992, 92)! The rhetoric of agrarian reform still drew national attention, but it made no concrete improvements for tenant farmers.

This precedent, indeed, created the basis for a history of land reform efforts in the Philippines. Agrarian reform—that is, reform that addresses the specific conditions of core peasantries—continued to be discussed as the essential feature of building a democratic nation. Liberals attempted to relieve rural social inequities; conservatives redirected them to benefit landholders (Putzel 1992). A series of land reform bills were passed, none of them worth much. "New lands" continued to be colonized, displacing earlier and less nationally prominent inhabitants. Technological inputs continued to be suggested as a solution to poverty. Big landowners, with renewed alliances with U.S. backers, continued to dominate politics. Agrarian reform became an ongoing program consisting of a lot of talk coupled with a few appeasements. Each new program or bill recognized this and declared itself a break with the feudal past. (In 1967 President Marcos said, "We have to put an end to the decades of official hedging and temporizing on the application of land reform laws" [quoted in Estrella 1969, 79].)[23] The rhetoric of national development required that attention be paid to the needs of poor farmers, but the organization of politics reproduced their subordinate positions. The advantage, perhaps, for core peasants, was that their concerns were being taken seriously. The disadvantage was that they were unable to make any of the basic changes they demanded.[24]

It is in this context, perhaps, that "everyday politics" and "everyday resistance" developed in core peasant areas. I am referring to an influential theoretical framework developed by James Scott and Benedict Kerkvliet and worked out, in relation to the Philippines, in Kerkvliet's wonderfully informative book *Everyday Politics in the Philippines* (1990; see also Scott and Kerkvliet 1986). This framework depends on the return of attributions of peasantness to core populations, which I discuss in the next section. It also depends on the history of core peasantries in nation building. Through this history, everything that core peasants do, however mundane, has become "political," that is, able to speak to nation-building concerns. In contrast, the everyday activities of upland, "tribal" groups in the Philippines are seen as "cultural" and those of Filipino Muslims are "religious." Only a core peasant can consistently be a political actor within the nation-making field of political science. I am not arguing that the personal is not political but rather that it is no accident that Kerkvliet picked a Central Luzon village of tenant farmers to represent the Philippines and understand its everyday politics. The way in which things core peasants do are political is shaped by their prominence in nation-building stories.

It seems quite right in this context to argue that there is a continuum of acts of resistance that range from footdragging, dissimulation, and evasion to protests and denunciations. Core peasants have gained their identities in relation to a long history of surveillance; from the perspective of those who would control them, too, *everything* they do is by definition an act of either docility or rebelliousness. What is missing in the analysis is a sense of the historical specificity of this kind of politicization. In this regard, Kerkvliet argues that the Philippine peasants he studied have a sense of entitlement to livelihood and dignity. It seems likely that these Central Luzon tenant farmers know about their centrality in Philippine discussions of the nation. Their sense of entitlement makes sense as a response to their elevation as populist protagonists; their claims are easy to make because they resound with those of elite nationalists who argue issues of livelihood and dignity by invoking their landscapes and bodies. As Kerkvliet argues, their sense of entitlement is not a sign of a universal moral economy; it draws from history and experience. I am suggesting that it also tells us about the culture of national politics in which these tenant farmers play a privileged role. It is only in this light that one can understand why these poor villagers bother to participate in conventional politics, including demonstrations, petitions, and other formal protests (e.g., Kerkvliet 1990, 141–42). The government actually listens to them. When tenants took over a piece of unused land in 1981, they actually got a hearing, although they did not win (190–98). In response to their complaints, the land was sold and redistributed, but it did not benefit the poor. This situation epitomizes their current allegorical role: as national protagonists, they can speak and stimulate reform, but the reform is unlikely to be that which they desire. Their protests — effective and ineffective at the same time — become "resistance" rather than paths to change. My reading points not to ordinary disadvantage, as Kerkvliet might have it, but to historically specific privilege of an ambivalent and not particularly enriching sort.

Scott and Kirkvliet's framework (1986) is important not just in specifying the dilemmas of Southeast Asian core peasants under regimes of national development but because it intervenes against the data-gathering programs that document these privileged national populations while erasing their historical construction. Peasant studies brought back scholars' awareness of the peasant character of these populations. It brought the peasant as a historical actor to the forefront of discussion and made it possible to imagine national histories that work for and against peasants rather than just being carried on their backs. Addressing the world as well as the academy, peasant studies showed that there was more to survival in the rural Third World than the cold war conflicts that inspired U.S. engagements in places such as Vietnam. At the same time, viewed from the perspective of present day concerns with cultural diversity and marginality, it is also possible to say that peasant studies further universalized and naturalized core peasant dilemmas, making it difficult to see what else was happening in the Third World countryside besides the reproduction or dissolution of allegorical peasantness.

THE REDISCOVERY OF THE PEASANT

> The peasant . . . does not operate an enterprise in the economic sense; he runs a household, not a business concern. — Eric Wolf

In the late 1960s, scholarship rediscovered the peasant nature of Third World national core populations, rescuing them from their cultural erasure and textual massification under "modernization as development" frameworks. Peasants became a new object of analysis as scholars describing rural communities in the Third World began to compare them to peasants in early modern Europe (Dalton 1972). Influenced by these comparisons, other scholars began to reconsider "peasant" stakes in protest and rebellion in both the Third World and European history (Hobsbawm 1973). Many disciplines were represented in the growing excitement. Social historians showed peasants to be subjects of neglected political histories. Anthropologists examined peasant values as well as the cultural ecology of peasant societies (Silverman 1979). Eric Wolf argued that anthropologists should attend to peasants because, as producers of surpluses transferred to elites, they illuminate important kinds of political economic hierarchies (1966). Meanwhile, an English translation of the work of Russian economist A. V. Chayanov, who wrote about family-farm-based economies in early-twentieth-century Russia, stimulated a burst of scholarly thinking about the dynamics of contemporary

Third World rural economies (1966). Instead of disappearing into the industrial economy, as both Marxist and non-Marxist theorists had prophesied, peasants had maintained a continuous presence in the rural Third World. Suddenly, the search was on for peasant social and economic characteristics.

Questions of how peasants relate to market economies, capitalist class relations, and state repression were central from the first; peasant studies became intertwined with theories of global inequality. The kinds of agrarian rebellions that had absorbed U.S. foreign policy experts began to interest scholars with a more sympathetic eye, and this led to discussions of peasant rebellion and consciousness. Fights broke out about who peasants were (Shanin 1990) and whether they were profit maximizing or risk averse (Popkin 1979; Scott 1976). In the 1980s, attention turned to "everyday resistance." Political ecology and subaltern studies began to develop. Peasant studies had become a lively source of theory building and intellectual debate in the social sciences.

Peasant studies stimulated an interest in the history of rural landscapes (e.g., Roseberry 1993). Exciting insights have been gained. For example, the looming importance of property in defining peasant landscapes became visible once peasants were viewed as participants in the making of history. Peasants' relationships with the environment are mediated through class-oriented access to resources. This is a key improvement over the populations versus resources frameworks of many national development theorists. Indeed, this insight helped give rise to the closely related fields of social ecology, political ecology, and liberation ecology (Guha 1994; Bryant and Bailey 1997; Peet and Watts 1996). In these fields, conservation is considered together with differential access to resources, state policies of administration and coercion, and histories of political negotiation and struggle. The long-term ecological adaptations of peasant communities often provide models for thinking about sustainable relations between humans and natural environments. One reason to develop an appreciation of the strengths and limits of the peasant studies of the 1970s, 1980s, and early 1990s is that their insights frame current social understandings of the environment—in Southeast Asia and beyond.

The "peasants" of peasant studies have both a broad comparative range and great historical depth; that is what makes them interesting subjects for discussion.[25] What groups diverse settings together for most analysts—and makes their inhabitants worth talking about—is their contrast with stereotypes of "modernity," whether as market rationalities, Enlightenment values, or the capitalist commodification of land

and labor. The fact that peasants have not disappeared, despite the coercions of imagined modernities, attests to the historical depth and continuity of their lifeways. Not that scholars ignored change: the point for many analysts was to study peasants in a "changing" world. Yet the key characteristic that made peasants a locus for thinking about change was the importance of continuity and reproduction in constituting peasant communities.

The focus on continuity and reproduction as the heritage of peasants encouraged the formation of models of peasantness. Here it was easy for notions of tradition associated with certain times and places to become naturalized as concommitants of the peasant situation. In areas where national governments were already considering certain core peasant populations to be national Everyman representatives, scholars continued to privilege these populations in their peasant models; not only were data about them available, but it was already clear that they played a part in national histories and political economies. The features of these "core" groups were accepted as the features of traditional rural people. The histories of how these particular populations had become central to national storytelling were overlooked. Furthermore, these characteristics were often further naturalized as necessary features of social reproduction itself.[26]

The frame of peasant continuity and reproduction is created and naturalized, in part, through unexamined assumptions about families and households. For many scholars, peasants *are* family-based farm households. Families reproduce, households reproduce, and each continues peasant social life. This connection between family, household, and social reproduction seems obvious, necessary, and natural in many studies of peasants.

One way to explore this problem follows the influence of Chayanov in defining peasants through the family farm. Chayanov argued that the distinctiveness of peasants has to do with family production and consumption, and peasant theorists, whether or not they agree with Chayanov's ideas, have tended to treat family-organized and male-headed households as irreducible units, the components of class differentiation, culture, morality, decision making, populist politics, and rebellion. Why do analysts begin with households? Family farm households make "peasant" landscapes; since male-dominated yet magically unified families are taken for granted as a human grouping, no attention is paid to the conditions under which these families are claimed and constituted. Could it be that peasant landscapes are reproduced through the historically specific constitution of families?

Feminist scholars have asked precisely this question, calling attention not only to the diversity, internal dynamism, and instability of peasant family household farms but to the historical circumstances under which even the most stable seeming ones must be reconstructed again and again. Diana Wong's study, *Peasants in the Making* (1987), is relevant here. Against the usual idea that Malaysia's Green Revolution undermined traditional peasant communities, Wong argues that it *made* peasants by segregating families as units of production. Wong used a specialized definition of the term *peasant* and included only family owned and operated farms. My "peasant allegories," which include sharecroppers and tenants, cast a wider net. However, Wong's definition is juxtaposed against Chayanov's model of the peasantry, in which the reproduction of families corresponds to the reproduction of traditional society. In the rice-growing area she studied, family farms were created by the high productivity of Green Revolution double cropping, the decreased labor requirements of combine harvesting and broadcast seeding, and the retrieval of land once leased to tenants. Before the Green Revolution, farming involved the poor working for the rich; no farm could survive as a single family affair. When new technologies decreased the need for labor, forms of family autonomy developed that cut off these forms of hierarchical social integration. Wong describes the Malay peasants she studied as poised in a nonreproductive historical moment in which "peasantization" seems likely to give way to capitalist class formation even as it emerges. Yet it is also a moment in which reproduction can be imagined. The family farm is traditional in the national fantasy; in achieving it even for a moment, peasants can speak from the privileged position of imagined historical depth.

Gillian Hart, writing of the same region, approaches the problem of the naturalization of households from another direction (1992). Malaysian state agencies, she argues, *wanted* to create unified farm households in the 1970s, yet despite their efforts this dream remained an illusion at least for the poor, obscuring differences between men's and women's economic strategies. In the 1970s and 1980s, poor women's labor gangs staged direct confrontations with landholders, while poor men, caught in webs of patronage, only grumbled as individuals. Indeed, the emerging national ideal of male family household headship was used to criticize poor men's inadequacies, further intimidating poor men and discouraging them from joining in their wives' protests (Hart 1991).

Wong's and Hart's analyses challenge the taken for granted status of peasant family household reproduction, forcing attention to the histories under which peasantness is shaped and imagined. They return us to the possibilities of studying peasant fantasies as well as peasant realities. They open a discussion of the formation of the peasant in Malaysia as well as in peasant studies.

THE LANDSCAPE OF RESISTANCE

> One cannot, after all, expect the fish to talk about the water.
> — James Scott

The British colonial administration created a racialized landscape on the Malay Peninsula.[27] After considering a few initial ideas about Chinese and Indian agricultural settlement, British administrators set their sights on attracting settlers from the Indonesian archipelago and making them, together with locals, a village-based "Malay peasantry" (Lim 1977, 19–20). Chinese and Indians would occupy other niches. Anxious to protect European interests in plantation agriculture, the British actively discouraged Malay farmers from planting commercial crops, especially (after 1905) the runaway success commodity, rubber. Although Malay smallholders eagerly planted rubber anyway, colonial policy discouraged this at every turn (Lim 1977). British administrators wanted Malays to grow rice, which was seen as the traditional peasant crop. They became concerned that Malays would sell their land and abandon peasant agriculture and village life. The 1891 Selangor Land Code pioneered the idea of preserving "customary lands," which could not be sold except to other Malays. This idea reached its fullest expression in the Malay Reservation Enactment of 1913, which established reserves of land that were available only to those of the Malay race and religion (103–38). In the process, the act legally determined who counted as a Malay and thus as a peasant (Ong 1987, 20).

Despite British commitments to peasant subsistence agriculture, economic autonomy was rarely a choice. Wong (1987, 31–39) describes how Malay elites in the North Kedah Plain, supported by British trade policies, turned their attention to land colonization, constructing drainage canals and claiming large landholdings to be worked by tenants. From the first, cultivators were burdened with obligations to landholders even as they faced the difficulties of clearing new fields; they were always in debt. Debt was a historically central feature of rural livelihood, not a recent deterioration of tradition, as colonial authorities imagined it.

The political autonomy of villages — which was imagined in some peasant models — was also never possible. From the beginning of British rule in the nineteenth century, Malay villages were cobbled together as sites for the negotiation of colonial administration. Immigrants were gathered, land was registered, and legal and illegal practices were sorted out. Shamsul (1986) describes Selangor settlements established in the wastelands around European plantations by means of illegal shifting cultivation. When land was registered to make "villages," shifting cultivation had to stop. He also describes how the *penghulu,* local chiefs who were converted by the British into colonial mediators, took charge of creating villages. When one village planted rubber despite colonial rules against it, the penghulu replaced the village leader and merged the village with others into a more obedient unit (33–38). Such events created village factions and oppositional movements. After independence, these were translated into party politics. Village leaders who wanted ties with the regime supported the United Malays National Organization (UMNO), the leading party, and became brokers of the patronage it lavished on Malay villagers. Oppositional sorts joined the Partai Islam SeMalaysia (PAS), developing a discourse of religious and moral superiority with which to oppose the patrons. Village men in particular imagined their agency as local political figures through a back-and-forth dialogue between patronage and compliance with the state and religious and moral opposition to the conduct of the patronage-empowered compliers.[28]

In working within discourses of morality, whether compliant or oppositional, village men drew on national rhetorics of the importance of Malay heritage. Shamsul points out that Malaysia's New Economic Policy, put into place in 1971, conflated "development" as economic and racial advancement for Malays (1986, 190–95). In this context, village evocations of race, religion, and family could draw on the transcendant legitimacy of national moral guidelines. Furthermore, urban anxieties about the loss of tradition made rhetorics of moral heritage even more influential. Aihwa Ong's study of rural Malay women working in electronics factories in Selangor in the late 1970s showed the importance of national concerns over these women's moral conduct (1987). In the context of public anxieties, there was tremendous pressure on the young women workers to consider themselves once and future peasants. They were expected to think of themselves as obedient daughters, send their money home, maintain solidary class and race identities, and prepare for reentry into village life after they were fired. The girls were not altogether opposed to being considered up-to-date "electric Minahs" or at least independent spirits who knew something about the town as well as the village. In the rhetoric that swirled around them, however, ideals of proper gender roles, moral families, and Malay peasant tradition were combined, providing a powerful imaginary of peasant decency. Villagers as well as urbanites had uses for these moral stances.

The 1970s was also the decade in which the Green Revolution changed the rice-growing countryside. In Kedah, the Muda Irrigation Scheme allowed double cropping of irrigated rice. High-yielding varieties were introduced, the use of fertilizers encouraged, and mechanization and credit made available. Most commentators agree that in the program's first years these changes raised productivity as well as rural incomes and employment opportunities (e.g., Scott 1985, 65). By the end of the decade, the differential advantages for rich and poor had become more obvious; without employment, some of the poor had begun to migrate away. This is the time in which Diana Wong found a consolidation of autonomous families as units of farm labor and sociality (1987). In the context of the emergence of national discourses of Malay family and tradition, it seems possible to imagine the power of family-based claims both within and beyond village politics.

All of this offers a frame through which to reread James C. Scott's important contribution to peasant studies, *Weapons of the Weak* (1985). Scott offers a careful description of a Kedah village affected by the Green Revolution. He is sensitive to the complaints the poor articulate about the behavior of the rich; through these complaints, they show that they see through the economic mystifications that elites use to justify their pursuit of wealth. Rather than being cowed by hegemonic ideas about social status, the poor defer in public but use "backstage" moments to gripe and disrupt elite exactions. This account has influenced scholarly appreciations of subaltern perspectives, not only because it draws attention to the agency of the weak but because it suggests that poor villagers can tell truths about elite ideologies and demystify capitalism and state power. Moreover, the truths they tell draw on their understanding of history and tradition. They critique the present from the perspective of an imagined past. For scholars, the power of this critical stance comes from its parallel course to that of social-justice-minded intellectuals who also criticize capitalism and state power by drawing attention to historical alternatives. That poor Malaysian peasants do the same allows readers to both empathize with and learn from them.

In his description of the village, Scott assumes that family-based households are units not only of production and consumption but of all social and political action. He is careful to distinguish among differentially wealthy households, but he tells us almost nothing about the internal affairs and histories that make families as households appear to be units. The social commentary he learns from peasants tells of class positions as they are understood from the perspective of family representatives. These representatives are often, though not always, married men.

Under what circumstances might married men speak for families? Why might they draw upon imagined pasts? I have been suggesting that a number of historical developments came together to make this a powerful rhetoric through which village men might imagine their agency in both compliance and opposition to state modernization projects. Like Wong (1987), Scott finds that families have consolidated their labor in response to Green Revolution opportunities. Like Shamsul (1986), he finds that political participation privileges Malay men, who both receive patronage benefits from the state as household heads and participate in morally charged griping sessions as members of the opposition party. In these roles men learn to draw on nationally charged rhetorics of tradition and morality. The "remembered village" that is called up in their critical comments is, then, both their own response to local conditions and a creative use of a more widespread discursive frame.

The specificity of the perspective of married men in this village is suggested by a number of anecdotes Scott tells. When young men react angrily to an incursion on the village road by a rice truck, which threatens the young men's income from transporting sacks of rice, the more mature household heads gather to discuss the situation, stop future incursions, and scold the boys for charging too much (1985, 212–20). When women transplanters boycott farmers who use combines to harvest their rice (thus depriving villagers of jobs), married men — including the husband of one of the organizers — describe the action as meaningless "idle talk" (249–53).[29] In each case, male household heads turn the more confrontational actions of others into their own symbolic politics. They articulate ideas of appropriate behavior that allow them to negotiate with each other but take for granted their power over those without their historically specific privileges — as men, as Malays, and as those who can claim to be representatives of both families and tradition.

I am suggesting that the allegorical power of these peasant perspectives derives from a particular historical moment. At this moment, reproduction can be imagined. It is imagined as a past that comes to haunt capitalist modernity in the voice of racially defined male household heads, who, since they "represent" current families and imagined past communities, speak for subalternity, poverty, and injustice.

There is nothing wrong with calling up this moment and these perspectives. This is powerful stuff. Using voices such as these, peasant studies summons up rich histories of inequality and resistance. Yet who is left out? What other stories might we want to tell alongside peasant allegories?

As a moment of contrast, consider the political perspectives scholars and activists learned from an only slightly later development in Malaysian politics: the protests of the "tribal" Penan against logging (see Brosius, this volume). Too marginal to tap the domain of peasant allegory, the Penan could not access a discourse of national heritage and traditional morality. They are not the Malay rice farmers national politicians imagine as the nation's historical and representative populace. They seem so far outside the circuit of national thinking that Malaysian politicians jumped to the conclusion that they were surely being encouraged by foreigners. The Penan cause must be an international setup, they argued, calling the campaign "eco-imperialism." Indeed, activists from northern countries sympathized with the Penan without ever considering that they are Malaysians. Tribal allegories portrayed the Penan as a culture without a state. They could be the key to a planetary alliance that bypasses nation-states entirely. In contrast, married Malay men, as peasants, speak for the long history of state rule and elite exploitation. They speak for the national family and the village family, for the elders of the past and the children of the future. They speak for long-settled landscapes that can only be perserved if elites reclaim their moral responsibility to the poor. Even in their disruptions, they stand for the people.

THE RETURN OF THE TRIBES

> There are many ecological lessons to be learned from an understanding of the structure of small-scale societies, but they are not necessarily those which some influential Green gurus have drawn attention to, or would approve of. — Roy Ellen

When environmentalists' concerns about the conservation of wild places around the world reached mammoth proportions in the late 1980s, a new space was created for discussion of the "tribes," the ones who live in those purportedly wild places. The new discussion drew on earlier histories of Fourth World, First Nation, and indigenous rights organizing; it also gained a new environmentalist specificity. Here tribes are defined by means of their cultural difference from nontribes; questions of class, colonialism, nationalism, and state rule are pushed to the side as issues of culture and nature take the floor.

This change of agenda has not been viewed positively by most experts on the rural Third World, who are steeped in peasant or national development studies. Tribalists are scolded not only for making up other people's cultures but for having an "unrealistic" view of the rural landscape. Indeed, they often do. Yet this awkwardness between storytelling and its objects can give us pause in thinking about the peasant landscapes scholars have come to recognize as the real. Peasant studies, and its inheritors in social justice ecologies, are also based on fantasy and storytelling. Allegory is what makes it possible for scholars and activists to consider our common past and future through rural landscapes.

This said, it is hard to be too sympathetic with some forms of tribalism. Some tribalism exists only in virtual reality and mass media. It has been at its most prominent in advertising, perhaps, as in the controversial campaign of the Body Shop to publicize its work with the Kayapo Indians (Corry 1993). These are easy targets for criticism. So, too, are the brave visions of one-world globalism offered by some tribalist activists, which glorify the possibilities of Internet connections among activists and ignore the social and technical requirements that make Internet connections meaningful.

Yet tribal allegories have allowed activists to forge promising visions and plans. As I mentioned at the beginning of this essay, juxtapositions between tribal and peasant allegories have shaped the excitement of environmentalism in Southeast Asia. In Indonesia, Malaysia, and the Philippines, environmentalist populisms have brought issues of national social justice together with international issues of deforestation, pollution, green marketing, and more. The movements are self-consciously nationalist. What is surprising is the transformation of older populist nationalisms to include cultural minorities. Tribalist agrarian agendas have expanded the meaning of populist nationalism by bringing new groups (uplanders, forest dwellers) and new issues (indigenous knowledge, biodiversity protection, community integrity) into the realm of sympathetic nationalist discussion.[30]

International organizations have also begun to promote hybrid peasant-tribal agendas. For example, "community-based conservation" (CBC) brings ideals of peasant livelihood improvement and tribal environmental management into a single international model.[31] The model promotes the idea that local communities can manage natural resources. International promoters of CBC projects come from the ranks of those who made their reputations in community-oriented peasant development. However, CBC encourages them to pay more attention to forests and the other "wild places" that are generally ignored in classic peasant allegories. The Ford Foundation's Poverty Alleviation Program, a CBC sponsor, took its model from small-scale irrigation works in core peasant areas of the Philippines; the program then moved to thinking about *forest* rights in Indonesia (Coward forthcoming). The program carried a "peasant" architecture for imagining community mobilization in order to address a "tribal" environmental problem. Yet to play a role in forest conservation the "local community" has been reimagined as culturally marked and naturally wise — that is, tribal — instead of economically and educationally disadvantaged — that is, peasant. The local communities of CBC are hybrids between peasantist and tribalist thinking.

Hybrids and juxtapositions create new possibilities for agrarian allegories that transform our stories of global futures. I conclude by reviewing key elements of familiar allegories.

PEASANTS, FARMERS, TRIBES: SOME FUTURES OF NATURE

Farmers are the ones who just use resources. Ideally, they are economic maximizers and contribute to the gross national product. We know about their futures because economists tell us about them. They are the ones about whom Vandana Shiva rightly complains that their enumeration leaves out both the "noneconomic" work of women and the regenerative work of nature (1989). It seems fair to say that their stories have embroiled governments and rural communities in plans that promote deforestation, desertification, erosion, salination, and pollution, not to mention poverty and exploitative labor. Yet in the early twenty-first century both peasants and tribes must measure themselves against the global contributions of farmers. Of course I am speaking of allegorical figures and not particular people.

The peasant figures rescued from national populations contribute long histories of national culture and struggle for livelihood and human dignity — as well as uppity disruption of elite and state plans that disregard them. They contribute the peaceful, fruitful landscapes for which our nations are known. We can't get rid of them, adherents say, because they are tenacious and determined fighters; they are allies in our struggles for a better national destiny. They hide their resistance behind compliance and thus remind us of the difficulties and commitments of social equity over the long run. Besides, their landscapes have the long-lasting stability we all want for the earth. Peasant figures are those who know best about the balance of nature and the systems requirements that keep subsistence and community and elite extractions going over many years and generations. They have ecosystems and social-political-economic systems. If the earth is made of nations and ecosystems, we must have peasants to sustain it. Our ability to imagine sustainability is a global contribution of the allegory of peasants.

Yet it is tribes who, like scientists, are thought to know the most about nature's secrets. Tribes are imagined as the keepers of biodiversity. Scientists cannot enumerate or maintain it without tribal help. The figures of tribal allegories know how to build landscapes and communities that do not separate people from their environments. They refuse the dichotomies of wild versus domestic and humans versus nature, and thus they help us learn to respect the variety and richness of nature. Tribal figures evade established nations, and so they reach beyond their borders. They teach us to think globally and act locally. They are the cultural nodes in global networks. If we are serious about tackling environmental problems that go beyond national jurisdictions, we must work together with, and follow the example of, these allegorical tribes.

Following World War II, a new wave of international environmentalism pulled together the scientific agenda of systems ecology and the moral agenda of preserving the balance of nature to build a social movement (Taylor and Buttel 1992). Within this movement, the national peasant protagonist was often used to imagine the possibilities of long-lasting social-natural stability and reproduction. The unboundedness of these systems analyses was central to their success in characterizing a better global future: just as natural systems take energy from anywhere, including outer space, and recycle it for their own reproduction, so, too, interconnected and hierarchical social systems can still provide models for productive social recycling and stability within parallel but self-reproducing niches, including nations. The intertwining of natural and social in the peasant agricultural landscape makes its fertile stability a particularly appealing model of sustainable futures.

The scientific rejection of ecosystem stability in the 1980s was only slowly felt in the environmentalist community, and many activists, to the horror of ecological scientists, still talk about the "balance of nature." Without its scientific underpinnings, however, the legitimacy of the environmental movement was in trouble (Worster 1994). When the movement floundered, a new form of science picked it up again: conservation biology. Conservation biologists brought a scientific theory and method to another moral cause, the protection of biodiversity. But the objects and assumptions of the environmentalism formed on this science and morality differed from those of the ecosystems era. Enter the tribes.

First, the focus turned to "wild" landscapes. Most conservation biologists assume an incompatibility between human use and nature's ability to flourish. Tribal landscapes, however, seem to represent a promising exception to human-nature incompatibility. Is this a crack through which humans might enter a renewed nature? Purist conservation biologists are still appalled at the idea. Peasant landscapes are clearly beyond the pale.

Second, the goal of preserving biodiversity can only be pursued at the global scale at which diversity can be measured. Nations mean nothing. The building of globalism is a contested affair, with many experts calling for a northern-dominated, culturally unmarked space of scientific observation. Tribal advocates have made themselves heard by offering an alternative: a global network linking varied nodes of culture and nature in a spirit of respect for diversity.

Peasants, in contrast, appear to have nothing to say about these issues. Instead, peasants maintain their environmentalist voice to call for social justice and national responsibility.

To draw attention to peasant and tribal allegories does not lead me to an evaluation or dismissal of their competing claims. Perhaps this is the beginning, however, of another kind of discussion.

ACKNOWLEDGMENTS

This essay was originally written in 1995. It was conceived as an opening to a conversation, and I feel privileged that it has already stimulated interchanges with a number of generous scholars. Benedict Anderson, Donald Moore, and James Scott contributed detailed, critical comments on the whole manuscript. Barbara Andaya, Warwick Anderson, Paulla Ebron, Corinne Hayden, Celia Lowe, Vicente Raphael, Craig Reynolds, and Ann Stoler offered references, suggestions, and warnings about my approach. I am grateful to all of them for their help, and I am all too aware that I was unable to fully absorb their suggestions in the final draft.

NOTES

1   These names are pseudonyms. My brief account of the work of these two men derives from 1994 fieldwork. For more on the Meratus Dayaks, see Tsing 1993.
2   For a useful introduction to Indonesian environmentalism, see Mayer 1996. For Philippine environmental alliances, see Broad and Cavanagh 1993. For some of the concerns of Malaysian environmentalists, see Sahabat Alam Malaysia 1987.
3   The standard references here are Said 1978 and Clifford and Marcus

1986. Scholarly critics of tribal cultural exoticization in Southeast Asian environmental movements include Brosius (this volume), Li 2000, and Zerner 1994a. My attempt to offer an analysis of the local benefits of tribalist storytelling can be found in Tsing 1999.

4   Classics in this tradition include Guha 1990 and Scott 1985. Scholarly critics of Southeast Asian environmental projects from a peasantist perspective include Peluso (1993, this volume) and Hirsh and Warren 1998.

5   A number of scholars have argued that peasants are an archaic social form of little relevance to today's world (e.g., Kearney 1996). In contrast, I find traces of peasant allegories everywhere — even as I trouble the naturalistic rhetoric through which scholars recount their earlier existence.

6   Environmental scholarship has been much informed — self-consciously and unselfconsciously — by these agrarian allegories. For example, peasant and tribal allegories about forests are strikingly different, and their divergence underlines the importance of paying attention to these formative stories. Both oppose the dominant developmental stereotype that holds that rural people necessarily destroy forests, yet each challenges this creed in different ways. The peasant story revolves around the terms of forest saving: why shouldn't local people strike back at elite enclosures? The tribal story questions assumptions about local use: when allowed to operate without state coercions, local people *are* conservationists. In peasant stories, forests are portrayed as luxury spaces protected by royalty for noble pleasures, by states for scientific timber management, and by urban elites for their aesthetic and recreational uses. Peasants rebel against the laws that cordon off the forests for the state and elites (e.g., Thompson 1975; Sahlins 1994; Kartodirdjo 1973; Guha 1990). Indeed, forest rebellion is often portrayed as constitutive of peasant political consciousness. In contrast, the main characteristic of tribes is their cultural *knowledge* of the forest. Tribes are good forest managers because they understand and care about forests. Precolonial Native Americans burned, not like peasants who burn to annoy the authorities but, like forest rangers, to promote particular forest successions (Cronon 1983). Tribal peoples are said to farm with the forest, not against it; in contrast to peasants who hold back weedy diversity, they promote biodiversity in their management (e.g., Posey 1985). There are, of course, ethnographic differences between the groups that form classic examples in each of these two literatures. The power of these stories to shape environmental scholarship, activism, and policy builds from — but moves beyond — this ethnographic specificity.

7   These works deal with the making of peasant landscapes during the colonial period. Other scholars have addressed the formation of peasantries in postcolonial events (e.g., Wong 1987; Takahashi 1972). In common, they refute the necessity of peasant social change from tradition to modernity. Instead, they show how the forms of peasant tradition are constructed in contingent histories.

8   Elson (1994, 32) usefully warns against attributing too much power to colonial policy, which was often unable to transform society in the ways it might have wished. However, for the purposes of my argument here, the imagination of rural society is equally as important as the successful com-

pletion of colonial projects. It is also worth noting that many of the issues most debated between historians who stress colonial construction and those who stress native agency, such as whether colonial policy in Java caused more hierarchy or more leveling and more communal tenure or more individual land claims, do not matter for the story I am trying to tell here.

9 Marx was not alone in his interpretation; conservative critics also found peasants conservative. According to Rosener (1994, 2), "Wilhelm Riehl lauded the conservative influence of the peasants during the 1848 Revolution and ascribed the salvation of Germany's princely thrones to it." Farr (1986, 9) traces images of conservative peasants in popular German rural novels after 1848.

10 A useful discussion of agrarian landscapes across Europe may be found in Scott 1998.

11 Gouda writes that "the principal portrayal of the rural scene in Holland [in the nineteenth century] was populated by savvy farmers who specialized in the production and well-paying export of cheese and butter and responded to oscillations in the foreign demand for agricultural goods with great alacrity" (1995, 126). Dutch historians portray their agricultural history as having left most feudal relations behind by the time of the seventeenth-century Republic, thus paving the way for specialization, export orientation, and the creation of large, capital-intensive farms, at least in coastal areas, by the nineteenth century (van Zanden 1994).

12 Until the beginning of the nineteenth century, the Dutch contracted with local Javanese rulers for specified quantities of export goods. In this "system of trade," they ignored the organization of production to work with indigenous elites (Elson 1994, 23).

13 Governer-General Van den Bosch explicitly used a model of the Dutch peasantry in imagining the traditional Javanese village; as with the Dutch *marke,* he argued, village stability was related to communal property (Boomgaard 1989, 8). The nineteenth century was a time of great debate about the marke in the Netherlands, as the state was moving to divide these collectively managed lands for the benefit of large landowners (van Zanden 1994, 32–43). It is not surprising that the marke influenced policy on Java; at the same time, however, more general European images and debates were often as significant as specific institutions.

14 Jan Breman's description of early colonial rural Java stresses the mobility of the population: nonterritorial patrons competed for the loyalties of a shifting agricultural populace, commerce required travel, laborers absconded, and villages were only one kind of settlement (1988).

15 Raffles, influenced by the British experience in India, argued that the village was the unit of Hindu civilization and that, although it had disintegrated somewhat in Java, it could be benevolently revived by the British (ibid., 3). On the scene already we see the disappearing peasant in need of restoration to a model itself faded through displacement and memory.

16 J. van Sevenhoven, the first director of cultivations, spoke of rural dwellings as "irregular, unordered, randomly situated in relation to each other and without the necessary means of securing them" (quoted in Elson 1994, 155).

17 Village leaders gained new access both to personal land and to land distribution and regulation. The gap between leaders and nonleaders rigidified: "Peasants who held land and did not have access to [the] favored group tended to become a more homogenous group, pliable and submissive in their attitude to their superiors and their fate" (ibid., 178).

18 Governor-General Van den Bosch said it succinctly: "I am trying to improve the security of our settlement on this island . . . [and] this must be based on a well-established aristocracy" (quoted in ibid., 180).

19 In *Agrarian Transformations,* a key scholarly work outlining relations between the state and rural society in Southeast Asia, only Javanese are mentioned under the heading "Indonesia" (Hart, Turton, and White 1989). Tania Li has recently published a response to this exclusion (1999); her volume was originally to be entitled *Upland Transformations* to echo the earlier volume title.

20 Population limitation was not a new idea; it was well developed in the colonial Southeast Asia of the early twentieth century. However, it became a national problem under international supervision after World War II, and in this guise it stimulated a great deal of new research, policy, and thinking.

21 Pelzer, describing this project of resettlement, mentions the problem of the tribes. "In certain parts of the islands," he writes, "the local non-Christian tribes resent the infiltration of lowland Filipinos and attack the settlers" (1945, 113). He suggests that the government should set aside tribal reservations, recapitulating the U.S. American landscape fantasy.

22 Note that the labels liberal and conservative are used quite differently in this twentieth-century American-influenced debate than in nineteenth-century European discourses such as that which characterized Dutch colonial disagreements.

23 Marcos was interested in dismantling the power of *some* key landholding families in order to empower his cronies and strengthen his personal rule (Hawes 1987). However, the rhetoric of empowering small farmers to participate in the national political process was, for him as for others, talk of nation building and not a plan for organizational change.

24 Putzel (1992) usefully takes this story up through the Aquino regime, showing how debates between liberals and conservatives have kept discussion of land reform at the center of Philippine politics without actually advancing any meaningful programs of reform.

25 As the excitement over peasant studies grew, the field came to encompass many kinds of historical and contemporary people; even precolonial Africans, once considered the urtribes, had been discovered to be peasants by the 1980s (Isaacman 1993, 229).

26 Theorists of peasant society often build their notions of peasant politics and culture too directly on the necessities of survival with limited technology plus biological reproduction plus general features of premodern social hierarchy (e.g., Langton 1998), neglecting the varied cultural alternatives for survival, reproduction, and hierarchy.

27 The states of East Malaysia — Sarawak and Sabah — were not actively "peasantized" under European rule. Their "too tribal" citizens are still

generally ignored in the national development literature as well as peasant studies.

28 Shamsul offers the story of one woman, the daughter-in-law of an important male leader, who became an influential local politician with her father-in-law's support (1986, 177–83). It has been possible for women to join party politics. However, this woman, promoted as a special case, needed to work mainly with men and in a predominantly male idiom. Hart (1991) also argues that Malay party politics has privileged men in relations of patronage that exclude women.

29 In a response to Scott, Hart (1991) argues that the direct protests of women transplanters should be contrasted with men's indirect grumblings in any evaluation of resistance.

30 In the 1980s, Michael Dove called the Kantu' of West Kalimantan, Indonesia, peasants; more recently, he has written about them as tribesmen. Dove (personal communication) points out that he was writing to development-oriented versus environmentalist audiences in these respective usages; this underlines the importance of the allegories the terms carry with them in mobilizing readers to imagine rural actors within action-oriented global scenarios.

31 Brosius, Tsing, and Zerner (1998) review some of the issues in this field, which we call "community-based natural resource management."

Ann Grodzins Gold

FOREIGN TREES

Lives and Landscapes in Rajasthan

Nostalgia may in fact be a vehicle of knowledge, rather than only
a yearning for something lost. It may be practiced in diverse ways,
where the issues for users become, on the one hand, the attachment
of appropriate feelings toward their own histories, products, and
capabilities, and on the other hand, their detachment from — and
active resistance to — disempowering conditions of
postcolonial life. — Debbora Battaglia

Over the last half century Rajasthan — like many other regions of South
Asia and the globe — has experienced mutually impacting and arguably
unprecedented pressures due to political, social, and economic transitions; technological development; population growth; and diminishing
natural resources. In December 1992, I returned to Ghatiyali, a large
village located in the Banas river basin (Ajmer District), where I had lived
over a decade earlier (Gold 1988). I intended to study cultural constructions of the environment by examining rituals associated with agriculture and herding. Before long, however, my collaborator, Bhoju Ram
Gujar, and I found ourselves eliciting complex chronicles of multifaceted
change.[1]

I knew vaguely from casual comments people had made during my
earlier residence in this area, and from the general literature on deforestation and the decline of common property resources in Rajasthan,
that the landscape had undergone radical transformations within the last
half century and thus within living memory.[2] I recalled persons telling me
in 1980 of a dense, dark, and dangerous forest populated with wild
animals and bandits, where now we saw scrubby, barren, largely open
land.[3] I found this hard to imagine and had paid it little special attention.
Most of my earlier research was concerned with the pressing realities in
human lives of invisible entities: deities, ghosts, and witches. I understood that such personified, imperceptible beings moved and motivated
the present in discernible ways. But the vanished trees and absent wildlife

did not then seem to me to be as pressing or vivid an imaginative reality; in that impression, I was mistaken.

Transformations in the landscape, I learned in 1993, have affected hearts and minds poignantly, even as do the changes in family composition and interpersonal relationships that lie at the heart of ghost and witch stories.[4] Hard in search of ideas about nature but a little baffled by where to find them, Bhoju Ram Gujar and I began to ask old people about the vanished trees. Bhoju was then a middle school teacher in his mid-thirties, the only member of his Gujar caste from Ghatiyali to hold a college degree.

Although we often initiated our interviews with questions about the visibly altered landscape, it soon became clear to both of us that environmental change was inseparable from a web of concurrent transformations in politics, technology, society, religion, family life, morality, and more. The eloquent accounts that so many villagers — most of them between fifty and eighty years of age — willingly gave us did not merely describe these processes but offered intellectual and emotional responses to them. Each person spoke from a particular position, in terms not only of age but of gender, caste, and economic status as well as the interview situation.[5] Nonetheless, their multiple tales converge closely on many topics and constitute a variegated but patterned discourse of change.[6]

Older or infirm persons were the easiest to find at home; old men, especially, were the only adults in the village with plenty of time and inclination to talk. We systematically sought out persons whose personal memories reach back at least to the early 1950s. Thus, the visions I transmit most particularly represent perspectives of an aging generation, a witness to pivotal change. I have very little formal interview testimony from members of the generation in its prime: persons between twenty and forty. In casual conversation with this cohort, which included in 1993 five sporadic employees, it seemed to me that recollections of the woods have been transmitted to them, though without the finer details of its biodiversity. All adults seemed minimally to know that today's landscape is starkly different from that of the past. For a separate but related project carried out during the same research period, I spent the better part of two months interviewing children, most of them between the ages of eight and fourteen, about their environmental knowledge (Gold and Gujar 1994). One of the questions I asked these children in 1993 concerned the former woods. Most responded animatedly and without hesitation were able to recount brief stories of wild animals heard from their elders.

To speculate on how much or how little old people's memories affect the action and aims of the generation currently most vigorous in production and politics would be presumptuous given my limited range of sources. I can say, however, that rural Rajasthan by and large — compared to the United States or modern Europe — is an oral culture, a culture of apprenticeship, and a culture where youths still listen to seniors with respect. Grandparents, moreover, often take a major role in caregiving and the practical education of young children, a factor that would serve to prolong collective memory. Readers should of course remain aware that I transcribe here the voices of a passing generation. I am confident, however, that this group's children and grandchildren have at least partially internalized their elders' messages. It is also well to keep in mind, when these voices speak memories, that memories are subject not only to selection and filtering but no doubt to embellishment. Layered as collective and social memories, they nonetheless bear a kind of historical truth force.[7]

Throughout this essay, I cite at length individual persons' words. Here I set down a synoptic synthesis of some recurring themes in aging Ghatiyalians' change stories. The end of princely rule marks conceptually — if not necessarily with precision — the beginning of this narrative. In the early 1950s, the drama of land reform took place, effectively eliminating the former rulers' highly oppressive taxation and conscripted labor systems. Villagers refer to this radical set of changes with the English word *settlement:* land titles were settled on the cultivators, written in the name of the farmer.[8]

Various technological innovations soon followed, more gradual than land reform but cumulatively of tremendous impact. Farming today is dominated (at least in people's minds) by the use of tractors to plow and threshing machines at harvest, by the application of chemical fertilizers, by the use of engine-driven pumps to irrigate, and by the preponderance of new varieties of wheat as the favored food grain (versus corn, millet, barley, and indigenous wheat species) and oilseed or spices as cash crops (versus cotton). Cotton, which I saw growing in 1980, appeared to be nearly absent in 1993. Coexisting with most forms of modernization, however, are continuing if waning practices, for example, plowing and threshing with oxen, fertilizing with composted manure, irrigating with oxen, cultivating older varieties of grain, and multicropping.

Associated with changes in production are changes in lifestyle. Improvements in economic conditions for small farmers have been accompanied by increases in conspicuous consumption, particularly in the form of stone houses and elaborate weddings and funeral celebrations. All such displays of wealth were in the past forbidden to middle-level farming and herding castes, the majority of the population then and now, by their jealous rulers. For the previously severely disadvantaged — the "scheduled castes" of Regars, Chamars, and Harijans — government programs have provided much: houses, land, wells, electricity.

Nevertheless, every person we interviewed, including members of these groups, spoke at times of deteriorations in both individual and community well-being. Such declines were notably in the good taste of food and its inherent power to nourish, which affects human health, strength, and character; these in turn impact on social graces and community harmony. Tap water — which runs for less than an hour a day from public and private taps — versus well water, grains grown with chemical fertilizers versus manure, and electrically milled versus stone ground flour form a proverbial triad blamed for many problems. The abandonment of local herbal remedies in favor of "English medicine" is associated with this syndrome. Indeed, one person elaborated an analogy between the effects of chemical fertilizer on the soil and Western medicine on the human body (both being at times likened to opium in their addictive nature).

Many with whom we spoke attributed the hot, short tempers people have today to eating grain grown with chemical fertilizers (referred to as "white," "English," or less often "foreign" as well as by the specific types in use: urea, DAP, and superphosphate) and spoke of a general dwindling of compassion in human hearts. But such changes are also attributed to a shortage of dairy foods (milk, yogurt, clarified butter), which are believed to enhance cool and refined temperaments. This shortage is due both to people selling more milk and butter, to the point of skimping at home so they can obtain cash with which to purchase consumer goods, and to smaller livestock herds (resulting in a shortage of manure and the need for chemical fertilizers). Decreased livestock is due, people explain, both to increased population, and the ensuing encroachment of agricultural cultivation on what was formerly common grazing land, and to fodder shortages resulting from deforestation and the advent of government-propagated trees (the central subject of this essay), whose leaves are inedible.

Along with individual health and good nature, community life has deteriorated, many say, as has religious virtue ('dharma') in the form of ritual observances. Most notably, rituals based on priestly knowledge, and reliance on Brahman priests in general, have greatly decreased, as have the intercaste barriers that supported Brahmans' claims to ritual superiority. Reliance on the gods, however, seems to be as powerful an emotional reality as ever.

It is risky to condense or flatten or epitomize a multidimensional and organically interdependent narrative such as this one. But in order to project images that may be perceived and understood I am ever forced to choose an angle, a lens, a focus. Elsewhere I have highlighted associations linking deforestation and declining morality to climate change (Gold 1998), associations linking vanished wildlife to the vanished nobility (Gold with Gujar 1997), and interpretations of neglected ritual as a sign of modernity (Gold 1999a). Here I shall circle round trees—and particularly one kind of tree.

Deforestation offers dramatic visible evidence to persons over forty of radical environmental transformations in the Rajasthani landscape. Ghatiyali, whose name derives from its valley location, is surrounded by hills—once densely wooded but now largely denuded. Each hill formation has a name, and some of these evoke the vanished woodlands. For example, one is called Wild Pig Hill and another Thieves Pass—each having once afforded shelter in its dense foliage to marauders, whether animal or human. The largest range is called *kāntolā*—which one person glossed as "where there once was deep jungle." The term appears to derive from *kānto* (thorn). Clearly, thorny trees are not new to this region. But the tree that inspires this essay seems to escalate pernicious thorniness to a previously unknown degree.

This currently dominant species in the environment of Ghatiyali is an aesthetically unpleasing, stubbly tree locally dubbed "foreign *bambūl*" (*vilāyatī bambūl; babūl* in Hindi) and often simply referred to as *vilāyatī* (foreign). This tree's Latin name is *Prosopis juliflora,* and it is not an acacia, as the Hindi would imply, but a kind of mimosa native to Mexico. In the United States, we are familiar with *Prosopis juliflora* as "mesquite," much valued for the flavor its smoke imparts. Significantly perhaps, I never once heard a Rajasthani resident exclaim that food tastes better when cooked over vilāyatī.[9]

In Ghatiyali and its environs, we were told, vilāyatī was initially introduced as an organic hedge to protect fields and mark boundaries. Seedling of almost every other kind of tree must be protected from livestock with elaborate improvised structures, and watered for several years as well, but vilāyatī—thorny and fast-growing—flourishes without human assistance. Because goats and other livestock do eat the seed pods, new trees sprout from their dung, and vilāyatī spreads quickly over the landscape. Farmers now claim that the trees have become unwelcome and hard to remove colonizers of agricultural land. Crops do not grow well in vilāyatī's company. Puncture wounds and splinters from their thorns cause dangerous infections and play havoc with bicycle tires. The presence of these foreign trees, however, has averted a severe fuel wood shortage. Government planners continue aggressively to promote vilā-yatī's propagation in plantations on otherwise barren or unproductive land.[10]

Although I've snagged my skirt and hair, scratched my limbs, and flattened my tires more than once, all because of vilāyatī, I was frankly surprised at the vehement dislike this plant evoked among herders and farmers, in spite of their evident and acknowledged dependence on it for the cooking of their daily bread. My aim here is not to debate the value or inappropriateness of vilāyatī for reforestation. Rather, my primary focus is on how village people feel about vilāyatī. I wish to explore the insinuation of foreign bambūl into the landscape, as it is so often nega-tively construed. I shall also consider how its eventual domination of the scenery intermeshes, conceptually and actually, with the other kinds of gross and subtle invasions and replacements that have so transformed these Rajasthanis' lives in the second half of the twentieth century.

A number of other verbally maligned but pragmatically incorporated elements of modern life in Ghatiyali are, like foreign trees, opposed to indigenous or local (desī) things but are either labeled "English" (an-grejī) — directly after the former colonizing power — or simply called by their foreign names. These include fertilizers, liquor, medicine, synthetic fabrics, and machinery. Like vilāyatī, these are avidly consumed and employed and the subjects of an ambivalent discourse. All such lin-guistically marked imports are associated with, and emblematic of, far-reaching changes that have diminished some aspects of life but that are by no means wished away. The nostalgia I evoke is more a wide-awake critique of the present than a dreamy yearning for the past.

Foreign carries a contrast with *local* or *indigenous*. As a noun, the primary meaning of *vilāyat* is "the land belonging to another," a foreign land. Most dictionaries also translate *vilayat* as England, Europe, and Iran or Turkistan, in that order. The RSK — beyond a general definition of *vilāyatī* as "foreign" — contains eleven entries beginning with this adjec-tive — many of them plants, although *bambūl* is not among them — and includes other items such as "foreign blue" from China. Clearly, thus to label an import that has become commonplace but remains identifiably not native has been a linguistic process for many years.[11]

Among trees, another species — presumably indigenous to the region — is called *desī bambūl* or "local bambūl." Although foreign and local *bambūl* appear to be similar, local bambūl is a true acacia: *Acacia nilo-tica*. Sharma and Tiagi report that this tree is "known as Babool locally and Babbul (Sanskrit), the decoction of the bark and fruits is used medicinally in Ayurveda. Incisions made on the stem yield a gum which carries medicinal value" (1979, 105). In the village, people often contrasted deśī bambūl, with its multiple uses, and vilāyatī, which is good "only for burning."[12] While deśī bambūl has become scarce around Ghatiyali, vilāyatī is everywhere.[13]

A hierarchical evaluation of local as superior versus foreign as problematic, evident in these tree appellations, is context dependent. When it comes to *ghī*, or clarified butter, "pure deśī" is synonymous with "the best" (and most expensive).[14] Opposed to it is ghī that is adulterated or totally fake (i.e., vegetable shortening). Regarding radios or tape decks, however (valued items notably foreign in their origins), people speak of deśī with derision; the economics are also reversed. A deśī tape recorder may be cheap, people advised us, but its sound is bad and it soon breaks.

I cannot help but be reminded of Salman Rushdie's use of a popular Hindi film song to epitomize or celebrate the identity crisis for Indians in this era of transnational flow: "Mera joota hai Japani/Ye patloon Inglistani/Sar pe lal topi Rusi — /Phir bhi dil hai Hindustani," which Rushdie translates poetically as "O my shoes are Japanese/These trousers English, if you please/On my head, red Russian hat — /My heart's Indian for all that" (1991, 11). It seems that the sense of being clothed in alien, transcultural fragments affects not just the filmgoing urban populace, or the non-resident Indians (NRIs) of whom Rushdie often writes, but rural people as well. The cheerful assertion of a deeper Indian identity vocalized in the song, however, may be a Bollywood fantasy of surface versus depth. While some persons with whom we spoke expressed comparable thoughts (or used similar strategies), others insisted that change had penetrated body chemistries and hearts.

Three substantial segments follow, each drawing on transcribed texts of interviews. In the first, I explore those local narratives of history and discourses on change in which the loss of the old, indigenous tree species is embedded. In the second, I track the advent of foreign trees and their impact on lives and landscapes. There follows a third section in which I explore visions of change beyond trees, showing how other imported goods and practices potently contrast to things "indigenous." I conclude with sketchy suggestions of how villagers' understandings of the past and appraisals of the present might offer realistic insights relevant to projects of ecological recovery.

While many of the experiences and images of change that unfolded in the meandering course of our oral-historical research undoubtedly reflect patterns existing in many parts of Rajasthan and throughout North India, it was often hard to keep this in mind. As stories of Ghatiyali's past unfolded, they made it appear unique: the stories of a singular place, of its named localities and inhabitants. In recorded history, Ghatiyali's past is embedded in that of a small kingdom (*thikānā*) called Sawar after its main fort and market town. Sawar's territory encompassed twenty-seven villages of which Ghatiyali was the largest next to the capital.

One former ruler's presence dominates Ghatiyali's remembered past: Vansh Pradip Singh. A strong personality, he reigned over Sawar for more than thirty years, from his ascension to the throne in 1914 until his death in 1947. In our interviews, Vansh Pradip Singh is usually referred to as the *darbār* — literally, "the court" — a term of reference commonly applied to rulers of big and little kingdoms in Rajasthan. This darbār had a strong interest in religious actions and was a particularly fervent protector of the forest and wildlife (Mathur 1977). During his reign, he shaped Sawar's environmental conditions with considerable deliberation.

When Bhoju and I began to inquire about the trees and animals that used to exist, our first, tentative questions evoked what were for me unexpectedly vehement and dramatic descriptions of how Vansh Pradip Singh had cared for wildlife more than he cared for the poor farmers from whose harvests he took the lion's share, whose labors he conscripted, and whose small human pleasures and dignities he and his agents severely curtailed. Indeed, everyone old enough to remember him told us, with various proportions of bitterness, astonishment, and admiration, how he had scattered popcorn for the wild boars that destroyed his subjects' crops and caused persons who harmed forest animals or cut reserved trees to be ignominiously beaten and fined.[15]

Vansh Pradip Singh died without progeny in 1947, resulting in a succession dispute over the Sawar throne that lasted until 1951, when his widow's adopted "son," Vrij Raj Singh — who was of the same generation as Vansh Pradip and already ruled nearby Chausala — was enthroned. Beginning during this four-year interregnum (and coinciding, coincidentally but not incidentally, with a tumultuous period in India's history), there was rapid decimation of trees and the animals that sheltered in them. Shortly after Vrij Raj Singh's succession to the Sawar royal seat, a series of land reform bills radically disempowered the former princes.

Within a single decade, as the tale was told, it seems that the densely wooded hills where tigers, deer, antelope, jackals, and destructive herds of wild boars once found sustenance and shelter were stripped almost bare. British records of administrative concern for forest conservation in Ajmer date back to well over half a century before the period focused on by our interviewees. Nonetheless, along with Ghatiyalians, historians working from archival evidence locate in the 1950s a period of unprecedented increase in deforestation throughout the region of former Rajputana (Haynes 1998, 1999; Richards, Haynes, and Hagen 1985). If Ghatiyalians often imply that the process began in this era, it may be that such rapid acceleration in the post-Independence decades overshadowed recollections of earlier and more gradual depletion.[16] In Ghatiyali, people strongly associate in their minds the former ruling kings, old growths of indigenous trees, and wild animals. These three came to an end together, and as the tales are told it appears that this was both a sweet and bitter transformation (Gold with Gujar 1997).

The term usually used in the local Rajasthani dialect for the designated "cattle guard" whose job it is to protect the trees from grazing livestock and firewood cutters is the same today as in the past: syāṇā.[17] But the sanctions today's government-appointed syāṇā wields, and his status in the village, are very different from those attributed to past guards, who were agents of the king. For, while these strong-arm officials abused their powers and exploited the people, the authority behind them was absolute — royal — and their vested interests were ultimately in maintenance. They were perhaps more hated, but less despised, than today's cattle guard — who as a government worker is almost by customary definition out to fill his own pockets.

Dayal Gujar, a former herder, probably in his sixties and forced by ill health to stay at home, explicitly connects the altered landscape with the changed political regime. Others with whom we spoke believed, along with Dayal Gujar, that no one charged with law enforcement in the present era possessed or could exercise an authoritative power in any way comparable to that of the great kings. This does not mean that people lament their passing, but they are aware of its consequences for local government's effectiveness.

Bhoju: For how many years did you graze goats?
Dayal: For forty years.
Bhoju: Between this time and that what are the differences?
Dayal: Four ānās to a rupee [i.e., the present is diminished, equal only to a quarter of what used to be].[18]

Bhoju: What are all the differences?

Dayal: At that time, there were many boars, many wild cows, many deer, living in herds of hundreds, in such large groups. There were antelopes, and the boars and the lions even came right up to the village. Just as the *rājā mahārājā* are now finished, the jungle, too, is finished. . . .

Bhoju: So in the time of the rājā mahārājā, what did the herders do?

Dayal: They herded goats.

Bhoju: But didn't they cut the small branches to get leaves?

Dayal: Yes, they did. But they just cut the small branches from above.

Bhoju: If they cut from above, how were the trees killed from below?

Dayal: In those times only the herders cut; others didn't come and cut the lower branches.

But after this, the kings were finished, their time was finished; then people began to cut the trees because there was no responsible authority (*zim-medārī*).

Bhoju: But what about the Forestry Department, the guard (syāṇā)?

Dayal: No, . . . the Congress came and they are all government workers, so there is no responsible authority.

Violence against trees was perpetuated at several levels of the social order and in varied settings. It was commonly said in Ghatiyali that the royal family members themselves had destroyed the shade trees along the seven-kilometer Sawar-Ghatiyali road. Vansh Pradip Singh had caused trees to be planted — a meritorious act recommended for kings in ancient Sanskrit texts.[19] His heirs had cut and sold them in the night. I was told it was done in the night because there would have been public protest otherwise. This selling of shade trees people viewed as an exemplary act of amoral selfishness.

Bhoju discussed these linked events with an elderly and educated Brahman, Suva Lal Chasta, and his somewhat younger castefellow, Bhairu Lal Chasta.

Suva Lal: Those who were to protect the jungle ate it. And besides that the rājā mahārājā thought, "The jungle is ours." So after Independence, they thought, "It is our property." So they arranged to have it cut and sell it fast. . . . Along the Sawar-Ghatiyali road, there were so many trees, every ten minutes on both sides. When they knew that the government was taking things over, they thought, "We planted these trees and they are ours."

Bhairu Lal: They weren't sorry. They had planted and watered them and raised them, and their rule was over, so they cut them.

Dayal Gujar also describes the selling of shade trees, giving an account similar to the Brahman men's.

> Dayal: He [Vansh Pradip Singh] thought, "Between the gate of the Sawar
> castle and Ghatiyali there should be shade for my people," and he planted
> trees all along the road: *nīm, pīpal,* and *ber* [all religiously valued species].
>
> Bhoju: Where did all those trees go?
>
> Dayal: They were eaten by the hungry [i.e., Vansh Pradip Singh's successors].
> They cut them all and sold them and ate them.
>
> Bhoju: Was this a sin (*pāp*) for them?
>
> Dayal: Yes.
>
> Bhoju: So why did they cut them?
>
> Dayal: People think it is a sin, but still they do it. What else can they do?
>
> Bhoju: Does God (*bhagvān*) punish this sin?
>
> Dayal: God inflicts much punishment. He will inflict punishment on Vansh
> Pradip Singh's successors or whoever cuts trees.

The lapse into sin by the rulers is emblematic of similar moral decay in
society at large, just as the cutting and selling of roadside shade trees is of
the greater commons problem and subsequent deforestation.

Today's forestry agent is perceived not only as amoral but as ineffective. Haidar Ali, a Muslim shopkeeper, contrasts the current
Forestry Department's work with the enforcement carried out in the
kings' era.

> Haidar Ali: The kinds of trees that once were no longer remain. The govern-
> ment servants sold them all and ate them, and people think it is just a game
> of sin (*pāp-līlā*). . . .[20] In the time of the rājā mahārājā there were twenty
> forestry guards, but nowadays the government sends only one man.

Nathu Lal Gujar, a herdsman with an elementary education, is paid by
community members to graze their cows and buffaloes collectively. He
spoke frankly of the current guard as subject to corruption.

> Nathu: The government should have the kind of guard (syāṇā) who will live
> on his salary. But this guard is like this: if I give ten rupees he "eats" my
> bribes (*bhrṣṭā khānā*), and if someone else gives five he eats his bribes, and
> he ought not to be like that.[21]

Ram Narayan Mali, a prosperous farmer, reinforced this motif.

> Ram Narayan: The government worker (*sarkārī kāramchārī*), the guard
> (syāṇā) — he is a very wrong person. He takes bribes and lets people cut the
> trees. He takes bribes, and he himself lets people cut the trees. He is a thief
> from head to toe [*ṭheṭ hū ṭheṭ tak chor hai,* literally, "from one end to the
> other]."

However, not everyone blames the government. Rup Lal Khati, an
older man of the carpenter caste, reflective and intelligent, attributes the

major share of blame to the community. He described the situation for us in terms of a classic commons problem.

> Rup Lal: Before people needed firewood, and today they need firewood, but when they saw that the wood was being used up, everyone thought "I need some for myself," and they cut it even faster. They stored in *advance. . . .[22] And if at that time people had only taken what they needed, then the jungle wouldn't have been finished and everyone, including the cows, goats, and buffaloes — all could have lived at ease.

The destruction of trees being understood as sinful is embedded in other concurrent degenerations both ecological and moral.[23] Haidar Ali's portrayal of the forestry agent, and all those who negotiate with him, as engaged in a "sin game" (pāp līlā) effectively expresses this convergence of wanton and irrational environmental destruction and lack of moral sensibilities (Gold 1998).

THE ADVENT OF VILĀYATĪ

I spoke with a very elderly blind Harijan woman, Gendi Bangi, about the changed landscape and the new dominant tree. Gendi was one of the few persons from the lower strata of society who expressed nostalgia for the grandeur of kings as well as for the old tree species. Royal patronage had meant something to her. Her grandsons, however, were quite articulate on the advantages for their community of the present era, in terms of both increased amenities and reduced oppression.

> Gendi: There used to be many cows and buffaloes, and in 1940, at the time of the famine,[24] we used to get leaves from the forest and grass, and we could still feed the livestock. There were *dhokaṛā* trees on the hills, and now there is only vilāyatī bambūl.
> Ann: Is vilāyatī bambūl good or bad?
> Gendi: It's bad.
> Ann: Why?
> Gendi: Because of the thorns.
> Ann: But for the cooking hearth . . . ?
> Gendi: It's good for burning, but dhokaṛā was good for burning, too, and it didn't have thorns.

Gendi bluntly states one contrast — salient to women, who bear the brunt of firewood collection — between the new and the old dominant tree species. Many people could readily list as many as ten or more trees that were numerous and important in the past, but only one species appeared on everyone's lists, and often it was the single tree mentioned: dhokaṛā. Forestry books confirm that this tree — *Anogeissus pendula* — is indeed the dominant indigenous species in the Banas basin, where Ghatiyali is located.[25]

Here is Dayal Gujar again, giving a more evenhanded account of the good and bad qualities of vilāyatī.

Bhoju: Today the government has planted vilāyatī bambūl. Is this harmful?

Dayal: No, it's a very good thing because we have firewood, and if not for that no tree would remain at all. . . . It's good for burning, but it's bad for animals. If we get splinters, it's bad. And beneath it, in its shade, no grass or crops will grow. There is poison in its shade. It is very bad for the fields.

Bhoju: Where does it come from?

Dayal: It comes from a foreign land (*vilāyat*) and that's why its called foreign (vilāyatī).

Bhoju: Which foreign land?

Dayal: I don't know. First we heard there was such a tree, but we hadn't seen it. It was planted in Devli [a nearby market town and military base], and then little by little it came in this direction. First it was only around our fields; then the Forestry Department planted it everywhere. It didn't exist during the time of the rājā mahārājā; there were only those other trees such as dhokaṛā, *pīlavāṇ, sālar, mīṭhā khaḍū,* and so forth.[26]

In our conversation with the Brahmans, Suva Lal and Bhairu Lal Chasta, we discussed changes in the weather, which they linked (as do many others) to changes in the tree cover on the hills.

Bhoju: Why has rain become less frequent?

Suva Lal: The most important reason is that trees have become fewer. All the trees were cut, and all that's left is vilāyatī, and it is not helpful in bringing rain, in drawing moisture. Other trees, such as nīm, deśī bambūl, dhokaṛā, they pulled the monsoon, and that is why there was much rain.

Bhoju: Was it because wild animals were finished off, and people weren't afraid of animals anymore, that they cut the jungle?

Bhairu Lal: No, it was because of population growth that the jungle was finished. Because people have increased, and they needed more wood, and there didn't used to be any vilāyatī bambūl, so that's why the jungle was finished.

Here, in a twist of logic, Bhairu Lal suggests that if other firewood, such as foreign bambūl, had been readily available in the past, the several preferred species of trees might have been spared. Moreover, in addition to selfishness and irresponsible government, he includes demographic pressures among the causalities determining deforestation.

Lalu Regar, an untouchable leatherworker, has a conviction, similar to that of the Brahmans, that recent poor rainfall is attributable to the change in the landscape.

> Lalu: Before there was jungle and so many trees from which we had rain; the trees made a wind that pulled the rain. . . . But today there is no jungle at all.
> Bhoju: When people know this, why don't they pay attention?
> Lalu: No, today people pay no attention, and so there are no trees left, only vilāyatī bambūl, nothing else.

When prompted, however, by a question about its value as fuel wood, Lalu Regar acknowledged with alacrity the importance of vilāyatī at the present time.

> Lalu: Yes, its very good that we have vilāyatī bambūl so we can eat; if not for it, women would always have a basket on their hip searching for cow dung, so it's good that we have vilāyatī.

Suva Lal Chasta's formulation that "All the trees were cut" and "all that's left is vilāyatī" and Lalu Regar's statement that nowadays there are "no trees left, only vilāyatī" are of course exaggerations. But these phrasings suggest that in some ways vilāyatī is truly thought of in a different fashion from all other tree species. In its difference, it does not count. Even children who have no memories of the old forest share their elders' differential evaluations of vilāyatī versus all other trees.[27] Thus thirteen-year-old eighth-grader Satya Narayan distinguishes vilāyatī from other sources of wood when discussing the moral dilemmas entailed by tree cutting. Although prompted by his teacher, Bhoju, to declare that it is sinful to cut trees because they have souls, Satya Narayan also frankly affirms that people need to cut them, no matter what the moral consequences may be. However, he exempts cutting vilāyatī from sin.

> Bhoju: Do you get sin from cutting trees?
> Satya Narayan: Yes.
> Bhoju: Why?
> Satya Narayan: Because we shouldn't cut them.
> Bhoju: Are trees and plants living things or nonliving things? [Note that the Hindi terms jīv and nirjīv, "living" and "nonliving," could also be translated as "souls" and "nonsouls."]
> Satya Narayan: They are living things.
> Bhoju: So when you know that trees and plants are living things, and that it is a sin to cut them, why do you cut them anyway?
> Satya Narayan: To get wood to burn, that's why.
> Bhoju: Are there any trees that it is no sin to cut?
> Satya Narayan: Foreign bambūl; it is no sin to cut them, and it is no sin to kill a poisonous animal.

In terms of the local ecology, this truly is the one tree that it does the least harm to cut. But in thus isolating foreign bambūl, and in connecting it with poisonous snakes, Satya Narayan identifies vilāyatī with things that are dangerous to humans.[28]

One of my part-time employees in the village, Shambhu North, created for me three albums with descriptions of local trees, shrubbery, and crops — assembling them with photographs and leaf samples and writing out brief descriptions of each plant's qualities and uses. Shambhu was educated to the ninth or tenth class and was familiar with agricultural work. He wrote from his own knowledge, which I take as fairly ordinary knowledge for a literate villager in his thirties. Here is what Shambhu's book has to say about vilāyatī bambūl.

> This tree's thorns are very poisonous and dangerous. If one slips inside some human being and ripens there — that is, becomes infected — it [the wound] fills with pus and is very painful. Sometimes people have to go to the hospital. If you don't get the thorn out of your foot, it makes a knot in that foot and for your whole life it keeps hurting. . . . Vilāyatī bambūl's wood has no special usefulness. . . . Vilāyatī's trunk is 90 percent crooked, and its wood has no work; all its wood goes for the work of burning. Among trees, this tree can be said to have no special importance. Even so, nowadays the government is sprinkling this bambūl's seeds in all the jungles of the country and raising plants and planting them. The reason is that it is very thorny and even sheep and goats don't eat it.

Shambhu thus summarizes major popular complaints about bambūl — curiously denigrating "the work of burning," which is of course invaluable. His entry on deśī bambūl is by contrast a paean of praise for its usefulness and contains a long list of useful items made from its wood, ranging from agricultural implements to doors and windows. He concludes, "This tree's wood is very strong, and from eating its seed pods goats become robust and their milk increases. And it has beautiful, beautiful round flowers of a yellow color."

Shambhu's language and attitude nicely epitomize a foreign versus local contrast embodied in the two trees.

OTHER FOREIGN GOODS AND BADS

The crooked foreign trees with their dangerous thorns, in whose shade it is no comfort to crouch but on whose wood people are dependent, are but one element in a complexly configured vision of ecological change in postcolonial times. A number of other items extremely important to the current village economy and lifestyle are also linguistically denoted in various ways as alien imports. Although some of these are usually called English (*angrejī*) rather than foreign, no consistent pattern is discernible in such variant usages.[29] Some of the most common and familiar items labeled alien include chemical fertilizer (*angrejī khād*, "English dung"), Western medicine (*angrejī davāī*, "English medicine"), and liquor sold in government stores (*angrejī śarāb*, "English wine"), which is explicitly opposed to the bootleg home brew most often drunk in association with sacrifices and feasts in honor of goddesses. In the case of farm machines and synthetic fabrics, their alien origin is not explicitly labeled but is clearly marked by the use of such foreign names as *thresher, tractor,* and *polyester.*

Still other things of relatively recent introduction have standard Hindi names — notably *chakkī* for "electric flour mill" and *nal* for "water tap." These equally contrast with previous practices both linguistically and physically. Chakkī contrasts with *ghattī* — the grindstone used for daily flour production that remains in a dusty corner of every home and is still worshiped by bride and groom as part of their prenuptial rites. Use of the nal contrasts strongly with getting water from the *kuā*, "well." Not only does the water taste different (to which I can testify), but the process of filling pots and buckets by those two modes is very different indeed. The power mill and the water tap are clearly perceived not only as innovations but as dependent on outsiders' engineering skills. Ordinary persons are impotent when power failures disable these services, and they have no recourse but to wait or return to the more laborious manual alternative.

Both chakkī and nal are regularly cited as items that have changed the very fabric and rhythms of daily existence: externally, most particularly for women, in terms of reducing labor time and generally altering daily work schedules; and internally, for everyone, in that electrically ground flour and tap water are both thought of as vaguely detrimental to health and strength. Men complain more of these losses; it is women who complain loudly of the inconvenience when not infrequent power shortages disrupt mill and tap functions. There is little genuine resistance from either gender to any of these foreign goods and devices.

Some persons tend to exaggerate, to radicalize verbally today's transformations. Often I was told, rhetorically and hyperbolically, "nobody plows with oxen anymore." More realistic estimates suggested that in 1993 half the village farmland, made up of mostly small plots, was still worked by oxen pulling wooden plows that the carpenter caste still produced. But in people's minds, or at least in their public discourse, the future had arrived. Similarly, I interviewed one man who I had heard knew about herbal medicines. He said immediately, "Nobody uses them anymore. Everyone goes to the dispensary for English medicine." Later in the conversation it emerged that just a few days earlier he had successfully treated a granddaughter's skin problem with a plant remedy he prepared himself, after a drugstore cure had failed to help her.

I acknowledge that such verbal maneuvers are in part self-conscious responses to the inquiries of a foreigner and a schoolteacher before whom persons might wish to profess adherence to the trappings of modernity. Nonetheless, I shall not dismiss them as hypocrisy. It strikes me that such totalizing statements are ways of adjusting; people see their worlds changing so quickly that in their imaginations they seek to internalize rather than resist the changes. As with the herbal remedy, further inquiries usually elicit gradations of predominance for most elements of the brave new technologies. The interview texts that follow highlight several key factors in the perceived complex of change, but even more vividly they show their intermeshing.

With Bhairu Phuleriya Mali, Ugma Nathji (another assistant) and I discussed his gardening practices and crops in detail. As a "flower-growing gardener," Bhairu was part of a community that took special pride in its knowledge and practice of produce cultivation. He began by telling us that every garden is like a shrine to Lord Shiva, in which one should never wear shoes.

When I bluntly turned the conversation to the subject of fertilizer, Bhairu's response, listing pros and cons, seemed to rehearse a familiar dialogue with himself.

Ann: Do you use "white" fertilizer or deśī?

Bhairu: From deśī fertilizer we get more flavor, but from white fertilizer they [the vegetables] get large but they don't taste good. . . . So, if you want to earn a lot, then put on "white," and if you want a good taste then put on deśī fertilizer. It [deśī] weighs more, though. Or you can put on both together: first deśī and later white; then it comes out well. Without some deśī fertilizer, they [the vegetables] won't be good. Better to use both, and the profits will be better.

Bhairu thus expresses measured, rationalized attitudes toward the use of foreign fertilizer in produce gardens, even while criticizing its effect on flavor.

The conversation then turned to grain crops.

Bhairu: In the past there was no mustard and no *kalyāṇ sonī* [one of the new varieties of wheat]. There was *bājā gehūṇ* (indigenous wheat) and barley (*jau*).[30] Besides these grains, nothing.

Ugma Nathji: And there was no English fertilizer, only desī fertilizers? What were they?

Bhairu: Goat dung and cow dung, besides them nothing. . . . And to make "green fertilizer" (*hariyā khād*) we planted *gauvar* and *sān* [hemp], if you couldn't afford cow dung and goat dung.[31]

Ugma Nathji: Which crops needed more water?

Bhairu: Today's crops need more—today's, like mustard and red peppers. Like, kalyāṇ sonī drinks twice as much as bājā gehūṅ and jau; and *koṭā phārmī, sonā rekhī*—these new seeds need five to seven waterings, but previously it was only three. . . .[32] We used to harvest only twenty *maunds* from one *bīghā*, and now we harvest thirty to thirty-five, but fertilizer and all causes five maunds of expense [i.e., the value of five maunds of grain must be spent]. Even so, there is some profit. . . . And in our field we never got more than twenty-five maunds. But my son is farming, and he puts on superphosphate and then waters, and then he plants wheat together with DAP, and twenty-five days later he irrigates with urea. Then he gets forty-five maunds of wheat in the same field where we used to get twenty-five—but with this much more fertilizer. And he uses an *engine to water. . . . He gets forty to forty-five maunds of wheat and has two thousand rupees expense [for everything]; so maybe he will receive thirty-five maunds profit. [Bhairu here subtracts the expenses as if they were maunds of grain.][33]

Ugma Nathji: And what kinds of sorrow did the farmers have long ago?

Bhairu: It was very painful to water with the *charas*, and your feet would get cold standing in the water, and all day the oxen suffered, and so did we. But now, with an *engine: comfort!

Although he complained about the tastelessness of vegetables cultivated with chemical fertilizers, for grain produced largely for the anonymous market Bhairu perceived the main problem with chemical fertilizers to be their cost. His praise for power irrigation, like most people's, is unmitigated.

Ugma Mali, a man in his early forties and thus younger than most of our interviewees, speaks, however, of other deficiencies in chemically nourished grain. Bhoju Ram was discussing the power mill with him, but Ugma's thoughts moved spontaneously to fertilizers.

Bhoju: Today's women don't do this [grind by hand]?

Ugma: Today all work is done with *machines; the flour mill *machine exists, so who will grind by hand? But, from being ground in the electric mill the grain loses its strength, and so we also lose our strength. . . . Because of the flour mill, and because of foreign (*videsī*) fertilizer, people have become weak.

Bhoju: Why?

Ugma: Because today is the era (*jamānā*) of *machines; all things are done with art [*kalā*, a term that in the village often implies not so much beauty as craftiness, artifice]. . . . When people used to make a pilgrimage to the Ganges River, they would go on foot or they might walk four *koś* [eight kilometers] to visit their friends; and the sacred Ganges seemed as close as Four Arms Temple [the central temple in the village]. But now you need money in your pocket, and you need a bicycle just to go one kilometer. . . . Before there was no money and fewer people, so there was a lot of love. But today everyone has money, and the population has grown, so there is no love; if anyone has work to do, they do it with money.

Ugma's free associations are worth noting here. Without prompting, he moves rapidly from the flour grinder to chemical fertilizer to general human weakness exemplified by the abandonment of religiously valued foot pilgrimages. He concludes, with a final flourish, by opposing money and love in the context of crunching population growth. Such trains of thought are not unusual.

Our conversation with Lalu Regar, a leatherworker—conducted in Bhoju Ram's own courtyard—also displays a characteristically interconnected way of thinking about various attributes of modernity:

Bhoju: When you farmed, what crops did you mostly plant?
Lalu: Deśī (indigenous) wheat and barley.
Bhoju: What's the difference between those crops and the present?
Lalu: There used to be more production; today it is less. Because we used to put on goat dung fertilizer, but for the past five to fifteen years we've been putting white fertilizer.
Bhoju: And has white fertilizer changed the land?
Lalu: It has made it alkaline.
Bhoju: If you put on fertilizer this year and not the next, what will happen?
Lalu: There will be no production at all.
Bhoju: When we know that if we use white fertilizer the land will become alkaline, why do we use it?
Lalu: Because we are crazy, that's why. Little by little the land has become like this: even if you put on full goat dung fertilizer and don't put on urea, you'll get no production. It has become an addict; it needs urea.[34]
Bhoju: So the land has got a bad habit?
Lalu: The land has begun asking a huge amount. The land has begun to collect rent from us.
Bhoju: The village council used to meet at Four-Arms Temple. Why don't they meet anymore?
Lalu: People have stopped of their own accord. Today there are no love and affection left; today—twenty to twenty-five years ago the whole village was unified.
Bhoju: What is the reason?

Lalu: Father of a Daughter [a common and mild expletive]! Today we have grain grown with white fertilizer, flour ground by the power mill, and water from the tap. So how can there be unity and love?

This kind of fluid move from politics to fertilizer, from communal harmony to tap water, is not at all rare in the discourse on change. Bhoju continued to question Lalu.

Bhoju: What shall we do? Go back and stop using all these new things?
Lalu: Sure [spoken with sarcasm].
Bhoju: Shall we tell our wives to grind flour?
Lalu: Sure.
Bhoju: Mine would tell me to grind.
Raji Gujar [Bhoju's mother, who has been listening]: I used to grind five kilograms of grain in one morning, but today's women couldn't do that.

Thus, we see vividly how different elements of changed existence are mutually reenforcing. Because health is "down," many assert, today's women could not grind flour by hand even if they wished to do so, but universally they do not. And one of the reasons why health is down is that grain milled by the chakkī loses its strength-giving capacity.[35] Moreover, among the reasons why women's behaviors today are judged as increasingly immodest are both the inner heat caused by chemical fertilizer and the free time granted by the advent of the chakkī and nal—which has made it easier for many women, especially from poorer families, to become day laborers, exposed to the company of strange men.

Synthetic cloth is another epitomizing feature of the ambivalently construed modernity complex, and it is also associated not only with poor health but with a decline in women's good character. In the previous era, daughters-in-law practiced perfect modesty and wore cotton; today they wear more revealing polyester coverings.

In another interview, which focused on the neglect of agricultural rituals (Gold 1995), a farmer named Amba Lal Loda described an entire ritual, confessed that he had failed to perform it this year, mentioned that as far as he knew only one of his fellow Lodas had done it, and then was asked by Bhoju to explain this neglect.

Bhoju: Why do people do this less often today?
Amba: Today people have forgotten everything.
Bhoju: What is the reason?
Amba: The things that existed before don't exist today; people used to wear *rejā*, and now they wear polyester.

The ways in which gods are worshiped and the cloth one wears next to one's skin are mutually implicated facets of the same transformative processes. The conditions of everyday life and the constitution of physical and moral selves have been altered along with the landscape.

CONCLUDING THOUGHTS

During my last weeks in the village (June-July 1993), a "plantation scheme" administered by the much maligned cattle guard was under way. The scheme involved local elementary school teachers who established a tree nursery in the schoolyard, raised funds for a watering system, and cared for what I was told numbered twenty thousand vilāyatī bambūl seedlings. After the monsoon broke, these were planted in rows on village "wasteland" — well beyond homes and farmlands in the hills toward Sawar. I photographed this project shortly before leaving the village. Cheerful groups of women laborers were carefully setting each baby tree in the earth, while the guard strutted among them, admonishing them not to be slack. No one to my knowledge opposed this project. Several people told me as a point of curiosity that it was funded by Japanese monies designated for improving India's environment. Foreigners with motives villagers find hard to fathom thus finance the propagation of unloved foreign trees.[36]

Geographer Paul Robbins has studied ecological change in western Rajasthan. He is convinced that *Prosopis juliflora* (which he calls *angrezī*, following residents of the districts where he worked in the former kingdom of Marwar) is less advantageous for afforestation in those arid lands than indigenous *khejarī* (*Prosopis cineraria*). Although Ghatiyalians hold no special brief for khejarī, they do, as we have seen, praise those species (notable dhokarā and deśī bambūl) indigenous to their region. Many of the faults Robbins identifies in *juliflora* coincide with those I heard repeated often in Ghatiyali. He writes that khejarī has stronger timber, for example. And he notes that *juliflora* has no appreciable understory of grass and herb communities since its leaves contain germination inhibitors that limit the growth of other species. Recall Dayal Gujar's "There is poison in its shade." Robbins paid attention to government agents involved in reforesting with *juliflora* as well as to local voices. He confirms villagers' perceptions of vilāyatī's alien perniciousness, contrasting it with an indigenous, traditionally valued species that strikes him as being more useful. Thus, having listened to both sides of the story, he concludes in favor of indigenous species and local knowledge (1998).

Some recent approaches to India's environmental crises critique "development" in both practice and ideology and propose to draw on traditional knowledge systems from a remote precolonial past for alternative sustainable strategies.[37] Emerging countercritiques of tendencies to romanticize indigenous ecological harmony call for caution if not full skepticism when considering such endeavors.[38] As many point out, it is impossible to draw a clean line between foreign and indigenous — whether speaking of historical practices or living species — let alone to label the one wholly detrimental to environmental conservation and the other wholly beneficent.[39]

While theoretical debate is ongoing around these issues, one recent publication seems to move this discourse forward to a proposal for future action. Gadgil and Guha in their hybrid alternative development paradigm, which they self-consciously and awkwardly call "conservative-liberal-socialism," suggest among other things a "fruitful utilization of the traditional knowledge and wisdom possessed by ecosystem people" (1995, 125). By their definition, *ecosystem people* are "people who depend on the natural environments of their own locality to meet most of their material needs" — and compose more than half the population of India (3). The majority of Ghatiyali's residents could be thus described if we lay stress on "*most*... material needs." Gadgil and Guha's suggestion does not call for a naive return, either politically or technologically, to some golden rural past. Rather, it is part of a complicated series of pragmatic proposals that include implementations of information flow and checks to ensure social equity.

What kinds of knowledge might Ghatiyalians contribute to projects of ecological recovery and future sustainability in India, South Asia, and beyond? There would be many specific items, from medicinal lore to agricultural techniques, that I have not discussed in this essay. But I would like to suggest that taken together, as part of a whole, the historical narratives and commentaries on the present assembled in these pages hint at ecological understandings of value to environmentalist thought and activism.

Elsewhere (Gold 1998) I have called these understandings "moral ecology." The chronicles of deforestation transcribed here present a merged vision of human morality with nature's bounty or depletion, as do the concerns that imported conveniences cause imbalance and degenerative addictions. Some voices provide a straightforward description of damage done to nature and the social order when indigenous trees are wantonly destroyed for selfish reasons and are replaced with alien species. Others suggest that the health of humans, the earth, and crops are necessarily founded on the same bases and — if we follow Lalu Regar and Amba Lal Loda — character and social life are implicated in the same web. To imbibe water from a different source or to treat the earth or the body with imported medicines may be understood to alter not only work routines but politics, rituals, and temperament.

Ghatiyalians' complex understandings of ecological interconnectedness have not moved them to work collectively toward ecological recovery. There are many reasons for this. Rapid and radical changes in polity and environment, as described in this essay, have left many people simultaneously stunned and scrambling. Most villagers are working as hard as possible — harder than ever before, as many assert — to take advantage of new technologies, cash crops, and educational and professional opportunities. Of course, some farmers resolutely continue to work traditionally because, they say, the food tastes better. But there is thus far no organized resistance to agro-technology that depletes the soil but creates profits, to reforestation projects that propagate despised tree species but keep firewood available, or to the colorful bolts of imported synthetic cloth that stock the local merchants' shelves and may increase discomfort but fade less rapidly than cotton.[40]

As nearly ecosystem people, Ghatiyalians' relations with their environment are neither harmoniously sacrosanct nor totally disenchanted and instrumental.[41] Bhairu Mali worships Lord Shiva in his garden and calculates the relative profits of chemical versus deśī fertilizer on his vegetables. Schoolchildren testify that it is sinful but inevitable to cut trees. Vilāyatī's thorny branches appear to cast an ominous penumbra (but no soothing shade) over Rajasthan's depleted landscape. But Ghatiyalians' understandings of the ways in which human health and community, trees and morality, lives and landscapes are interwoven inform their active struggles to lead a good life. Some attempt to work within the constraints of such a moral ecology; others deliberately defy it, remaining aware of their actions' human and environmental costs. Their words, respectfully transmitted here, testify to enduring sensibilities and future possibilities.

ACKNOWLEDGMENTS

Fieldwork in Rajasthan was supported by a senior research Fulbright fellowship administered by the Council for International Exchange of Scholars in the United States and by the United States Educational Foundation in India. I am very grateful to these institutions and equally to the Institute for Economic Growth of Delhi University, where I was affiliated. There professors T. N. Madan and Bina Agarwal offered sage counsel and warm hospitality. Conversations with Ram Guha in Delhi and Hilo were crucial to the initial and final stages of this essay's production. I thank all other thoughtful and enthusiastic participants in the Environmental Discourses conference and particularly — for specific suggestions — Amita Baviskar, J. Peter Brosius, Paul Greenough, Ravi Rajan, and Anna Tsing. For contributions at various stages, I also thank Lila Devi Chauhan, Daniel Gold, Brian Greenberg, Shubhra Gururani, Ron Herring, Anirudh Krishna, Shambhu Nath, Ugma Nathji, Paul Robbins, and anonymous reviewers for Duke University Press. To none of the above named institutions or persons should any blame attach.

NOTES

1 Bhoju Ram Gujar and I have worked together since 1979, and it is difficult to disentangle our respective contributions to this research. Throughout the essay, I attempt to make my "authority" transparent to our fundamental collaboration (see Gujar and Gold 1992). Our coauthored work (Gold and Gujar 2002) treats more fully many materials included in this essay and incorporates additional fieldwork undertaken in 1997.

2 See Jodha 1985, 1990.

3 When using my own words, I employ *forest* to describe a a wooded area. When translating interviews, I use *forest* if the speaker said *van* and *jungle* if he or she said *jangal*. A certain amount of confusion arises from the different meanings of *jangal* and *jungle* as they have evolved over time in Indian languages and English. Appadurai notes "the radical rupture between our modern Western conception of jungle (as a dank, luxuriant, moist place) and the ancient Indian category, which referred to a dry and austere natural setting, which was nevertheless ideal for human subsistence practices" (1988a, 206; see also Zimmermann 1987). The English implications have, however, slipped back into Hindi, I believe. For example, the *Rajasthani Sabad Kos* (Lalas 1962–78; hereafter RSK) offers as definition number 1 for *jangal* "*van*" and "*araṇya*" which are both terms for forest. Definition number 3 is "*registān*" or "desert." For further elucidation of *jungle* and *jangal* in South Asia, see Dove 1992a.

4 For some recent, varied explorations of emotional and poetic ties between persons and the changing, contested landscapes they inhabit, see, for example, Brightman 1993; Cronon 1983; Roseman 1991; Sen 1992; and Tsing 1993.

5 For a methodological discussion of this fieldwork in relation to oral his-

tory, and of our evolving collaborative research, see Gold with Gujar 1997, where we focus on one striking instance of two persons relating a single event in divergent narratives. See also Gold and Gujar 2002.

6 Litfin's definition of *discourse,* in the context of environmental politics, as "sets of linguistic practices and rhetorical strategies embedded in a network of social relations" (1994, 3) is serviceable here.

7 See Fentress and Wickham 1992 on memory as not necessarily producing history but nonetheless crucial for understanding it and above all for the way history is implicated in identity. For carefully surveyed approaches to the relationship between memory and history, Hutton 1993 is helpful.

8 For two important studies of land reform in Rajasthan, see Singh 1964; and Rosin 1987. Herring 1983 provides a comparative study of the process in other regions of South Asia.

9 Thanks go to Amita Baviskar for pointing this out to me. Maheshwari and Singh (1965, 129) confirm the identification of vilāyatī bambūl as mesquite.

10 See Shiva 1991, 123–80, on conflicts over afforestation and the appropriation of so-called wastelands for social forestry. See also Brara 1992 for important, ethnographically informed insights into conflicting government and village perceptions of wasteland in Rajasthan. Bhandari's survey of plants in western Rajasthan dates *juliflora*'s introduction into Jodhpur District to 1914; he notes that "It is a hardy plant, grows fast and is likely to be very useful for afforesting arid land" ([1978] 1990, 137).

11 Memory eventually fades, we may presume. Corn and tomatoes — both brought to Rajasthan in some distant century from the Americas via Europe — are thought to be indigenous.

12 See, however, Rajendran (1995, 20), who — based on observations in South India — claims that *juliflora* is a gold mine, that its charcoal is highly valued, that it can restore saline soil, and it is even good for making furniture. The latter two claims, at least, Ghatiyalians vehemently deny! My thanks go to to Roger Jeffery for sending me this reference.

13 Botanically, vilāyatī is more closely related to the indigenous *khejarī* (*Prosopis cineraria*) than it is to local bambūl (*Acacia nilotica*). Some khejarī grows around Ghatiyali, but it was never predominant. People are aware of its great religious value for the Vishnoi community but grant it no special importance.

14 It is well beyond my scope here, but undoubtedly relevant, to contemplate the politics of deśī as it has evolved and changed in the past century in India, from Gandhi's *svadeshi* movement and the struggle against colonialism to the current resurgence of Hindu nationalism.

15 See S. Guha 1999b for nuanced historical research on Maharashtrian kings and their relationships with trees and landscape. See also R. Guha 2000; and Murali 1995 for resistance to government forest policies in other regions of India. Sahlins 1994; Schulte 1994; and Thompson 1975 offer European examples of contests over hunting and other forest rights.

16 Gold and Gujar 2002 explores this history in greater detail. See Sivaramakrishnan 1995a for a very helpful discussion of colonial forest policy and its self-interested appraisals of indigenous practices.

17 For a literary reference to this figure's potential to abuse peasants in the days of kings, see my translation of the oral epic of King Bharthari as performed in Ghatiyali (Gold 1992, 86–87).

18 In the old Indian currency, there were sixteen ānās in a rupee. Today, in spite of the decimal system, people still refer to one-quarter of a rupee as "four ānās" and use these fourths of a rupee as common figures of speech for estimated percentages.

19 Kane's *History of Dharmaśāstra* includes the following statements concerning the proper relationship between rulers and trees: "trees have life since they feel pain and pleasure and grow though cut" and "the king should award . . . [fines] against those who wrongfully cut a tree" (1974, vol. 2, pt. 2, 895). For strong associations between kingship and environmental well-being, see also Ludden 1984.

20 Haidar Ali used Hindu terminology in spite of his Muslim identity. Bhoju interpreted his idiosyncratic usage as meaning that "no one is responsible for anything; you can use money to pay for sin."

21 *Bhṛṣṭā* means "corruption, depravity, wantonness"; in the RSK, definition 2 of *bhṛṣṭācār* is "bribe." Bhoju orally translated this phrase as "eats shit" — as it is commonly understood. On village perceptions of government corruption, see Gupta 1995.

22 An asterisk preceding a translated word indicates that the English word was used originally.

23 See Wadley 1994 for similar perceptions from Uttar Pradesh, a different North Indian region with a different local history.

24 Gendi Bangi uses the *samvat* year 1996, which is c. C.E. 1940; Kachhawaha (1985) confirms that 1940 was indeed a famine year in Ajmer District.

25 See Shetty and Singh 1987, 22–23; and Sharma and Tiagi 1979, 155.

26 The RSK is not terribly helpful on these species. It defines pīlavaṇ not as a tree but as a "thick-stemmed vine which climbs on trees." Vaguely, it describes sālar as "a special kind of tree" used in Ayurvedic medicine. Shetty and Singh, however, identify this as *Boswellia serrata,* a species associated with the mixed deciduous forests dominated by dhokaṛā (1987, 22). For mīṭhā khaḍū, or "sweet khaḍū" (a variant spelling) as "a special kind of medium-sized tree."

27 See Gold and Gujar 1994 for a discussion of Ghatiyali children's attitudes toward, and knowledge about, the environment.

28 Snakes are beaten to death on sight in Ghatiyali.

29 The trees called vilāyatī in Ghatiyali, for example, are called angrejī in Jodhpur District (Robbins 1998).

30 I have been unable to locate this particular wheat variety in any source except Shambhu Nath's survey, which lists a *bajyā gehūn* (1993). It should not be confused with milet (*bājrā*). A number of persons spoke generally of deśī wheat, opposing it to native species on two counts: better flavor and less need for water.

31 I have identified these green manures as Hindi *gavar, Cyamopsis tetragonoloba* (Bhandari [1978] 1990, 104), and Hindi *san* or "hemp," *Crotolaria juncea,* whose uses (as described by Maheshwari and Singh) in-

clude "making ropes, mats, cordage and paper. The flowers and fruits are eaten as vegetable and the green stem and leaves make good manure" (1965, 49).

32 These are local language variants on other new wheat species promoted in Rajasthan; probably their names are interpretable as "Kota farming" and "golden furrow." Kota is an important city in the region.

33 Only a fairly prosperous farmer would follow this complex and expensive fertilizing and irrigation strategy.

34 Lalu uses a term for opium addict.

35 For lack of space, I have left out other interviews that contrast the strength obtained from the old grains, especially barley, with that derived from wheat bread; see, however, Gupta 1998; and Vasavi 1994.

36 Thanks to Anirudh Krishna, I was able to look at one of the documents produced by the Japanese group (SAPROF 1991). From it, we learn that with full good intentions by the project organizers villagers are assumed to "mismanage" so-called wasteland. The recommended strategy for field personnel is to engage villagers' self-interest but never to tap their knowledge — a familiar development mentality. See also Brara 1992.

37 For one of the earliest and most influential statements along these lines, see Shiva 1988 on "maldevelopment." Other sources are too numerous to cite; see, for example, Banuri and Marglin 1993; Gadgil and Guha 1992; and Kothari and Parajuli 1993.

38 See, for example, Agarwal 1991; Greenough 2001; and Greenberg, Sinha, and Gururani 1997.

39 Discussion of these complexities is well beyond my scope here. For an admirable deconstruction of the false category "indigenous," see Gupta 1998. For ecological aspects of colonialism, see Grove 1995. For measured historical contextualization of colonial policies, see Sivaramakrishnan 1995. For overviews of issues in South Asian environmental history, see Grove, Damodaran, and Sangwan 1998a; and Guha 2000, 211–22.

40 I had an ongoing humorous debate throughout 1993 with Bhoju's wife, Bali, on cotton versus synthetic fabric. She thought my wearing of cotton somewhat eccentric, foolish, and unfashionable, and it troubled and puzzled her that I defended it. When I brought her new baby two cotton shirts from America, she discovered in the hot season that the infant remained free of skin rashes only when wearing these, and she washed them constantly in order to avoid dressing her baby in locally purchased synthetic outfits. The irony of this did not escape her, as we both knew that cotton was supposed to be deśī.

41 See Baviskar 1995 for an eloquent discussion of similarly indeterminate relations between religious values and environmental practice among *adivasi* villagers in the contested Narmada Valley.

PART 2

Toward Livable Environments:

Compromises and Campaigns

States of Nature/States in Nature

Paul Greenough

PATHOGENS, PUGMARKS, AND

POLITICAL "EMERGENCY"

The 1970s South Asian Debate on Nature

Does humanity really need so much biological diversity?
— Mostafa K. Tolba and Osama A. El-Kholy

Nature is forever being made and remade in speech and text, not least when science and the state collaborate to alter the fate of highlighted species. In India and Bangladesh in the 1970s, ambitious projects to eradicate smallpox and preserve wild tigers were taken up by the government, stirring debate over efforts to — in effect — rewrite the inventory of nature. Distinct as the projects were, they exemplified the capacity of modern states to shift the boundary between the human and non-human — whether by rooting out an offending virus where it hides in the bodies of men, women, and children or by rejiggering the forest to foster wild tigers' impulses to hunt and mate. Both projects were highly visible and required public justification. Indian politicians and officials were particularly vocal, explaining themselves variously, sometimes in the language of science, sometimes in terms of regional traditions or diplomacy, and occasionally with reference to the rulers' personal enthusiasms. Ordinary villagers, however, saw Project Tiger and Smallpox Zero (as the projects were called) in a different light: the vaccinators who pushed their way into homes and biologists who sponsored man-eaters were clearly labeled abusers. Subalterns thus squared off with scientists and officials in spontaneous debates, while supporters chimed in by way of newspaper commentaries. Of course, criticizing the tiger and small-pox projects in India was also a way to attack the government, especially after 1975, when the prime minister brushed aside constitutional niceties and took a forced march approach to development. Some of the sparring from this period is reviewed below, and while the voices are hardly representative they capture a distinctive time of dialogue when state and society struggled discursively to define Indian nature. Among those whose words are examined are Indira Gandhi; various European, Bangladeshi, and Indian environmentalists, epidemiologists, and conservation biologists; central and local health officials; a tribal patriarch; writers of letters to the editor; and a handful of angry peasants and tribals.[1]

Paralleling this first dialogue over nature is a second one in which a Critic interrogates the Author—not for whimsy's sake but as a way of yoking together ideas—disease eradication and tiger conservation—that are disjunctive and would otherwise fly apart.[2]

CRITIC: Then why yoke them at all?

AUTHOR: I have to, they are co-contextual. In the first place, the projects that I'm describing overlapped in time. The one reached a climax in 1975; the other was launched in 1973. Both were regional theaters of larger, global campaigns, and in both outsiders weighed in with forceful arguments about South Asia's global responsibilities. For example, it was urged by European biologists that only in the forests of India and the mangrove swamps of Bangladesh were there wild tigers in sufficient numbers to make an effort to save them worthwhile. At nearly the same time, it was pointed out by World Health Organization (WHO) epidemiologists that the most fatal strain of smallpox, already eradicated everywhere else, still flourished in Bangladesh and India. The relevant global organizations—on the one hand, the World Wildlife Fund (WWF) and the International Union for the Conservation of Nature (IUCN) and on the other, WHO—regularly focused international media on these regional singularities. The Indian government knew exactly how to respond to such attention and threw itself into Smallpox Zero and Project Tiger; it then used its successes to boost national prestige and heal particularly urgent diplomatic rifts.[3] Remember that India had greatly annoyed the Americans in late 1971 by sending troops and tanks into East Bengal to support the Bangladeshi liberation struggle. Subsequently, in May 1974, India angered the Western powers and once again threatened Pakistan by detonating a secretly prepared nuclear bomb. In the following year, Indira Gandhi imposed an internal "Emergency" that suspended Indian democracy for two and a half years (1975–77), further isolating the country. Yet by embracing tiger conservation and bringing the smallpox campaign to a successful conclusion the Indian government raised the country's international standing while exhibiting its scientific and technical prowess. Even in Bangladesh, where there was far less public discussion, there was a tendency to use these projects for diplomatic gain. In short, I think we'll learn about the interconnectedness between projects of health and conservation as well as diplomacy and development during the 1970s if we take them all together.

CRITIC: Maybe. It sound ambitious. What else?

AUTHOR: Second, there was an astonishing symmetry in the matter of scale—tigers are large and visible, viruses are small and unseen—and in the projects' overt goals. Project Tiger was intended to *save* a species from extinction whereas Smallpox Zero was intended to *extinguish* a species. Both claimed to rest on science and both were externally driven efforts to alter evolution. The projects were mirror images of each other, and because of these numerous symmetries I think it's important to ask: what was the working concept of nature that authorized such opposite goals?

CRITIC: Well, maybe as you say, there were symmetries—even symmetries that took the form of contradictions. So what? Governments can't be expected to be more consistent than ordinary citizens even in their embrace of science. But I have another concern, which is that your smallpox viruses don't really seem to me to be a part of "nature"; I mean forests and tigers, okay, but as you say, no one can even see your viruses.

AUTHOR: They're not my viruses. And in any case you're making my points for me! The concept of nature in science is unitary: it holds that all living organisms, from viruses to mammals, are governed by the same DNA chemistry and the same evolutionary pressures. Modern states foster this understanding of nature, one in which pathogenic germs and wild tigers evoke parallel forms of official control. Visible or not, viruses were definitely on the same official platter with tigers. But should the South Asian public, which was largely innocent of this understanding, have had to learn this lesson from the agents of regional governments eager to please foreign critics and scientific organizations?

CRITIC: Now I'm not sure where you are going. You sound like a populist. Maybe the symmetry of science stuff is a little too neat?

AUTHOR: You be the judge.

SMALLPOX ZERO

In India, a large health bureaucracy, stretching from New Delhi to state capitals, district headquarters, and nearly 560,000 villages, was put in place more than fifty years ago to carry out health and disease control activities as directed by the Ministry of Health.[4] The first Smallpox Eradication Program (SEP) was established inside this structure in 1962 with the goal of immunizing 80 percent of the population. Eradicating smallpox meant halting the transmission of a virus that had uniquely adapted itself through centuries of evolution to human beings alone; there were no extrahuman or animal sources of infection.[5] But by 1964, after 80 percent coverage had in fact been achieved in some Indian states, it was recognized that transmission was still occurring among the remaining 20 percent — slum dwellers, migrant workers, poor fishermen, villagers in inaccessible regions — and was undoing the benefit of mass immunization. From 1964 to 1967, the goal was raised to 100 percent coverage, with particular attention being paid to the densely populated smallpox-endemic states of Bihar, Madhya Pradesh, Uttar Pradesh, and West Bengal. Another review in 1967 concluded that the incidence of smallpox was rising, not falling, and that only 10 percent of the actual cases were being reported. From 1968 to 1972, in the years when the WHO launched the global smallpox eradication program, the existing Indian SEP underwent an administrative shake-up; reporting was renovated, the production of freeze-dried vaccine was instituted, and the rapid detection of outbreaks and their containment by mobile vaccination teams was begun. Numerous outbreaks continued to occur, however; between 1970 and 1973, more than 130,000 new cases were reported. By any measure, northeastern India and Bangladesh were the world's largest reservoirs of smallpox. Because the most severe form of the disease (*Variola major*) had disappeared everywhere else, world attention turned to South Asia (Basu Jezek, and Ward 1979, 20–34; Fenner et al. 1988, 719–53).[6]

There were reasons why South Asia was a particularly difficult site for smallpox eradication. The population was huge and moved easily by road and rail over long distances and between rural and urban settings; itinerant groups and remote settlements fostered low-intensity ("smoldering") chains of infection; the infrastructure for producing and transporting vaccine was acknowledged to be defective; and the administrative culture in some state health services discouraged subordinates from reporting outbreaks to their superiors. In the face of these difficulties, senior Indian and Bangladeshi health officials, with WHO urging and support, instituted an intensified SEP program in 1974. First, they turned from mass vaccination to a more focused "containment" strategy that involved surrounding known outbreaks with rings of intense vaccination. Effective containment depended on "active surveillance," that is, on ferreting out smallpox outbreaks instead of waiting for them to be reported slowly through channels (including postcard notification).[7] Second, to assist with the changed vaccination strategy, WHO pressured India and Bangladesh to accept the services of epidemiologists from Europe, Japan, and the United States; a few dozen of these experts arrived and began to work closely with SEP officials right down to the level of outbreaks in individual villages.[8] Jeep- and motorcycle-equipped surveillance teams roamed near and far, searching for cases in markets, schools, pilgrimage sites, docks, tea shops, and slums. They made repeated village to village and then house to house searches on a scale and with an intensity that had been attempted before only in census operations. The public was offered cash rewards for revealing hidden cases, and schoolchildren were asked to report cases in their homes. Then, whenever outbreaks had been pinpointed, containment teams surrounded affected wards or villages and vaccinated everyone within, regardless of prior immunization status. Patients ill with smallpox were confined to their homes and all their contacts vaccinated. Supervision was increased, and guards were posted. The staff of the SEP was required to keep up-to-date records, including charts showing the sequence of transmission for every case and outbreak.

Despite these stringent measures, the SEP in India came close to collapse in the first six months of 1974. There was an explosion of cases in Bihar and Madhya Pradesh, and the largest number of new cases in years was reported in May. This epidemic spike coincided with the testing of India's first nuclear bomb, which led at once to waspish internal and foreign commentary: how could India have a nuclear capacity yet not be able to control smallpox? At the same time, the country was in the middle of a crippling rail strike, and there were widespread political disturbances in Bihar and Gujarat. Both the strike, which lasted for twenty-two days, and the political movement, which went on for months, were crushed by the government (Gupte 1992, 433–34; Jayakar 1992, 259–61; Gandhi 1984, 84–90, 113–14). In the middle of the same year, senior WHO advisers got into a serious disagreement with India's director general of health services and the Bihar health minister over eradication strategy; these officials had lost faith in the new surveillance/containment approach and advocated a return to mass vaccination (Fenner et al. 1988, 765–69). In desperation, WHO's regional directors appealed to the central minister for health and family planning, Dr. Karan Singh, who overruled his subordinates' objections. But there had been a deal: WHO arranged for an infusion of millions of dollars to appoint dozens more foreign epidemiologists to come to India to shore up the surveillance/containment operations. In Bangladesh, similar high-level calls for a return to mass vaccination were also rebuffed early in 1975 (835–37). After June of 1974, the number of foreign epidemiologists in India doubled to about one hundred; half were sent to the key state of Bihar on short-term assignments. In Bangladesh, where similar arrangements lagged by a few months, expatriate epidemiologists arrived in numbers early in 1975. The foreigners were equipped with jeeps, motorcycles, gasoline, and suitcases of cash with which to hire guards and vaccination personnel, print leaflets, pay rewards for the discovery of outbreaks, and make other on-the-spot arrangements. While the foreign epidemiologists were denominated "advisers," they in fact took control of smallpox eradication in rural districts (757, 773, 777; Joarder, Tarantola, and Tulloch, 1980, 206–8, 214–15).

Villagers often ran away or fought back. Wherever there was resistance to containment, SEP methods became coercive (Greenough 1995). In fact, the practice of containment was modified at least twice in ways that made coercion more likely. Initially, containment had only meant vaccinating the known contacts of active smallpox cases; the contacts' names were elicited from patients through interviews — a classic public health method — and health workers then followed up to determine whether the contacts had been vaccinated. If they had been, they were excused from further trouble. Expatriate epidemiologists, however, didn't speak local languages and were impatient at having to rely for translation on their Indian and Bangladeshi coworkers; they argued that interviews were time consuming, especially when patients were too ill to speak. At the foreigners' urging, containment was redefined early in 1974 to mean that wherever active smallpox was detected *everyone* in the village had to be vaccinated whatever their immune status; proof of prior immunization (e.g., by exhibiting a vaccination scar) was deemed irrelevant. The new containment goal was called "focally intense ring vaccination"; as a practical matter, vaccinating teams no longer spoke with villagers caught inside the ring. The reasons were explained by a foreign epidemiologist.

> The standard containment framework, limited as it [was] to known contacts, was therefore too narrow to be sure and took far too long to complete. . . . we wanted to restructure containment so that it would not be highly dependent upon a well-motivated and talented interviewer. . . . For these compelling reasons we abandoned the specific contact approach to containment and adopted in its stead the concept of focally intense ring vaccination. Translated into the context of Bangladesh, the ring becomes the village. Based on the observation that the Bengali village in its entirety functions as a loose extended family, and also on the assumption that most if not all of the actual contacts are in this readily defined population, the village became the outbreak containment unit. The village is smallpox's least common denominator in rural Bangladesh, and village containment is a logical extension of the one infected village equals one outbreak concept. The minimum containment target became the entire population of any village with even one case of smallpox. (Music 1976, 35).

Later, in 1974 and 1975, during the last phase of the eradication campaign, containment was again redefined: *everyone* living within 1.5 kilometers of a known outbreak had to be vaccinated, and this radius was gradually increased as the number of outbreaks decreased. The first redefinition had muted the villagers; the second effaced the village. Containment began to resemble veterinary medicine, for which a single infection causes a whole herd to be regarded as suspect.

Containment, however defined, frequently produced chaos in the affected villages.

> The initial stage in the evolution of a coherent containment policy was marked by an almost military style attack on infected villages. . . . In the hit-and-run excitement of such a campaign, women and children were often pulled out from under beds, from behind doors, from within latrines, etc. People were chased and, when caught, vaccinated. Many misunderstandings arose and tempers often flared in these heated situations. Attempts were made to secure the cooperation and "blessing" of village headmen, thereby putting social pressure on the villagers to stand their ground and accept vaccination. Still, however, some form of minor chaos was the rule, as headmen's authority did not extend into individual's homes. . . . Known infected villages were revisited — often repeatedly — to check for new cases and leftouts. Almost invariably a chase or forcible vaccination ensued in such circumstances. . . . We considered the villagers to have an understandable though irrational fear of vaccination. . . . We just couldn't let people get smallpox and die needlessly. We went from door to door and vaccinated. When they ran, we chased. When they locked their doors, we broke down their doors and vaccinated them. (Music 1976, 35–38)[9]

CRITIC: Earlier you said you were interested in voices of resistance, but I haven't heard any voices yet.

AUTHOR: You're right, I did say that; wait just a minute.

Containment teams generally had their way, and sustained resistance was infrequent. When resistance did occur, it ranged from flight to loud protest. The SEP teams, always fearful that new outbreaks would undo their hard work, met resistance with coercion. The expatriate WHO advisers often initiated it. Their rule was to vaccinate everyone, and they felt obliged to demonstrate to Indian and Bangladeshi subordinates as well as villagers that exceptions would not be tolerated. An account from rural Bangladesh in 1973 indicates how coercion arose from resistance. In this instance, one man refused

> to let anyone into his house or to come out to be vaccinated. When he left his house he locked the women and children inside with a padlock. When he came home he barred it from within. The [sanitary inspector, a local-level health

worker] had tried three times to convince the family to take vaccination. I waited for the man to come home and when he did I told him that he had to take vaccination and to let his wife and children be vaccinated. He refused, went inside and barred the door. I broke the door down and vaccinated — with a struggle — every member of his family, including the man. He was very angry and told me he was going to initiate a case against me. Approximately three months later I was told by the local magistrate that a case had been registered against me but that it had been thrown out of court. (Music 1976, 46–47)

Another source describes an unusually violent encounter in 1975 in an Adibasi (aboriginal) village in eastern Jharkhand (India). The narrator was a WHO physician-epidemiologist who spoke fluent Hindi.

In the middle of the night an intruder burst through the door of the simple adobe hut. He was a government vaccinator, under orders to break resistance against smallpox vaccination. Lakshmi Singh awoke screaming and scrambled to hide herself. Her husband leaped out of bed, grabbed an ax, and chased the intruder into the courtyard. Outside, a squad of doctors and policemen quickly overpowered Mohan Singh. The instant he was pinned to the ground, a second vaccinator jabbed smallpox vaccine into his arm. Mohan Singh, a wiry 40 year-old leader of the Ho tribe, squirmed away from the needle, causing the vaccination site to bleed. The government team held him until they had injected enough vaccine; then they seized his wife. Pausing only to suck out some vaccine, Mohan Singh pulled a bamboo pole from the roof and attacked the strangers holding his wife. While two policemen rebuffed him, the rest of the team overpowered the whole family and vaccinated each in turn. Lakshmi Singh bit deep into one doctor's hand, but to no avail. (Brilliant and Brilliant 1978:1)

After seeing his family vaccinated, Mohan Singh addressed the containment team and his fellow villagers, who had been assembled, in the following terms.

"My dharma [moral duty] is to surrender to God's will. Only God can decide who gets sickness and who does not. It is my duty to resist your needles. We must resist your needles. We would die resisting if that is necessary. My family and I have not yielded. We have done our duty. We can be proud of having been firm in our faith. It is not a sin to be overpowered by so many strangers in the middle of the night. Daily you have come to me and told me it is your dharma to prevent this disease with your needles. We have sent you away. Tonight you have broken my door and used force. You say you act in accordance with your duty. I have acted according to mine. It is over. God will decide." (Brilliant and Brilliant 1978:1)

The American physician who was the source of this account admits to being troubled by the attack on Mohan Singh's house.[10] At the time, it seemed justified: a smallpox outbreak was occurring in the nearby city of Jamshedpur, hundreds of cases were being exported to elsewhere in India, and one case had been traced to the Ho village. In recognition of Mohan Singh's status as chief, and of the obvious advantage of enlisting his authority, he had been given a few days by the SEP team to change his mind. But Mohan Singh's view of disease as a test of faith never wavered, and he and his village were eventually vaccinated in a military-style operation. This display of force — massed policemen and jeeps at midnight — gives the account a peculiar vividness, but there was no difference in principle between this episode and the Bangladeshi case described earlier: local norms had no standing.[11]

CRITIC: What are we supposed to make of these stories? Are you suggesting that if the vaccinators had been kinder and gentler they wouldn't have been guilty of allowing the virus to escape? As you say, the whole world was watching.

AUTHOR: The big picture of eradication is unclouded; smallpox was a historic killer, and now it's gone. What these examples show, though, is how implacable epidemiologists became when articulate opponents resisted their incomprehensibly "veterinary" procedures. Resistance threatened the authority of the state and agencies like WHO, while the patently archaic arguments made by resisters in defense of patriarchy, fate, dharma, and so on only steeled the SEP team's resolve and made real dialogue unnecessary. Occasionally — very occasionally — resistance was so fierce that the epidemiologists themselves were violently attacked (Greenough 1995).

PROJECT TIGER

India is the custodian of more than 60 percent of the world's wild tigers; the total would be lower but for Project Tiger, a chain of 25 reserves — up from 9 in 1973 — that encompass 33,000 square kilometers of closed forest, savanna, and mangrove swamp. The Project Tiger reserves are directly administered by the states under the central direction of the government of India and are major components in a system of 75 national parks and 425 wildlife sanctuaries — many of which are now part of larger "biodiversity reserves" — that cover 140,000 square kilometers or about 4 percent of India's surface area (Nath 1993, 1–3; Project Tiger 1993).[12] Project Tiger reserves have been sited inside or adjacent to protected forests in diverse biogeographic zones to ensure that genetic variation will occur and thus enhance the tigers' chances for survival.[13] Most

Indian states have been allocated at least one Project Tiger reserve, and tiger conservation has been effectively nationalized.[14]

The goal of Project Tiger was to bring the South Asian sub-species (Panthera tigris) back from the edge of extinction.[15] At its Tenth General Assembly meeting, held in New Delhi in December 1969, the IUCN determined that, while other tiger subspecies have dwindled in numbers to near hopeless levels, the estimated fifteen hundred to two thousand members of the Indian subspecies were a viable breeding population. A special obligation was placed on India, Bangladesh, Nepal, and Bhutan — but especially on India, which had the administrative experience and scientific resources — to embrace tiger conservation. Indian biologists generally favored Project Tiger as part of a wider conservation effort, and the Indian government obligingly banned tiger hunting and the sale of tiger skins in 1970. Shortly afterward the government passed a comprehensive Wildlife Protection Act. Following a special plea made directly to Prime Minister Indira Gandhi in 1972 by an IUCN representative, Guy Mountfort, the Indian government set up a task force within the Indian Board for Wild Life, chaired by Dr. Karan Singh, minister for health and family planning, to develop an outline plan. It was this plan, with the ringingly military title Project Tiger, that established the policy frame that shaped Indian tiger conservation for nearly thirty years (Indian Board for Wild Life 1972).

CRITIC: I have to ask: was this the same Karan Singh you mentioned before, the man who supported the SEP surveillance and containment strategy in 1974, when some Indian officials wanted to return to mass vaccination?

AUTHOR: Yes, it was the same Karan Singh. He was the last royal ruler of Jammu and Kashmir and had made a smooth transition to electoral politics. Both Jawaharlal Nehru and Indira Gandhi entrusted him with high-profile scientific and environmental tasks, especially those requiring negotiations with Europeans. In addition to serving as union minister for health and family planning, Singh held the portfolio for tourism and civil aviation.

The Project Tiger task force began in 1972 by taking a nationwide "tiger census," which found a total population of 1,827 animals (the figure was conservatively rounded down to 1,800). The task force instituted a conservation program called the "ecosystem approach," which was urged on it by the "Cat Survival Group" within IUCN (Indian Board for Wild Life 1972, 14). The premise of the ecosystem approach was the need to provide an extensive range for adult tigers: each required a minimum of ten square kilometers of undisturbed hunting territory. A further premise was that the minimum tiger population required for sustained reproduction was 300. This suggested the need for reserves of at least three thousand square kilometers, each with a "core" where tigers could hunt and breed undisturbed. Karan Singh's task force, however, showed political realism in opting instead for reserves that averaged less than fifteen hundred square kilometers.[16] Singh noted that "vast areas could not be sequestered in a developing country like India with an ever increasing population now of over 570 millions." The tiger reserves were in most cases embedded in state forests that already restricted many kinds of human use and were under the control of the Ministry of Forests. While foreign experts predicted that Indian tigers could not sustain their numbers in India's less than optimally sized reserves, they had little actual evidence that this was the case. The task force predicted that sooner or later Indian tigers would roam outside the reserves (Indian Board for Wild Life 1972, 1, 12–21, 31–32).

In the task force's 1972 plan, each tiger reserve was given an interior core, entirely for tigers and off limits to humans, and a surrounding forest "buffer zone," where villagers would be allowed limited access for cultivation and the collection of minor forest products. In accordance with the ecosystem approach, the cores were to be carefully bounded and all existing roads blocked off; stock grazing and commercial timbering were to be suspended; depleted prey species (mostly deer) would have their habitats restored; fire protection would be provided during the dry season; and silted watercourses would be restored. In short, the existing forest landscape was to be reengineered. An additional step envisioned by the 1972 plan was the forced removal of more than sixty thousand tribals whose villages lay within the forest cores; hundreds were removed for each tiger being protected, and tribals were allowed to remain in only a few of the buffer areas.[17] With the African model of big game tourism in mind, rangers were to be given jeeps and two-way radios to secure the boundaries of the cores, and forest guards enforced this separation with techniques aptly called "fines and fences."

Substantial funding for Project Tiger was provided by the WWF, IUCN, and other bilateral donors, and with one exception every aspect of the planned tiger conservation system was implemented. Eight reserves were established in 1973, and a ninth was added in 1975 (sixteen more have subsequently been declared). The exception was a network of forest "corridors" through which the excess tiger population in one reserve was supposed to "spill over" into another (Indian Board for Wild Life 1972). Between 1973 and 1993, India's population grew by nearly 300 million, and 100 million cattle were added to existing herds (India 1993a, 15). As early as 1976, a review found that the buffer zones were being steadily degraded by grazing animals and encroachments, while large development projects (such as road building and mining) were taking a toll. Nonetheless, scientific studies and anecdotal evidence strongly suggested that tigers had begun to increase in numbers (International Union for the Conservation of Nature 1976).

Project Tiger accelerated after June 1975 when Prime Minister Gandhi arrested her real and imagined enemies, suspended civil liberties, amended the Constitution to her liking, and imposed tight controls on the press and other media.[18] A marked characteristic of the Emergency period was the prime minister's effort to centralize major development projects in her office. One result, as commentators have noted, was that official data in this period lost all objectivity: only good news and favorable statistics were acceptable (Center for the Study of Developing Societies 1995). However, Project Tiger reports had always been presented favorably, perhaps because Mrs. Gandhi's personal interest in conservation was well known. In any case, in 1975, even before the declaration of the Emergency, the forest minister of Uttar Pradesh (UP), the most populous Indian state, announced with fanfare that protected tigers in UP had increased by almost 100 percent since 1970 (when hunting had been banned) — from four hundred to nearly eight hundred animals (*Times of India*, 14 January 1975). Within two weeks, a Kerala research team called in reporters to announce that the number of tigers in their reserve had increased from thirty-five to sixty — a rise of 70 percent — in only two years. The Kerala surveyors had conducted a census in the Periyar-Thekkady tiger sanctuary "by identifying the pugmarks [prints of splayed paws] and the width of strides of tigers that haunt water holds. The survey team, searching through the forests, [had] covered 50 km a day with the aid of 20 guides from the hill tribes" (*Times of India*, 28 January 1975). These increasingly fanciful claims flushed out the national director of Project Tiger, K. S. Sankhala, who called his own press conference in New Delhi to denounce them as "grossly exaggerated." Sankhala explained that "the breeding habits of the tiger are such that their population can increase at the most by eight percent a year" (*Times of India*, 3 February 1973).

Numbers have always been important to Project Tiger. A common argument for tiger conservation was the stark contrast between the eighteen hundred animals detected by the tiger census of 1972 and an estimate of forty thousand wild tigers in India in 1900 (Indian Board for Wild Life 1972, 8–11). While the forty thousand figure (proposed in 1966 by E. P. Gee) had been based on arbitrary assumptions and was dismissed as fantastically high by specialists, it was cited by the task force when Project Tiger was established and is still widely repeated.[19] In contrast to Gee's armchair approach, the "scientific census" of 1972 had tried to determine a baseline population through empirical methods. Unlike the respondents to a human census, however, tigers do not wait to be surveyed, and indirect methods have to be used, particularly the recording of fresh pugmarks. Pugmark counting is not a science, to say the least, and is susceptible to observers' biases; in addition, tigers are highly mobile and can move rapidly among survey sites so that the same animal can be counted more than once. A 1976 IUCN review of the project observed the following.

> Statements on increases in tiger populations, in particular, are fraught with hazards. In the first place, the pug mark census method, whilst almost certainly the best currently available for this situation, can only be regarded as an approximation of the true figure and, in any case, few tiger reserves have taken regular pug mark counts since 1972. . . . Under these circumstances [of tiger mobility], only a nationwide enumeration of tigers can give a reasonable indication of the true situation, and here again, caution will be necessary. The data from the 1972 tiger counts were subjected to particularly stringent analysis and several Project and territorial forest officers with whom we discussed the subject consider the total figure [eighteen hundred] to have been an underestimate of the true number. (International Union for the Conservation of Nature 1976, 23)

In other words, both "baselines" on which Project Tiger rested were inaccurate — forty thousand for 1900 was improbably high, and eighteen hundred for 1972 was improbably low — and the only practical method for estimating tiger numbers was admitted to be faulty.

In June of 1978, the *Times of India,* tipped off by an article in the English press, ran an editorial that caused a storm. (By this time, Mrs. Gandhi and her Congress Party had been expelled from office, although they would return in 1980 and Indira Gandhi would serve as prime minister until her death in 1984.) While the article aimed to provide accurate information about the current state of Project Tiger, it also turned a knife in the still raw wound of the Emergency. Entitled "Tiger Tales," it read as follows.

> One of the strangest emergency "excesses" — details of which are only now coming to light — concerns the over-enthusiastic PR campaign for Project Tiger. Launched with great fanfare in 1973 with an initial budget of Rs. 4 crores [40 million rupees] (including one million dollars from the World Wildlife Fund) to save the big cat from extinction, the project really came into the limelight during the emergency when extravagant claims were made

on its behalf. Last January, for instance, the project director, Mr. K. S. Sankhala, asserted that the number of tigers in the country had risen from 1,800 in 1972 to 2,500, thanks to improved conditions in the nine reserves which come under the project. But this rosy view was challenged by three top "cat specialists" who were sent to India by the Swiss-based wwf: according to them, no tiger population has ever increased by more than 2 percent a year, whereas Mr. Sankhala's statistics projected an increase three times greater. Not surprisingly the adverse report which the specialists submitted to the Agriculture Ministry (which sponsored Project Tiger) was never made public. This is by no means all. The present acting director, who took over when Mr. Sankhala retired prematurely last November, has also complained about the wasteful expenditure on fancy equipment — including electronic calculators! — by the project authorities. These revelations are disturbing because the tiger may be in much greater danger today than is commonly believed. Now that Project Tiger is about to enter its second phase, it is surely time that the government made a sober assessment of what exactly it has achieved. Since some wildlife experts here are still defending the project, the controversy should be settled immediately. The first need is to take a more thorough census of tigers in the nine reserves. (*Times of India*, 11 June 1978)

"Tiger Tales" put the fat in the fire; Project Tiger authorities were for the first time asked to justify themselves without a patron in the prime minister's office. Was there a "suppressed" wwf study? Had Sankhala been guilty of overestimating the number of tigers? Were tigers under graver threat in 1978 than in 1972? Political revenge was lurking in the background (the *Times of India* was one of dozens of newspapers shut down during the Emergency), but at the heart of the editorial was a simple question: were Indian tigers increasing or decreasing in number? Two weeks later the *Times of India* returned to the fray.

The controversy over Project Tiger refuses to die down. The Madhya Pradesh authorities have just produced figures to show that there were only 45 tigers in Kanha National Park last year — apparently 13 less than in the previous year. Since there is no reason to believe that conservation measures in the sanctuary were any worse in 1977 than they were in 1976, this seems to confirm the allegation that over-zealous Project Tiger officials made exaggerated claims regarding the rise in the numbers of the big cats during the Emergency. In other words there were far fewer than 58 tigers in Kanha in 1976.... It is certainly time that these controversies were finally resolved and the poor tigers left to breed in peace. (*Times of India*, 29 June 1978)

Eventually wwf scientists were drawn into the controversy, doing what they could from Europe to support Project Tiger managers and draw attention away from indefensible announcements about tiger numbers.[20]

It appears that tigers cannot be accurately counted and that uncertainty is as endemic to their study as to the study of many other wildlife populations. In the meantime, pugmark counting continues. While some Project Tiger field directors claim that pugmarks are as distinctive as fingerprints, Arjan Singh, a noted tiger specialist, says that "It's all nonsense, I've been tracking tigers almost every day now for 40 years and even I am unable to differentiate from pugmarks alone between tigers of the same size and sex, unless there's some abnormality — and even that doesn't always show up" (quoted in Ward 1987, 56–57). Arin Ghosh, a past director of Project Tiger, notes that "the tiger census figures have come in for criticism from all quarters. There has been no improvement in the methodology which is practically still the same. We still depend on pug-mark analysis, which brings in lot of individualistic considerations in the finally arrived at figures" (Project Tiger 1993, 15–16). In the end, the debate over numbers cannot be resolved; while rising trends were discernible through the 1970s and 1980s, firm baselines and accurate numbers were beyond anyone's grasp.[21]

CRITIC: Are you emphasizing this numbers and counting business for some reason?

AUTHOR: Yes. I find it instructive to compare the degree of surveillance demanded by the smallpox eradication campaign — at one point in the mid-1970s there were repeated house to house searches over nearly half of India and every case was tracked — with the sketchy methods sufficient to keep Project Tiger afloat. Smallpox Zero nearly collapsed when the numbers turned against the eradicators in 1974, whereas Project Tiger steamed forward despite the critical 1977 WWF evaluation without any good numbers at all. Nature in the grip of politics had sometimes to be precisely counted, while at other times precision could be elided.

CRITIC: Maybe numbers aren't as central to these large state enterprises as you assume?

AUTHOR: No, no — they live and die by them. There's a regional history of setting targets and then inventing numbers to more than meet them. It derives from subordinates' need under colonialism to discourage too much scrutiny. Watchdog agencies and investigative journalism in the region are weak, and that, too, encourages unrealistic official pronouncements. But my main point is that, even though the *Times of India* blew the whistle about absurdly false tiger numbers, the prime minister's office persevered with the project.[22]

And in fact the results for Project Tiger did improve within a few years. At the 1979 symposium in New Delhi, the weight of opinion among naturalists was that tiger numbers really were rising; tiger reserves had meanwhile increased from nine to eleven, and government funding was promised for another five years. Foreign delegates at the 1979 symposium congratulated Indian personnel for their achievements, especially the "excellent manner in which [field staff members] were able to achieve the difficult task of shifting villages from within the tiger reserve to the outside." One speaker from Rajasthan observed that he "had not detected any unhappiness among the villagers for being shifted from the area occupied by their forefathers [i.e., the Ranthambhore tiger reserve]. . . . Project Tiger had clearly demonstrated that to achieve success one had to go to the people" (India 1979b: 11–12). But this was too rosy. Other speakers drew attention to signs of hostility to tiger conservation by villagers residing in the buffer zones and beyond; a particular concern was that tiger predation on domestic cattle and the villagers themselves (i.e., man-killing) was generating "management problems." Arjan Singh, the tiger specialist, predicted that "the tiger reserves were reaching or would soon reach points of saturation . . . and this would induce the tigers to move into the peripheral areas where they were likely to create many problems when they came into conflict with man and his interests" (India 1979a, 9). While Singh advocated "translocation," that is, sedating man-killers in the buffer zones in order to return them to the core areas, others favored shooting man-killers at once to avoid public anger.[23] Apart from villagers' hostility there were other threats to Project Tiger: military and engineering activities near the reserves were disrupting tiger mating, herbicides and pesticides (e.g., Follidol) were drifting into the reserves from cultivated fields and reducing the numbers of wild prey species, Project Tiger staff and Forest Department staff were constantly feuding, and the protected forests surrounding the reserves were being rapidly logged (21–25; see also India 1979b). Discussions of how best to ensure the well-being of tigers in a context of rapid development and intense economic activity, and of the need to neutralize opposition among villagers and local officials, were jarring developments in a symposium principally oriented toward reporting scientific research on ecology and game management.

In truth, rural India didn't favor Project Tiger. Only a few weeks after it was inaugurated in April 1973 a perceptive letter had appeared in the *Times of India.*

> I am just back from a grueling three day visit to Kolkaz in the Melghat [Maharashtra] which has recently been named as one of the areas in which Project Tiger is to be initiated. Though a considerable amount of traveling

was done along the forest roads both by day and night, we saw no trace of the tiger and/or panther and several of the local inhabitants plainly stated that the project would not have their support for they could not afford to feed tigers which lived on their cattle. There are over a hundred villages in the area and as soon as a kill is detected, the carcass was poisoned and the tiger, which seldom survived, was buried entirely leaving no trace of its disappearance. During the visit we heard three shots at night. Those were no doubt directed at deer or lesser game; their removal will force the tiger to kill more domestic animals and lead to more tigers being poisoned. This is a big problem which cannot be solved by the tabling of pious resolutions and the budgeting of large amounts. It will not be possible to save the tiger alone. The forests and all their other inhabitants will have to be considered and this will only be possible with the collaboration of the public who are most intimately in touch with the problem, i.e. the genuine *shikaris* [hunters] and naturalists. [Signed] Humayun Abdul Ali, Bombay. (8 May 1973)

The writer was prophetic in his anticipation of opposition to Project Tiger, and he pinpointed the reason: "saving the tiger alone" transgressed cultivators' judgment that tigers are vermin. A huge educational effort would be required to reverse this judgment, which was based in rural Indians' long familiarity with tigers and their belief that tigers roaming through paddy and cane fields is unacceptable. Each year between 1975 and 1985 fifty human lives along with those of hundreds of cattle, buffaloes, and goats were taken by tigers (Jackson 1985, 11). Rancorous demands for compensation came from the human victims' families and the owners of slaughtered herd animals, and settling these claims took up more and more of park directors' time. Rural animosity varied from reserve to reserve according to the extent of tiger attacks (which depended in turn on tiger density in the cores, the size of the buffers, the proximity of settlements, etc.), but what leaps out is villagers' strongly felt sense of injustice: they realized that there was greater official concern for tigers than for humans. Further, the swiftness with which forest guards demanded bribes before granting illegal access to the buffers for gathering firewood and other minor forest products contrasted badly with long delays in receiving official compensation for losses.[24]

Geoffrey Ward, a journalist who documented these issues for years, found hostility right on the surface.

I stopped beside a field [near the Dudhwa tiger preserve, Uttar Pradesh] where an old man was plowing behind a haggard bullock. His name was Kanthulal and he had lived there all his life. Things had been much better before the park was established, he said; he had been able to collect his firewood without fear of arrest, could buy timber and thatch to shore up his house in the monsoon. Hunters had kept the tigers down. Now he lived in fear. The wife of a boyhood friend had been killed cutting cane; he himself had twice seen tigers padding along the road and often saw their fresh pugmarks on his way to the fields in the early morning. Two young cyclists stopped and walked their bicycles across the ruts to join us. They agreed. "Government cares only about tigers," one said. "They do not care about us." "We might as well be dogs," the third man added. "In my village no one stirs from his hut once the sun has gone down." . . . No one who lived around the park seemed to have a good word to say about it. Nor did most of the villagers who clustered in and around the other reserves I visited seem anything but resentful of the parks' existence, and their smoldering hostility sometimes flares into open warfare. (1987, 62).

By the end of the 1970s and throughout the 1980s, tiger conservationists were on the defensive; international acclaim for Project Tiger was overtaken by unflagging domestic criticism. Defending the reserves was becoming hard work, and project managers found themselves struggling with village leaders, local politicians, and journalists. The central government had invented Project Tiger without preparing public opinion; now the government found itself vulnerable. Opposition politicians began to press hard in the late 1970s on a specific popular concern: tiger attacks on humans outside the reserves. A 1978 *Times of India* article, "Keeping Track of Man-Eaters," deplored the politicization of episodes of man-killing near the Dudhwa tiger reserve in the state of Uttar Pradesh.

The [Forest] department's efforts in combating the menace is being thwarted by publicity-seeking politicians pandering to mass phobia. Attempts have been made to inflame public hostility and even link the sugarcane crisis to the depredations of the animals. The district authorities have been flooded with complaints from farmers that the man-eaters are operating in their territory. They have also persuaded some families to turn down the Rs. 1000 compensation and offers of jobs to kin of the deceased on the plea that it is inadequate. The Forest department has appealed to the government to enhance this aid to Rs. 5000. . . . The authorities are also alarmed at reports that a large number of people is missing, and the man-eaters have been blamed for the unfortunate incidents. It is feared that unscrupulous elements are taking advantage of the situation to settle old scores and personal enmities. (11 June 1978)

By framing this report around "panderers" and "unscrupulous elements," the journalist discounted villagers' losses. Other accounts from the period make it clear that enraged villagers were prepared to strike back.

Eighteen tigers and 30 or more leopards are believed to have been killed in and around [Sariska Park, Rajasthan] in the six years before Fateh [Fateh Singh Rathore, field director] took up this new post in 1988. He has rounded up some of the alleged offenders. A local tribesmen confessed to having done the actual shooting with an ancient muzzle-loader, but he was reportedly aided and abetted by nearby villagers eager to ensure the safety of their sheep and goats and cattle, by poorly paid forest department personnel just as eager for a share of the profits, and by a big-time smuggler in Delhi who paid the poor hunter just a thousand rupees (then worth $75) for each tiger skin. (Ward 1992, 16)

Villagers living near tiger reserves rarely hesitated to poison or shoot them for cash, or out of revenge or from spite, whenever the opportunity arose (Jackson 1985).

In 1989, twenty-six years after Project Tiger began, another "census" was taken. The tiger population in the whole country was determined to be 4,344 — an increase of more than 2,500 since 1972; within the reserves proper, the number of resident tigers was believed to have risen from 273 to 1,327. On the basis of these figures, Project Tiger was deemed to be a success (Project Tiger 1993).[25] Nonetheless, difficulties of several sorts confronted project managers. Tourism, the great hope for the extra revenues needed to sustain the tiger operations, had barely materialized and was always unevenly distributed — only a few sites, such as Corbett and Dudhwa National Parks, saw many visitors. Development projects near or in the reserves, on hold during the Indira and Rajiv Gandhi years from the early 1970s to the late 1980s, resumed. Armed rebel groups moved boldly into several tiger reserves, where they established their headquarters, and local poachers in league with the traditional Chinese medicine market decimated the animals (Project Tiger 1993). Arin Ghosh has suggested that Project Tiger reached the limits of its effectiveness in the 1980s and has since gone into decline (interview with the author, New Delhi, 1 July 1995).

CRITIC: Well, I think I see what you are getting at. In the smallpox eradication story, there was a climactic moment when health managers and epidemiologists got the satisfaction of publicly saying "we did it!" even though "doing" it was pretty rough on the ground. Here you're telling another kind of story, "the rise and fall of Project Tiger," right?

AUTHOR: Not quite. Project Tiger is actually alive and well. It never lost its global supporters, and the most viable tiger reserves have obtained millions of dollars from the United Nations Development Program (UNDP) and the World Bank to institute new approaches based on conciliating residents living around the reserves (IIPA 1994; UNDP

1995). I *was* trying to make the point in these stories that to extinguish a species and preserve one from extinction are very similar undertakings. Both exemplify hypermodern ambitions that originate with a small set of scientific arbiters who must persuade others to act. It obviously makes a difference what the species in question is. It also matters whether those being persuaded are powerful rulers, who can command an army of subordinates, or humble villagers preoccupied with daily subsistence. The international appeals made in the 1970s emphasized South Asia's exceptionalism — India was the last hope for a viable tiger population, Bangladesh was the last redoubt of the smallpox virus, and so on — and one can see the diplomatic calculation in this. But India in particular was peculiarly open in this decade to elite scientific appeals from abroad; WHO and IUCN were pushing on an open door. In choosing to eradicate smallpox and conserve tigers, India brought characteristic legitimizing practices and governing structures to bear on grand projects, evoking characteristic public opposition and resistance. Why India was open to such appeals in this period, however, is an interesting question and the one I want to turn to next. Okay?

CRITIC: Do I have a choice?

THE PRIME MINISTER OF NATURE

Three generations of the Nehru-Gandhi family filled the office of the prime minister of India almost continuously from 1947 through 1989: Jawaharlal Nehru (1889–1964, r. 1947–64), Indira Gandhi (1917–84, r. 1967–77, 1980–84), and Rajiv Gandhi (1944–89, r. 1984–89). As a child Jawaharlal Nehru was provided with every possible social and cultural advantage within the framework of colonial rule. Reared in a highly Anglicized and politically connected household in Allahabad, he enjoyed an elite education first at Harrow and then at Cambridge, where he took a bachelor of science degree in the natural sciences, followed by legal training as a barrister in the Inns of Court (Nanda 1974, 102, 128–29). When Nehru returned to India after World War I he became a conduit of characteristically modern European attitudes toward nature, holding, for example, that nature must surrender its treasures for human use (nature as a resource) but also that nature can uniquely refresh those who have lived too long in cities (nature as a refuge). Subsequently, while in prison for his leading role in the national struggle, he read widely and came to appreciate aspects of Indian tradition that he found compatible with a modern outlook and that he thought would help furnish free

India's cultural needs. For instance, his family's practice of vacationing in Kashmir and hill stations, where they communed with scenes of natural sublimity, and their fondness for both tame and wild animals, which they believed embodied untutored wisdom, set an example while strengthening a distinctive style of patrician leadership (Nehru 1942: 568–69).

Nehru and his daughter Indira presented themselves to the Indian public as more cultivated than other Indian politicians and never hesitated to assert a commonality with the great emperors Ashoka (r. 272–32 B.C.E.) and Akbar (r. 1556–1605), by consensus wise rulers who had protected India's forests and wildlife from the greed of inferior men. Occasionally they invoked the teachings of Buddha and Mahavira, great saints of the fifth century B.C.E., whose compassion extended to the suffering of all embodied souls, including trees, animals, and even insects. These allusions attracted the attention of privileged foreigners, enhancing the Nehrus' mystique abroad while softening the intensity of their striving at home.

Indira's biographers agree that her childhood was marked by great loneliness; her father often traveled or was in prison, and her mother was chronically ill and died in a sanitarium when Indira was eighteen. By her own account, she found that pets and gardens made life more bearable. Her strong attraction to animals and plants was not considered unusual — her relatives were equally smitten.

> I [am] also reminded that one of my earliest associations with animals was with snakes because my mother's brother was not only a keen botanist but had a passion for snakes. When I was, I suppose, not more than six or so, we used to come to Delhi and stay with my grandmother. Anything you opened out popped a snake. It might be a cigarette box, it might be a drawer or it might be a pipe in the bathroom, much of course to the distress of my grandmother. And later, when he was grown up, he kept two pythons . . . in his garden as pets. Unfortunately, on his marriage he had to give them away. (1986d, 224).

It was Indira's acerbic view, probably formed as a child and never relinquished even after marriage to a mild-mannered parliamentarian, Feroze Gandhi (unrelated to the Mahatma), that the main virtue of animals and plants is that they do not speak, whereas human contact takes place through the intermediacy of words, which are often bent or misconstrued. Hence her revealing statement that "with plants and animals I could be myself" (1986b, 218). Later, as the most powerful adult in India, she felt free to draw on her own childhood to prescribe love of nature for the nation's children, who "should be trained to observe and to enjoy the loveliness of the ordinary things that surround us—trees, flowers, hills, beaches, animals, even stones; they must also be brought up to love animals and their natural environment" (1986a, 216).

As prime minister, Mrs. Gandhi's commitment to forest protection and wildlife conservation was genuine and exemplary, and when environmental degradation and resource depletion became matters of state in the early 1970s she raised her personal preferences to the level of national policy. She spoke regularly about environmental problems (1975, 1982, 1986a, 1986b, 1986c, 1986d, 1986e), and she drew on the skills of first-rate advisers as speechwriters for these occasions. Over time, the vocabulary in these addresses became more precise and scientifically based, indicating that professionals had her ear. She hectored local officials about wildlife and forestry programs in which she took an interest, threatening to dismiss those who were derelict, and she visited game sanctuaries and national parks. It was only late in her term of office that she stopped these visits, giving as her reason the fact that the "swarming" of security men caused the animals distress (1986d, 225). Among heads of state in the 1970s, she was clearly far ahead in her understanding of conservation, pollution control, and biodiversity issues (Jayakar 1992, 247–48). Within the Indian government, a Committee on Environmental Coordination was set up in 1972 and a Department of the Environment in 1980; both were administratively situated under the prime minister.[26] The Fourth Five Year Plan (1969–74) articulated for the first time a need to integrate environmental concerns into economic development planning (Ramakrishna 1985, 915). Among other enactments, her government promulgated a Wildlife Protection Act in 1972, a Water Protection and Control of Pollution Act in 1974, and the Forty-second Amendment to the Constitution in 1976, which wrested control of forestry, wildlife, and population policy away from the states. An important part of the amendment added a clause that stated "It shall be the duty of every citizen . . . to protect and improve the natural environment, including forests, lakes, rivers and wildlife and to have compassion for living creatures." Further legislation followed, with a Forests Conservation Act in 1980 and a National Wild Life Action Plan in 1983. In the early 1980s, she also took the chair of the Indian Board for Wild Life (IBWL), the primary framer of wildlife conservation policy in India.

Mrs. Gandhi had a clear sense of the relationship between nationalist politics and environmental concern. She believed they strengthened each other because an attachment to terrain becomes in time an attachment to the nation and, as she pointed out in a speech in 1983, nationalism and environmentalism had similar genealogies in India. She wrote that "the beginnings of the movement for the study of natural history in India happened to coincide with the birth of the Indian National Congress and the start of the Freedom Movement. The bond between the two was provided by [the Englishman] A. O. Hume, the founder of the Indian National Congress, for his contribution to ornithology was no less significant. The flight of birds is itself an expression of the desire to be free and to rise high above the mundane" (1986d, 224). This pairing of anti-imperialist struggle and bird flight is not fanciful. Her first serious reckoning with birds dated from 1942, when she was jailed along with her father for participating in a major uprising (the Quit India campaign) against British rule: "I did not know much about birds until the high walls of Naini prison shut us off from them, and for the first time I paid attention to bird songs. I noted the sounds and later on my release my father sent me Dr. Salim Ali's book (a famous bird-watcher's guide)" (224).[27]

She seems always to have realized that, while wild nature is to be preserved and appreciated on spiritual and aesthetic grounds, nature had another, utilitarian value for peasants and tribals who rely on the forests and commons for food, fuel, fodder, and other useful products. "We cannot allow people to think that we worry more about animals and plants than about the underprivileged," she told an audience at the Bombay Natural History Society in 1983 (1986d, 225). Indeed, she instructed state forest ministers and environmentalists to follow Mahatma Gandhi's prescription before taking major decisions—that is, to conjure up the face of the *daridranarayan*, the God who comes to earth in the form of a poor man to test the virtue and generosity of the rich (1986c, 219). She further noted that, while peasants and tribals no doubt push cultivation to the limits and overrun the forests in pursuit of subsistence, these were manageable excesses; the real environmental villains were the multinational corporations that were poised to plunder India's resources (Jayakar 1993, 408–9). These were crushing environmental dilemmas: how to achieve economic development without denuding the Indian landscape, how to obtain capital without letting foreign investors make off with the country's natural wealth, how to reverse the environmental impact of a huge and growing population without coercion and without having to apologize to the West for failing to check India's growth rate, and how to preserve rural traditions and values that celebrated the fertility of nature? These became common themes in her later public statements. She responded to both internal and foreign critics, who thought her environmental initiatives either wildly quixotic or a regrettable brake on economic growth. The internal dissenters were easier to answer because, despite the debacle of the Emergency, her party generally maintained comfortable majorities in the Lok Sabha (Parliament). In responding to foreign critics, she was apt to note that the industrialized nations began to nag India only after depleting their own resources and that in any case the West's exaggerated consumption, warmaking, and pollution were out of proportion to its limited population.

At a United Nations conference entitled Man and the Environment held in Stockholm in 1972, Mrs. Gandhi instructed the Indian delegation to propose a special "principle on wildlife conservation," which was eventually accepted and incorporated into the Declaration on the Human Environment. In the keynote speech, she ranged over most aspects of the global crisis as seen from the perspective of the developing nations. She warned against focusing on environmentalism without addressing broader political and economic issues, and she managed to touch on distinctively Nehruvian themes such as love of nature, the importance of science, and the continuity of values from antiquity. She waded into her foreign critics, tying their rapacious pasts and present day economic practices directly to the conference's environmental theme.

> Many of the advanced countries of today have reached their present affluence through domination of other races and countries, and exploitation of their own masses and their own natural resources. Their sheer ruthlessness . . . gave them a head start. . . . We do not wish to impoverish the environment further and yet we cannot for a moment forget the grim poverty of large numbers of people . . . we cannot prevent them from combing the forest for their livelihood, from poaching and despoiling the vegetation. . . . The environment cannot be improved in conditions of poverty. Nor can poverty be eradicated without the use of science and technology. . . . It is an over-simplification to blame all the world's problems on increasing population. Countries with but a small fraction of world population consume the bulk of the world's production of minerals, fossil fuels and so on. . . . There are grave misgivings that the discussion of ecology may be designed to distract attention from the problems of war and poverty. . . . The most urgent and basic question is that of peace. . . . What ecological project can survive a war? . . . Life is one and the world is one, and all these questions are interlined. The population explosion, poverty, ignorance, disease, the pollution of our surroundings, the stockpiling of nuclear weapons and biological and chemical agents of destruction, all are part of a vicious circle. Each is important and urgent but dealing with them one by one would be wasted effort. . . . [Modern man] must again learn to invoke the energy of growing things and to recognize, as did the ancients in India centuries ago, that one can take from the earth and from the atmosphere only so much as one puts back into them. (1982, 60–67)

CRITIC: Amazing. "The environment cannot be improved in conditions of poverty" and "There are grave misgivings that the discussion of ecology may be designed to distract attention from the problems of war and poverty." These sentiments are pretty impressive for a politician in 1972. I see what you mean when you say that Mrs. Gandhi was ahead of her time.

AUTHOR: Yes, it's still uncommon for politicians to speak so clearly about the downward-interlocking relationships that link industrialization to overconsumption, poverty, pollution, disease, and war. Indira Gandhi really was the first prime minister of nature — other politicians have been dressed in that mantle since — and she used the language of environmental concern to hurl bolts at her domestic and foreign critics. The problem was that she so often got it wrong.

CRITIC: What do you mean?

AUTHOR: I mean that she was simultaneously too pessimistic, too trusting, and too self-confident. For example, she assumed there was an unbridgeable contradiction between development and conservation; she always spoke as if degraded landscapes, extinction of species, and rank pollution were inevitable. Given these assumptions, she took it for granted — like the colonial rulers before her — that the choicest parts of nature needed protection from tribals and land-poor wretches and that the colonial practices such as "fines and fences" should, if anything, be strengthened. In important ways, she distrusted ordinary people and fell completely into the hands of global organizations that reinforced the notion that she and her family were the sole effective caretakers of India's scientific promise and natural heritage. The arrival in the 1970s of messengers from the West bearing smallpox eradication and tiger conservation found her more than willing to unleash an army of vaccinators on villagers and to expel thousands of tribals from their forest homes. Neither of these projects was democratically debated before India committed itself to action.

CRITIC: You're so critical! Don't you see *any* good in what she tried to do?

AUTHOR: Yes, of course I do. She was impressively willing to invest political capital in environmentalism, and Project Tiger and Smallpox Zero are global monuments in wildlife conservation and disease control. But, look, there's still the question of *how* great things are accomplished — you have to admit that smallpox eradication and tiger conservation were jammed down the throats of Indian tribals and peasants. It was the *other* Gandhi — Mohandas, the Mahatma — who insisted that process was more important than pace, something that seems increasingly apt in an age of heightened concern about the democratic process and human rights. Indira's forced pace violated these concerns. I also happen to think that there have been serious aftereffects from the excesses of the 1970s, including popular hostility toward conservation and enduring distrust of state-led medical interventions (Greenough 2002, 2003).

In the last decade, historians have coined two telling terms — *authoritarian biologist* (Guha 1997) and *conquering epidemiologist* (Leavitt 1996, 238–48) — to pinpoint new forms of arrogance that have been authorized by unchecked expertise backed by state power. In this perspective, South Asian successes in eradicating smallpox and enlarging the tiger population in the 1970s conjured up their own nemesis: popular hostility toward green agendas and ambivalence over even basic public health measures. Although conservation and vaccination had been occurring separately in various parts of South Asia since the turn of the twentieth century, it was a novel development in the region's environmental history when the state asserted agency on both fronts, for similar reasons, in the same decade and throughout an entire country. But the state didn't have it all its own way. Tribals, peasants, journalists, and ordinary citizens in the 1970s pushed back against state-led efforts to reconfigure nature in India and Bangladesh. Nature was remade anyway, of course, because of the intensity of the states' incredible agendas: the all-out extermination of a submicroscopic virus and the all-out protection of a "charismatic megafauna," the tiger. But opposition to this new nature was heard in the press and on the street; it was diffuse and lopsided because the power of articulation rested overwhelmingly with government. Physical resistance was reactive and had to wait until an outrageous government demand or a gross dereliction of duty sparked an outrage — for example, when doors were broken down to force vaccinations or when man-eating tigers were tranquilized and allowed to continue their depredations. Then a patchy democratic debate on biodiversity erupted, and subaltern anger spilled over into action. On these occasions, "nature" was not simply the sum of extant biodiversity but the ground for voiced ire, ridicule, and hatred of unchecked state power.

ACKNOWLEDGMENTS

I acknowledge with gratitude incisive comments received from fellow participants during and after the conference Environmental Narratives in South and Southeast Asia, sponsored by the Social Science Research Council and held in

Hilo, Hawaii, in December 1995. I also acknowledge the helpful research assistance of Ned Bertz during 1998–99. Critical suggestions by an anonymous reviewer for Duke University Press were helpful in improving the logic of the essay.

NOTES

1 Nearly all the "voices" in this essay are mediated texts, and only a few are based on interviews, as noted.

2 This dialogue is intended to suggest the liveliness of a transcript rather than the elegance of a drama. The format was suggested by a rereading of Mahatma Gandhi's dialogue between a "Reader" and an "Editor" in *Hind Swaraj* (1909). A contrived dialogue has the merit of letting the author make statements non sequitur.

3 Bangladesh was also the scene of a successful smallpox eradication campaign in 1975, and its continuation of colonial era tiger protection practices in the mangrove forests along the Bay of Bengal were greatly valued by global wildlife conservation agencies.

4 The name Smallpox Zero was adopted in India in January 1975 to initiate the final phase of eradication; I use it here to summarize the Smallpox Eradication Program activity in South Asia as a whole after 1973 (Basu, Jezek, and Ward 1979, 30).

5 Fenner et al. (1988, 719–25) discuss this early effort in admiring terms because India's first eradication program was ambitious and carefully organized. Only later would its failings become evident.

6 By world attention, I mean the attention of the global public health community. Because an earlier effort at malaria eradication in the 1950s and 1960s had largely failed, there was anxiety that WHO and its collaborating Ministry of Health allies would be ridiculed if smallpox eradication also turned out to have been a wasted effort. South Asia was the last eradication site for *Variola major,* the severest form of the disease, with fatality rates between 20 and 40 percent of those infected. A weaker strain, *Variola minor,* with fatality rates of 1 percent or less, was endemic in eastern Africa and was not eradicated until 1977.

7 Surveillance and containment had first been used successfully in West Africa. Taken together, they offered very considerable technical, logistic and cost advantages over routine mass vaccination. See Fenner et al. 1988, 484–515.

8 "Indian officials had some reluctance about accepting international physicians . . . in part because there was a surplus of underemployed Indian doctors. [Regional WHO director William] Foege used a long train ride to persuade one of the top officials of the Ministry of Health and Family Welfare that the practice of teaming foreign epidemiologists with Indian counterparts would enhance the program's chance for success. . . . This had not been the only occasion when Foege found the trains of India to be a useful venue for doing business. In an office, it was sometimes difficult to

Pathogens, Pugmarks, and "Emergency"   227

get past the amenities. But on a long train trip there was ample time to reach agreements. The six-foot seven-inch Foege became a familiar figure to the trainmen across the northern part of the country" (Ogden 1987, 102).

9   Chaos was incompatible with long-term SEP methods, and the Bangladesh program subsequently hired vaccinators in the affected villages rather than launching military-style containment raids, which greatly lessened the coercive aspect (Music 1976, 40).

10 Dr. Lawrence B. Brilliant, telephone interview, San Francisco, July 1992.

11 In the Bangladeshi case, an appeal was made to legal norms, hence the court case initiated against the SEP leader. In Mohan Singh's case, the objections were explicitly religious, and he invoked the most distinctive moral principle in Indian thought, dharma, which is understood to have the sanction of destiny (Weightman and Pandey 1978, 217–27). When Mohan Singh had faced down his midnight visitors, he assumed that they, too, were under the religious compulsions of dharma.

12 Nepal and Bangladesh each have three tiger preserves. For population estimates of wild tigers through 1998, see the Tiger Information Center Web site, which is managed by the National Fish and Wildlife Foundation: ⟨http://www.5tigers.org⟩. The government of India's official Project Tiger Web site is at ⟨http://envfor.nic.in/pt/pt.html⟩.

13 Some of the assumptions made in the mid-1970s about the biology of tiger conservation were, in retrospect, too sanguine; in the last thirty years, both the animal science and the human sociology of park-based conservation have been greatly elaborated. See Seidensticker, Christie, and Jackson 1999.

14 "The tiger reserves are situated in eight different states in all four corners of the country from Assam to Rajasthan and from Uttar Pradesh to Mysore. When completed they are intended to function as focal points of domestic and foreign tourism, thus contributing towards the emotional integration of the country" (Indian Board for Wildlife 1972, 8). Tiger Reserves are directly supervised by state-level field directors who report to the chief wildlife warden of the state, and Project Tiger is placed nationally under the control of the Directorate of Project Tiger within the Ministry of Environment and Forests.

15 The IUCN placed the Indian tiger in the *Red Book of Rare and Endangered Species* in 1970 (World Wildlife Fund 1971, 2). Three tiger subspecies have become extinct in the last seventy years; see the Tiger Information Center Web site at ⟨http://www.5tigers.org/Basics/Subsp_distribution/basics2.htm⟩.

16 Together the core and buffer areas of four reserves came to less than one thousand square kilometers, and two others were less than fifteen hundred (International Union for Conservation of Nature and Natural Resources 1976, 5, table 1).

17 The basic project planning document anticipated the ratio of protected tigers to displaced tribals at 1 to 624 (IIPA 1994).

18 The thirty-month Emergency was India's one episode of "home-grown authoritarianism" (in a phrase of Ashish Nandy) since Independence in

1947. Mrs. Gandhi miscalculated her popular support, and she and the Congress Party were ejected from national office in the elections of 1977. The coalition of opponents in the interim, some of whom were former supporters in Mrs. Gandhi's party, fumbled, and she returned to the premiership in 1980. She remained in office until she was assassinated in 1984.

19 "Mr. J. C. Daniel questioned the authenticity of the often quoted figure of 40,000 tigers that were estimated by Mr. E. P. Gee. . . . He was skeptical about this high figure and cautioned against its use in official circles, as this was misleading" (India 1979a, 13). The forty thousand tiger figure for 1900 can be found in nearly every tourist guide to India.

20 Peter Jackson, director of information for WWF in Switzerland, tried to quiet the controversy in a letter to the editor of the *Times of India* in July 1978: The WWF report, he wrote, "was not suppressed by the government, nor is its circulation restricted. There was delay in its release largely due to the general elections and change in the chairmanship of the project. Since release was authorized late last year some 70 copies have been distributed to journalists. No one has been refused copies. . . . A great deal has been made of whether there has been an increase or not in the tiger population. The report certainly urged great caution in assessing wildlife trends, largely on the grounds of lack of data on normal fluctuations in species populations. It remarked that the data from the 1972 tiger counts was [sic] subjected to particularly stringent analysis, and several directors of tiger reserves considered the total estimate of 1,827 tigers to be an underestimate. But discussion of this issue should not be inflated to a major dispute. . . . The Project has moved beyond simple protection of the tiger and its prey—which continues to be all important, as your editorial rightly emphasises—and now the emphasis is shifting to scientific management and monitoring programmes, for which a basis has already been laid with the help of scientists whose services have been provided by the WWF. I should like to put the project in perspective by recording the view expressed by a senior Indian official, which is shared by WWF, that Project Tiger represents the conservation of whole natural ecosystems, which have important crucial influence on water regimes in surrounding agricultural areas, protection of soils, and local climates. It is to benefit human populations, not merely to save a spectacular animal. . . . No project fulfills everything that is expected of it, but it can be said that Project Tiger has been a notable success, not only in India but in a world context" (*Times of India*, 9 July 1978).

21 Under special conditions of tiger research, scientists have succeeded in tranquilizing and collaring a few tigers at a time; the method is not suited to large-scale tracking of thousands of tigers. See Goghate and Chundawat 1997; and Vanak 1997.

22 The 1978–79 controversy over tiger numbers occurred during the years of the Janata Party government, which was sandwiched between Indira Gandhi's premierships. Neither of the prime ministers in this interval, Morarji Desai or Charan Singh, moved to cancel Project Tiger or Smallpox Zero. The controversy over tiger numbers has continued since the

1970s. In 1999, the Indian government opted to conduct tiger censuses every year.

23 The policy of shooting man-killers was motivated in part by public relations concerns: "in our opinion the only practical method of dealing with aberrant animals . . . is to shoot them, as quickly and efficiently as possible, to avoid further loss of human life and public opposition to conservation of the species that such animals engender" (International Union for the Conservation of Nature 1975, 25).

24 The family of a human victim in the 1970s received Rs 1,000; in the 1980s, this was raised to Rs 5,000. On the other hand, anyone who killed a tiger was fined Rs 5,000 and jailed for six months (Ward 1987, 61). Paying compensation for cattle and similar losses was an established but not uncontroversial practice. For example, J. C. Taylor of the Wildlife Preservation Society, Dehra Dun, speaking before the International Tiger Symposium in 1979, objected "to the practice of awarding compensation to the people whose cattle were preyed upon occasionally by tigers in the forests. He was of the opinion that this encouraged the people to continue with the grazing of domestic livestock in the tiger habitat" (India 1979a, 12). Compensation gradually increased until in 1987 loss of a cow or buffalo was worth Rs 2,000 if it was killed outside the tiger reserve or government forest; there was no compensation if the killing occurred while the animals were grazing in a protected forest or tiger reserve.

25 While the numbers were substantial, expert opinion now holds that the Indian tiger population reached a peak in the 1980s and has since declined. The problem of pugmark counting has been noted; there are also issues in population biology, including cycles in reproductive success among tigers, that make short-term comparisons of totals problematic. Further, any statement of numbers of tigers in India has to distinguish between animals living within the tiger reserves (relatively easier to count) and animals outside the reserves (relatively difficult to count).

26 The department became a full-fledged Ministry of Environment, Forests, and Wildlife in 1985 and has served as the focal point in the administrative structure for planning, promotion, and coordination of environmental programs (India 1990, 183).

27 Until his death in 1987, Salim Ali was India's best-known naturalist; he served for many years as secretary of the Bombay Natural History Society, India's premier nongovernmental conservation institution. Ali maintained a productive personal relationship with the Nehru family for decades, which he comments on in his autobiography (1985). Also see Lewis 2003, chap. 2.

Nancy Lee Peluso

TERRITORIALIZING LOCAL

STRUGGLES FOR RESOURCE CONTROL

A Look at Environmental Discourses and

Politics in Indonesia

Territorial strategies of resource control have played important roles in the claiming and allocation of resources by indigenous groups, communities, and government natural resource management agencies even prior to colonialism.[1] The late colonial period in Southeast Asia, however, is notably characterized by the emergence of an increasing number of territorial states. Using land and forest laws, these colonial and nascent national bureaucratic states established territorial mechanisms through which states and state agencies could control both resources and the activities of their subjects seeking access to those resources (Peluso and Vandergeest 2001; Vandergeest and Peluso 1995; Peluso 1992; Barber 1989).

Scholarly analyses of such practices have typically focused on the analysis of the state and its agencies, despite the concurrent growth of both individual- and community-level territorializing practices (Vandergeest and Peluso 1995; Sivaramakrishnan 1997, 1999; Sundar 2001; Menzies, 1994; but compare Sack 1986). These studies have largely argued for a focus on the processes of internal territorialization that characterized the period following the international boundary-setting activities of colonial or independent nation-state formation (Passi 1996; Mann 1993; Foucault 1979). The main contribution of the internal territorialization argument has been to show how territorial processes such as administrative territorialization, land use zoning, and the allocation of land management jurisdiction to forestry departments and other land management agencies have helped constitute and consolidate state power (Vandergeest and Peluso 1995).

State territorialization policies have, in fact, always faced local and regional challenges to their territorial sovereignty. In these, local and regional actors have emphasized more localized, identity-based territorial strategies of resource ownership and control as a means of mounting counterclaims or reclaims to contested or appropriated resources. In other words, even at the local level, land claims for coralling access to floral and faunal species are gaining priority over other sorts of resource claims and management strategies. Such transformations constitute both direct and indirect responses to state discourses of territorial resource management in that they are either formulated purposefully or emerge unintentionally under newly constrained circumstances. This essay examines these two ways in which local discourses of property rights are becoming territorialized in the province of West Kalimantan, Indonesia, i.e. through intentional practices and as effects.

Two distinct cases are made. The first shows how environmental nongovernmental organizations (NGOs) are strategically reinventing the means of both expressing and communicating "customary" rights by emphasizing the landed dimensions of customary claims to forest resources. This is accomplished not only in the terms used to discuss resource rights but in the practices they use to document claims. The mapping of village resource territories, as well as the translation of localized resource management terms, play a leading role in these processes. NGOs have inspired many local communities, and actually assisted them, to make such maps. The second example shows a more subtle territorialization of resource rights/claims, one that gradually emerges as villagers respond to the new parameters of acting created by state efforts to rezone and restrict local people's resource-related activities. In this instance, villagers are moving toward territorial interpretations of individual property rights and away from a previous intergenerational tenurial practice of families sharing rights in long-living fruit trees. Both state and local practices help produce new sorts of territoriality.

The two cases complement each other. The mapping effort depends on an understanding of territorialized ethnicities that constituted the basis of Dutch colonial land law until the end of the Indonesian revolution in 1949. Somewhat ironically, given the association with colonial rule (in the past), these "old" territorial imaginings express some people's current and anticipated future claims on maps. The main technique used to represent these claims is "countermapping" (Peluso 1995), and it is not in any way a part of some local "traditional" practice. It is, rather, a very contemporary form of representing local/regional claims that allegedly preceded the formation of the Indonesian nation-state. The countermap is believed to have the potential to embody a certain legitimacy, as it expresses a claim in a language (landed or territorial claims) and uses a "text" (a map) understood (and used in other forms) by powerful actors in the Indonesian government and international conservation NGOs.

As with the mapping project, the current resource practices of the villagers need to be understood as part of a larger process of transformation — indeed, as producing a new, hybridized discourse. This discourse is constructed through the merging of the colonial legacy of selectively reified customary rights with contemporary territorial claiming strategies. Although the two cases I present here involve different locations and sets of actors, the changes in discursive and practical activity throughout West Kalimantan are facilitated by the spreading counter-mapping movement and general awareness of it. Changes in the language — and imagining — of property and in the everyday practices producing property relations, are stimulated or grow out of the changes in a more broadly shared language of claims and rights. I examine changes in the ways in which inheritence practices are transforming access to land and trees. The ways in which people talk about their plans to allocate their property to their heirs provide another illustration of the shift in local property discourses. Common rights in long-living trees, held by multiple generations of heirs, are slowly being replaced with a notion that property rights in land supersede or dominate all forms of property in trees and other terrestrial resources. Thus, local territorialization is not only a product of intentional changes from the government but can also emerge from a context of more gradually changing everyday practices.

Following a brief theoretical discussion on territoriality, I outline local territorial and nonterritorial claims in forests, land, and trees that are relevant to the corner of West Kalimantan that I reference. I then provide a sketch of the recent historical role of mapping in forest management in West Kalimantan. The second half of the essay focuses on the two case studies.

THE DIALECTICS OF TERRITORIALITY

In conceptualizing territoriality, Sack's (1986, 19) simple definition is the most useful: "the attempt by an individual or group to affect, influence, or control people, phenomena, and relationships by delimiting and asserting control over a geographic area." Explicit resource control through territorialization works by determining how people may use resources found within spatial boundaries. Although territoriality is a type of activity in space, it is not the same as variation across space. The study of the spatial location of activities (e.g., Soja 1989) is thus not the same as the study of how activities are regulated by territorial strategies, although Soja's argument that "the space of physical nature . . . is liter-

Territorializing Local Struggles 233

ally made social" through its appropriation (or management) by contending actors is relevant (Soja 1985).[2] Moreover, a discussion of territoriality is by definition more focused and different than the concern with spatial politics or the debates on space and place that have recently exploded in the geographical, anthropological, and rural sociological literature (e.g., Massey 1994). Most of the time these miss the territorial dimension of spatialized politics.

As I have discussed at length elsewhere, all modern states divide their territories into complex and overlapping political and economic zones, rearrange people and resources within these units, and create regulations delineating how and by whom these areas can be used (Vandergeest and Peluso 1995).[3] These zones are administered by agencies whose jurisdictions are territorial as well as functional. Because the territories are represented on maps, modern cartography plays a central role in the implementation and legitimation of territorial rule (see, e.g., Anderson 1991; and Winichakul 1994). Further, property rights in land—variously called "alienated" land or "private property"—are also represented on maps and administered by the state in virtually all nation-states today. Indeed, the term *alienated* refers to a sort of excision of some authority formerly exercised or claimed by the state with regard to the land within its national territory. Sketch or surveyors' maps often accompany land titles or deeds and are also a tool state agencies use to rationalize and record the geographic location of a particular piece of land that is "privately owned." Importantly, however, such alienated land still remains within the jurisdiction of state territory. Its recording in state files is a means of control (Kain and Baigent 1992).

Territorialization can refer to any attempt to exclude or include people by reference to an area of land marked or even simply known by geographic boundaries (Menzies 1994). Boundaries must be understood if they are to serve their purposes as such (Rose 1994). Sack (1986, 21–22) claims that territorial classification and control of resources often replace the regulation of access to specific resources within a territorial zone. This view can be misleading, however. More often, territorial controls supersede or precede—rather than replace—other types of regulation (see, e.g., Sivaramakrishnan 1999).

The long-distance perspective afforded by modern mapping techniques is key to representing the territories groups claim in what Lefebvre has called "abstract space" (1979; see also Anderson 1991). Maps do more than represent territory; they are instruments by means of which state agencies draw boundaries and establish the claims enforced by their courts of law, thus producing territories (Harley 1988). Modern maps are meant to be scientifically accurate, meaning that they claim to present abstract space in specific ratios to verifiable external referents. As Anderson has pointed out, mapping situates space in a global grid defined by latitudes and longitudes and composes empty boxes (as it were) to be filled through the state-administered census (1991, 170ff.; Winichakul 1994; see also Smith 1984, 68). Spatial situating is also important for the mapping of natural resources such as forests, minerals, water, or soils. Maps thus enable the communication of territorial boundaries by using the allegedly universal language of global location. Map readers can verify whether or not the location of a particular village, township, farm, house, elevation, or soil type corresponds to its representation on the standard grid underlying the map (Vandergeest and Peluso 1995).

The examples presented below support Sivaramakrishan's (1999) explanation of territorialization as the process by means of which a variety of resource rules or access rights are subsumed, but not always eliminated, under land rights. In other words, land control becomes not the only but the most important element in a resource control strategy. Property arrangements affecting particular species of forest trees and wildlife, for example, as well as other mechanisms of resource access such as labor arrangements and marketing controls, became subordinate to land control even though they may continue to be applied at the same time (Ribot and Peluso 2003). Further, the discursive forms of claiming use territorial terms — *boundaries, spaces, zones, areas, plots,* and so on — to describe the realms within which a claimant aspires to hold rights. Indeed, it might be argued that only a fine line separates the *combination* of various sorts of rights to and controls on resources — territorially and nonterritorially — and the *domination* of one sort by another. As the cases described here show, however, the subtle changes in perceptions and practices of resource rights and property claims (i.e., emergent "effects") can be just as telling as direct and open strategies for laying claim to land-based resource territories. Words, like maps, matter.

DAYAK TERRITORIAL AND NONTERRITORIAL RESOURCE MANAGEMENT CLAIMS

Dayak forest and land management practices typically have included both territorial and nonterritorial components.[4] These are schematically described below.

Swidden cultivation, which has until recently been practiced by more rural Dayaks, has always imparted some kind of territorial rights. Recognized by a community because of the labor entailed in clearing mature forest, after the death of the clearers territorial rights were vested in either the clearers' direct descendants or their resident longhouse or village (see Appell n.d.; Sather 1990; Peluso 1996). In recent generations — that is, since at least the turn of the century — these land rights have often been held in common by the clearer's descent group. Individuals could make claims on the family's commonly owned swidden farms, for example, when a descendent invested their labor to clear the secondary growth and plant a new swidden. Sometimes certain plots of land would be cleared and planted repeatedly by an individual, and over time that plot would be recognized as "his" or "hers." Whether or not that particular piece of land would then be inherited by a favored child or grandchild, however, would depend on many circumstantial factors and would have to be explored empirically. Simply put, such practices inevitably varied within and across villages.

Swiddening, for many groups, is a form of rotational agro-forestry practiced on a broad regional basis. It involves the management not only of swidden fields but of swidden fallows in multiple stages of development, including standing forests. This management of standing forests is important to note here because in Kalimantan such management — and it cannot be recognized as anything less — was never legally recognized as a territorial claim through the end of Suharto's rule in 1998, although some colonial administrators in the first part of the twentieth century argued for its recognition (Peluso and Vandergeest 2001). Only land that was recognized as "under permanent agriculture," recently swiddened, or in relatively early stages of regeneration were recognized generally as "customary land" (*tanah adat*). Mature forest was treated as if it were pristine or virgin rather than the product of a longer period of regrowth enabled by the specific decisions local people had made.[5]

Recent research has shown that as Dayak farmers in West Kalimantan rely less on swiddens for food, and either buy rice and vegetables or extend and intensify rice production in irrigated and rain-fed permanent fields, they are converting their swidden fallows on the hillsides to more intensively managed forests, forest gardens, or agro-forests (1985; Potter 1987; Colfer 1987; Peluso and Padoch 1996). Other evidence shows that the management of such agro-forestry systems does not depend solely on easy access to markets — it precedes commercialization (Dove 1996;

236 Nancy Lee Peluso

Padoch and Peters 1993; Padoch 1994; Tsing 1999; Peluso 1996). In addition, forest management is not restricted to areas where wet field rice cultivation is impossible; on the contrary, the management of standing forests and woodlands is likely a long tradition common throughout much of the island. However, as access to markets for tree and other forest products increases, the transformation of the settled landscape from one dominated by field crops plus lightly managed fallows to one dominated by heavily managed, economically important trees is notable. A telling aspect of this transformation is that it has frequently taken place without any direct government intervention or encouragement (Peluso and Padoch 1996).

Dayak forest managers differentiate activities within different types of forest, although they do not always establish rigid land use categories. Dayaks we worked with in West Kalimantan managed a range of forest types, each with different origins, species compositions, uses, and combinations of forest products. The borders between these land use types are blurred and uses overlap (see Peluso and Padoch 1996 for details). Importantly, these forest management categories are almost never understood or officially recognized by government forest managers. They are not labeled on the forest maps of Kalimantan, for example, as people's forests, or swidden fallows. They tend to be labelled as degraded land, secondary forest, or deforestation.

Nonterritorial Claims

Nonterritorial claims guide access to and control of specific forest and garden products. These products, such as clumps of rattan, clusters of resin-producing trees, or lone honey trees, are often held by the individuals who find, protect, encourage, or otherwise manage them. Some such products are cultivated, such as rattan, resins, and ironwood. Whether planted, protected, or encouraged, the rights to these products are inherited, often bilaterally, that is with both male and female descendants having rights to ancestral resources. Once trees or other forest resources are planted or otherwise claimed, others may not arbitrarily clear them to use the land. The land is tied up — giving implicit territorial control to the individuals and groups who claim these trees and their products. At the same time, when many trees are claimed by many people in one location, territorial control becomes impossible unless one person buys up the rights to all the trees in the area. Local management thus has territorial effects.

Consolidation of ownership may be further constrained in groups that proscribe the buying and selling of ancestral property. Perhaps for this reason the village or longhouse often holds the territorial rights to the standing forest (planted or spontaneously occurring) within which those nonterritorial resources are found. Individuals, households, or descent groups can hold and inherit or otherwise transfer nonterritorial or species rights to resources that exist within that forest area. This produces a combination of village territoriality and individual rights to resources.

Unfortunately, as I will explain, the state's claim to nearly all standing forest causes it to legally recognize only the rights of individuals to specific forest products and not the rights of the village to the particular forest territory.[6]

INDONESIAN STATE FOREST MANAGEMENT AND FOREST MAPPING

Territoriality in Indonesian national forest management goes back to the Domeinverklaring, which was passed in 1870 as part of the Agrarian Act of the Netherlands East Indies, in which all land was declared the property or "domain" of the state. Land that could be shown to be under cultivation or other use was declared "native land" and subjected to "native" or "customary" (*adat*) law, as part of a legal code separate from the land code that guided property rights in land leased by the colonial government, Chinese, and Japanese entrepreneurs. Free land — that is, all land that was neither in the category of native land nor alienated to private claimants at the time the territorial colonial state began to operate in Java — was subject to direct government jurisdiction, and it was out of this category of state land that the forests of Java were carved. Native lands were not immediately mapped but often constituted a kind of residual category remaining after forests or agricultural leases, were surveyed, gazetted, and demarcated in the field and on maps.

A form of zoning thus began, based on land use and cover. Forests — regarded generally as "natural" and "uncultivated" or "unmanaged" — became government territory while agricultural fields became native territory.[7] In other words, the Domeinverklaring reinforced colonial officials' assumptions about local agricultural systems and the relations between forests and fields — that is that they were separated and separable entities for conceptual, practical, and legal purposes. One immediate outcome of this law/policy, which followed the passing of the first "real" forestry laws in 1865, was that the teak forest regions of Java were rapidly surveyed, gazetted, and demarcated as government property

(Peluso 1992). The colonial Forest Service (*Boschwezen*) in its various institutional forms was given jurisdiction over all forest lands. Their actual control was strongest in those areas where plans for direct government management were completed. However, the claims of the Forest Service to these forests and the lands surrounding them continued to be contested by local people (Peluso 1992).

The Domeinverklaring was passed in the Netherlands East Indies colonial territory of Java. Regional colonial administrators in the Borneo territories, including the Western Borneo District, challenged its relevance and legality in Borneo in the 1920s and 1930s when colonial foresters wanted to create territorial management units outside Java (GOI 1986; Potter 1988; Peluso and Vandergeest 2001). The legal outcome of this was that Western Borneo (now West Kalimantan), like the rest of the territories on Borneo, did not have a political forest of the sort possible on Java until well after the formation of the Indonesian Republic in the mid–twentieth century.

The priorities of the Sukarno government after independence from colonialism did not include significant investment in "Outer Island" forestry, including in West Kalimantan.[8] Indeed, by the early 1960s West Kalimantan had become the site of a massive militarization project as part of *Konfrontasi*, Sukarno's low-intensity conflict with the Federation of Malaysia.[9] By then as well, Sukarno's economic policies had also discouraged foreign investment in Indonesian enterprises.

When Suharto took over from Sukarno in 1966, Konfrontasi was declared over and a new regime emphasis was adopted: development. In 1967, both Foreign Investment Act 1 and Forestry Act 5 were passed, enabling the establishment of timber concessions and foreign investment in logging enterprises. Political forests would soon dominate the national territorial landscape of West Kalimantan.

The formation of political forests based on territorial principles was aided both conceptually — at the national level — and legally by the passage of the Basic Agrarian Law (BAL) in 1960 (under Sukarno). The BAL formally eliminated the special legal differences between native or customary lands (*tanah adat*) and other kinds of private property — that is, those alienated lands carved out of state land for purposes other than forestry. This meant that claimants to customary lands could acquire legal titles to their land; it also meant that such lands could be formally parcelized and legally sold to other Indonesian citizens. Having a single legal code for land administration (as well as for other legal spheres) was seen as a unifying mechanism for the nascent nation. At the same time, it diminished the jurisdiction and authority of some local groups over lands — "ethnic" territories — they had claimed as theirs under Dutch rule.

Forests were now coded as state land even when their boundaries had not been formally demarcated or surveyed. As a result, although swidden cultivation, the primary agricultural practice in West Kalimantan (particularly within the extensive inland forests), involved a series of field and forest stages of management and use, local people's claims to forest were never recognized. Only two kinds of local management claims enjoyed some legal recognition.

> 1. Claims to lands that had been cleared of forest and continuously planted, with a three-year fallow period between plantings allowed. Cleared land, according to the BAL, resulted in the formal recognition of territorial rights.
> 2. Claims to specific products that individuals or groups of individuals could prove they had owned and managed. Such forest products could have either commercial or subsistence value and included various sorts of forest resin trees, fruit trees, rattans, bird's nest caves, and "honey trees."

However, no product rights granted to local people carried with them any territorial rights. There was, then, in practice, no recognition of the local forest use and management activities that had helped create or shape the composition of the forest — for example, enrichment planting, the imposition of harvesting restrictions, and so on. Forests, political now by definition, had been declared the territorial domain of the state.

Because of Sukarno's policies concerning investment, little large-scale timbering took place anywhere in the Outer Islands of Indonesia until 1967, although some operations went on in parts of Sumatra and East Kalimantan (e.g., Obidzinsky 2002). The Forest Act of 1967 changed all that. Almost immediately, forests were carved into timber concessions — many of which overlapped — and allocated to political friends and supporters of the Suharto government.[10] By the end of 1989, some 561 timber concessions were in operation outside Java. More than half of them, or 294, were located in the four Indonesian provinces on Borneo — West, East, South, and Central Kalimantan (FAO/GOI, cited in Potter 1996).

State management activities since 1967 have included three major mapping exercises, which have been described at length elsewhere (Peluso 1995; Potter 1996; Moniaga 1993; REPPROT Report, West Kalimantan 1990; GOI 1986). It is important to point out however, that these government mapping projects began with the quintessential exercise of drawing "lines on the map," an exercise undertaken by government foresters, other officials, and timber company executives sitting around tables in Jakarta. This system later was replaced with a process called "consensus mapping," which used high-powered GIS tools and involved field and planning officials from various ministries with interests in landed resources. Finally, the World Bank and the FAO's Forestry Division aided the government in developing a mapping component for a highly ambitious regional planning program aimed primarily at planning resettlement into converted forest areas of Kalimantan and other Outer Islands.

In the two latter mapping endeavors, the "empty spaces" on earlier maps were "filled in" by zoning land uses and scientifically categorizing the land's physical characteristics. This filling in, however, did not include the documentation of local people's claims or even situating most forest-based villages on official forestry maps. Local villages — and thereby local claims — were kept off forest maps. Planners did not know the boundaries and types of customary claims throughout the region; nor were they even sure how many people lived near or inside the forests, on which many depended heavily for their livelihoods (Moniaga 1993).

Indonesian law still nodded to the fact that notions of customary land, law, and practice (*tanah adat, hukum adat,* and *hak ulayat*) held some sway throughout Indonesia and that, given the history of forest mapping (or lack of the political forest) under colonialism, these claims and practices frequently occurred within territories subsequently categorized as state forests. Forest Law 5, for example, states that the adat rights of indigenous peoples to land and resources should be respected, except when these conflict with national law or the "public interest." This clause, however, had little effect during the Suharto regime (see, e.g., Moniaga 1993; Ngo 1995; Lynch and Talbot 1995; and Peluso 1995).

In sum, state territorialization of resource management in Kalimantan has involved de facto and de jure definition of land categories (and subsequently zones), the mapping and filling in of maps with biophysical characteristics of the land, and the creation of "empty" or "abstract" spaces on maps and in textual plans that ignored local people's management activities and territorial claims.[11] These territorial management categories are reinforced in practice by the allocation of permits, the establishment of restricted production activities within particular zones (such as those determining which species and size classes of trees can be harvested), the imposition of marketing procedures, and so on. In other words, territorialization is not a totalizing process but a simplification (Scott 1998), one in which resource access is managed/controlled by the state in multiple ways — of which territorial zoning constitutes an initial or primary means. This has led to the creation of a whole set of terms and tools for representing authority—the creation of a discourse of resource management that self-consciously includes maps, zones, and land-use categories. All of these are forms of property rights involving, by definition, territorial power.

CASE 1: NGOS, MAPPING, AND TERRITORIALIZATION

My first example of local territorialization involves Indonesian environmental NGOs that are using land rights as a key forum for advocacy. A key component to the NGO strategy is countermapping, so-called because it is viewed as providing an alternative vision to maps and claims made by government, industry, and "Big Conservation" (i.e., internationally based conservation organizations) (Peluso 1995).

Using a method developed by Jeff Fox of the East-West Center (1990), local activists, sometimes with the help of international consultants and government officials, use sketch maps to delineate land and resource territories and standing forest resources that forest villages claimed according to local custom or practice. In some cases, they matched their sketch maps to points on the Global Positioning System (GPS) and Indonesian forest planning maps using sophisticated software, just as government cartographers do. This countermapping has been generally used by NGOs to identify what they call customary forest tenure boundaries. The process and products are meant to illustrate how indigenous ways of organizing and allocating space support or conflict with the government's objectives of forest management. The mappers talk to villagers about land tenure and inheritance, the nature of individual and community decisions regarding resource use, and the ways in which villagers have dealt with outsiders seeking access to local resources. They then record this information on sketch maps.

These sketch maps are not the final product. The field data are matched with official land-use data and topographic maps to create more high-tech maps, which are used to make claims to government and large international nongovernment agencies. Such opportunities may come up when new development projects or conflicting land uses are planned for the same areas.

One goal of these efforts is to appropriate the state's techniques and manner of representation to bolster the legitimacy of local claims to resources and what is represented as indigenous forms of zoning. Nevertheless, one practical effect of using maps and territorialized language and concepts is that nonterritorial claims are reinvented and rerepresented as claims to the land itself. By using the very language of territory, the NGOs compel the translation of concepts of property and use that derive from other ways of thinking and forms of practice.

Countermappers also hope to "fill in" the zones and conceptual environments created by government mapping exercises, by placing real people in the spaces of these mapped zones. For some NGOs, this means associating numbers of residents categorized according to the languages they speak at home with various forest territories as a form of data about who lives where, how long, and so on. The maps thus produce new forms of territorializing ethnicity and strengthening unrecognized local claims to state forests. In districts that are ethnically mixed, the mapmakers often assign a majority ethnicity, or use terms such as "native customary land," which ignore changes in ethnic territorial identities that come with the elimination of the plural legal codes.

In practice, therefore, countermapping accomplishes some of the same things as formal government mapping does. It asserts permanent claims to both territorial and nonterritorial resources. It covers differences in forms of claim. It seeks a historicity to some claims while it ignores others. And, oddly enough, it does what colonial officers were never able to accomplish: it maps the extent of village territories and the various intensive and extensive land and forest uses. While it eschews the government's overarching claims to forests, it uses some of the categories of contemporary forest management — for example, forest protection — in order to legitimize its claims to the very government authorities it wants to deny direct controls. Finally, these new notions of territoriality reflect an earlier time and earlier systems of authority and celebrate both the "timelessness" and the dynamic nature of adat.

One of the fears of those who have opposed the codification of customary rights under colonialism or early Indonesian nation-state building was that codes would have the potential to "freeze" inevitably dynamic social processes (Lev 1983; Supamo 1950). In a similar vein, countermaps, as written documents, have been imagined as potential freezers (Peluso 1995). However, just as the strictest of legal provisions is subjected to contestation almost from its inception, it seems unlikely that disputes and contests over either village claims to resources in a particular territory or the countermaps depicting those claims will fail to occur. The question remains, however, just how powerful will new maps be, and in what contexts?

During a research trip taken through Sanggau, West Kalimantan, in 1992, for example, Christine Padoch of the New York Botanical Garden and I encountered a particularly salient example of the potential complexity of claims and their persistence over time despite radical social and environmental change. We visited a village that claimed to have occupied its current territory since approximately 1920. The inhabitants had "purchased" the right to occupy the territory from its previous occupants, a group that spoke a different language but shared many of the agro-forestry and property practices of the incoming group.

The terms of the transfer of occupancy and use rights had been negotiated between the two heads of adat and included the rights to the swidden fallows left behind by the previous occupants and two relatively large *tembawang* (fruit forests). Tembawang are the sites of abandoned longhouses or clusters of houses — the name given to a former residential site after everyone has moved away. Longhouses and other settlements were typically surrounded by fruit trees that people had planted or that had sprouted from seeds tossed off the verandas. Tembawang are thus constituted of many fruit trees and almost always include multiple trees of durian — the most favored of local fruits (Padoch and Peters 1993). Durian means many things as a resource (see below and Peluso 1996a), one of them being as a marker of a former longhouse site and therefore imputing a property right.

When the transaction is negotiated for turning over a former occupants' home site to the newcomers, the terms of that exchange are meant to reflect the labor invested by the previous occupants in creating value by managing for certain resources. Fields, standing trees, and tembawang sites are all counted and calculated. In addition, a ritual activity intended to appease the ancestors who had performed this labor and cleared the way, so to speak, for the new occupants to move in and enjoy the fruit, must be carried out.

In this case, however, the move of one group out and the other one in did not occur simultaneously. The first group had decided to move late in the nineteenth century after two devastating head-hunting raids on the settlement. Having lost women, children, old people, and able-bodied men, the survivors fled to a place farther down river, abandoning their forests and field sites. The new group moved in after "pacification" of head-hunting by the Dutch a couple of decades later. It was at this time — twenty years after the site's abandonment — that the negotiations and ritual transfer took place.

Once transferred, neither the lands nor the event passed out of the memory of the old occupants. In approximately 1977, more than fifty years after the ritual transfer, one of the "new" occupants decided to swidden a site in the forest in which two or three durian trees were growing and would need to be cut. News of his intent made its way to the other village, as the cutting of durian trees is an important event, given their important social and ritual meanings (Peluso 1996a). The head of custom (*kepala adat*) from the downriver village traveled upriver and demanded that a series of additional customary fines be paid. These included payment to the former occupants as a village, to the direct descendants of the trees' planter, and for the ritual appeasement of the trees' planters and subsequent heirs who had passed. The "new" villagers did not object; they paid the fees (fines). Why? This cluster of durian trees, technically a small tembawang, had been overlooked in the original transfer of rights of occupancy. Both because they acknowledged the importance of the customary claim and perhaps because they feared some kind of spiritual retribution if the ancestors of the tree planters were not ritually recognized, the villagers, particularly the prospective swiddener, were willing to recognize the old claim.

Even over two or more generations, then, the territorial and resource claims of one group continued to be recognized by new occupants. Had a map been made at the time of transfer, perhaps the small cluster of durian trees would not have been marked. The failure to write it down at the time of transfer could later be used in a strict legal sense to dispute the claims of the first village. But at the same time the fact that such arrangements were possible so long after resettlement raises questions about the finality of the finalities predicted by a formal legal change in procedure and documentation. Would a countermap have affected the outcome?

TERRITORIALIZED VILLAGE DISCOURSE

My second example of territorialization has to do with changes that people in the village of Bagak have made in their land and forest management practices. This is not a village where NGOs have been active. These villagers have transformed their local landscape in response to government zoning policies and definitions of the territory since the 1930s and in response to changes in market access. They have also changed the way they talk about their resources, more often using words that refer to places (such as gardens) than to the trees themselves. In the past, property rights in trees dominated the discursive and inheritance practice. Today property relations in land are becoming much more of a focus. I focus here on that process.

Over the years, the village's boundaries have become fixed, both by government delineation of village boundaries and the actual filling up of the spaces outside their boundaries. Bagak is bounded on the south by a small (three-thousand-hectare) nature reserve. To the east are both the agricultural lands of adjacent villages and special transmigration settlements for retired police and Air Force officers. To the west is a Catholic mission and school, and to the north is an extensive rubber plantation established on the lands of another village. Since 1980, the plantation has been worked by those villagers and some four thousand Javanese transmigrants who were settled there by a government program.

In the context of these changes over the past three generations, villagers have altered their living and working environment. They changed it most recently from a largely forested landscape dominated by swidden fields and fallows with patches of managed forests to a landscape dominated by forests of economic trees, particularly fruit and rubber, and including some self-sown timber, fuel wood, and medicinal species. The relationships among land, trees, and the systems of tenure around them have been revolutionized by changes in the regional political ecology. By the mid-1990s, economic trees — fruit and rubber — dominated the landscape. As one woman said, "Rubber is our daily rice. And fruit brings windfall profits in good production years." The following is a brief interpretive history of land use and territory and some meanings of the working landscapes in Bagak (see Peluso 1996 for further details).

Oral histories and landscape markers indicate that Bagak villagers have lived in the same general area for at least two hundred years. Every thirty to fifty years, the villagers moved their longhouse sites very short distances — fifteen to twenty minutes' walk away — either because the trees near the longhouse had grown too large or illness had struck the occupants, or because they couldn't accommodate population growth. When they left a site, they would take transportable materials with them and plant durian and other fruit trees in the spaces left by the removal of the structure. The site was henceforth called *timawokng*, the Selako term for "tembawang." This movement created the patched local landscape of swidden fields, fruit forests, and fallows in various states of management or regrowth. The rights in the fruit trees of the tembawang were passed down bilaterally through the generations to the members of the planters' descent groups. Because durian trees live for hundreds of years, each tree came to be owned by more and more people each generation. Durian trees are particularly important symbols of kinship and are highly valued for the descent groups' own fruit consumption, for local exchanges of hospitality, and for sale in local, regional, and national markets. Cutting productive trees is both a bad idea economically and ritually dangerous. The local expression that "selling durian trees is like selling your grandparents" expresses the significance of these amazing trees. Ownership of and access to these trees — not the land they occupy — was an important aspect of local people's identities both collectively and individually.[12]

In 1920, Dutch colonial authorities initiated plans to turn the upper slopes of the mountain complex, including about a third of their village lands, into a nature reserve — a watershed protection area. The initial line for the reserve border was drawn where a water catchment device was to be constructed, encompassing all of the village's current and former living sites, the sites of their ancestral forests, agricultural land, and durian trees. The longhouse occupants were ordered to move off the mountain and forfeit these ancestral rights. To enforce this, Dutch officials negotiated with local leaders to convince people that they had no choice but to move to the lower slopes of the mountain. Even after they moved out of the watershed protection area, however, the head of the village continued to negotiate with the Dutch to change the lower boundary on the reserve. He wanted them to concede the rights of local people who had planted trees or converted forest to swidden fields within the territories appropriated by the Dutch engineers.

Ultimately, the Dutch moved the reserve boundary above the old longhouse sites, restoring a good deal of the people's territory, and gave them full control over the ancestral trees and forest below the reserve line. The boundaries of the reserve and the resources within are actively contested, however, although in unorganized, informal, or invisible ways. Villagers today still harvest durian and other fruits planted by their ancestors within the reserve border; they also continue to plant new fruit and rubber gardens within the border. Relatively open contestation has been most prevalent during times of political upheaval. During the Japanese occupation (1942 to 1945), the Indonesian revolution, and the early years of Indonesian independence, villagers made extensive swiddens within the reserve boundaries and planted rubber and fruit in the fallows, when Government surveillance of state forests was practically nonexistent.

By planting tree crops, people are also staking claims in the control of the hillside's upper slopes, thereby negotiating new forms of old territorial and nonterritorial resource claims. Whereas previously they had claimed the lands encompassed by the reserve by clearing forest, now they were reclaiming them by planting trees. They have no formal rights over any reserve land; yet in practice they have created an effective buffer zone and gained resource territory inside the reserve border.

Villagers' assumptions of control appears in another context as well. When colonial authorities rearranged the village's social and productive space by moving villagers off the mountain, they did more than superimpose a new set of territorial rules about land and forest use. They created a territorially bounded landscape complete with new terms to indicate government zoning categories. But the villagers have their own set of territorial terms. Whereas officials would refer to "being inside" or "outside reserve," local people refer to places throughout the landscape more specifically by the names of the ancestors who planted durian trees there, who had swiddened there, or who had been involved in some memorable event in those places (e.g., the place where Jon fell from the tree). They have their own zones, which do not actually concede the primacy of the government's classifications (and the intended limits on their activities). In a sense these give them control of those places. Using their own terms recalls both their ancestral claims to the reserve territory and practices of place-naming that hark back to earlier times.

After the formation of Indonesia, and in particular since the changes in the land and forest laws, the villagers' ability to move or open up new forest for settlement has been significantly reduced. As the village became more sedentary, people's interest in planting rubber escalated. They began planting rubber in swidden fallows, which shifted the landscape composition. The expansion of rubber gardens intensified after the establishment of the nature reserve. Rubber and fruit trees eventually came to dominate the landscape, encroaching on swidden fields and less intensively managed fallows. As the amount of land available for swidden declined, people could not produce enough of their staple food and more frequently bought rice.

This land use revolution has seen some land use categories expand at the expense of others. It has also generated changes in the sorts of places where trees are planted. Durian is no longer found only in former living sites; people are planting durian trees in swidden fallows and even in declining stands of rubber (which themselves had been planted in swidden fallows). Durian trees are thus clustered into what people are calling "gardens," using a term they had used earlier to refer to the clustered planting of rubber trees (*kabotn*). By 1990, 85 percent of Bagak villagers owned productive rubber trees (which means they had gardens because rubber trees would not be planted alone). In addition, some 97 percent of sample households have planted durian trees in their swidden fallows; at least 41 percent have planted mixed durian and rubber gardens. Durian trees, in fact, occupy 71 percent of the old and medium-aged fruit forest's total basal area. By planting durian trees in specialized and mixed gardens, people are deploying new sorts of territoriality in their "traditional" land use practices.

These changes in tree planting practices alter property rights in land, especially in parcels formerly regarded as swidden fallows. One material effect of planting trees that live 40 years (rubber) or over 150 years (durian) appears in the ways land is tied up. When trees are planted in parcels recultivated every 10, 20, or 30 years, property rights as well as landscape — and the conceptions and practices that accompanied the earlier practices — are inevitably changed. For rubber, this type of change is not major in terms of its meaning as a resource. Rubber has always been only a commercial crop. Durian, on the other hand, still represents kinship and ancestors as well as livelihood.

Some people plant trees or gardens of trees for their children and other heirs, indicating their intent at planting time. These new fruit trees in new kinds of places represent new practices and meanings. In this way durian trees are beginning to be thought of as territorial resources.

At the same time, the new practices are not frozen, and the old ones are being reinterpreted all the time. Not every descent group has privatized or territorialized rights to the trees they would have all held in common in earlier times. Ancestral trees, whether growing in the tembawang or other places still retain a great deal of meaning and value for many villagers.

These processes have changed the ways in which people are valuing, talking about, and acting in relation to resources. They also have led to new types of property relations and everyday practices. Without countermaps or NGOs, but in response to similar sets of changes brought on by changing regional, national, and global politics, the people of Bagak are progressively territorializing their notions of resource rights.

CONCLUSION

In the cases discussed here, we saw that villagers in this section of western Borneo are territorializing their resource use, talk about property, and inheritance practices. At the same time, some villagers still talk about property relations in trees rather than in land. While national and regional government land use projects are changing the regional political ecology, the globalization of claims on tropical forest resources and social movements calling for indigenous people to formalize their resource claims are reverberating locally just as they coalesce with simultaneous local processes. Territorialized spaces, in other words, are being produced locally as well as nationally and globally (Lefebvre 1979).

Nongovernmental organizations and others involved with countermapping are engaged in more conscious, strategic territorialization processes. Through territorial politics and practices, they aim to decenter state power and replace it in the control of local people. Yet countermapping NGOs have explicitly chosen to use the state tools and terms of territorial power. Maps, GPS, and so on are powerful forms of communication as well as means of making claims; clearly they are technologies of state power. Thus, at the same time that NGOs are making counterclaims, they are accepting the terms set by the state. In this process, they are inevitably aiding in the incorporation of these localities into state maps, state-defined categories, and state mechanisms for controlling resource use.

These forms of territorialization—particularly when they involve mapping the residual memories of idealized pasts and ethnicizing or racializing the resource landscape in the process—represent sharp sides of a potentially double-edged sword. While the territorial strategies and tactics discussed here may seem to promise the return of resource control to local claimants, they also run the risk of creating serious problems for the very people they are meant to serve. Even when mapped claims are allocated to whole groups, as in community mapping, they are nevertheless privatized group rights. They therefore create the conditions for conflict that exclusivity and enclosure bring with them. In regions characterized by a great deal of migration, intermarriage, and other forms of blurred ethnic and political allegiances, confusion, if not conflict, is likely to ensue.[13]

Conversely, when looking at options for people whose individual and group claims were never fully acknowledged by a national government, making countermaps seems to be a practical way to establish property rights or at least to create documents that can be used for negotiation. It remains true, however, that once rights to resources are territorialized and mapped or documented in ways recognizable by the state, the state gains a certain power over those resources and the people claiming them. The state becomes a recognized arbiter and mediator of both access and rights. Increased visibility to the state and its disciplining mechanisms carries its own risks, which mappers and their constituencies must remember.

Both cases in Kalimantan illustrate that territorialization is a dynamic process, an expression of relationships that emerge and operate across localities, national spaces, and global networks. These cases show that territorialized spatial practices are not only responses to events or processes at one level of analysis or another but are simultaneously produced at multiple levels (Massey 1994). If countermaps constitute a new spatial practice as a territorializing mechanism for making claims, the acts of making and interpreting the maps, as well as the maps themselves, help transform local discourses of property rights. In the process, concepts that come from different eras — such as "customary rights" — can be translated or transformed in the present. They may thereby attain more or different meanings and power — not only on the maps but in speech and the ways in which people relate to each other and their environments.

NOTES

This essay was written in 1995, and while it has been updated, it was impossible to comprehensively rewrite it to reflect all the ways my thinking about territoriality have changed.

1 This is not to say that land has always been the primary focus of resource claims for management. Landed or territorial claims could be and often were combined with or separated from claims on other resources (e.g., trees, crops, or water) and on control of production processes associated with particular resources.

2 Soja (1971) has discussed territoriality in the sense that I use it here; see also Paasi 1996.

3 This section draws heavily on arguments made by Vandergeest (1996). It also refers to arguments I have made (Peluso 1995, 1992). See also Barber 1989; Sack 1986; Vandergeest 1996; and Peluso and Vandergeest 2001 for developments in our thinking about territoriality and territorialization.

4 I use the term *Dayak* to refer collectively to the non-Muslim peoples of the interior of Borneo. The specific people among whom I carried out this research are also known as Salako and Kendayatn, and they speak languages of the same name. They live primarily in the western districts of West Kalimantan. Some of the material in this section, however, specifically that on the practice of swidden cultivation, is generally true of various Dayak peoples around the island. Specific aspects of property rights may vary, but the differentiation of individual and group rights is true for virtually all of them. See also Dove 1985.

5 Much of this has changed since 1996 and the subsequent decentralization. A discussion of these changes is beyond the scope of this essay.

6 Again, these comments refer to the circumstances during the Suharto regime. For recent changes in these village property rights, see, for example, Wadley 2000.

7 See Peluso and Vandergeest 2001 for a systematic explanation of this colonial era process of creating state domains and carving forests out of these new state lands in the territories of what are today the nation-states of Indonesia, Malaysia, and Thailand.

8 The Outer Islands is a colonial category that refers to the territories under Netherlands East Indies control outside of Java, Madura, and Bali. The largest of these included the Borneo territories, Sumatra, and Sulawesi. The term is still used frequently in common parlance following indepen-

dence, for lack of a better way to refer collectively to Indonesian islands other than Java, Bali, and Madura.

9 The *Konfrontasi,* or Confrontation, took place from 1963 to 1966. Tens of thousands of troops were stationed in West Kalimantan, including in barracks located in the villages referred to in this essay, as well as on surrounding military bases. On Confrontation in general, see Mackie 1980. On the buildup in West Kalimantan see Peluso and Harwell 2001; Davidson and Kammen 2002.

10 Early on, provincial governors, district officers, and village leaders also allocated timber concessions, until the central government passed a law stating that territorial concessions could only be granted by the minister of forestry. On this early period, see Manning 1971. A recent dissertation by Obidzinsky 2003 gives further details.

11 On abstract space, see LeFebvre 1979; and Anderson 1991.

12 The history, property rights in, and meaning of durian trees are discussed in detail in Peluso 1986.

13 Indeed violent ethnic conflict did emerge in this region in 1996–97 and 1999, a situation at least partially attributable to new local territorialities.

K. Sivaramakrishnan

SCIENTIFIC FORESTRY AND

GENEAOLOGIES OF DEVELOPMENT

IN BENGAL

The scrubby sal (*Shorea robusta*) forests of Southwest Bengal have been resuscitated in the last two decades. Much of the credit for this dramatic transformation of the rugged landscape has justifiably been given to joint forest management (JFM) by the foresters, development experts, and villagers involved. But the gains of JFM have remained precarious. Conflict over its institutionalization has accompanied the spread of JFM to other parts of Bengal and the rest of India. One realm of contention has been the struggle around silvicultural aspects of microplanning.[1] Several development experts with many years of experience in promoting and evaluating JFM have noted the scant role of villagers in forest management decisions (Arora and Khare 1994, 10). Such failure to devolve decision making under JFM particularly afflicts matters silvicultural. Even as JFM becomes an icon of success among participatory forestry programs implemented in India and other "developing" countries around the world in the early twenty-first century, the silvicultural sciences on which it rests remain caught in paradigms from earlier times of "custodial" and industrial forestry.

In this essay, I will explore the production of this contested domain of silviculture in JFM and argue that it has been wrought in several histories—of ecology, politics, and scientific discourse.[2] I will therefore undertake a genealogy of the discourse of scientific forestry through the history of sal forest regeneration in colonial Bengal. Genealogy, as a historical ontology with particular reference to power, is used and illumined as a method in Foucault's *Discipline and Punish* (1979).[3] Genealogy allows us to historicize the production of scientific forestry as a discourse (a complex of ideas and social practices) through the analysis of colonial state building, for "the critical thrust of genealogy is simply to uncover power strategies involved in the genesis of power/knowledge relations in order to disturb the unitary, global form these take and reveal their historical and hence contingent character" (Cohen and Arato 1992, 292).

We are rightly cautioned that all genealogies are selective, but the concept is nonetheless vital and generative because it reminds us that all ideas ramify backward and at key historical moments they spread horizontally into their contemporary context (Appadurai 1988b, 40). Therefore, when analyzing the burgeoning JFM program as it spread across India's forests in the 1990s, we have to examine the relationship between this historical moment and one that occurred about one hundred years earlier, when scientific forestry similarly expanded across the subcontinent.

Scientific forestry was constructed in colonial Bengal by valorizing certain kinds of knowledge and thereby privileging attendant modes of forest management. The forms and patterns of rule that were established during the nineteenth century in India were shaped by the flow of information and the categories through which it was absorbed and transformed into what might be lumped together as colonial knowledge (Bayly 1993, 3–43). In this essay, I examine the formation of colonial knowledge (information, ideologies, perceptions, and the lessons of practical experience) in the realm of forest regeneration, which itself was part of a larger process through which managerial mentalities and institutions were formed. By focusing on policy formulation and implementation, as well as the relationship between enacted policy, outcomes and reforms, I wish to zoom in on the points of knowledge production, codification, and transmission. The last two procedures show us the ways in which knowledge is sought to be transformed into institutions of government,[4] illuminating the constant struggle in state building over supplanting, and/or using with modification, existing local structures of authority and government.[5]

By considering the conflicted and experimental ways in which sal silviculture was sought to be standardized in colonial working plans, my essay advances two arguments: first, that the scientific and technical discourse surrounding JFM is shaped by a historical legacy; and second, that such environmental development discourses are continuously under production through entanglement with debates about the locus of governance.[6] By historical legacy I refer not merely to a foreshadowing or sense of déjà vu but to a pattern of disputes about the disposition of knowledge and technical jurisdictions through which management regimes were generated. Management implies at once a technical and administrative universe of action. By defining technical jurisdictions, management impinges on rights and achieves an explicitly political aspect.

Through representations of the forest, definition of expertise, and manipulation of local structures of authority, colonial foresters created a body of knowledge about natural regeneration for sal forests in eastern India. They worked with, and sometimes against, the vanguard parties charged with establishing the colonial state on its frontiers. In Bengal, these frontiers were often the forested fringes of settled cultivation. Managerial knowledge was defined and the landscape partitioned by the colonial state into discrete jurisdictions, which were then subject to different modes of management.[7]

My discussion thus locates the history of scientific discourse in the related histories of politics and landscapes. A lot of the politics involved was internal to the forestry and larger colonial bureaucracy, but the unravelling of this politics is educative because it tells us about enduring mechanisms of state building. For the same reason, I am less concerned with drawing distinctions between local and foreign knowledge, and more interested in the production of knowledge in specific political-ecological-historical settings. In this essay the term local knowledge is used not to denote the distinct cultural categories of an indigenous people. I use this term in a manner that implies local knowledge is situated practice and, to that extent, is neither a system nor an alternative rationality.[8] I refer more to the intimate acquaintance with a locality, its landscape, and the social relations of production and environmental management that people develop as they work to change its appearance. Such special knowledge of a place and its spatial history is produced by those who traverse it intensively to make something of the place for their purposes.[9]

I am concerned with such localized production of information and the processes of translating it into standard terms that made possible a project such as scientific forestry. Historians and sociologists of science have frequently explored the ideological and intellectual processes in which particular branches of science developed.[10] I would suggest that such an approach pays insufficient attention to sites of application, that is, to places where these sciences become technological practices. The terrain of implementation leaves a strong impression on the production and transformation of scientific knowledge.[11] When these sites enter the processes of knowledge production in a specific domain such as forestry, they bring with them much else that is going on there. One of the important things that creeps into the generation of scientific knowledge is the issue of government.

This happens in at least two ways. First, forestry as land management becomes entangled in such wider issues of land administration as agriculture, revenue, and stable local arrangements of production. Second,

the pressure on forest departments to develop, standardize and dissemi-
nate universal and replicable scientific management models that mesh
with larger bureaucratic forms of government influences their selection
and codification of procedures. There is, then, a tension between fitting
forestry into a wider universe of managed landscapes of production and
identifying it as a distinct, separate, professionalized activity. The work
done under this tension suggests a constant production and transformation of science in its applications, often with the context being development. We need to track these changes.[12]

In *Representing and Intervening* (1983), Ian Hacking provided a landmark study that shifted the focus of scientific studies toward practice by
stressing the "doing" aspects of science as much as the representing. He
later emphasized the multiplicity, patchiness, and heterogeneity of the
space in which scientists work (1992). More research in the history of
science has moved in this direction of looking to the social to understand
the ways in which rules and practices shape each other (Pickering 1992).
The discussion of interests I have suggested allows us to understand how
the stabilization of science takes certain routes and not others as the
open-ended processes of experimentation unfold. But when scientists
continually explore their way out of a problem, with experience as their
guide, their interests intersect with ecological processes. As this essay
will discuss further, foresters were interested in growing sal in large
contiguous blocs along convenient conversion and transport networks
for timber. Their silvicultural options were soon limited to natural regeneration. Ecology here is itself a product of human preception and
intervention, not fully autonomous but not entirely imagined either. So
scientific forestry focused on devising silvicultural systems where concentrated natural regeneration of sal could easily be obtained. This condition of science as historical practice is what this essay wishes to explore
and illustrate using the case of forestry in Bengal.[13]

The institutionalization and professionalization of forest management
through its engagement with issues of governance, resource conservation, and enhanced productivity also brought scientific forestry into the
realm of emerging development discourse in the late nineteenth century.
It may be true that "we do not yet know enough about the global,
regional and especially local historical geographies of development — as
an idea, discipline, strategy or site of resistance — to say much with any
certainty about its complex past" (Crush 1995a, 8). We then need a
genealogy of development with which to trace the recurrence of ideas,
imagery, and tropes of development across a range of nineteenth- and
twentieth-century contexts. This may be found in the genealogy of spe-

cific elements such as scientific forestry, for it, too, works to produce the normalizing strategies of the modern state and the idea of irreducible difference between modern and premodern societies that characterize development.

FORESTRY AS SCIENCE AND PRACTICE:
A DEVELOPMENT REGIME

In 1884, Sir Dietrich Brandis, the first inspector general of Indian forests, drew a distinction between a modular science that could be transposed from the European laboratory, so to speak, into the Indian field site and a location-specific forest protection program in which local knowledge was the best asset of the forest guard (1884). But this neat division could not always be sustained in practice. Cultural operations were often crucially dependant on local ecological knowledge and understanding the social mechanisms by means of which scarce labor could be secured for silvicultural tasks. In performing the routines of forestry and through their sporting pursuits, forest officers assumed the mantle of authority and scientific expertise that became central to their functioning by the end of the nineteenth century.[14] But at the moment of translating silvicultural prescription into action in any coupe, compartment, or bloc, the mantle sometimes slipped, tugged away by a shift in the locus of necessary knowledge to reveal the precarious relationship between assumptions and practice. In the words of a novel written in 1909 and set in forested Bengal, "when it is time to work the forest, *burra sahib* will need Dulall to mark the trees, as no one can tell which can be cut" (Gouldsbury 1909, 243). These were the travails of moving from lumbering to forest regeneration, which meant that the Bengal Forest Department had to change from building a regime of restrictions around the forests to detailing a set of interventions in them.

Forestry, in this respect, was part of a wider process noticeable in the late nineteenth century when increasing intervention in agricultural production and its justification by appeal to a rhetoric of conservation went hand in hand.[15] Following the Famine Commission reports and the creation of an Agriculture Department in 1885, a new managerial assertiveness was discernible in the whole rural landscape of production.[16] The possibility of transforming the floral and crop composition of this landscape was perceived through the powerful lens of institutionalized science. As the conservator of Bengal put it, describing the Kurseong forests a few years before the first working plan in North Bengal was prepared, "we should here step in and assist nature . . . and by these means add greatly to the value of the estate."[17]

Working plans came to symbolize this confidence of the scientific forester. But visualizing a terrain where science could plan unimpeded the manipulation of the forest compelled a more complete enumeration and disposal of local rights that might obscure the vision. Forest settlements therefore became a necessary prerequisite, and where they could not be concluded working plans remained an ideal seldom realized. The lasting irony of the situation was that these plans aspired to define a universal code but their implementation was always caught up in securing and controlling local ecological and political knowledge.[18] The more working plans were reworked in an attempt to render them into modular prescriptions, the more their successive revisers became disconcertingly aware of specific regional ecological histories that slowed the drive to modularity. These paradoxes of working plans also reflect the ways in which forest management was caught up in a wider tension in colonial governance between central direction and local autonomy.

Forest administration emerged at a time when the colonial state (by 1880) had become a huge investor in India and was manned by a large and disciplined bureaucracy that conceived of itself as the custodian of public welfare.[19] This increased governance created a massive documentation project that has now been widely discussed in the literature.[20] As a result, to use David Ludden's words, "India's development regime evolved on coherent, consistent lines after 1870, the trend being towards more ramified and centralized state power" (1992b, 264). To a limited extent, this evolutionary view of the state centralization process is salient. In many ways, the postcolonial pattern of democratic socialism and centralized planning carried these tendencies further. To this, we must add the redefinition of *expertise* in terms of the high technology, complicated science, and environmental uncertainty that privileged metropolitan agency in the identification of environmental problems, outlining solutions and mooting federal legislation even while bringing into sharp relief local conflicts over resources.

We have also to remember that "the system inherited from colonial times was in many ways more decentralised than centralised. With the arrival of democratically elected governments . . . the balance was tilted heavily towards centralization" (Mukarji 1989, 468). The case of forestry seems to largely exemplify this wider finding. Therefore, JFM can be seen as an effort to regain the greater flexibility that existed in local government during colonial times. But the argument here is that JFM is fruitfully examined not as a break from tradition or the recovery of a temporarily abandoned approach but as the re-creation, through a process of engagement and modification, of a complex set of themes in governance that came to the fore in the late nineteenth century. The point is that we have to reevaluate epochal transitions in Indian historiography by looking closely at important, if attenuated, continuities in state building and the culture of politics.

Recently the questions of whether there was a sharp disjunction between colonial and precolonial forest policy and, if there was, when it occurred have been well discussed (R. Guha 1983, 1989; Grove 1993, 1995; Rangarajan 1994; Skaria 1998; S. Guha 1995a). There were apparent continuities between precolonial and colonial states, notably in forest destruction and monopolization of valuable forest resources. The differences can be seen in ideologies and concomitant technologies rule. Arguably, British forest policy as it emerged after 1858, when India was formally integrated into the empire, bore the stamp of forest regulation and management that had been carried on in different provinces as they came under East India Company rule.[21] Systematic forestry could only commence after the stabilization of British rule in the aftermath of the uprising of 1857 (Stebbing 1923, 2:4).[22] In Bengal, many of the areas that would become reserved forests came under British control only by the 1860s.[23] In other conquered areas, the flow of detailed information about the landscape and people also only thickened in the latter part of the nineteenth century (Ball 1880; Hooker 1854; Waddell 1899; Forsyth 1889; Hunter 1868; Balfour 1862; Anonymous 1853; Jackson and Ricketts 1854; Jackson 1854; Lewin 1869). It is in this sense that the late nineteenth century is particularly significant for major aspects of the genealogy we would seek for scientific forestry as development discourse.

Crafted in this expanding world of empire and information, the development regime for sal forests in Bengal began to take the shape that is discernible in contemporary JFM during the period from 1893 to 1937 when political consolidation converged with technocratic assertion. This essay, confined as it is to the latter process, necessarily dwells on the way in which expertise in forest management was defined by different elements in the colonial state in which it was seen to repose and on how it was deployed. The natural regeneration of sal, the most valued tree in Bengal forests, became an elusive goal for scientific forestry by the end of the colonial period, despite a tremendous research effort. During those frustrating years, the production of detailed reports, compendia, manuals, calendars, agricultural censuses, and of course working plans created a textual basis for fixing and transferring expertise.[24] Such textualization in agriculture was a managerial act that established an instrumental attitude toward farming. From a situation in which farm practice was expertise, peasant wisdom was moved to the category of folklore even as it was appropriated and transmogrified into the scientific format of statistical tables or maps and reports (Ludden 1992a, 270).[25] Similar things happened in forestry.

The mechanisms that categorized expertise and directed the forms in which it would be deployed gave control over technologies of improvement to different agencies of the state and made official research the sole arbiter of what constituted progressive innovation. Thus, even in a scheme based on natural regeneration the Forest Department assumed that it would define the scientific modes of such regeneration and hence took upon itself the task of training people in the apparently simple task of protection, enhancement, and release of woody growth. This powerful legacy in sal silviculture has been carried through into the working of JFM in Bengal today, even though there has been no recent research on natural regeneration and the colonial experience in the matter was never satisfactory.

Offering a general explanation of such processes and an agenda for their analysis, Arturo Escobar says that "the demarcation of fields and their assignment to experts . . . is a significant feature of the rise and consolidation of the modern state. What should be emphasised however is how institutions utilize a set of practices in the construction of their problems through which they control policy themes, enforce exclusions and affect social relations" (Escobar 1988, 435).[26] But the "modern state" was not the steamroller projected here. If we look closely within the broad contours provided by Ecobar's framework, we find that the constitution of expertise was always conditioned by the exigencies of particular contexts. Realized at an uneven pace and in diverse forms, the processes identified by Escobar were constituted through significant regional variations in Bengal.

The emergence of scientific forestry and rational management in late-nineteenth-century Bengal is then best analyzed as a product not only of intellectual revolutions and transformations in the organization of knowledge in Europe but of the practical circumstances of controlling land and labor and manipulating tree species that became valuable at different points in the history of forest management in India.[27] However, assigning knowledge or material conditions the determining role in policy is likely to prove unsatisfactory. Representations are intimately connected to the production of knowledge and thereby its codification in government into legal and policy instruments. At the same time, law and policy as instruments of power are shaped not only by this knowledge but by practice and experience.[28] The British administrators engaged in framing forest policy clearly brought with them ideas about what was appropriate from their European experience, but they also encountered and described a pattern of forest use that they displaced only partially after disparaging it. Grounded thus in regional histories of conquest and ecology, forest management still emerged as a development regime. That is why we have to see how "a corpus of knowledge, techniques and scientific discourses is formed and becomes entangled with the practice of power" (Foucault 1979, 23).

Prefigured by an unprecedented territorialization of forest control after 1860, codified information, standard techniques, and rigorous management became central to scientific forestry through a recognition that these had not been attempted in the past by native states.[29] Reconsidering the nature of state formation in medieval and early modern India, historians are concluding that precolonial states in India had little control over production and distribution and that what they did have came through social intermediation largely unregulated by "the state." Precolonial political culture produced multiple overlapping levels and arenas of authority more than centralized states. Even the Mughal state was more patrimonial than bureaucratic, and its centralization was more ideological than operative (Ludden 1992b, 266; Subrahmanyam 1992, 291–322).

The British colonial process of state building in India regarded traditional society as something to be both reformed and preserved so as to retain elements of social hierarchy and stability that would facilitate governance, but at the same time it intervened freely in the agrarian economy by treating it as an autonomous domain open to progressive action (Bayly 1990; Washbrook 1981).

The development of forest management and silviculture in the mixed deciduous forests of Bengal fits within the broad scheme of domination that was put in place in the nineteenth century. There is growing evidence that no previous ruler had such a sustained policy of intrusive exploitation or regulation of forested tracts.[30]

An allied feature that converged with the processes of state formation briefly outlined above was the urban bias in determining forest value and use. Forest science flourished where central states began to rationalize administration, as in eighteenth-century Germany and later in France. This process narrowed the focus of management on wood. As one historian of German forestry notes, "identifying wood mass as the crucial variable of forestry set the stage for quantitative forest management"

(Lowood 1990, 326). As the measures of wood mass and volume were perfected, the urge to grow an accurately measurable forest increased. But the measurable forest needed more accurate estimation also because its principal products, greatly reduced in diversity, participated in world markets. Plantations of valuable trees were created through an impressive network that supplied seeds and planting material across continents.

But initially forest conservancy in Bengal, as in the rest of India, commenced with the urge to directly control, systematize, and regulate the extraction of timber from what was perceived as the rapidly dwindling hardwood forest wealth of the subcontinent. The rhetoric of conservancy espoused both the "environmental" tones of watershed management, species conservation, and wildlife protection and the strident political-economic realities of territorial expansion, the establishment of British rule in strategic regions, and development of the infrastructure for administering empire.[31] While both strains of conservancy ultimately facilitated the disempowerment of local communities in the forests and expedited capital accumulation through forest exploitation, they created in their discordances interstitial spaces for the modulation of forest policy.

Protection, reservation, extraction, and marketing of timber were gradually followed by a growing interest in regeneration, particularly by natural methods, of the principal timber species, which were teak and sal. The period broadly coinciding with the first three decades of the twentieth century witnessed burgeoning research on silvics and the structural qualities of many hardwoods and a few softwoods such as *Pinus longifolia* (Champion 1975; Rodger 1925). Such research and the dissemination of intensive silvicultural systems through working plans were complementary aspects of scientific forestry that placed new demands on forest management. There was a conflicted expansion of knowledge and a contested growth of managerial arrangements through which scientific forestry was professionalized and institutionalized in the sal forests of Bengal.

The rest of this essay will therefore consider certain programmatic aspects of scientific forestry that illuminate its constitution through demarcation, inventory, protection, regeneration, working plans, and silviculture. In particular, I will take up the vicissitudes of preparing and implementing working plans, and the concomitant reduction of forestry to silvicultural models, to illustrate the two main features through which scientific forestry developed. The first, which can be called *management by demarcation and exclusion,* aimed at simplifying land use in state forests by regulating local access. The second, which can be called *man-*

agement by inventory and controlled regeneration, complicated the earlier regulation of people with the added regulation and transformation of tree growth. In combination, these types of managerial aspirations sought to move the locus of expertise and direction up and out into the higher echelons of the forest service. At their most ambitious, working plans were to serve as powerful instruments that would permit the inspector general of forests to dictate which trees were to be grown where and how and when they would be harvested. Through the cases of working plan preparation and the tentative, often baffled, silviculture they document, the following sections evaluate the making and unmaking of scientific forestry against the standard of this grand ideal.

WORKING PLANS AS INSTRUMENTS OF REMOTE CONTROL

The first, albeit simple, working plan in India was introduced by Munro, who was superintendent of Travancore forests in 1837. This was largely an exercise in the enumeration of trees by size and thus an estimate of the harvestible timber in any year. Linear surveys introduced by Brandis in the 1870s to estimate the growing stock were the basis of early working plans. In 1874, Schlich drew up a preliminary working plan for the Buxa reserve, where the problem of water in the dry season had necessitated reconsideration of timber conversion and removal operations (Stebbing 1926, 3: 199; Bengal Forest Administration Report 1875–76; Hatt 1905, 5).[32] But progress was slow, and by 1884–85 only 109 square miles of reserves were being administered under regularly sanctioned working plans. In 1884, Schlich centralized in the office of the inspector general of forests the control and preparation of working plans. This hastened things somewhat, and by 1899 twenty thousand square miles of government forests were covered by working plans, of which nineteen hundred were in Bengal (Stebbing 1923 2:592–98).

Local governments were to use the working plan as an instrument that would balance the "reasonable requirements of neighbouring populations" with the "exigencies of sound forest conservancy." Forest settlements that would ascertain and finally record all admissible rights of village communities and private persons in forest lands and their products were introduced as a necessary corollary of working plans.[33] The plans themselves were declared to be the most important job of the forest officer, as the forest department quickly recognized them as the key to professional continuity in forest management.[34] Struggles to perfect these plans reflect the transformation of forest management into predominantly a scientific issue. But such recasting of the terms of argument did not necessarily alter the elements that were the subject of contention. A stable silvicultural system and the locus of its governance remained the most pressing issues.

There are many definitions of working plans, but their most important feature was the effort to reduce control into a matter of holding local agencies to plan prescriptions. As one of the last colonial inspectors general of forests wrote, "a working plan is a forecasted framework for the management of a forest over a considerable period, often 120 years, with a detailed plan of what to do in the next 10–15 years to achieve the ultimate result."[35] These working plans were seen as restoring normalcy to the state forests, which would consist of normal age classes, normal increase, and normal growing stock in compartments, blocs, and coupes (Schlich 1876, 104–7). The object of the plan was often limited to showing the quantum of timber and firewood that could be removed without detriment to a continuous output and what works of improvement were desirable.[36] These plans were not, however, introduced as soon as a forest was taken over or reserved.

For any forest area, the initial decade after its reservation was one of limited forest management. Operations were confined to forest protection, selection, and improvement felling; creeper cutting to release advance growth; and conversion of sapling sal into timber. In Bengal, the general pattern was one in which reservation mostly took place in the 1880s, initiation of planning in the 1890s, and approval of short-term (ten- to twenty-year) plans in the period 1900–1910. During this period, nontimber products such as bamboo, grazing fees, lac, and *mahua* flowers in Southwest Bengal were seen as a significant component of forest revenues.[37] Quite often the working plan for a particular division was taken up when competing demands grew, such as the spread of tea gardens in Darjeeling District, which caused a sharp increase in the demand for firewood.[38]

Within twenty years of preparing the first working plans in North Bengal, however, the systems of management prescribed under them came under a cloud, as they were not yielding the desired regeneration of sal. The inspector general of forests, after inspecting the Jalpaiguri and Buxa forest divisions, observed that the "forest conditions in Bengal were more diverse than any other province and with more intensive methods of management plans must be revised more frequently."[39] Yet the revision to the Jalpaiguri plan simplified the landscape classification of its predecessor from eight to four—sal, mixed, evergreen, and savannah.[40] Seeking to control these revisions, the inspector general of forests deputed the imperial superintendent of working plans to collect "necessary local knowledge" from Bengal. The state government refused to organize the tour, suggesting that it would impair service discipline and arguing further that providing local knowledge was the task of the regional government, since such knowledge pertained to the demand and supply of timber and the extraction facilities available.

The real argument soon narrowed to the silvicultural prescriptions. While the inspector general of forests was perturbed that Bengal was adopting annual plans of operation that smacked of a lack of professionalism, the Bengal conservator was adamant that these were appropriate, as "through silvicultural control centralised control of forest management can go too far."[41] This official went on to forcefully present the case for granting local officers full freedom to experiment with various silvicultural techniques, as working plans should not be cluttered with prescriptions not justified by the poor levels of local knowledge.[42] The outcome was a curtailed tour by the imperial superintendent of working plans. The controversy admirably illustrates the way in which planning and professionalization, valorized by scientific forestry, repeatedly became the issues around which more important disputes about regional autonomy and central control in forest management were reenacted.

Let us take another example. The first Singhbhum working plan was prepared in 1903. By this time, there were several plans already in operation, or in advanced stages of preparation, for different North Bengal areas.[43] These plans came up for revision, often prior to the end of their initial duration. At that time, the changes made in the plan usually incorporated the practical deviations that had been carried out and sometimes noticed in the annual reports. In Singhbhum, for instance, the plan had been to continue selective felling of sal timber from a 32 square mile area of good valley-type forests, half of which had been taken out in 1895–98 to supply sleepers for the East India Railway. For the rest of the 693 square miles of reserves in Singhhum, the plan called for fire protection for sal regeneration, something that had already covered 64 percent of the reserves, up from a mere 12 percent in 1895.[44] At the time, the projected revenue from timber operations (major products) was expected to exceed that from *sabai* grass (a minor product) sales.[45] But the inspector general of forests ruled in 1915 that the poorer quality hill forests, being of little value in the production of timber, should be given up to sabai grass production. This would entail burning the forest floor and creating large blocs for the production of sabai grass.[46] At the same time, with the introduction of concentrated regeneration blocs, the working plan was also to be revised to include a regular engineering scheme covering the

Scientific Forestry and Development   265

extraction, conversion, and transport of timber. The elaboration of such a scheme hinged on the prior completion of procedures alloting specific areas to blocs and determining a sequence of coupes in the first bloc. Mechanized timber extraction hinged on a prior reorganization of silvicultural practice and thus a reordering of the landscape into more systematic and compact blocs of evenly aged tree crops.[47] As management became more intensive, Singhbhum was divided into Saranda, Kolhan, Porahat, and Chaibassa, with separate plans for each division, by 1925. The uniform system, under which partial clear-cutting had been prescribed, was introduced under all these plans. But the monopoly contractor for timber, the Bengal Timber Trading Company, was mostly in arrears in its cutting, thereby largely keeping prescriptions at bay (Stebbing 1926, 3:254).

During the same period, the inspector general of forests and a silviculturist visiting Jalpaiguri and Buxa had also recommended taking up artificial regeneration since the evergreen undergrowth in fire-protected natural regeneration areas was suppressing sal.[48] Three hundred acres of experimental sowings of sal and fifty acres of other species annually were approved as deviations from the working plans in 1917. The revision of working plans paid great attention to problems of regeneration. Removal and exploitation of both major and minor products remained under a regime of permits and concessions to contractors. Shaw Wallace and Company, for instance, had the monopoly for collecting nettle fiber from the reserved forests of Darjeeling, while Burn and Company had the timber and bamboo concessions in the Darjeeling and Jalpaiguri forests.[49]

The significant patterns that emerge in working plan revisions are revealed by the case of the Darjeeling plan, which was altered several times in the space of thirty years. Darjeeling forests ranged in elevation from 12,000 feet above sea level in Singalila to 600 feet in the Teesta Valley. The ground was steep, with deep gorges and rapid mountain torrents. Hill and valley forests covered an area of 115 square miles.[50] The upper hill forests (above 9,000 feet) were mainly silver fir and rhododendron. The middle hills (5,000 to 9,000 feet) chiefly contained oak, walnut, toon, laurel, maple, champ, and alnus. Sal was found in the valley forests (600 to 3,000 feet).[51] The middle and upper hill forests had been worked departmentally for three years beginning in 1865 and then under the permit system till they came under Manson's plan of 1892.[52]

This plan prescribed a 160-year rotation in five 32-year periods, with the first and last bloc closed to grazing. The first bloc was to be regenerated by means of concentrated felling over one-sixteenth of the area annually under the shelter wood system. Soon after the introduction of the plan, a summary forest settlement extinguished private rights in all the forests.[53] Osmaston revised this plan in 1902, and shelter wood was removed in all the ten original coupes, but no new regeneration felling was undertaken. Due to inadequate removal of overwood under the Manson plan, plantings had failed to become established (Government of Bengal 1935, 29).

In 1912, Grieve's plan was introduced to avoid a second felling such as the one that had destroyed much of the regeneration following the first felling. He excluded all areas open to grazing, put all regenerated areas under a plantation working circle, and divided the rest of the forest into high and coppice working circles. We can see the emerging separation of the managed forest into discrete compartments subject to distinct treatments. More significantly, a clear separation came to mark forests open to grazing and those managed for the production of fuel wood and timber. The plan proposed selected felling in groups, relying on natural regeneration after mature stems had been removed. In areas open to grazing, regeneration was assumed to be impossible, and so green felling was confined to the closed areas, from which all stems over two feet in diameter would be removed in 50 years. Overruling the local officers, the inspector general of forests changed this plan to one of regeneration felling in groups, which would remove all first- and second-class trees from closed areas in 50 years and would rely on open forests and plantations to yield products for the second and third 50-year periods in the 150-year rotation.[54]

In 1920, the plan was revised again. The failure of natural regeneration and crop improvement methods had led to the adoption of taungya cultivation of sal. Clear-cutting and taungya sowings remained the prescriptions in later working plan revisions in North Bengal sal forests of the Duars, although in some cases, as in Buxa, the division of the regeneration areas into sal conversion and softwood working circles brought various blocs under rotations of different durations.[55]

Table 1 shows the slow progress made in the preparation of working plans in the nineteenth century. By 1920, while coverage had increased, working plans still only covered half the notified forest areas of Bengal, the reason in part being the frequent revisions undertaken in existing plans, which kept designated officers from covering new areas.[56] But even where plans were prepared and closely supervised, for which Bengal appointed a full time silviculturist, their translation into forest management was poor. The inspector general of forests, touring Bengal in 1936, was constrained to remark that the situation in sal divisions was

TABLE I. Forest Survey and Working Plan Coverage in Bengal Divisions by 1900 (in sq mi)

Division	Surveyed	Not Surveyed	Working Plan	No Plan
Darjeeling		114	38	76
Tista		212	212	
Kurseong		109.5		109.5
Jalpaiguri	183		183	
Buxa	309			309
Palamau		268		268
Santhal Parganas		1,435		435
Hazaribagh		90		90
Singhbhum		1,247		1,247
Sundarbans		4,174	4,174	
Chittagong		1,523		1,523
Angul		251		251
Puri		401		401

Source: Adapted from information provided in Ribbentrop 1900.

not satisfactory, plantation work was behind prescription, and mortality was increasing, while in areas where artificial regeneration had failed there was no alternative in sight.

His words echoed, in the frustration expressed about securing sal regeneration, the report of the sal management tour led by Herbert Champion a few years earlier, who had documented the large variety of localized problems being faced in devising standard silvicutural systems for sal forests.[57] Some of the problems were created by the frequent revisions of working plans when prescribed rotations proved to be insufficient to raise timber-quality trees or exotics such as cryptomeria were declared to be unsuitable as firewood. While the Finance Department found these changes indicative of hasty and incomplete planning, the foresters began to justify the revisions as central to scientific management.[58] Separate regeneration experiments were also introduced for hill sal, Upper Bhabhar sal, Lower Bhabhar sal, Terai sal, and coppice sal in Southwest Bengal. In Jalpaiguri in 1936 research had begun on the effects of controlled burning on the regeneration of *khair* and *sissoo*.[59]

Recognizing the local peculiarities of conditions of sal regeneration and a few other desired species certainly undermined the centralizing expertise claims of the working plans and hindered their use as instruments of control by the inspector general of forests. But there were advantages, and the benefits gained from working plans were sometimes of a different nature. As the inspector general of forests noted in 1942, working plans had become more exact and scientific with increased intensity of management but chiefly in terms of superior surveillance and estimation of growing stock or merchantable timber. He observed that "those parts of India which have the best arrangements for working plans and the best control are just those parts which are providing the most supplies . . . because they know what they have and where it is."[60]

The overall pattern that emerged under the working plans placed better-quality forests under conversion to the uniform system, with a rotation or conversion period of sixty to one hundred years. Three or four blocs were formed with roughly equal areas of teak and sal. The area allotted to the first bloc was regenerated with shelter woods, while selected felling and thinning was continued in the third and fourth blocs. Forests deemed to be of poorer quality were placed under a coppice working circle to produce small timber and firewood on a thirty to forty year rotation.[61] As will become more apparent in the following section, by making conversion to the uniform system the ultimate aspiration of any working plan, the entire forest management regime in Bengal was placed on a scale of approximation to scientific forestry with very little being close to the top of the scale. This served both as a powerful incentive to achieve the ideal and as a way of accommodating deviations and distortions.

SILVICULTURAL MODELS AND ELUSIVE PARTICULARITIES

From the beginning, natural regeneration was the favored method of crop development, and for this purpose Brandis favored the training of recruits to the Indian Forest Service in Europe, where this method was successfully used for high-volume timber production (Stebbing 1922–62, 2:47). This was not by any means a recent innovation since natural regeneration through coppice for fuel wood and selected felling for timber had emerged by the fourteenth century as standard forestry practices (Fernow 1907, 38). The main crop improvement activities were creeper cutting and improvement felling. Cleanliness of crops (absence of creepers) became a measure of whether foresters and guards were working hard on their beats. The main idea underlying improvement felling was to "favor the valuable species and eliminate the less valuable and those interfering with the growth of the former."[62]

Subsidiary work would encourage the younger classes by removing the weeds and low growth that choked them and would lighten the cover overhead by girdling or removing inferior species of trees. Thinning aimed to achieve similar ends of improving light for valuable species regeneration and producing evenly aged crops.[63] Experienced foresters often confessed to their diaries that it was far from an exact science, yet for each species a model forest was envisioned through thinning alone.[64] Table 2 shows what a model sal forest would consist of in Bengal.

The ideal was light and frequent thinning, but lack of men and money made this unattainable in Bengal, where rapid forest growth made underthinning the main problem (Homfray 1936, 4–6). The chief purpose of thinning was to attain the largest possible timber trees per acre, with straight, well-formed boles, an ideal as aesthetic as it was commercial. Noting the reluctance of marking officers to take out trees of large girth that were forked or crooked, Homfray wrote, "it cannot be too carefully impressed on thinning officers that the chief point about the tree is its shape and not its site" (9).[65] Work progressed better where valued species appeared in unmixed stands, a condition that crop improvement aspired to create, imitate, or stimulate. But by 1915 prescriptions for intensification in sal management included moving into the regeneration bloc system, and here crop improvement was introduced into every felling series on a continuous basis as improvement felling became a management practice in forests of all age classes instead of a forest-harvesting technique allied with selected felling.[66]

By 1925, selection and improvement fellings were being replaced in Bengal with concentrated regeneration under taungya or various coppice systems, aspiring to the shelter wood compartments or unifom system. But, except for North Bengal taungyas, where clear-cutting and artificial regeneration were essential to securing sal growth, the transition remained mostly an ideal. Progress toward the ideal was interrupted by wars, which increased timber demands in sharp spikes; recurrent labor problems; and financial stringencies. But the most significant thing about incomplete, unattained, and constantly revised working plans and silvicultural arrangements was the repudiation by local governments of central direction and control after a point. Typically, the local officials would emphasize the need for short-term and revisable schemes that were transformed gradually into long-term plans. Such rejection or resistance, which challenged notions of absolute expertise residing at the center, emerged as part of the development regime in the forests of Bengal.

TABLE 2. The Model Sal Forest in Bengal

Age (years)	Number of Dominant Stems per Acre after Thinning	Average Height of Dominant Stems in Feet
5	1,450	20
6	1,200	24
7	1,000	27
8	850	30
9	650	34
10	550	38
15	330	56
20	240	72
25	190	83
30	150	92

Source: Compiled from information in Homfray 1936, 30.

Changes in silvicultural practices necessitated the modification of all access rules of production and forest protection. With the shift to regeneration by blocs, which was considered permanent, provisional arrangements such as selection and improvement felling were displaced, and this change required closing protected forests for longer periods (twenty to thirty years).[67] As closer attention was paid to tree crops that maximized valuable species in evenly aged stands, concomitant changes in silvicultural practice altered labor requirements. Subordinate departmental employees skilled in the organization of tasks such as thinning and cleaning became necessary and were sought through the pool of trained personnel recruited at the Kurseong Forest School.[68] Silvicultural tasks such as thinning always posed a challenge when the benefits of scientific prescription were realized only through local and intimate knowledge of the managed forest. This displaced the balance of expertise down the forester hierarchy, making the guards and rangers key personnel in identifying trees to be marked or determining the intensity of thinning in any season.[69] Periodic thinning thus became not only a management operation but the performative moment when expertise, like ritual knowledge, was passed on to younger generations of specialists in the making.

Prior to 1910, all the sal forests in Bengal were worked under the selection method with some improvement felling, a system necessitated

TABLE 3. Silviculture Systems in Late Colonial Bengal Forestry (in sq mi)

Systems / Year	1926–27	1936–37	1943–44
Clear-cutting	1,033	591	637
Selection and improvement	1,061	5,199	4,234
Coppice	33	47	131
Unregulated and protection	4,674	947	1,062
Total	6,801	6,784	6,064

Source: Adapted from figures provided in Stebbing 1922–62, 4:293.

by the supply of large sal trees being scant and dispersed through the forests (McIntire 1909, 6).[70] In the decade following World War I, radical changes were introduced in the silviculture of sal. By the late 1920s, Shebbeare, the conservator of forests in Bengal, who fifteen years earlier had pioneered taungya experiments in sal in North Bengal, could report that taungya had become the single most important means of regenerating sal forests. Taungya was a method of raising pure plantations that was labor intensive and required land preparation by means of clear-cutting and the firing of scrub. But the advantage was that the outcome was easily managed for timber. Taungya working plans were simple. They prescribed clear-cutting and restocking $1r$ of the total area every year, where r was the length of rotation, usually eighty years.[71] One consequence of taungya and the switch to concentrated regeneration of any other sort was that trees such as mahua, which were valued mainly for their nontimber forest product yields to villagers, were also removed under silvicultural prescriptions. Under earlier selection systems, they were left alone in recognition of their utility for local people.

During 1926–39, most sal forests were brought under the uniform system, but within the next ten years this was given up, as it was found that natural regeneration of sal could not be obtained through canopy manipulation (Stebbing 1922–62, 4:84–86).[72] As the sal study tour report had noted, the conversion to the uniform system was predicated on the belief that regeneration de novo could be established in sal forests through the management of edaphic and light factors. But the highly mixed results had revealed that success was limited to regions with existing adequate advance growth, which was "due to the past history of the forest, not the purposeful action of the forest officer" (Anonymous 1934; Smythies 1940, 193–99; Warren 1940, 334–40; Raynor 1940, 525–29;

Warren 1941, 116–23; De 1941, 283–91; Griffith and Gupta 1948). Ironically, this was a condition that could only obtain under conditions not subject to the criteria of scientific management, namely, financial prudence and standardized silviculture. Field foresters in the late 1920s were finding that sal seedlings became established in situations of varying light that were possible only under an uneven aged canopy. Felling to simulate these conditions would be uneconomical and would violate the ideal of concentrated regeneration blocs (Osmaston 1929). Conversion to the uniform system had failed on several counts. First, preparatory felling did not induce regeneration; second, final removal of overwood damaged established crops; third, the debris from concentrated felling posed a pest and fire hazard; and, fourth, in damp areas weeds became rampant (643).

While Osmaston recommended giving up concentrated regeneration for a revised group selection system, he also stressed the importance of an understory of *Mallotus phillipinensis*, *Woodfordia floribunda*, *Wendlandia tinctora*, and *Indigofera pulchella* to minimize canopy drip and suppress grass (648–54). Another forester noted the damage to sal from deer, which had increased with the depletion of their predator carnivors, hunted as vermin, and the reduction of inedible shrubs in the regeneration areas, making sal and important associates such as *Haldu adina cordifolia* more vulnerable, as deer quickly learned to prefer areas in the forest exclusively stocked with plants palatable to them (Smythies 1929, 514–15).

Thus, by the 1930s the debate on sal regeneration had systematically brought into question every foundational aspect of scientific forestry posited over the previous fifty years. The blanket exclusion of fire and grazing in regeneration areas; the distinction between valuable and valueless trees and efforts to eliminate the latter to maximize the former; the aesthetic and managerial ideal of the model forest consisting of evenly aged, orderly stands of desired trees; and the possibility of laying down plans that would prescribe treatments and procedures for 80 to 150 years on the basis of conjured models — all this and more had become suspect.[73]

From different sites, a consensus on mixed overwoods and intermediate story vegetation was developing, but its composition and treatment defied generalization (Osmaston 1929; Chaturvedi 1931; Davis 1931; Stracey 1931). That sal needed a mixed canopy of trees and shrubs of all heights became increasingly clear. The crop itself should preferably be irregular, interspersed with associates and under an undulating broken canopy (Anonymous 1934, 4–5). Seedlings germinated better under mixed cover than one of pure sal, as this was lighter, leaves from such a canopy degenerated more easily after falling, and a mixed canopy suppressed weeds without suppressing sal (Davis 1944, 1948).

Thus did the uniform system come under critical scrutiny. On the eve of World War II, the national silvicultural conference was still calling for research on sal regeneration and the problems of pure teak plantations, pointing to the enduring problems in the silviculture of the two most valued species of Indian forests.[74] The same issues were revived as Indian foresters convened for sal and teak regeneration planning after India's first post-Independence national forest policy was announced in 1952. In short, scientific forestry remained a development discourse under production.

DEVELOPMENT REGIMES AND HISTORICAL PROCESSES

Forest guards — often assigned to lead tricky silvicultural operations on their beat — mahouts, and the toils of the field forester all generated information that was schematized to develop scientific forestry in Bengal as a complex of knowledge and technologies of power.[75] In this way, they contributed to processes that redefined forest conservancy and provided it with several distinct elements: a clear delimitation of its domain — *demarcation;* identification of indigenous vegetation and its valuation — *inventory;* enumerating, simplifying, and circumscribing the bundle of usufructuary and other rights of local people — *reservation/protection;* devising a scheme of management that would produce the most desirable woods in the quickest time — *regeneration/plantation;* and formalizing the arrangements through codes, manuals, and the division of responsibility among forestry officials in order to ensure the establishment of routines — *working plan.* These elements were and remain crucial to the definition of scientific expertise and the privileging of its role in forest management, but they also contain traces of what has now widely come to be called development discourse.[76]

I am not speaking of development here as a received doctrine or cultural schema.[77] Dogged by uncertainty, conflict within its agencies, and attritional resistance from the local political configurations that it had sought to co-opt, scientific forestry remained a discourse continually under production. I have argued, therefore, that historicizing such discourse is a basic task that has to be undertaken before studying its effects. One benefit of such an approach is that "by tracking development historically, one can appreciate the complex origins of what came to be the unitary meaning of development that seemed to surface in the late colonial period in and around the second world war" (Watts 1995, 49). I have further suggested that identifying the locus of production for any particular variant of a discourse should be integral to any such historical inquiry. The constellations of debates and expertise that surrounded scientific forestry one hundred years ago remain salient through the forest management institutions that emerged then and exist today, hence the importance of a historical approach that takes us into the making and unmaking of colonial science as a development regime.

In the latter part of the nineteenth century, changes were made with the introduction of formal forest management, the elaboration of a system of scientific forestry, and finally the assertion of a strongly centralizing state forestry regime that encompassed production of large volumes of timber, other forest revenues, and the conservation of the environment. In the early decades of the twentieth century, while nation building and conservation came to dominate the rhetoric of governance, the idea of development being the legitimate mission of the national state was continually reinvented. The several transformations of this idea and the force it exercised on forest management bind the past and the present together. The discourse of development has a long history, then, precisely because it is not a received doctrine.[78] This essay is an effort to demonstrate its continuous production and negotiation through processes of state building in the forests of Bengal spanning the colonial and entering the postcolonial period.

At the same time, despite a fairly draconian law that itself came out of heated debate within the colonial state, forest management as practice remained enmeshed within the wider world of agrarian production relations; hence rules, policy resolutions, and working plans frequently created a discordance between grand designs and particular contexts that made room for negotiation. Through this pragmatic resolution — allowing decentralization, greater rights, and responsibilities at the local level — developmentalist states have passed on, or been made to concede, greater power and flexibility to petty officialdom, rural elites, and forest users in various forest management regimes. Hence it is possible to say, without consolidating the colonial state in any particular way, that there emerged a development regime that held within it a tension between central authority and local control over natural resources. That tension was carried over many epochal divides to remain with us in the current debates about JFM.

In this essay, I have focused on scientific forestry as it was created in colonial Bengal through the strategies designed for forest regeneration, in particular the management of silviculture and the preparation of working plans. The reason for doing so is that JFM is a field full of arguments about these very elements of scientific forestry. But there are important differences that suggest that colonial discourse is both re-created and refashioned in contemporary politics.

As laid out, the argument advanced here recognizes that recent scholarship on development, like that of Arturo Escobar, acknowledges a comparability between colonial discourse and development. James Ferguson does the same with notions of improvement, conservation, and development. Yet both of these powerful analysts of development firmly locate the production of a distinct development discourse in the decolonization period after 1945 and in the corridors of Western development agencies, principally the World Bank (Ferguson 1994, 67–68; Escobar 1995a, 9, 23).[79] They also focus on the effects of development discourse working as a system of knowledges. They conform thus to the currently dominant mode of analysis in which development is treated as a schematic representation of the Third World and thereby the agent of certain political consequences, including those whereby local "targeted populations" absorb and manipulate the discourses of development (Appfel-Marglin and Marglin 1990; Dubois 1991; Parajuli 1991; Esteva 1992).[80] In contrast, I propose a deeper genealogy for development in general and suggest that the particular case of conservation and development, or the management of natural resources on the fringes of development, reveals a conflicted and contested production of development discourse.

Scientific forestry, with its focus on the efficient and systematic production of timber in the "public interest," clearly enunciated the productionist agendas that we take as having characterized developmentalist state policies in the twentieth century. On the other hand, the authors and propagators of scientific forestry launched a sustained critique of shifting cultivation, deplored private forest management, and inquired into the relations between deforestation and desiccation. This aspect of their work helped formulate the discourse of conservation so carefully identified and traced back to the seventeenth century in *Green Imperialism* (Grove 1995). I am suggesting that by conflating conservation with colonialism's civilizing mission by the end of the nineteenth century, scientific forestry took on another important feature of development discourse — the notion of progress. Emerging thus as a development regime, colonial scientific forestry became a complex of changing institutions and ideas informing postcolonial forestry.

But my purpose here is not only to suggest the importance of a colonial prehistory or genealogy to any notion of modern development. I have also demonstrated, through a discussion of the making and unmaking of scientific forestry in Bengal, the constructed quality of development discourse and revealed its distinctive production in particular locations. Thus, my analysis seeks to critique and move beyond recent poststructuralist anthropology of the development concept.[81] In outlining this critique, I have suggested that we must constantly question whatever is presented as "natural," inherently systematic, or uniformly powerful, and see it in the light of its historical production.[82] The analysis of production is important because it illuminates the everyday practices and procedures through which discourses become visible in historical contexts. What this essay has done is to identify a repertoire of procedures that crystallized in the colonial regime and have become the politically charged resource for contemporary forest management debates in Bengal.

ACKNOWLEDGMENTS

The research on which this essay is based was carried out as part of a larger project entitled Revising Laws of the Jungle: Changing Peasant-State Relations in the Forests of Bengal. The research was assisted by a grant from the Joint Committee on South Asia of the Social Science Research Council and the American Council of Learned Societies with funds provided by the Andrew W. Mellon Foundation and the Ford Foundation. Financial support for this project was also provided by the Wenner-Gren Foundation for Anthropological Research, New York; the Center for International and Area Studies, Yale University; and the Program in Agrarian Studies, Yale University. I thank Mark Ashton, Indrani Chatterjee, John Cinnamon, Renald Clerisme, Susan Darlington, Margaret Everett, Vinay Gidwani, Ramachandra Guha, Sumit Guha, William Kelly, David Ludden, Patricia Mathews, Nancy Peluso, James C. Scott, Saroj Sivaramakrishnan, and Heinzpeter Znoj for reading and commenting on earlier versions. Discussions of the previous version with Paul Greenough, Anna Tsing, and others at the conference Environmental Discourses and Human Welfare in South and Southeast Asia held on 28–30 December 1995, were invaluable for revising the essay. Residual shortcomings are entirely my responsibility. This essay is a long version of another article (Sivaramakrishnan 2000). Permission granted by Institute of Social Studies, the Hague, to reuse materials from it, is gratefully acknowledged.

1 *Microplanning* refers to the participatory plans that are prepared by foresters and forest protection committees (set up under JFM) for the jointly managed forests. Defining the realm of silviculture in these plans and conceding that realm to the expert prescriptions of foresters are proving difficult. Such effort re-creates the patterns of conflict between local agency and central direction that were etched into the landscape of the managed forest in colonial times.

2 *Silviculture* as it is used in this essay refers to the art of producing and tending a forest. It comprises, at the very least, the theory and practice of controlling forest establishment, composition, structure, and growth. See Smith 1986, 1–28.

3 It was first defined by Foucault in 1970 in a lecture on discourse and language and was later elaborated in his 1971 essay "Nietzsche, Genealogy, History." See Bouchard 1977.

4 I use the term *procedures* in the specific sense given to it by de Certeau, who says that, although procedures are schemas of operation or technical manipulation, they are also flexible and respond to diverse local objectives and thus mediate between strategy and the more formal aspects of discourse (1988, 43–46).

5 I should clarify here that I am not drawing a sharp distinction between indigenous society and the foreign state. After all, for foresters from about the 1880s, the struggle I refer to included dealing with belligerent district officers who resented intrusions into their domains of authority.

6 For a similar argument with regard to discourses of community and conservation in Thailand, see Darlington, this volume.

7 A fine discussion of this historical process as functional territorialization of state resource control may be found in Vandergeest and Peluso 1995. Also see Peluso, this volume.

8 This corrective to "indigenous knowledge systems" approaches is provided in Agrawal 1995 and the essays in Hobart 1993. See also Arturo Escobar's review of the Hobart volume (1995c) for a fine discussion of new ways to theorize local knowledge.

9 Local knowledge is most usefully recognized by its "inseparability from a particular place in the sense of embeddedness in a particular labor process" (Kloppenburg 1991, 522). This formulation is also central to much feminist analysis of science, which emphasizes the importance of producing knowledge through sensuous activity, experience that is specifically local. See, for instance, Harraway 1988; Harding 1986; and Smith 1987.

10 Scholarly discussions of science as representation have flowered into the sociology of scientific knowledge. Notable exemplars are Barnes 1977; Bloor 1976; Collins 1992; and Gooding 1990.

11 The relationship between science and practice, and the practitioner debates in which institutionalized "basic science" is shaped, are well discussed in the context of late-nineteenth-century American medicine in

Warner 1991. I am grateful to Warwick Anderson for alerting me to Warner's work and its endorsement of my approach.

12 For recent work that stresses the fact that scientific ideas were not imported into colonies and were more often in a process of continuous construction, reconstruction, and transformation there, see several essays in Reingold and Rothenburg 1987, especially Chambers 1987.

13 I am thus arguing that "scientific knowledge has to be seen as intrinsically historical, in that its specific contents are a function of the temporally emergent contingencies of its production" (Pickering 1995, 209).

14 The memoirs of many foresters reveal this; see Forsyth 1889; Wilmot 1910; Stebbing 1920; and Best 1935.

15 Here the distinction between conservation and preservation is useful to bear in mind. The former combined utilitarian and developmentalist ideas in environmental management, underpinning soil conservation, water management, sustained yield forestry, and so on; the latter inspired more directly the creation of wilderness areas, parks, and sanctuaries. See Hays 1959 for a discussion of these ideas in the context of American environmentalism. A growing body of scholarship on Africa suggests the same trends there in the late nineteenth and early twentieth centuries; see Grove 1989; Anderson 1984; Beinart 1984, 1989; and Peters 1994.

16 Oriental and India Office Collections P/2934, Bengal Revenue Proceedings (Agri), Jan. 1887, Misc/1/29–30, A Proceedings, no. 510T, dated Calcutta, 19 October 1886, from M. Finucane, Director Agriculture to Secretary, Government of Bengal, Revenue.

17 Oriental and India Office Collections P/3871, Bengal Revenue Proceedings (For), May–July 1891, A Proceedings, 98–121, July 1891, Head 4, Collection 2, no. 2669F–G, dated Darjeeling, 30 Dec. 1890, E. P. Dansey, Officiating. Chief Forester, Bengal, to Secretary, Government of Bengal, Revenue, p. 13.

18 Both Michael Adas (1990, 95–108) and David Ludden (1989, 101–30) have pointed out the translation of local knowledge that was basic to the creation of colonial science and its codification as discourses of rule through classification, standardization, and textualization.

19 David Ludden makes the argument for the process of colonial state formation in general (1992b). Dietrich Brandis recognized similar trends in forest administration in particular (1884).

20 David Ludden has described the process with respect to agricultural surveys and settlements (Ludden 1992a). For colonial anthropology, see Dirks 1992a; for forestry, see Sivaramakrishnan 1995b. The wider theoretical implications of the process are discussed in Cohn and Dirks 1988; and Prakash 1990.

21 The focus during the company Raj remained on individual tree species, leading to protracted efforts to conserve, manage, and monopolize teak in South India, West India, and Burma. See Anonymous 1871; Falconer 1852; Brandis 1860; Bryant 1994; Cleghorn 1861; Birdwood 1910; Stebbing 1922; Rangarajan 1994; Grove 1995; and Skaria 1998. In Bengal, the first half of the nineteenth century was similarly a period of sporadically knowing and taming the wild. Surveying natural wealth, cataloging it, and

making forested terrain more habitable by means of "vermin eradication" were important interventions into a landscape earlier seen as impenetrable and unknowable (Sivaramakrishnan 1996a, chap. 4).

22 Stebbing (1922) specifically credits the viceroyalty of John Lawrence (1863–69) as being the period when forest conservancy was systematically introduced in India.

23 The sal forests of the *duars* came under British control in 1865 with the conclusion of the Bhutan war and the cession of the area east of the Tista River. See ibid., 2:5.

24 Commenting on the discursive strategies whereby expertise is constituted as the exclusive preserve of development agencies, Tim Mitchell observes that "the discourse of international development constitutes itself . . . as an expertise and intelligence that stands completely apart from the country and people it describes" (1991, 19). This theme of objectification and depoliticization recurs in all critiques of development discourse.

25 Similarly, scientific forestry in Europe had already declared the restoration of forests to be a task beyond the reach of mere preventive laws and something that called for scientific expertise. See Harrison 1992, 117; and Lowood 1990.

26 David Harvey calls this "perspectivism" and points out that it led to rules of rational practice and the idea that the expert as a creative individual is always capable of a view from the outside—a totalizing vision (1989, 244–46).

27 Nancy Peluso has done an admirable job of analyzing forest policy in terms of these three aspects of control in Java (1992). Mahesh Rangarajan has looked at forest management in nineteenth-century Central India from the same perspective; he attends carefully to changes in the silvicultural agenda — cast in terms of scientific advance — as political-economic conditions changed (1998).

28 E. P. Thompson gives us an excellent discussion of this complex fusion in which forest law takes shape in both agrarian practice and conflicting representations when he says that "the forest in fact was so by virtue of legal and administrative designation rather than by any unitary organization" (1975, 28–29).

29 Dietrich Brandis, a careful and often sympathetic commentator, writes that "In the Central Provinces forests have been preserved by malguzars or landholders on their estates, because the timber or bamboo in them was valuable and could be converted to money. In the drier parts of Northwestern India, where forests are scarce, there has been a tendency towards the preservation of forests, either as sacred groves or for hunting, or in some cases to provide fuel for iron smelting, to protect the water supply in springs and streams, to provide fuel for towns, or to secure a supply of cattle fodder in times of drought and scarcity. But there has been no organized and effective action to accomplish these objects" (1884, 460).

30 Mahesh Rangarajan (1992, 26) makes this case specifically for the Central Provinces, as do Ramachandra Guha (1989) for the western Himalaya, Richard P. Tucker (1989) for Assam and Kerala, Ajay Skaria (1992) and

David Hardiman (1994) for the Dangs of Gujarat, Sumit Guha (1995a) for western India, and Gadgil and Guha (1992) for India generally.

31 Temple (1880) reproduces minutes penned by the governor of Bombay, Sir Richard Temple, on the forests of different districts and states of the province. Temple had been lieutenant governor of Bengal before this assignment. See Cleghorn et al. 1852; and Clutterbuck 1927.

32 Schlich's plan had proposed annual removals of 5,785 trees over five feet in girth in the next eight years. This turned out to be a very optimistic estimate.

33 Oriental and India Office Collections P/2800, Bengal Revenue Proceedings, Jan.-Feb. 1886, A Proceedings, 32, Jan. 1886, Head I (RR), Collection 1, no. 21F, dated Simla, 31 Aug. 1885, Government of India Home Resolution.

34 National Archives of India (NAI) Government of India Rev and Agri (For), A Proceedings, 12–16, file 45 of 1901, July 1901, no. 128For, dated Cal 5 Jan. 1901, Government of Bengal, Revenue Resolution, p. 1026.

35 NAI Government of India Education, Health, and Lands (For), File 13–3/42—F&L 1942, S. H. Howard, Inspector General of Forests, inspection note for the forests of Bengal, December 1941 and January 1942, p. 1.

36 Oriental and India Office Collections P/7034, Bengal Revenue Proceedings (For), 1905, A Proceedings, 71–77, Dec. 1905, File 9R/1, no. 271, dated Darjeeling, 11 Jan. 1905, A. L. McIntire, Chief Forester, Bengal, to Secretary, Government of Bengal, Revenue, p. 122.

37 Oriental and India Office Collections P/7033, Bengal Revenue Proceedings (For), 1915, A Proceedings, 14–16, June 1905, File 3W/9, no. 11, Working Plan, dated Cal 23 Jan. 1905, S. Eardley Wilmot, Inspector General of Forests, to Chief Forester, Bengal; no. 1233T–R, dated Darjeeling, 15 June 1905, M. C. McAlpin, Undersecretary, Government of Bengal, Revenue, to Chief Forester, Bengal, pp. 150–53; Oriental and India Office Collections P/7034, Bengal Revenue Proceedings (For), Oct.–Dec. 1905, A Proceedings, 60–64, Dec. 1905, File 3W/4, no. 297, dated Darjeeling, 6 Feb. 1905, Chief Forester, Bengal, to Secretary, Government of Bengal, Revenue; no. 527, dated Cal 7 Jan. 1905, A. L. McIntire, Chief Forester, Bengal, to Inspector General of Forests, pp. 107–9.

38 Oriental and India Office Collections P/6561, Bengal Revenue Proceedings (For), A Proceedings, 19–25, July 1903, File 3W/3, no. 14, dated Cal 29 Jan. 1903, R. C. Wroughton, Inspector General of Forests, to Secretary, Government of Bengal, Revenue; no. 584T–R dated Darjeeling, 22 May 1903, A. Earle, Officiating Rev. Secretary, Government of Bengal, to Chief Forester, Bengal, p. 17.

39 NAI Government of India Rev and Agri (For), A Proceedings, 28–32, File 162 of 1915, July 1915, inspection note dated 28 Mar. 1915, of Buxa and Jalpaiguri, by G. S. Hart, Inspector General of Forests, p. 4.

40 Trafford, Jalpaiguri Working Plan, 4.

41 West Bengal Secretariat Record Room, Calcutta, Government of Bengal, Revenue (For), File 6D/4, B Proceedings, 20–24, Nov. 1907, no. 1857/320–7, dated Simla, 6 Sep. 1907, S. Eardley Wilmot, Inspector General of

Forests, to Chief Secretary, Government of Bengal; no. 2219JR, dated Cal 2 Oct. 1907, Chief Secretary, Government of Bengal, to Inspector General of Forests; no. 11/C, dated Simla, 11 Oct. 1907, Inspector General of Forests to Chief Secretary, Government of Bengal, pp. 1–5.

42 West Bengal Secretariat Record Room, Calcutta, Government of Bengal, Revenue (For), File 6D/4, B Proceedings, 20–24, Nov. 1907, note dated 24 Sep. 1907, by A. L. McIntire, Chief Forester, Bengal, in keep with papers, pp. 9–10.

43 Oriental and India Office Collections P/7034, Bengal Revenue Proceedings (For), A Proceedings, 71–77, Dec. 1905, File 9R/1, no. 271, dated Darjeeling, 11 Jan. 1905, A. L. McIntire, Chief Forester, Bengal, to Secretary, Government of Bengal, Revenue, pp. 122–23. Also see Haines 1905; Trafford, Jalpaiguri Working Plan; Hatt, Buxa Working Plan; Tinne, Tista Working Plan; and Grieve, Darjeeling Working Plan.

44 Oriental and India Office Collections P/7034, Bengal Revenue Proceedings (For), Oct-Dec 1905, A Proceedings, 60–64, Dec. 1905, File 3W/4, no. 297, dated Darjeeling, 6 Feb. 1905, Chief Forester, Bengal, to Secretary, Government of Bengal, Revenue; no. 527, dated Cal 7 Jan. 1905, A. L. McIntire, Chief Forester, Bengal, to Inspector General of Forests, pp. 108–9.

45 The distinction made between major and minor products indicated the priorities of forest management, especially in the matter of transforming the character of the forest under working plans. The idea was to increase the yield of major products. These were further classified into valuable and less valuable or jungle trees. I have discussed this schematization as it emerged as an all-India feature of forest management elsewhere (Sivaramakrishnan 1995a). Prasad (1994, 78–90) discusses these classifications and their implications for forest management in the Central Provinces.

46 NAI Government of India Rev and Agri (For), A Proceedings, 35, File 136 of 1916, May 1916, no 376/24–Working Plan, dated Simla, 17 May 1916, G. S. Hart, Inspector General of Forests, to Secretary Rev, Government of Bengal and Orissa, p. 1.

47 Ibid., 2.

48 NAI Government of India Rev and Agri (For), A Proceedings, 24–26, File no 311 of 1915, Feb. 1916, no. 12319, Government of Bengal, Revenue, Resolution dated Cal 17 Dec. 1915, p. 2.

49 NAI Government of India Rev and Agri (For), A Proceedings, 23–25, File 286 of 1916, Jan. 1917, no. 10091–For, dated Cal 18 Dec. 1916, Government of Bengal, Revenue, Resolution, p. 1.

50 Grieve, Darjeeling Working Plan, 1.

51 Ibid., 5.

52 Under the permit system of forest working, the sale of individual stems at a fixed price per tree led to the removal over time of the best trees, leaving the defective trees in the forest.

53 No. 1449, dated 26 Mar. 1896, from Deputy Commissioner, Darjeeling, to Commissioner, Rajshahi; no. 909G, dated 12–14 Sep. 1896, from Deputy Commissioner, Darjeeling, to Chief Forester, Bengal, cited in Grieve, Darjeeling Working Plan.

54   NAI Government of India Rev and Agri (For), A Proceedings, 5–7, File 54 of 1917, Feb. 1917, inspection note on the Darjeeling and Kurseong Hill Forests by G. S. Hart, Inspector General of Forests, dated 28 Dec. 1916, pp. 3–4. According to one official history, this alteration of the plan was based on a misunderstanding. The author (unknown but probably the chief forester, Bengal, of the time, E. O. Shebbeare) notes that the idea of selected felling in groups was unworkble, but, as Grieve's proposal was confused with the group method of Europe, the inspector general of forests approved the modified plan. See Government of Bengal 1935, 31.

55   NAI Government of India, A Proceedings, Government of India, Education, Health, and Lands (For), File 13–3/42–F&L 1942, inspection note by Inspector General of Forests on the forests of Bengal, Dec. 1941 and Jan. 1942, p. 5; Government of Bengal 1935, 31.

56   NAI Government of India Rev and Agri (For), A Proceedings, 3–5, File 9 of 1920, Jan. 1920, Government of Bengal, Revenue, Resolution no. 9655–For, p. 13.

57   NAI Government of India Education, Health, and Lands (For), A Proceedings, 67, file 19–4/36–F 1936, no. 102, dated 20 Mar. 1936, C. G. Trevor, Inspector General of Forests, to Secretary Government of India, p. 2; Champion 1975.

58   West Bengal Secretariat Record Room, Calcutta Government of Bengal, Forest and Excise (For), File 3W/16, B Proceedings, 47–51, Dec. 1939, no. 12664/1W–1, dated Alipore, 21 Oct. 1935, W. Meiklejohn, Chief Forester, Bengal, to Secretary, Government of Bengal, Agri and Industries, pp. 1–2; note dated 23 Jan. 1936 by W Meiklejohn, Chief Forester, Bengal, in keep with papers on file, 7.

59   West Bengal Secretariat Record Room, Calcutta, Government of Bengal, Forest and Excise (For), File 9R–46 of 1940, and File 9R–12, A Proceedings, 1–3, Mar. 1941, no. 2519/1R–56, dated Darjeeling, 29 Mar. 1941, W. Meiklejohn, Senior Chief Forester, Bengal, to Secretary, Government of Bengal, Forest and Excise Dept, p. 35.

60   NAI Government of India Education, Health, and Lands (For), File 13–3/42–F&L 1942, inspection note by the Inspector General of Forests on the forests of Bengal, Dec. 1941 and Jan. 1942, p. 2.

61   See, for example, Sinha 1962; Phillips 1924; and Stebbing 1962 4:115–16. This does not apply to sal forests of North Bengal, where taungya had been introduced, and other forests of Bengal, such as those in Chittagong and Sundarbans, where sal was not the most valuable species.

62   Stebbing 1922–62, 2:576–78.

63   Oriental and India Office Collections P/10122, Bengal Revenue Proceedings (For), 1917, A Proceedings, 4–6, Mar. 1917, File 3I/1, inspection note by Inspector General of Forests, G. S. Hart, on Darjeeling forests, dated 28 Dec. 1916; no. 85F/54–1, dated Simla, 14 Feb. 1917, A. E. Gilliat, Under Secretary, Government of India, Rev and Agri, to Secretary, Government of Bengal, Revenue, pp. 16–17.

64   One forester was candid enough to assert that "no two officers would mark exactly the same tree in a given area" (CSACL, Wimbush Papers, un-

dated typescript entitled "Life in the Indian Forest Service, 1907–1935,"
88–89).

65 Since the marking of trees was often left to village *mandals* (headmen), forest guards, and even intelligent coolies, omission of crooked trees may have been deliberate, as these were needed for making plows.

66 NAI Government of India Rev and Agri (For), A Proceedings, 28–32, File 162 of 1915, July 1915, inspection note of Buxa and Jalpaiguri, dated 28 Mar. 1915, by G. S. Hart, Inspector General of Forests, p. 17.

67 NAI Government of India Rev and Agri (For), A Proceedings, 43–46, File 124 of 1916, May 1916, no 174For, dated 3 May 1916, Officiating Secretary, Revenue Punjab, to Government of India.

68 NAI Government of India Rev and Agri (For), A Proceedings, 5–7, File 54 of 1917, Feb 1917, inspection note on the Darjeeling and Kurseong Hill Forests by G. S. Hart, Inspector General of Forests, dated 28 Dec. 1916, pp. 2–3.

69 The respect that senior foresters had for the local knowledge of the venerable guard of long standing is well conveyed in Gouldsbury 1909. Homfray writes in his authoritative manual on thinnings, that "village mandals, guards and especially intelligent coolies . . . know a good deal about silviculture" (1936, 11). Stebbing notes (1926, 3:460) that in France, too, the inspector would carry out thinnings after assembling all guards and rangers, and the oldest forest guard would be the acknowledged expert.

70 For selected felling, the minimum prescribed diameter was two feet, that is, a girth of six feet.

71 Oriental and India Office Collections P/11712, Bengal Revenue Proceedings (For), 1928, A Proceedings, 20–24, April 1928, File 9R/19 of 1927, no. 5191/R–53, dated 26 Sep. 1927, E. O. Shebbeare, Chief Forester, Bengal, to Secretary, Government of Bengal, Revenue, p. 39.

72 The work of R. S. Hole and E. A. Smythies initially, and the supplementary research of a host of other field foresters, was the basis for the shift to the shelter wood compartment system, notably Hole 1919; Smythies 1920; Makins 1920; Bailey 1924; and Ford-Robertson 1927.

73 For a detailed discussion of fire and grazing in the definition of scientific forestry in Bengal, see chapter 6 of Sivaramakrishnan 1996.

74 National Archives of India, New Delhi, Government of India Education, Health, and Lands (For), A Proceedings, File 22–4/41–F&L, 1941, no. 14803/40–IV–130, dated 14 Nov. 1940, S. H. Howard, President, Forest Research Institute, to Secretary, Government of India, pp. 6–7.

75 For instance, in thinning operations, about which more will be said later, forest guards were required to work ahead of the officer so to present a clear view. See Homfray 1936, 29.

76 For definitions of *discourse* of *development,* see several essays in Sachs 1992; Ferguson 1994; Escobar 1995; and Mitchell 1991. The characteristic of importance to us is the ability of development discourse to comprehend any situation requiring "improvement" or "development" through nonlocal technical expertise that can then offer modular and generalized solutions.

77 My usage of the term follows Ortner 1989.

78 I am extending here David Ludden's argument (1992b) that postcolonial Indian development discourse was shaped by the colonial governmental forms that emerged in the latter part of the nineteenth century. More recently, a longer European history of development has been presented by Michael Cowen and Robert Shenton (1995, 29–33). In this context, see also Hettne 1990.

79 The invention of development in the 1940s and 1950s is also argued with historical evidence from British colonial policy debates by Cooper (1991).

80 See Pigg 1992 and Woost 1993 for instances in which development as a received and systematic discourse engages other discourses in a local setting in South Asia.

81 Principal expositions are Mitchell 1988; Ferguson 1994; and Escobar 1995a. A recent South Asian ethnography using the development concept as it is characterized in these influential writings is Pigg 1993. Cooper (1995) does venture into the recent history of development discourse in West Africa. Chatterjee (1993, 200–19) similarly discusses the early-twentieth-century history of the rise of development planning ideas and their subsequent adoption by the Nehru government. But this limited historicization still excludes the scientific, conservationist, and social reformist aspects of development discourse that have a deeper and more contested history. It is my contention that concentrating on these neglected facets of development discourse reveals more clearly the influence of struggles at various levels on the processes of state building.

82 Dirks 1990, 25–33; Dirks 1992a; and Holston 1989, 120–30, make this point with reference to the caste system in India and urban planning in Brazil.

Uneasy Allies

Amita Baviskar

TRIBAL POLITICS

AND DISCOURSES OF

INDIAN ENVIRONMENTALISM

In India, state-led developmentalism has recently been challenged by the discourse of environmentalism. Among the various streams of environmentalism, ecological Marxism has been the most dominant. Its marrying of two concerns — social justice and ecological sustainability — has made this ideology highly appealing to social activists working with tribal communities in western India. Yet closer examination reveals that the dynamics of tribal politics often strain the discourse of environmentalism and have an ambivalent attitude toward development. This essay analyzes conflicts between middle-class activists and tribal leaders within a trade union of tribal peasants in Madhya Pradesh and argues that their disparate political strategies and postures stem from sharp differences in the ways in which they conceptualize the place of the "tribal" in relation to "nature." The essay shows that the discourse of environmentalism is not consistent or finished but consists of the interweaving of often contradictory political thought and action.

The Indian state legitimizes its current policies for structural adjustment and liberalization by promising economic growth and prosperity for all. Opponents point to the havoc that these policies seem to necessarily entail for the rural poor and the natural resource base that supports them and assert once more the need for a different model of welfare. Among these models, "sustainable development" appears today to be the most influential theoretical framework shaping the political practices of environmental activists in tribal India. *Our Common Future,* the landmark report of the World Commission on Environment and Development of 1987, defined *sustainable development* as that which "meets the needs of the present without compromising the ability of future generations to meet their own needs" (WECD 1987, 43). The report contains within it two key concepts: that overriding priority should be given to the essential needs of the world's poor and that ecological sustainability is inseparable from social equity. The appeal of this ideology for activists lies in its combination of two important concerns—social justice and ecological conservation. Despite the co-optation of the vocabulary of sustainable development by sections of the Establishment, the ideology endures as an overarching utopia, anchored in analyses of political economy and prescriptions for social change, that unifies activists' attempts to transform the tribal people and landscapes with which they work.

ACTIVISTS AND TRIBAL LEADERS: ALTERNATIVE VISIONS

Despite the best efforts of activists to mobilize tribal groups for sustainable development, this utopia appears to be as distant as ever. Instead, wherever middle-class activist intervention has been absent, *adivasi* (tribal) assertion has taken a different direction altogether, toward a kind of minority identity politics that is ambivalent in its orientation toward the principles of sustainable development.[1] How does one explain this? This essay argues that the theories of social change that inform the work of activists and tribal leaders start from different premises about the relationships between rural people and their environment. These premises are strongly influenced by the social locations of the actors who make them, their cultural background, and their experiences. While middle-class activists and adivasi leaders share certain common concerns, their competing conceptions of the "tribal" and the environment create a degree of mutual antipathy that has so far prevented their coming together. These varying conceptions partly stem from the emerging differentiation of the tribal community into two distinct classes, a process accelerated by the intervention of the state and market forces. This essay tries to explore claims about tribal relationships with nature by looking at politics within a tribal trade union, focusing on the relationship between the middle-class activists who started it and the tribal activists who are now emerging as its leaders.[2] The trade union is part of a regionwide federation of tribal groups, and the same conflicts can be seen at the regional level too.

In my previous work, I focused on the dissonance between the tribal relationship with nature and its representation by urban environmentalist supporters of the Narmada Bachao Andolan (Movement to Save the Narmada), an antidam campaign (Baviskar 1995). In that work, I also described the political organization of tribal people into a trade union called Khedut Mazdoor Chetna Sangath (Organization for the Consciousness of Workers and Peasants), which fights the state for rights to forest land. The four years that have elapsed since the fieldwork for that

290   Amita Baviskar

study have been marked by the emergence of an internal debate between activists and adivasi leaders in the Sangath. The implications of this debate extend to wider issues such as tribal identity, natural resource use policies, and the future of tribal groups in India. This essay examines the debate by drawing on participant observation and discussions with activists, tribal leaders, and ordinary union members from my perspective as an associate who worked as an apprentice activist during 1992–93. Although I am now involved only peripherally with the union's work, I stay in close touch with developments in the area through periodic visits and meetings with friends.

This essay begins with a brief description of the political economy of the local environment, the origins of the Sangath and its activities. This is followed by a general discussion of the economic imperatives of structural adjustment and liberalization in Madhya Pradesh (the state in which the Sangath works) and the rise of identity politics in the state. This statewide situation helps contextualize political developments within the Sangath. The essay then settles down to examine more closely the position of activists and tribal leaders and the strategies adopted by the tribal rank and file. It concludes by evaluating the differing stances of these groups with respect to sustainable development and the assumptions about nature and culture that underpin the concept.

ALIRAJPUR: FROM THE PAST TO THE PRESENT

The Alirajpur *tehsil* (administrative subdivision) in Jhabua District lies in the southwest corner of Madhya Pradesh in western India along the Narmada River. The area is mountainous and sparsely settled; the hills are covered with dry deciduous mixed teak forests, which have been largely cleared for cultivation. The appearance of isolation is misleading, for the Bhil and Bhilala population of the region has dealt with successive waves of Rajput, Maratha, and British invaders and settlers. For more than four hundred years, adivasis have struggled against the inroads made by states and markets, which have transformed their relationship with their environment and nonadivasis (Baviskar 1995, 49–78).

In the early part of the twentieth century, while other parts of India mobilized against the British, the Bhils of western Madhya Pradesh were uncharacteristically quiescent. The only memorable political action of that time was the Lal Topi Andolan, which happened in the north of the region and took the form of a campaign against forced labor and the payment of rent to feudal landowners. This campaign adopted Sanskritization as a strategy: as Christians and twice-born castes were exempt from corvée, adivasis had begun converting to Christianity in order to avoid forced labor. Mama Baleshwar, a social reformer, approached the *Shankaracharya* (Hindu pontiff) of Puri and apprised him of the mass exodus of adivasis from the Hindu fold. The Shankaracharya agreed to Mama Baleshwar's suggestion that adivasis be allowed to wear the scared thread of the twice born, a symbol that would exempt them from corvée, on the condition that adivasis foresake liquor and meat. This ingenious ploy enabled thousands of adivasis to avoid forced labor (Baviskar 1995, 79–80).

In 1949, when India became free, the Bhils became citizens and subjects of an independent nation-state. One of the first acts of the new government was to conduct a land survey, formally issuing titles to lands that were then being cultivated and classifying most of the remaining lands as the property of the Forest Department. The region was designated a Scheduled Area in 1950, and the state was charged by the Indian Constitution with the responsibility of "promoting with special care the educational and economic interests of the weaker sections [the Scheduled Tribes] and protecting them from social injustice and all forms of exploitation" (Government of India 1978, 4). In practice, however, the state has performed its role as guardian only fitfully, initiating half-hearted welfare schemes such as the Integrated Tribal Development Program.[3] The state's refusal to recognize tribal rights to forest lands and allow tribal communities control over their productive economy subverted the project of tribal welfare from the very start. The most grievous blow to the tribal cause came from the state's enthusiastic pursuit of a strategy of national development based on industrialization. Mineral-rich forested areas and the upper reaches of rivers in the hills, prime landscapes for resource extraction, have been gradually acquired by the state "in the national interest" by pushing out the resident tribal population. Physical displacement in some cases and resource displacement in others have impoverished the lives of the majority of Bhils.

However, a tiny group of Bhils — those who were economically and politically more powerful, whose ancestors as village headmen had turned to their advantage their mediating role between the villagers and the state — were in a position to seize the opportunities offered by tribal development programs and gain access to jobs on the lower rungs of the government bureaucracy. Over time, with the spread of state education, this section grew. While development has brought economic security and lower-middle-class respectability to this group, its movement away from the land and into a class dominated by nontribals has engendered a strong desire to shed the stigma of tribal identity and adopt caste Hindu practices. At the same time, the initial conditions of relative privilege that enabled this group of petty officials to emerge also gave rise to the current tribal leadership. However, the demographics of representative democracy ensure that tribal leaders, despite their prosperity, maintain their tribal identity in terms of overt markers such as language, dress, and name in order to retain the allegiance of people in their constituencies.

Forty-five years after independence, rural Alirajpur presents a dismal picture in terms of various human development indicators: just 4.6 percent of the population is literate; only 2 percent of rural women can read and write. Of the tehsil's total rural population of 196,000, only 14 percent has access to government medical services. A mere 55, or 16 percent, of the 339 villages in the tehsil are electrified. Most villages have no source of safe drinking water (GOI 1981). A part of the Bhil belt, which stretches from western Rajasthan through Gujarat and Madhya Pradesh to Maharashtra, the population of Alirajpur is overwhelmingly tribal; almost 89 percent of rural people belong to the Bhil and Bhilala tribes. Another 6.7 percent belong to various Scheduled Castes. Trade and commerce and the entire state administration in Alirajpur are dominated by nonadivasis, with adivasis relegated to petty posts. There is a sharp social divide between adivasis and nonadivasis, with the latter regarding the former as savage, backward, and contemptible.

LOCAL POLITICAL ECONOMY: LAND, LIVESTOCK, AND FORESTS

Jhabua is one of India's poorest districts. Almost all the people of Alirajpur make their living from the land. Eighty-three percent of adult workers cultivate their own land, and another 8 percent work as agricultural laborers. People grow maize, *jowar* (sorghum), and *bajra* (pearl millet) and several kinds of pulses, mainly for self-consumption. Oilseeds such as groundnuts and sesame are primarily grown for sale. Although people grow as many as twenty different crops, agricultural productivity is low due to thin soils and unpredictable rains. Only 8 percent of the total cultivated area of Jhabua District is irrigated. Out of the district's total of 97,674 agricultural holdings, 91,507 (93.6 percent) are classified by the government as uneconomic (District Rural Development Agency 1993). With a growing population, more and more people are dependent on increasingly tiny, partitioned plots.

With marginal legal landholdings, people rely heavily on livestock and the forest to sustain themselves. Access to the forest enables adivasis to own large herds of livestock—draft animals, a few cows, and several goats. More affluent adivasis keep buffaloes and large herds of goats. While there is little significant differentiation in the size of legal landholdings among adivasis, the size of livestock herds tends to vary quite a bit.

With crown densities of 40 percent or less, the forests of Alirajpur are classified as highly degraded. Yet they are as central to the tribal economy as legal landholdings and livestock. Through the seasons of the year, the cycle of collecting various forest products marches along with the cycle of agriculture (Baviskar 1995, 142–47). Adivasi homes, constructed entirely of teak, bamboo, and *anjan,* with floors of packed mud and cow dung, are built almost entirely of forest products.[4] Besides providing house-building material, the forest yields fodder, fuel, fiber, fruit, medicines, edible gums, and numerous other items. The continuity between the forest, animal husbandry, and cultivation is reiterated through rituals and taboos that seek to control and manage nature. The dependence on the forest is also expressed in the *gayana,* the Bhilala myth of creation, in which teak and *khakhra* are accorded as much importance as jowar.[5]

Access to the forest enables the adivasis of Alirajpur to hold their own economically. Besides meeting their consumption needs, they trade forest products along with some of their agricultural products for merchandise such as cloth, jewelery, iron implements, and salt. And in years when the rains fail people fall back on the forest for survival by selling wood. As one adivasi observed, "during a drought, the forest is our money-lender." Whereas people from other drought-stricken areas are forced to migrate in search of a livelihood, the adivasis of Alirajpur who still have access to the forest manage to stave off starvation and avoid migration by selling forest products. During a particularly lean summer, when asked why he and his fellow villagers had not migrated for *mazdoori* (wage labor), one Bhilala man replied, "we are doing *cheek ki mazdoori* right here." That is, villagers survived by collecting and selling the aromatic resin exuded from the *halai* tree.[6]

NEVAD: FIELDS IN THE FOREST

The most significant contribution of the reserve forest to the local subsistence economy is *nevad.* The word *nevad* literally means "new field," a place cleared for cultivation. However, now it refers only to fields that encroach on forest lands. The statistics about nevad speak for themselves: more than a thousand claims for regularization were submitted on one day in May 1994 in Sondwa administrative block alone. These revealed that each household cultivated nevad holdings that were three to ten times larger than its legal holdings. Since the size of legal holdings is too small for subsistence, it becomes imperative to supplement them with nevad cultivation. Nevad fields tend to be tiny patches of cleared forest, usually discreetly tucked away in the high hills. The land is generally sloping, with friable soils. But, despite its drawbacks, this land keeps the adivasi economy of Alirajpur on its feet. While there are no precise records about the extent of encroachments in Jhabua, it has been estimated that, for Madhya Pradesh as a whole, out of a total of 15.5 million hectares of forest land, 1.6 million (more than 10 percent) has been lost to encroachment (Buch 1991, 12).[7] While the Sangath argues that forests belonged to adivasis before they were privatized by the state and felled extensively in the 1930s, and that the process of land settlement in 1949 was simply land alienation since it left out many holdings deep in the forest, the rights of adivasis to forest encroachments are continually contested by the state.

Since nevad is crucial for adivasi survival, every attempt by the Forest Department to repossess nevad fields has met with widespread resistance. Adivasis have made frequent representations to the administration to settle their claims through negotiation but have been rebuffed. The Forest Department has rarely tried to find an amicable solution to this conflict, preferring to enforce its claim with the unilateral use of force. Most confrontations have been sparked when Forest Department parties have suddenly descended on an area and started digging cattle proof trenches (CPTs) preliminary to planting, attempting to cordon off an area that may include grazing lands as well as nevad fields. A particularly charged encounter occurred in March 1991 in Kiti village when the police fired to disperse assembled villagers (both men and women) from Kiti, Keldi, and Vakner, who had been peacefully resisting CPT work. In another instance, forest guards came with a herd of cattle and set them to graze on standing crops in nevad fields that belonged to Semlani village in August 1993. Very often, the Forest Department provokes a confrontation by setting its laborers to dig holes in the middle of nevad fields, ostensibly for planting trees, as was done in Pujara ki Chauki village. Because this work will never attract local cooperation, the Forest Department brings in laborers from distant villages under armed escort. In the instances in which the Forest Department's attempts to reclaim nevad led to retaliation in the form of villagers throwing stones, the crisis was precipitated mainly because of the state's use of force at the outset.

Besides the violent mass confrontations that have occurred in villages such as Kiti, Semlani, Pujara ki Chauki, Umrath, Khodamba, and so on, the conflict over the forest has also been a ceaseless war of attrition in which the Forest Department uses legal weapons such as litigation and confiscation. The registration of thousands of cases, many of them on trumped up charges, against adivasis for violating forest laws have trapped people on a treadmill of visits to the police lockup and the court. People also risk having their livestock confiscated and must pay to get them back. If a pair of bullocks is confiscated at the time of plowing during the crucial agricultural season, it can cripple an adivasi household's economic prospects for the entire year.

The state's legal actions against nevad were supplemented with illegal ones. Villagers recount the beatings they suffered in the hands of forest guards. They remember times when the *nakedar* (forest officer) or ranger would enter their village and order that a feast of chicken and *pannia* (break cooked between leaves) and *mahua* liquor be served for the pleasure of the officers. Earlier, forest guards would simply demand and receive a jar of *ghee* (clarified butter) or a bag of groundnuts; no one dared resist. When called on, an adivasi had to put aside his work and escort the forest official to the next village, carrying his bag for him. A constant accompaniment to these demands were the monetary bribes that villagers had to pay to persuade the Forest Department to look the other way.

ORGANIZING FOR SUSTAINABLE DEVELOPMENT: THE SANGATH AT WORK

Since 1982, the Forest Department's ability to get away with such blatant abuse of power has been sharply curtailed by the formation of the Sangath. The Sangath began work in Sondwa block as a subcenter of the Social Work and Research Centre (SWRC), an organization with its headquarters at Tilonia, Rajasthan. The SWRC is famous as a rural nongovernmental organization (NGO) engaged in grassroots development through the use of appropriate technology, handicraft cooperatives, and improvements in community health and education. However, the activists chose to abandon SWRC's community development model of social work and instead engaged in direct political action through collective organization and mobilization of adivasis against the state and the market. They first organized a successful strike against a local contractor working on a public works project who was employing local laborers without paying them minimum wages. They went on to organize villagers against exploitation and harassment by forest officials. Now the Sangath works in about ninety-five villages in Sondwa and Sorwa blocks of Alirajpur tehsil. Besides the issue of land rights and forest management, the Sangath tries to ensure that public development funds and welfare services actually reach the villages and are not siphoned off by a corrupt administration. The union works in the area of education, using local history, music, and myths to revive a sense of pride in the adivasi heritage. It tries to revitalize customary modes of dispute resolution within the community, avoiding recourse to the police and courts. The union runs a cooperative shop at its headquarters in Attha village. Although the number of full-time workers keeps changing, the Sangath has a core of three full-time activists and three tribal leaders. It has begun paying special attention to training adivasi youth for continuing political activism. In terms of its origins, organizational structure, and ideology, the Sangath is similar to other organizations—Adivasi Mukti Sangathan, Kashtakari Sanghatana, Shramik Sanghatana—in the region.

The centrality of nevad in the lives of adivasis makes it a key political issue for the Sangath. The administration's refusal to negotiate drew the Sangath toward more aggressive tactics like mass demonstrations, hunger strikes, and the obstruction of forest-related work. These have ended much of the petty violence and corruption of the Forest Department. The Sangath claims that its work is not limited to defending nevad. According to a pamphlet distributed for publicity and fund-raising purposes, "its objective is the wider cause of empowering adivasis in their struggle to live with dignity, without being exploited and cheated, with control over the resources and processes that so vitally affect them." To this end, the Sangath has tried to work on several fronts—organizing the cooperative shop, teaching literacy in Bhili and Bhilali, initiating a soil and water conservation program, and generally strengthening adivasis' ability to stand up for their rights. For its efforts, the Sangath has been frequently called a "naxalite" organization that incites simple adivasis to violence.[8] For the most part, the local administration has chosen to treat the mobilization around the forest rights issue as a law and order problem to be suppressed with state violence.

The adivasis of Alirajpur are living on the edge, forced to cultivate nevad fields on fragile hill slopes and collect forest products in order to avoid migration in search of work. Because adivasis have no security of tenure and live under the constant threat of eviction, they cannot invest in improving their land. Their poverty prevents them from planting tree crops that have long gestation periods, and the illegality of their position precludes their receiving loans from the government to make their agriculture more productive. In this situation, the first step toward sustainable development has to be recognition of adivasis' rights to the forest. Without access to their primary means of production, it is almost impossible for adivasis to survive in Alirajpur. However, the Sangath argues that access alone is not enough; as long as control is vested with the Forest Department, the forests will continue to be destroyed due to illicit felling by contractors and expensive afforestation programs will be launched without any lasting benefits. At the same time, forests are also being destroyed due to increasing adivasi numbers and their land hunger. The Sangath argues that the solution lies in local control. Only when local communities have the power to decide how they should best manage the forest to meet their needs can they choose to set aside some areas for protection. With security of tenure for nevad, they can invest in land improvement measures.

With the intervention of the Sangath, as adivasis have secured partial control over the forest for the last fifteen years they have initiated some conservation measures. The villages of Attha, Gendra, and Umrath, which are members of the Sangath, have tried to improve nevad fields and manage the rest of the forest for sustainable fodder and fuel yields. Labor collectives have worked on bunding and gully plugging to prevent soil erosion from the fields.[9] One year villagers ran a nursery to grow saplings for planting. These efforts have resulted in a marked improvement in forest regeneration and in checking soil erosion, but they remain limited to a handful of villages. Their future is also highly uncertain, partly because of the possibility of fresh state initiatives to remove encroachments and partly because of the organizational crises that periodically affect the Sangath. The few full-time activists bear the burden of coordinating activities in ninety-five villages; despite the flexible structure that the Sangath of necessity maintains, sometimes chaos prevails. Or there are occasions when critical institutional support from the Sangath is not forthcoming because the activists are dealing with something else. Yet nevad fields need inputs on a scale that the Sangath cannot meet. Only the state can ensure that a comprehensive soil and water conservation program covers the entire watershed. But the government is unwilling to make this long-term investment in land resources, as it feels that to do so on nevad lands would be construed as recognizing adivasi rights to the forest. The mutual hostility and suspicion that mark the relationship between the state and the Sangath seem to rule out the possibility of finding a middle ground of cooperation.

The small experiments undertaken by the Sangath indicate people's preference for an approach in which they have control over the conservation program and their rights are secured. However, a small financial base prevents them from expanding the scale of their activities and from undertaking works that require more purchased materials (e.g., for water harvesting) or paying workers for wages foregone. Unlike most NGOs, the Sangath raises most of its funds from its members, impoverished though they are. All households pay union dues and contribute in kind to the running of the union. Most of the work is done voluntarily. Only the six full-time activists receive small stipends. Specific projects are funded by small grants from Indian NGOs and by donations from supporters. The organization recently received a grant of Rs 2.4 lakhs (approximately U.S.$6,900) from the Council for the Advancement of People's Action and Rural Technology (CAPART), a government institution, for soil and water conservation — its largest grant so far.[10] This discussion of the union's funding is important if we are to gauge the kind of financial straitjacket within which the Sangath operates. This situation is a direct consequence of the organization's decision to chart a path of political confrontation with the state. The kind of political goodwill required to secure funds from donor agencies has never been the Sangath's happy lot. At the same time, it has ideological reservations about accepting foreign funding or any kind of work with a large budget, feeling that it makes the organization less accountable to its membership. This choice has ruled out the possibility of undertaking the kind of resource-intensive land development work that many NGOs have been able to do.

So far, the Sangath has managed to maintain the production economy of Alirajpur's adivasis with respect to their access to the forest. In the future, though, if forests continue to be converted into nevad, people will face problems in securing fuel, fodder, and other forest products. Some villages that have cleared almost all their forests face this situation already. Arriving at a land use balance between field and forest through collective management of the remaining forest and the prevention of further encroachments is going to be essential for the continued survival of the forest-based economy of Alirajpur. At the moment, people feel an urgent need for agricultural land that overrides all other considerations. However, forests are also a crucial component of the adivasi economy. At present, people are being forced to choose between the two — either land or forest — and necessity compels them to choose the former. If forests are to survive, it is essential that existing agricultural lands be made more productive through protective irrigation, soil fertility improvement, and checking soil erosion. A strategy of this sort requires enormous decentralized planning, sustained resources and stable structures of management. In the present context of the political uncertainty about people's rights to land, such a strategy remains a distant dream. Even if the political issue of land rights were to be somehow resolved, there would need to be a sea change in the state's pattern of relating to tribal people, a movement toward recognizing their right to have greater control over development planning and practice. More concretely, state-initiated conservation schemes such as Joint Forest Management would stand a greater chance of success if they acknowledged that, in this case, people want to grow food first and trees later. Greater flexibility in state programs would help people to combine food and tree crops in ways that best suited their priorities.

Although the Sangath has secured a degree of temporary stability for the production economy of Alirajpur's adivasis, its achievements have been miniscule in terms of the overall vision of sustainable development. Local access has not been converted into local control and management in most of the member villages, despite persistent efforts by the activists to set up village-level committees to manage natural resources. In some Sangath-controlled areas, the virtual absence of the Forest Department has created a free-for-all with extensive clearing of forests for nevad. Valuable gum-yielding trees such as halai are being tapped so intensively that villagers say that no trees of this species will be left after a few years. Recourse to seasonal migration increases every year in the region. The situation of grinding poverty that marks the region has not changed substantially.

THE SANGATH UTOPIA

It would be useful at this point to delineate the version of sustainable development that drives the Sangath's work. This ideology is not available as an articulated doctrine but emerges from an analysis of the Sangath's practices and activists' statements on specific issues. As one may expect from work in progress, many aspects of Sangath ideology are not fully worked out and are somewhat tentative formulations. This model envisages an economy and polity that are largely autonomous from external control, that are internally equitable, and that allow natural resources to be replenished and expanded in a way that first satisfies the subsistence needs of the local population. If basic requirements cannot be met locally, it is incumbent on the state to provide them. Control over decision-making processes as well as the management of resources would rest primarily with the *gram sabha* (all the adults of a village or hamlet), the body that is best informed about local specificities. The focus on subsistence in the sustainable development model is a way of emphasizing that resource use and management remain limited to that which is necessary to meet basic needs without entering into the ever-rising spiral of demand for consumption which would be ecologically hard to sustain. Thus, control brings with it responsibility toward all the members of the community and deprived people everywhere and toward maintaining ecological productivity for the future. According to the Sangath, the decentralization of power also entails recognizing the legitimacy of local concerns and knowledge, which are undervalued and ignored by centralized systems.

Whereas other attempts to bring about sustainable development have tried to create model villages such as Ralegan Siddhi or Sukhomajri (Pangare and Pangare 1992; Chambers, Saxena, and Shah 1989), the Sangath has chosen to mobilize politically in a regionwide fight for rights to natural resources, supplemented by a revival of the tribal history of resistance, customs of dispute resolution, and traditional knowledge about herbal medicine and forest use. The Sangath has also participated in nationwide mobilizations on issues such as the proposed Forest bill, liberalization (Azadi Bachao Andolan), state repression of the Chhattisgarh Mukti Morcha (a powerful trade union in eastern Madhya Pradesh), displacement (through its participation in the Narmada Bachao Andolan), and many other wider struggles. Despite these efforts, the Sangath's project of sustainable development faces an even more serious threat in Madhya Pradesh today.

In 1994, the Madhya Pradesh government launched an aggressive program intended to shed the state's industrially backward image by courting private industry with incentives such as attractive tax breaks and fast clearances in order to fully exploit the state's rich endowment of mineral and agricultural resources. Proposed investment since 1991 exceeds Rs 36,000 crore, next only to Gujarat, Maharashtra, and Uttar Pradesh (Chakravarti 1995, 167). Its location in the heart of the country and good connections by road and rail make Madhya Pradesh ideal for the sourcing and distribution of manufactured goods. Industrialists are also drawn by the availability of relatively docile and cheap labor. Some of the investment is a spillover from the neighboring states of Gujarat and Maharashtra. The state has agreed to supplement hydropower projects currently under construction with six private thermal power plants and four naptha/gas plants to meet critical power requirements. For a state in which more than 60 percent of the population lives below the poverty line, the slogan of "Let's Talk Business" signifies the government's resolve to prosper by capitalizing on the opportunities thrown up by the new climate of liberalization.

The new liberalization policies were welcomed by Madhya Pradesh's business community. They were accorded a more mixed response by the urban middle class, which looks forward to improved transport and power infrastructure but is apprehensive about the worsening of already severe water scarcity. In the fertile plains of the Malwa region, most farmers are upbeat about increased demand for cash crops such as soybeans, cotton, oilseeds, and sugarcane. Opposition to liberalization has emerged only in tribal areas in the form of protest against projects that threaten to displace people. For instance, Bastar is a heavily forested, mineral rich, predominantly tribal region in southeast Madhya Pradesh with major heavy industry to its north. In this district, which has experienced resistance to proposed dams, a demand now frequently voiced by tribal leaders and activists is that half the shares of any private industry set up in the region should be distributed among the tribal people, the real owners of the region's resources. While this demand seeks to decentralize the liberalization process and secure a degree of control for the local population, it does not address broader questions about the model of intensive resource extraction that is being promoted. These demands on the part of tribal leaders have been largely polemical, and the state has ignored them so far. There has also been low-key naxalite activity in Bastar for several years, but it has not seriously impeded the state's plans. At present, the state's partnership with private industry steams ahead unchallenged.

The statewide mobilization for industrialization provides the context within which sustainable development becomes even harder to achieve than before. The state is committed to transferring natural resources to private industry. The only future envisaged by the state for those who depend on these resources for sustenance is that they join the pool of cheap compliant labor that is one of the attractions drawing private capital to the state. At another level, though, the state proclaims its commitment to improving rural livelihoods by promoting greater industrial demand for agricultural products. However, the tribal farmers of Alirajpur, whose land barely provides enough food to see them through the year, are unlikely to be the beneficiaries of this process.

While the winds of liberalization sweep through Madhya Pradesh, another current is also affecting the political climate of the state. This is the rise of *dalit* (backward class) politics as an influential factor in state-level politics.[11] In a state where 23 percent of the population consists of Scheduled Tribes (compared to 7 percent in India as a whole) and another 14 percent belongs to the Scheduled Castes, and where the tribal population is heavily concentrated in particular districts, dalit support is crucial for electoral success. The ruling Congress Party is presently headed by (upper-caste) Chief Minister Digvijay Singh who has so far managed to keep tribal leaders on his side with great agility. The success, if limited, of backward-caste-based political parties in Uttar Pradesh (the Bahujan Samaj Party) and Bihar (Janata Dal) has reinforced the belief of Madhya Pradesh's tribal politicians in the electoral potential of mobilizing on the basis of dalit identity. The confidence that dalit support can make or break the state government has led one tribal member of parliament, Jhabua's Dilip Singh Bhuria, to demand that Madhya Pradesh be given a tribal chief minister. Since 53 out of the ruling party's 174 members of the Legislative Assembly in the state are tribals, this demand has political potential.

Simultaneous with the rise of dalit politics in representative government at the state level, yet independent of it, is the emergence of an interstate movement of tribal assertion. In the entire Bhil belt, which stretches from Maharashtra to Madhya Pradesh and from Gujarat to Rajasthan, broadly two kinds of mobilizations have attempted to remake adivasi identity. The first movement is illustrated by the Sangath's politics, which focuses on rights to natural resources. This politics links the issue of adivasi identity to their material exploitation and argues that political control over resources is essential for gaining self-respect and dignity vis-à-vis nontribal oppressors. (An exemplary tribal leader is Vahru Sonavane.) The second movement seeks to remake adivasi identity by emulating upper-caste Hindu practices in order to shed the "backward, savage" image of adivasis. The action consists of joining various religious sects such as the Ramanand *panth*, Kabir panth, and Gayatri Parivar. While the former movement asserts itself by espousing a revival of tribal culture, the latter seeks to erase its adivasi past in order to claim higher status in the Hindu hierarchy. While Sangath politics shares with state-level dalit politics an explicit orientation toward capturing power, it differs from dalit politics in its understanding of what power should be used for—a difference that we shall examine later. The religious revival movement has stayed aloof from any clear political stand, concentrating instead on self-improvement under the slogan "tum badloge, yug badlega" (if you change, the age will change).

The failure of the sustainable development model espoused by activists is linked to the stumbling progress of the political project initiated by the Sangath, which focuses on local control. The state not only refuses to relinquish its power over natural resources and the financial resources needed to invest in local employment for land improvement but in fact has launched an intensive program of industrialization that makes local control even more difficult. While people have fought as Sangath members to gain access to the forest and have gained a temporary reprieve through their efforts, their economic and political disadvantages vis-à-vis the state prevent them from realizing more fully the model of sustainable development. Under these circumstances, tribal leaders in the Sangath feel increasingly drawn to dalit politics, which promises to bring power into their hands. They are willing to shelve the model of sustainable development for the time being, arguing that capturing power would automatically enable them to use it. This argument fails to persuade the activists, who point out that state-level tribal leaders such as Dilip Singh Bhuria or Arvind Netam are simply interested in controlling the lucrative flow of resources from the state for their own benefit; although these leaders claim to represent exploited adivasis, they are not committed to challenging the model of development that impoverishes them. Instead of questioning the resource-intensive pattern of industrialization being promoted by the nontribal state leadership, these tribal leaders seek only to enlarge their share of the benefits. Only a tribal leadership committed to the cause of sustainable development would genuinely transform the lives of poor adivasis.

The activists' criticism of state-level tribal leadership touches a sensitive chord. In effect, the activists are arguing that they are better representatives of the interests of adivasis than adivasi leaders! That is, activists claim to understand tribal needs and desires better than the representatives from their own community. In order to understand this presumption, we have to examine the activists more closely.

THE ACTIVISTS

As mentioned earlier, I use the term *activist* to denote those youths who left their urban (usually metropolitan), upper-middle-class lives to settle in Alirajpur and work among the adivasis. The Sangath was founded by one such activist, who teamed up with a tribal leader twelve years ago. For most of the activists I know, the shift to work in an unusual profession, in an place far from home, was the result of a personal ideological and moral crisis. Most felt oppressed by the inequalities that surrounded them and felt guilty and helpless that their class position made them relatively privileged. All felt compelled to leave the comfort of familiar environs to seek out Gandhi's "last man" — the poorest and most oppressed — and work for his welfare. Doing this frequently involved rebellion against family pressures to settle into more conventional careers, against ingrained middle-class values of conformism, and against the desire to be comfortable and secure.[12] Many activists spoke also of their alienation from their urban environment and of their perception that urban life was counterfeit, artificial. In the city, they believed that "true India" lived not around them but in the distant villages. As one activist expressed it, "You feel that the people in the village are more real [than urban people], their lives matter more." After a while, she went on to add, "I suppose I think they are more real because being with them makes *me* feel more real." So the activists derive their sense of identity and worth from their engagement with the lives of adivasis. A decade or two earlier, the activist may have joined the naxalites or (less likely) the Sarvodaya movement. In the 1980s, with environmentalism added to the agenda for social transformation, they took to sustainable development.

Amar, the activist who founded the Sangath, is now in his late thirties. Like other activists, he avoids using his last name, which would reveal his (upper) caste identity. Amar left training as an architect to become a political activist in Alirajpur, attracted by a chance remark he heard at the swrc Tilonia that "the adivasis of Alirajpur were very fierce." His partnership with Vesta, the adivasi leader, led to the creation of the Sangath.

Unlike other activists, Amar did not come to the field with much theoretical baggage apart from a notion of social justice as his navigational principle. His ideology evolved in village meetings, nightlong conversations, and observing and participating in adivasis' everyday lives. In those days, the Sangath concentrated on fighting the Forest Department. Its ideological horizons expanded to encompass sustainable development only when it entered the nascent antidam movement, a struggle that sharply articulated a challenge to the modernization-industrialization-urbanization paradigm of development. Participation in the Andolan protest enabled the Sangath activists to relate their work to a wider, analytically more sophisticated, political framework. The leap from the concrete to the abstract was wryly summed up by an activist: "Earlier we couldn't see beyond the *patvari* or *nakedar* (lower-level revenue or forest officer); now we challenge the entire model of development." The antidam movement also put the activists in touch with a regionwide network of similar organizations that it had mobilized. Activists now meet frequently with other organizations to demonstrate solidarity and strength through joint political action as well as to keep up with friends. Amar met his wife, now an activist with the Sangath, when she came to work with the Andolan.

As the activists' political understanding has evolved toward sustainable development, so has his or her concern about the "authenticity" of different political actions (Baviskar 1997). An ideal activist is someone who has succeeded in erasing the contradictions between belief and practice. For instance, Amar abandoned the Tilonia model of rural development because he felt that, even though it claimed to work for the empowerment of villagers, it continued to rely heavily on outside resources over which the villagers had no control. The political objectives of an authentic organization would be blunted if its agenda were shaped more by its donor agencies than by its members.

Within the Sangath, the concern for squaring practice with ideology permeates most aspects of organizational relations as well as activists' lifestyles, which are markedly unencumbered with material possessions. Amar recalls that initially their frugality bordered on the ascetic: they would have heated arguments about whether to use oil for cooking (because the villagers could not afford to use it). Over the years, the austerities have become less rigorous—standards changed as activists mellowed and as consumerism made inroads into Alirajpur. Now activists are less troubled or embarrassed by the occasional visit to a restaurant or the cinema. In fact, visits home are often welcome respites from arduous rurality, a chance to briefly luxuriate in metropolitan middle-class comforts.

ACTIVISTS AS ATAVISTS: A RETURN TO A PRISTINE WORLD?

The intellectual streams shaping the ideology of Indian environmental activists have been described by Guha as "Crusading Gandhian," upholding the precapitalist village as the ideal of social and ecological harmony; "appropriate technology," which emphasizes the use of resource-conserving, labor-intensive technology; and the "Ecological Marxist," which holds that political and economic equity must be achieved prior to ecological conservation (Guha 1988). All of these streams have shaped the model of sustainable development, as has another minor current: "Adivasi assertion," that is, the notion that tribal people who despite their exploitation maintain and use complex systems of knowledge for managing natural resources sustainably are ideal stewards of the land (Baviskar 1995, 44–47). In this theoretical edifice, power is concentrated in the hands of a centralized state that represents mainly the interests of the urban-industrial complex. Political action, therefore, is aimed at liberating the poor tribal villager and the natural resources that rightfully belong to him or her from the clutches of the state. Thus, adivasis are simultaneously people who possess the answer to the development dilemma and people who have to be protected and helped to become more resourceful politically.

This analysis lands the activist in a dilemma. On the one hand, there is a strong urge to respect the beliefs and sentiments of the adivasis; on the other, there is an equally strong urge to transform adivasi consciousness. The same is true for adivasi institutions: activists simultaneously profess the desire to revive local institutions even as they seek to modify them irrevocably. For instance, traditional adivasi dispute-resolution practices only allowed men to arbitrate; women are never accorded the status of elders. Activists feel uncomfortable with the systematic way in which adivasi society downgrades its female members, yet their inherent belief in cultural plurality keeps them from protesting.[13] While activists claim to believe in letting adivasis decide their own agenda, activists' ideology, and their very presence and intervention, transform the terms under which an agenda for action is set. There is a strong desire on the part of the activist to believe that adivasi struggle is spontaneous and to erase the intervention of the activist.

This desire to believe in autochthonous action gives rise to piquant situations. For example, a public meeting was organized by eminent journalists and social commentators Prabhash Joshi and Nikhil Chakravarty at the Gandhi Peace Foundation in Delhi on 12 March 1995 to address the issues raised by the tribal critique of development. The speakers at the daylong meeting included Medha Patkar (of Narmada Bachao Andolan), Swami Agnivesh (Bandhua Mukti Morcha [Campaign for the Liberation of Bonded Laborers]), Sundarlal Bahuguna (Chipko and Tehri Bachao Andolan), Siddhraj Dhadda (a veteran Gandhian from Rajasthan), Dr B. D. Sharma (former Commissioner for Scheduled Castes and Tribes), and Justice Rajinder Sachchar (People's Union for Democratic Rights) — something of a who's who of prominent public figures active in "alternative politics." However, the very first speakers were not celebrities at all but three tribal leaders from the

Narmada Valley. They spoke in their own language, Bhilali, and activists translated their speeches into Hindi for the rest of the audience. During the translations, I noticed that something odd was consistently occurring. Both of the activist-translators edited out every reference to their own intervention! So one tribal leader's statement that "we were suffering because the state was totally unjust. Then Medhabai, Silvybai [referring to the activists] came and went around the villages, they taught us to come together and fight" was translated by the activists as "we were suffering because the state was totally unjust, so we came together and fought." Thus, activists perceive the key role that they have played in building alliances between feuding villages, transforming adivasi consciousness and the terms of conflict between them and the state (Baviskar 1995, 179–84), as embarrassing and do not speak of it at all. This elision is not simply due to modesty but also stems from a belief that authentic adivasi struggles must be unmediated by the presence of "outside" agencies.[14]

Another factor with which activists refuse to come to terms is perhaps the most serious in its implications for the future of adivasi society: proletarianization. As mentioned before, the crisis of ecological productivity in Alirajpur is inexorably pushing people into the circuit of labor migration, so that larger numbers of adivasis stay away for longer periods of time to work in Gujarat in intensive agriculture or the construction industry.[15] Besides the ecological "push" factors, there is also the pull that adivasis, especially the young, feel toward earning cash and being able to afford a wristwatch, a new sari, or some other manufactured product. But seasonal migration has no place in the activists' vision of creating sustainable communities in tribal areas. All their developmental efforts are geared toward re-creating self-provisioning village republics that will, they hope, obviate the need for *mazdoori* (wage labor); they make no attempt to organize workers as members of an agricultural or industrial proletariat. Given the likelihood that adivasis' steadily increasing participation in the labor force will only grow with liberalization, this reluctance on the part of activists to come to terms with an unpleasant fact of life appears inexplicable.

Activists assert their faith in the model of sustainable development, which will secure the welfare of adivasis as well as the environment, where there is no role for "adivasis as proletarians." However, the model is far from being achieved, adivasis are increasingly proletarianized, and activists refuse to change their diagnosis and prescription for social change. I would argue that activists' refusal to accept the fact that adivasis are proletarians, and the failure to mobilize them politically as members of a working class that faces exploitation from new agents, labor contractors, and landowners instead of the Forest Department, stems from the belief that the best future for adivasis has to be close to nature. That is, they believe that adivasi culture is authentic and alive only when it retains its links to nature. If the activists perceived the threat to the tribal-nature relationship as primarily an issue of rights to livelihood and self-determination, would they not intercede on behalf of adivasis in all aspects of their productive life — as laborers as well as peasants? The singular focus on livelihood derived from self-cultivation and the forest can be explained partly in terms of the activists' own preconceptions that the place of adivasis in the proper scheme of things should be close to nature. Although for most adivasis, too, a life on the land is still the preferred self-image, increasing reliance on migration is causing this ideal to recede ever farther over the horizon.

ADIVASI LEADERS: THE STRUGGLE FOR SELF-RULE AND SELF-RESPECT

The activists' stand is at considerable variance with that of state-level tribal politicians. For the former, political mobilization for control over natural resources is simply a means to an end, that is, sustainable development. For the latter, political control over the state is the key that holds the answer to all questions about development. As mentioned earlier, the adivasi leaders within the Sangath are increasingly drawn to the latter ideology. The reasons for this can be traced in the growing frustration that tribal leaders feel, a frustration that stems partly from the political scenario without and their role within the Sangath.

The Sangath has four full-time adivasi leaders, who receive modest salaries, as well as about twenty part-time volunteer activists who are farmers. Of the adivasi leaders, Vesta, at forty, is the oldest. Since his school days, Vesta has been unafraid of speaking out against corrupt officials. In fact, when Amar came to Alirajpur, someone directed him to Vesta as a kindred spirit. Vesta allowed Amar to stay with him for several months and they gradually began working together. During his years with the Sangath, Vesta has remained steadfast in maintaining that the organization should remain modest in its endeavors, retaining its original focus on corruption. He is unwilling to participate in the antidam Andolan movement or to travel to events organized by other groups. It is a sad irony that Vesta was the person most brutally tortured by the police and the Alirajpur subdivisional magistrate in connection with the antidam struggle (Baviskar 1995, 210–11). This experience demoralized Vesta's family. Because his family becomes nervous in his absence, fearing that Vesta has been picked up by the police, Vesta has become homebound, which severely hampers his work. Vesta is married, with five daughters; he has recently taken a second wife. He supports his large family by continuing to cultivate some land in his village, although he lives in Sondwa, the block headquarters.

The most articulate adivasi leader in the Sangath is Mahesh, who has studied in college. Mahesh has always been deeply interested in furthering his understanding of political theory and reads voraciously. In his enjoyment of ideological debates, he comes closest to the stereotype of the left-wing intellectual. Among the adivasi leaders, Mahesh, more than anyone, could have successfully aspired to obtaining a government job, but he chose not to do so. His decision to work with the Sangath is constantly attacked by his family, which feels that he could have commanded a better status in a *sarkari naukri* (government job). Of the other two tribal leaders, Isha, a college student, joined the Sangath through the Andolan, which worked in his village (which was slated to be submerged by the dam). Budh Singh is from Mahesh's village and learned to read and write from him. Budh Singh's father participated in the Lal Topi Andolan in the 1940s and was drawn to the activist cause and lifestyle. Budh Singh subsequently changed his name to Adivasi Budh Singh Azad—a proclamation of adivasi pride.[16] Both Isha and Budh Singh have worked in the Sangath for five years.

The adivasi leaders are distinguished from other adivasi members of the Sangath by their literacy and the fact that they draw a salary and are not primarily dependent on agriculture for a living. Whereas other adivasi men wear cotton drawers or loincloths, the leaders dress in trousers and shirts, sometimes made from *khadi* (hand-spun, hand-loomed cloth popularized by Gandhi). Although their dress, demeanor, and command over nonlocal knowledge is close to those of the activists, and the charisma of certain individuals may make them more popular than the activists, they are generally not accorded the same respect as are the activists by Sangath members. People tend to be more easily convinced of the wisdom of a particular course of action if the program is espoused by an activist rather than an adivasi leader. To some extent, the presence of the activists tends to exercise the banyan tree effect in that other plants cannot grow in their shade.

Their passage through the formal education system, their choice to give up manual work, and their awareness of other life chances make adivasi leaders highly ambivalent about the tribal-nature relationship advocated by the activists as an ideal. They can empathize with the statement of Amarsinh Chaudhri, a tribal leader and former chief minister of Gujarat, that "today the tribals have a relationship with forests and the land because they have no other means and choices. If they could come out of the forests they could gain so much more. Their land holdings are very small so they have to depend on fruits, leaves and gum. If they get good land, they will grow better type of grains; their entire habits will change" (*Indian Express*, 22 September 1988). Thus, life in the forest is not desired by adivasis but is forced on them. If they had more control over resources, they could be masters of their own destinies.

These beliefs are expressed in a letter written by the adivasi leader who is the president of the Sangath: "Tribal areas have everything: coal, iron, minerals, rivers, roads. We need to start a region-wide struggle to block access. . . . I can't swallow the line that we should be satisfied with small battles and small victories. . . . If we establish our control over resources, all our enemies will be automatically defeated." This view echoes the stand taken by the widely discussed "Report of Members of Parliament and Experts to make Recommendations on the Salient Features of the Law for Extending Provisions of the Constitution (73d Amendment Act, 1992) to Scheduled Areas," known as the Bhuria Committee Report (after its chairman Dilip Singh Bhuria, MP from Jhabua, the district of which Alirajpur is a part). The report is based on the constitutional provision that *panchayati raj* (local government) institutions in tribal areas may be formed in ways that accommodate traditional tribal structures of authority. The committee recommended that tribal areas be made autonomous and

> management of land, forest, water, air [and other] resources should be vested in the gram sabha. The gram sabhas should be federated upwards into autonomous district councils along the lines of those existing in north-east India. Further, "the tribal people have been marginalized in the process of industrialization and urbanization, leading to strong resentment among them. . . . It has been our stand that the tribal community should be regarded as in command of the economic resources. In this view of the matter, in a resource-based industry, the partnership of the village community and the outside capitalist-financiers should be recognized." (Sharma 1995, 46–48)

While activists dismiss tribal leaders who focus exclusively on self-rule for adivasi areas as self-serving politicians and assert that sustainable development must be the ultimate goal, adivasi leaders accuse activists of conspiring to keep adivasis backward by suppressing their voices. In a three-state rally organized in January 1995 in Alirajpur, a Chaudhri tribal leader from Gujarat took this stand and declared that, as non-tribals, activists have no right to speak at tribal forums. The activists were deeply offended, and in the bitter recriminations that followed, the adivasi Sangath president defended the Chaudhri leader, saying that

> for thousands of years, we dalits have been cheated time and again. But so far we have never cheated established society; we have hesitated to even ask the names or caste of anyone who has come to our village. . . . We have now started doubting you activists who have come out from big cities like Delhi, Bombay, Calcutta or from palatial houses, but this does not mean that you should doubt us in turn. The wounds that the so-called upper class people had inflicted on us, and are inflicting on us even today, are still fresh. That is why we can doubt you without a qualm: where do these alleged well-wishers want to take our society? The tradition of using our society any way you like must be ended.

The anger and pain that marked this speech brought into the open the long-simmering resentment of tribal leaders toward activists. The idealism of the latter, their definition of the struggle in terms of sustainable development, and their unwillingness to negotiate more pragmatic compromises are seen by adivasi leaders as utopian and politically risky endeavors. By making Sangath members wait for sustainable development, activists seem to be forcing them to forego any chance of capitalizing on the ongoing wave of dalit politics, which to many adivasi leaders appears to be the only viable political strategy, at the moment. The desire of activists to remain "ideologically pure" and undertake a politically more ambitious and risky strategy is seen by many tribal leaders as arrogance made possible by the economic security that activists can always count on due to their literate skills and middle-class family backgrounds.

Equal remuneration in the Sangath notwithstanding, the economic differences between activists and tribal leaders are resented by the latter. If funds are solicited from the outside, middle-class skills and connections always prevail. Activists also receive larger subsidies from their families than do tribal leaders. Even though the differences in living standards may not be very marked, tribal leaders are conscious that activists have given up what they, the leaders, can never even aspire to achieve. When a Chaudhri tribal leader from Gujarat comes in his own jeep to Alirajpur and spends money freely on long distance phone calls, the adivasi leaders of Alirajpur do feel a tinge of envy. Another arena in which adivasi leaders feel their relative lack of power keenly is in interactions with nonadivasi and adivasi government officials. Tribal leaders resent the fact that when they visit them in the company of activists the officials speak only to the activists, often using English and ignoring the presence of the adivasis. Although the activists try to ensure that this will not happen, the officials respond only to the presence of people they consider closer to their own status. This also happens at press conferences and other gatherings. Thus, an equally articulate and able tribal spokesperson finds himself or herself sidelined because of the activist's presence.

The discriminatory treatment meted out to tribal leaders has led some of them to shift their focus to a movement for greater dignity and self-respect. As discussed earlier, one stream of this movement is accommodated within the Sangath's ideology that the issue of dignity is inseparable from the issue of control over the material relations of production. Thus, adivasis should make their distinctive cultural identity the source of their strength in what is primarily a political struggle. However, for some tribal leaders the project of gaining self-respect cannot wait for political control. They have therefore opened a dialogue with the religious reformist stream, which promises self-respect at the price of shedding particular adivasi practices. Besides the adoption of Hinduized religious practices—giving up meat, liquor, and so on—some adivasis have also changed their tribal names to Kshatriya-sounding names, adding Kshatriya *jaat* (warrior caste) names as their surnames. Thus, a Bhil adivasi called Pema, son of Gutia, might have his name changed to Prem Singh Solanki. This transformation usually occurs at the time of school enrollment. Boys who get to school give up the traditional loincloth in favor of trousers; girls wear saris like urban women. Most profoundly, school education in Alirajpur has inculcated in youth a strong feeling that working on the land is demeaning. Their aspirations turn away from the land toward white-collar jobs.

The adivasi leaders' diverse strategies for seeking self-respect are criticized by the activists, who see these as side issues. They point out that the pre-occupation with dignity is limited for the most part to a privileged segment of adivasis who are already secure about their livelihood and can afford to spend their collective energies on strategies of upward mobility, rising in the eyes of nonadivasis. The Chaudhri leader from Gujarat who spoke of forging a regionwide tribal identity and attacked activists for speaking on behalf of adivasis, is criticized by activists for receiving funds from an indigenous people's rights organization abroad. This leader is particularly reviled by activists because he champions the cause of all adivasis and obscures the fact that much of the Chaudhri tribe in Gujarat is a fairly prosperous landowning group (Shah 1991,

289–93) and that its class position is quite different from that of the poor Bhils of Alirajpur. The small, relatively affluent segment of adivasis would like to believe that its particular concerns about dignity are shared by all adivasis, but for the vast majority in their community the key issues are still related to natural resources. Adivasi leaders who move away from these concerns are accused of betraying the very people they claim to represent.

THE MASSES: VOICES FROM THE WAYSIDE?

Left out of this debate are most adivasis, who still depend on the natural environment for sustenance and find themselves increasingly unable to survive on the land. For these adivasis, both ecological sustainability and cultural dignity remain somewhat remote concerns. They make the most of the opportunities for cultivating nevad and harvesting forest products that their struggle in the Sangath has secured for them even as they strike out further and further in search of wage labor to make ends meet. Even though seasonal migration is eating into the hill economy, the Sangath has no strategy to strengthen its members' bargaining power vis-à-vis labor contractors and employers. This failure may eventually erode the hitherto cordial relationship between activists and Sangath members (Baviskar 1995, 188–91). If the activists desire to maintain their role in political action, they will be compelled to address the issue of migration.

A rare acknowledgment of adivasis' situation as migrant laborers is a song composed by an activist, which has been a raging hit at Sangath meetings for more than a year because of its evocative imagery of what it means to be a mazdoor.

Moonde dauba meline, kakhoma gudara ghaline,
Navsarima phirine, tadma bartha hoovine,
Haurine taav vethine,
Poyha padya re apu jeeve hata kaurine,
Poyha kunin re, tharla kun re?
Malik kun re, majur kun re?

With the tin kept on our heads, the quilt clutched under one arm,
Wandering in Navsari, sleeping out in the cold,
Enduring fever and chills,
We earned some money by breaking apart body and soul,
Who gets the money, who has nothing?
Who is the owner, who is the labourer?

CONCLUSION: WARRING VISIONS OR A NEW ENVIRONMENTALISM?

The literature in environmental sociology tends, by and large, to identify particular actors with particular environmental discourses. The "discourse of development," for instance, has been dominated by the modern state, a key agent of ecological and social change because of its role in initiating nationalist strategies of industrial and urban development. The same state can, in response to pressures exerted by international environmental movements, modify its policies to preserve pockets of "wilderness" even as it further intensifies natural resource extraction to meet the needs of structural adjustment policies. In the balance, the discourse of "national development" still prevails over green rhetoric.[17] The counterpoint to the discourse of development is supposed to be the discourse of environmentalism. In India, the environmentalist discourse has been dominated by ecological Marxists, who believe that political action must be aimed at achieving sustainable development.[18] So far, there has been a consensus that participants in tribal/peasant movements around forest issues represent ecological Marxism in action (Guha 1989). Not enough attention has been focused on the different groups, with their disparate ideologies, who comprise these movements. I have attempted such an exercise in this essay, with a view to understanding the political strategies and postures that tribal movements end up adopting as a result of trying to accommodate the conflicts and compromises that come with collaboration. I have argued that the only "pure" environmentalists in these movements are the activists from middle-class backgrounds who are engaged in facilitating tribal mobilization. For these activists, ecological conservation is possible only when tribal people have control over natural resources *and* remain faithful to the principles of sustainable development. The refusal of the tribal leadership to accept the latter condition has been seen by the activists as a betrayal of the cause of adivasis. I have argued that the differentiation of the adivasi community has created a dilemma that is difficult to resolve within the present terms of debate. The emergence of an adivasi "middle class" that is not directly dependent on the land has complicated the picture by challenging the notion that the only viable future for tribal people is "close to nature." At the same time, the class tensions between activists and tribal leaders have vitiated work within the Sangath and in the regional tribal movement so that each questions the other's authority to speak. Yet one hesitates to side with the activists and allege that the tribal leadership has sold out to the state's dominant discourse of development. In the larger pecking order of

Indian society, Dilip Singh Bhuria will always remain a dalit, even if he becomes the chief minister of Madhya Pradesh.

This essay deals with ongoing processes that are dynamic and open-ended. It describes only the emerging lines of conflict and cooperation without attempting to speculate on whether they will succeed. At present, some tribal movements for regional autonomy, such as Jharkhand, are discredited due to charges of corruption against their leadership, their constituencies betrayed. There is a danger of something similar happening in Madhya Pradesh too. The viability of sustainable development at the regional level is untested; its visionary charter is not even a complete blueprint yet. These differing conceptions of utopia are not watertight compartments. As Sangath members, activists, and adivasis talk and work together and learn from each other, their essential solidarity comes to the fore whenever the Sangath has to respond to an acute, state-induced crisis. This underlying unity leads one to think that the current bitterness will ultimately contribute to an enrichment of ideas and understanding on all sides. It must be remembered that ideological coherence is a luxury usually absent during praxis.

The current debate between adivasi leaders and activists represents a democratization of the environmentalist discourse. So far, the ideological debates over who is or is not an ecological Marxist have been dominated by middle-class activists, who are able to draw on literate intellectual traditions and metropolitan ideologies and have almost exclusively defined what sustainable development is and who constitutes a fitting torchbearer for the cause. Their explanations and interpretations of tribal movements have been accepted largely without comment by sympathetic observers in the "outside world." Now, for the first time, other participants in the movement, drawing largely on their experience on the ground, are questioning the authority of the activists to represent others and are modifying the very terms of the debate by linking it to issues such as dalit identity. The gates to the ideological arena are being torn off their hinges as previously excluded groups barge in and demand to play, even if it means changing the game. In the process of negotiating these complex claims and counterclaims, it may appear that the cause of "nature" is being neglected. But nature—the biophysical habitat as well as the intrinsic qualities of different social groups—remains at the heart of the discussion. Meanwhile, just as they have spread their economic risks by pursuing an ecologically diverse livelihood strategy, the adivasis of Alirajpur spread their political risks by participating in both activists' and tribal leaders' strategies, even as they vote with their feet and migrate for work.

1 The term *adivasi* derives from the Sanskrit roots *adi* (first, original) and *vasi* (inhabitant) and refers to India's Scheduled Tribes. Although the term suggests that tribal people are "indigenous" in the American sense of being clearly distinguished from white settlers, this is not historically true for India, where the boundaries between tribal groups and others have always been porous. Using the term *tribe* alone has its own problems (Hardiman 1987, 11–17). I prefer to use *adivasi*, for it suggests a specifically Indian experience of autonomy and subjugation and not the least because this is how tribal people in Central India refer to themselves.

2 To avoid clumsy and long-winded usage, I shall use the term *activists* only to refer to the middle-class youth from urban backgrounds who have settled in the tribal region. I shall use the term *tribal leaders* or *adivasi leaders* in reference to local activists who have joined the union.

3 For a description of welfare programs in Alirajpur, see Baviskar 1994, 2497.

4 Anjan is *Hardwickia binata*.

5 Khakhra is *Butea monosperma*.

6 *Halai* is *Boswellia serrata*.

7 After prolonged agitation by the Sangath, the Forest Department conducted a survey of encroachments in Sondwa block in 1988. The survey revealed that almost every cultivator had supplemented his or her legal holdings with several small plots of nevad. In Anjanvara, a village of thirty-three households, fourteen cases of encroachment (with most cases representing joint cultivation by two or more brothers) amounting to 192 hectares of forest land were recorded. Most of these fields have been cultivated since 1970 and some even earlier.

8 Naxalite groups practice the Marxist-Leninist tactics of armed struggle against oppressive landowners and state officials. The first wave of naxalism occurred in West Bengal in the late 1960s and was suppressed by the Left Front state government. At present, parts of Bihar and a pocket of east-central India (where the borders of Madhya Pradesh, Maharashtra, Andhra Pradesh, and Orissa meet) are naxalite strongholds.

9 Most of this work is voluntary and is based on a labor-sharing custom called *laah* in which a household's labor-intensive tasks are shared by every household in the village, which sends one person to help with the work in return for a feast. All households, in turn, are entitled to reciprocal help. In 1990–91, the Sangath also paid people by using funds from Jawahar Rozgar Yojna (a government employment program) in panchayats where its members had been elected.

10 Compare this to a five-year grant of $185,000 awarded by the International Labor Organization in 1988 to a unit of the Self-Employed Women's Association (SEWA) in neighboring Gujarat, which resulted in the afforestation of exactly eleven hectares of land. The resource intensity of such projects raises doubts about their replicability in larger areas, while their dependence on external funding calls into question the accountability of the organization to the local people among whom it works.

11 Although the term *dalit* (literally, "oppressed") is usually used to denote only the Scheduled Castes, I shall employ it in the sense argued for by tribal activists in Madhya Pradesh, that is, to refer to all the oppressed — Scheduled Castes, Scheduled Tribes, and some of the other backward classes.

12 However, in some cases, especially in places with a progressive tradition of middle-class participation in social reform (e.g., Brahman Pune), activists emerged from fairly supportive environments.

13 Here I refer only to those activists who feel a sense of disquiet at the paternalism that inevitably creeps into a relationship that they would like to be egalitarian. Many activists who arrive with the intention of doing "social work" — upliftment and improvement — feel quite at ease with paternalism.

14 This is an interesting inversion of the state's belief that adivasis resist only when they are "misled" or "incited" by outside activists. Perhaps activists play down their own roles in order to avoid providing ammunition for a government attack. The ironic outcome is that both the state and the activists themselves end up devaluing and distorting the latter's contribution.

15 This is true for large parts of the Bhil belt; entire adivasi villages from the Mahi-Kadana area in Gujarat are deserted, except for the aged, eight months of the year. The rest of the population returns only during the monsoons to harvest a crop and then returns to wage labor. For a detailed account of this phenomenon, see Breman 1985.

16 *Azad* is a Hindi word meaning "free." It was also the title adopted by a renowned activist of the independence movement, Chandrashekhar Azad, who was born in Jhabua.

17 India still has not witnessed the phenomenon of the state championing what may be called "ecological Fordism" — American-style green consumerism as the path to economic prosperity (see Gore 1992).

18 Gadgil and Guha 1995; and Center for Science and Environment 1985 provide good illustrations of the analysis and ideology of Ecological Marxism.

J. Peter Brosius

VOICES FOR THE

BORNEO RAIN FOREST

Writing the History of an

Environmental Campaign

Two thousand miles northwest of PNG . . . thousands of indigenous
people in Sarawak, Malaysia linked arms in human barricades to
block the logging roads deep inside the tropical rain forest in a desperate
effort to stop indiscriminate and destructive logging. . . . Although these
resistance fighters had little chance against the powerful forces arrayed
against them, their courage inspired international protests that are
still continuing.

One of the Sarawak peoples, the Penan, sent a delegation to the
United States with the help of an environmental group, the Friends of
the Earth. They walked into my office one winter day, looking a little
like visitors from another millennium, their straw headgear and wooden
bracelets the only remnants of the culture they left behind, wearing
borrowed sweaters as protection against the unaccustomed cold. Using
a translator who had painstakingly learned their language, the Penans
described how the logging companies had set up floodlights to continue
their destruction of the forest all through the night as well as the day.
Like the shell-shocked inhabitants of a city under siege, they described
how not even the monsoon rains slowed the chain saws and logging
machinery that was destroying the ancestral
home of their people.

These are the front lines of the war against nature now raging
throughout the world. These words from the Penans are hauntingly
similar to the pleas of the Ethiopians invaded by Mussolini's forces in
1935 and the calls for help from Hungary when Soviet tanks rolled
through its streets in 1956. — Al Gore, *Earth in the Balance: Ecology
and the Human Spirit*, pp. 283–5

Because I'm an earthling on this plant.
— Jerry Garcia, explaining why he was testifying on behalf
of the Penan before the U.S. Congress, July 11, 1989

On the morning of 5 July 1991, a group of eight individuals from the United States, the United Kingdom, Germany, and Australia walked onto the grounds of a timber camp at the mouth of the Baram River in Sarawak, East Malaysia, climbed up the booms of several barges, and chained themselves there. They hung banners from their perches, played guitars, and ignored the entreaties of the officials who asked them to come down. After some eight hours, they were brought down by police and arrested. To the great frustration of the authorities, they had hidden their passports and gave as their names things such as Chipko Mendes Penan, Stop the Logging, Save the Forests, and Let the Truth Prevail, names that duly appeared on the mug shots taken at Miri police head-quarters. When subsequently their identities were established, they were tried, and most were sentenced to sixty days in prison. They were there to protest the destruction of Sarawak's forests by timber companies and the effects of that destruction on a small group of hunter-gatherers, the Penan.

This single action was but one small piece of a much larger environmental campaign over the Sarawak rain forests that had been growing since 1987. If one could venture to suggest a starting date for this campaign, it would be 31 March 1987. On that day, Penan in over a dozen locations erected blockades against logging companies that were encroaching on their lands. It was not long before photographic images of these blockades, accompanied by transcripts of Penan statements, made their way to Japan, Australia, Europe, and North America. The result was a dramatic upsurge in interest in the Penan among numerous northern environmental and indigenous rights organizations. Within a very short time, the Penan became the focus of a broad-based transnational campaign to stop the logging in Sarawak. The momentum of this campaign grew through the late 1980s and early 1990s. In a manner analogous to the case of the Kayapó of Brazil, the Penan struggle had a very high international media profile and was supported by numerous prominent political figures and celebrities. For a while at least, the spotlight of global environmental activism was focused directly on Sarawak. In a series of interviews I conducted with European and American environmentalists, Penan resistance to logging was repeatedly cited as an exemplar of the way in which indigenous peoples can assert control over their own destinies and in the process halt the loss of global biodiversity.

The Malaysian government responded vigorously to this campaign, criticizing what they portrayed as northern "ecocolonialism" and making compelling counterarguments about northern consumption. In the process of formulating their response, Malaysia came to play an increasingly visible role on the world diplomatic stage. It emerged as a leader among the nonaligned countries and played a key role in directing the shift in the North-South debate toward an explicit critique of northern environmentalism. This was most clearly seen in the highly visible role played by the Malaysian prime minister, Dr. Mahatir Mohamed, at the 1992 Earth Summit in Rio de Janeiro. Much of Dr. Mahatir's rhetoric was formulated as an explicit response to critics of the Malaysian government's policy on logging and the effects of that policy on the welfare of the Penan. It is a remarkable state of affairs that a small group of forest nomads living in a remote part of Borneo should have become a central focus in a debate that has global repercussions.

The Sarawak campaign is of considerable historical significance. Northern nongovernmental organizations (NGOs) never expected such an aggressive response from Malaysia, nor did they anticipate that Malaysian NGOs would themselves eventually find common cause with their own government. Though certainly not the only factor, the fallout from the international Sarawak campaign has fundamentally transformed the way in which northern NGOs campaign over issues affecting the South.

This campaign has been the subject of my research for the last several years. It is my aim to produce an ethnographic-historical account not merely of Penan resistance to logging but of the campaign itself. I am interested in examining the discursive and institutional contours of the campaign in order to understand how various agents—the Penan, the Malaysian government, Malaysian NGOs, northern mainstream NGOs and northern grassroots NGOs—have each constructed and contested the terms of the debate. In conducting this research, I have drawn on a range of sources: interviews, environmentalist campaign literature, hagiographic Malaysian political tracts, newspaper accounts of speeches by prominent Malaysian politicians, and the like. It is a project that has taken me not only to the encampments of nomadic Penan but to the offices of the Ministry of Primary Industries in Kuala Lumpur, the offices of the Rainforest Action Network in San Francisco, the World Wide Fund for Nature (WWF) international headquarters outside of Geneva, the halls of Parliament in Vienna, the offices of the International Tropical Timber Organization in Yokohama, and to New York, London, Copenhagen, Munich, Basel, Sydney, and elsewhere.

My purpose in the present discussion is to consider what each of these sites has to do with the others and to describe my attempts to comprehend the Sarawak campaign. The approach that I take here is genealogical in the sense that I address a series of broader theoretical issues in reference to the process of my own attempts to understand this campaign at various stages and in various ways. This project, I believe, has important implications not only for interrogating the nature of ethnographic writing but for theorizing environmental discourses.

At its most basic level, ethnographic writing concerns the problem of bringing coherence to some set of observations about the world. An ethnographic account is a kind of crystallization, a setting into form. The simple question I ask myself as I continue to examine the Sarawak campaign is "How do I write about it?" In the present discussion, I intend to combine the task of describing some of the broad outlines of the campaign with a discussion of the issues I have confronted in the act of trying to produce a coherent account of it. Why, the reader might ask, is this problematic? The Sarawak campaign certainly appears to be in some way coherent. That coherence, however, is illusory.

First, this is an ethnographic context that has no site. Certainly it is in some sense about a particular place in Borneo — the interior Baram District of Sarawak — but as often as not that place is as imagined as it is real: a site of pristine innocence, captured in the titles of books that have appeared in conjunction with the campaign — such as *Nomads of the Dawn* (1995) — and films — such as *Into the Heart of the Last Paradise* (1988). Is it really about that place or does it merely make use of images from that place — arresting images of loincloth-clad indigenous peoples standing at blockades — to speak to larger issues such as indigenous wisdom, the fate of rain forests, and the future of the planet?

Not only is it not *about* one site, but it is not carried on at any single site. The "campaign" is a series of direct actions (climbing timber barges, fasts in front of the Swiss Parliament, attempts to blockade the Rotterdam harbor), decisions by the Austrian Parliament to restrict the importation of tropical timber, resolutions by the European Parliament, congressional resolutions condemning Sarawak timber, press conferences, benefit concerts, newsletters, letter-writing campaigns, faxes, e-mail messages, and NGO strategizing meetings.

This campaign not only lacks a site; it also lacks an issue. That is to say, the "issue" may be very different to any number of differentially positioned (or repositioned) observers at different points in time. The issue, then, is both a function of the position of different agents and of the way in which it is in turn actively produced and constructed by such agents. Thus, while for one NGO the problem of logging in Sarawak may be one of a corrupt political system, for another group it may a problem of northern consumption, for the Malaysian government a problem of instigators, and for the Penan the failure of the queen to return.

Finally, the context in which this campaign is embedded is not station-

322   J. Peter Brosius

ary. Environmental discourses themselves are changing, responding to critiques of elitism and charges that they ignore social justice issues, that they are a form of neocolonialism, or that they ignore North-South imbalances. Institutions are emerging and evolving. Actions in spaces that were thinkable ten years ago no longer are. Environmental politics and discourses are moving very fast. The Sarawak campaign is embedded within this temporal stream. Locating and describing it are thus very difficult tasks. And yet it is not just a thing of fragments, of disconnected events. There is a degree of coherence around the issue of logging and indigenous rights in Sarawak, and the campaign itself has had that tangible quality referred to as momentum. The problem, then, is one of locating that coherence or locating divergent axes along which coherence might be made apparent in the form of an ethnographic-historical account.

INTERSECTIONS: THE DEVELOPMENT OF THE SARAWAK CAMPAIGN

In order to pursue this discussion, it is necessary to provide some background on how the situation in Sarawak developed and how it evolved into such a highly visible international campaign. This story begins at the intersection of three developments.

There is first the story of logging in Sarawak. The movement of large-scale mechanized logging into the interior of Sarawak has occurred rather quickly — mostly since the 1970s. Sarawak is today a major supplier of tropical hardwood on international markets and, at least until recently, was experiencing one of the highest rates of deforestation in the world. Timber operations have now nearly reached the Indonesian border in several places, and Malaysian timber companies have begun to move into Laos, Papua New Guinea, Surinam, Brazil, Cameroon, and elsewhere.[1]

Logging has a dramatic effect on the lives of Penan. The most immediate effect is on the forest resources that they depend on for subsistence and trade: sago palms, which form the basis of Penan subsistence, are uprooted by bulldozers, the trees from which they get fruit are felled, game disappears, rivers become silted, rattan is destroyed, and graves are obliterated. For Penan, logging means hunger. But what is of as much concern to the Penan as the privation caused by logging is the way in which logging has altered the landscape in which they live. Though to all appearances a complete wilderness, the landscape is one imbued with biographical and cultural significance. There exists a strong coherence between the physical landscape, history, genealogy, and identities of individuals and communities. With logging, the cultural density of the landscape — all those sites with biographical, social, and historical significance — is obliterated.[2]

A second development is the proliferation and growth of rain forest and indigenous rights movements on a global scale.[3] The Sarawak campaign exists within a larger context of concern about the fate of rain forests and indigenous peoples, a concern that began to grow perceptibly during the 1980s. What is remarkable when one examines the history of the rain forest movement is how suddenly it came into existence. The mid-1980s was a period in which rain forest groups were forming throughout Europe, the United Kingdom, Australia, Japan, and the United States, and existing environmental groups such as Friends of the Earth and Greenpeace were expanding their own involvement in tropical forest issues. Also important in the growth of the rain forest movement was the increasing role played by southern NGOs. Here the case of Malaysia is particularly significant. Increasingly through the 1980s, the city of Penang became a center of intellectual development in Third World environmental politics. By the late 1980s, Penang was home to five interlinked NGOs: Sahabat Alam Malaysia (SAM, Friends of the Earth–Malaysia), Consumer Association of Penang (CAP), World Rainforest Movement (WRM), Third World Network (TWN), and Asia-Pacific Peoples Environmental Network (APPEN). This group of NGOs, and SAM in particular, played a major role in the unfolding campaign.

The third element on which to triangulate this story concerns the figure of Swiss artist Bruno Manser. In 1984, after coming to Sarawak as part of a cave-exploring expedition, Manser disappeared into the forest and took up residence with a band of nomadic Penan. He remained among various nomadic groups for six and a half years. The story of the blockades and Manser are inextricably linked. More than any other single individual, it is Manser who is most responsible for bringing the situation of the Penan to world attention. Beginning in 1985, Manser began writing to a number of Malaysian and international environmental organizations. In a very short time, reporters, northern filmmakers, and environmentalists, as well as Malaysian security forces, began to seek him out in the forest. At the same time that Manser was working to make their situation known outside of Sarawak, he was simultaneously engaged in organizing the normally retiring Penan to resist. He traveled extensively throughout the Baram and Limbang areas, organizing meetings at which Penan aired their grievances about the activities of timber companies, discussed cases of harassment by loggers and police, and considered the possibility of erecting blockades.[4]

GENEALOGY: "NEGOTIATING CITIZENSHIP"

Elucidating the perspective I argue for here requires that I provide a brief overview of the course of my thinking about how best to describe the Sarawak campaign. The shifts I describe are discernible in a series of articles published in the last several years. My work can be divided into two types. On the one hand, I have written a number of pieces that examine particular fragments of the Sarawak campaign. For instance, I published one article that examined why some groups of Penan have resisted logging while others have acquiesced (Brosius 1997b). In another piece, I considered environmentalist representations of indigenous knowledge, in particular the subtle discursive shift that occurs when "knowledge" becomes an essentialized "wisdom" (1997a). In yet another piece, I examined some of the difficulties of translating Penan conceptions of landscape into the language of transnational environmental activism (2001). All of these accounts are fragments, detailed examinations of particular parts of the larger story. They do not represent attempts to provide anything like a comprehensive account of the history of the Sarawak campaign (to the extent that such a thing can be said to exist). On the other hand, I have written two pieces that attempt to provide a broader overview of the campaign. The first was a 1993 essay entitled "Negotiating Citizenship in a Commodified Landscape."[5] This article, written for a Social Science Research Council conference entitled Cultural Citizenship in Southeast Asia, organized by Renato Rosaldo, was my first attempt to try to bring some coherence to the story of the Sarawak campaign. Central to this piece was an examination of the forms of rhetoric employed by three of the parties involved: (1) the Penan, (2) the Malaysian government, and (3) northern environmentalists. It seemed to me then that what lay behind the political impasse that gave rise to the campaign was a fundamental disagreement over concepts such as *indigenous, conservation,* and *development.* I was interested in how each party had constructed the Penan and their relationship with the rain forest, the nation-state, or the fate of the planet. It seemed to me that the best way to approach this was to provide a multiplicity of often discordant voices. My second attempt to provide a more complete account of the Sarawak campaign recently appeared in the *American An-*

thropologist (1999b). It is the first piece that I wish to focus on here, as a way of elucidating how my perspective on the Sarawak campaign has shifted.

In "Negotiating Citizenship," I first examined the Penan perspective. I considered Penan conceptions of landscape, influenced by my reading of a number of authors who had been looking at the links between landscape, history, and sentiment: Renato Rosaldo's *Ilongot Headhunting* (1980), Steven Feld's *Sound and Sentiment* (1982), Fred Myers's *Pintupi Country, Pintupi Self* (1986), and the work of Keith Basso (1984, 1988), among others. I then considered the Penan response to logging. I examined the kinds of arguments Penan deployed in trying to familiarize themselves with government officials and company employees. These were arguments used to convince people who were unwilling or unable to appreciate their situation. I also examined Penan ideas about the moral accountability of those who would destroy the forest and the moral calculus they employed in describing why they felt compelled to erect blockades. Penan expressed utter frustration with what they described as the deafness of the government. I described how, seeing a sudden influx of Euro-American environmentalists, Penan transformed mere colonial nostalgia into a real expectation that the queen of England would return to once again "hold" them: seeing white people, they often said, was like seeing their parents come back to life.

I next considered the environmentalist perspective, in particular that of the Euro-American activists who had so dramatically internationalized the campaign and against whom the Malaysian government responded so strongly. I described the role of Bruno Manser in the campaign and how the photographs of indigenous hunter-gatherers standing in front of blockades, facing off against police and bulldozers, had provided such galvinizing images around which to mobilize international support. I was particularly interested in exploring the romanticized, essentialized images of Penan being deployed by environmentalists, exemplified in statements like this from the film *Blowpipes and Bulldozers* (1988): "The Penan are shy, gentle people who avoid the sun and move through the forest like swift and elusive ghosts, always ready to vanish without trace at the smallest alarm."

I was profoundly concerned that such representations objectify and dehumanize the Penan and that the subtext of this idyllic portrayal is that the claims of these people are more valid because they are aesthetically appealing to Euro-American audiences. I was also interested in environmentalist claims about the global significance of the Penan and, by extension, the ways in which northern environmentalism had become a discourse of globalism. Thus, for instance, the film *The Penan: A Disappearing Civilization in Borneo* (1989) ends with the statement: "What is taking place in Sarawak is a holocaust, a biological and cultural holocaust affecting the entire global ecosystem. . . . These Borneo natives, through their courageous stand, have become the guardians of these last whispers of antiquity. . . . Their struggle for survival is the struggle of all humanity. Their loss is our loss. Their future, our own." My thinking about environmentalist rhetoric was particularly influenced by the work of Mary Louise Pratt. In *Imperial Eyes: Travel Writing and Transculturation* (1992) Pratt examines "how travel books by Europeans about non-European parts of the world went (and go) about creating the 'domestic subject' of Euroimperialism" (4). She introduces the idea of anticonquest narratives, that is, "the strategies of representation whereby European bourgeois subjects seek to secure their innocence in the same moment as they assert European hegemony" (7). This argument seemed to me to have a certain relevance to the Sarawak campaign, given environmentalist declarations of solidarity with indigenous peoples and proclamations about a global biological heritage.

Finally, I examined the Malaysian government perspective on the Sarawak campaign.[6] In particular, I focused on the government imperative that Penan should enter the "mainstream" of Malaysian society and the way in which development stands as a totalizing discourse of legitimation, positioned against the counteridealogies of colonialism, communism, and environmentalism. In many cases, this took the form of trivializing commentary on the situation of the Penan. So, for instance, Prime Minister Mahatir stated that "We don't intend to turn the Penan into human zoological specimens to be gawked at by tourists and studied by anthropologists while the rest of the world passes them by . . . it's our policy to eventually bring all jungle dwellers into the mainstream. . . . There is nothing romantic about these helpless, half-starved and disease-ridden people" (World Rainforest Movement and Sahabat Alam Malaysia 1990, 140). Penan were variously portrayed as "confused" or merely acting up because they were being "instigated," misbehaving children under foreign influence, deluded objects of pity to whom only sympathy was due.

I also examined how the government responded to the international pressure being exerted on behalf of the Penan. For instance, one government publication stated that "It is questionable whether western critics who take upon themselves to judge what's good for the Penans would have wanted their forebears to have remained as cave and forest dwellers as they are pleading so strongly that the Penans should be left alone in the jungle, as if they were an endangered species. It is high time environmentalists treat Penans as humans and not as part of the biodiversity" (Ministry of Primary Industries 1992, 19).

The rest of this 1993 piece was a commentary on the implications of these contested images of Penan for thinking about cultural citizenship. My readings of works such as Harrison's *Forests: The Shadow of Civilization* (1992) and Short's *Imagined Country* (1991) directed me toward recognizing how the forest, or more correctly the place of the Penan within the forest, became a pivot for debates about their place as citizens in the Malaysian nation-state. Short argues that "National environmental ideologies use the myths of wilderness, countryside and city in establishing and maintaining a national identity" (55). Through development, this becomes a historical project, a project of futurity. To the extent that Penan resist, or are perceived to resist, development, and to the degree that they are seen to embrace the colonial legacy as embodied in northern environmental activists, they represent a threat to Malaysia's attempt to construct a national biography.

AUTO-CRITIQUE

This analysis of the Sarawak campaign provided an opportunity to present a number of entertaining quotes and vignettes and to bring a certain coherence to the campaign. Yet, as I have begun to produce a more comprehensive account of the history of the Sarawak campaign, one that takes more account of some of the complexities that have characterized it, I have become increasingly dissatisfied with the approach I took in 1993. A number of things led me to feel this way. One was the reaction of audiences and readers to this type of account. They were generally moved by my account of Penan resistance, aghast at the audacity of the Malaysian response, and amused by the romanticism of environmentalists. I began to think a great deal about how my portrayal of the situation affected audiences. I was troubled, for instance, when one individual commented that my portrayal of environmentalists read like something from the Wise Use movement. Many more interviews with environmentalists in the mid-1990s made me realize that it was problematic to equate the images deployed in a campaign with what actually constituted that campaign. Such images are a kind of mask — one worn for very deliberate purposes and one that obscures a great deal about what may actually be occurring behind the scenes in a campaign.

Aside from these misgivings, I also began to feel that this approach wasn't able to tell me much that was new or interesting about the campaign or environmental discourses in general. In particular, I did not feel that my previous approach could tell me much about how environmental discourses configure (or are configured by) emerging forms of political agency. This campaign was transformed from one with a singular focus on the imperative to stop the progress of bulldozers — what I have referred to elsewhere as the Fern Gully allegory — to one forced to contend with the emergence of the Uruguay Round of the General Agreement on Tariffs and Trade (GATT), post-Earth Summit conventions, International Tropical Timber Organization (ITTO) criteria indicators of sustainability, and the North-South debate. A campaign such as this is not merely the sum total of a series of points of contestation among actors with a diversity of perspectives.

I began to articulate this auto-critique more clearly as I recently read over the transcripts of an interview I conducted in Sweden during the summer of 1994 with journalist-activist Anne Daniya Usher. At several points during the course of the interview, I referred to the "complexity of the issue" or to the ways in which the issue had become more complex. Finally, she stopped and asked me with some annoyance to clarify what I meant by saying that "the issue" had become more complex. A long discussion ensued, as I negotiated the terrain between being someone who had my own analysis of the situation and someone who was carrying on an interview and wanted to hear another person's analysis. What Anne Usher was trying to convey was her annoyance over my suggestion that the issue had become *more* complex. The issue has always been complex, she asserted: it is merely that northern environmentalists had only lately become aware of these complexities. Although I think that in fact the issue *did* become more complex, her insistence forced me to clarify how an issue such as this may in fact look very different to any number of differentially positioned (and repositioned) observers at different points in time. The issue is a function of both the positions of different agents and of the ways in which it is actively produced and constructed by such agents.

Since 1993, I have also become increasingly concerned that my research is part of a larger trend in the ethnographic study of environmental movements and discourses and that this is leading toward routinization. As I noted in a recent article, there are several recognizable trends in contemporary treatments of environmentalism: (1) a sustained critique of romantic, essentialized images; (2) an emphasis on contestation; and (3) an interest in the transnationality of environmental discourses (1999a).

The first, the critique of romantic, essentialized images, was a central element in a 1993 essay (reprinted Brosius 2003). Compelling though such critiques may be, they not only place us politically on what I consider to be the wrong side of these issues, but they elide most of what is interesting and significant about environmental discourses. By focusing on easily refuted romantic images, we evade any real engagement with the politics of nature and how those politics play out in particular local contexts. The second trend, an emphasis on contestation, was also central to my 1993 piece. One can find numerous examples of this in the titles of a number of books from a range of disciplines over the past several years: *Contested Lands: Conflict and Compromise in New Jersey's Pine Barrens* (Mason 1992), *Contested Frontiers in Amazonia* (Schmink and Wood 1992), *Contesting Earth's Future: Radical Ecology and Postmodernity* (Zimmerman 1994), *Contested Arctic: Indigenous Peoples, Industrial States, and the Circumpolar Environment* (Smith and McCarter 1997), and *Contested Landscape: The Politics of Wilderness in Utah and the West* (Goodman and McCool 1999).

While this emphasis on contestation provides a useful foundation for elucidating the multiple positions and perspectives of a spectrum of actors involved in particular environmental debates, it is nonetheless problematic in several respects. In focusing on contestation, we treat environmental discourses as if they are relatively immutable, deployed by actors with fixed interests, positions, or perspectives. We fail to consider the extent to which such discourses may be subject to reformulation in response to critiques, because new linkages are recognized, because of changes in the positioning of various actors, or for other reasons.[7] We also fail to see how certain voices are able to edge others out, how certain voices may be co-opted, and how certain voices may be taken to be irrelevant. How does the process of forcing open spaces for newly emerging political agents occur? How or why do such spaces close on others? Finally, we fail to see that strategic decisions may be made about the deployment of particular discursive elements in ways that depart from what we take to be the core values of those deploying them.[8] In short, if we hope to understand the processes by means of which emerging forms of political agency are constituted, it defeats our purpose to consider these debates merely as a matter of multivocality, of differently positioned actors giving voice to contested representations. Such an approach hinders our ability to recognize the dynamism that characterizes environmental discourses and elides the agency of the actors that deploy them.

The third trend in the analysis of environmental discourses is that we have linked them to transnational discourses. Transnationalism is, of course, an idea being spoken about across a range of disciplines. While it has led us to numerous insights concerning processes of cultural production, it has also created certain problems. When we bring the idea of the transnational to bear on environmental discourses, we tend to assume, often implicitly, that the rhetorics and images that provide the basis for local environmental and indigenous rights groups to constitute themselves as political agents are of metropolitan origin. At the same time we recognize that northern NGOs are disseminating local discourses, genericizing them so that they partake of globally valorized discourses. We thereby situate these discourses as suitable subjects for critique. This places us in a precarious position. For all the transnationality of the discourses adopted, transformed, and deployed by particular actors — for all those qualities that allow a First Nations activist in British Columbia to communicate via the Internet with a Chinese indigenous rights activist in Sarawak — we must recognize that the stakes for these actors are local. By paying so much attention to the transnational aspects of these discourses, we obscure the reality of locality. A single transnational discourse of indigenaity may fall on the ears of a diversity of elites in many nations whose varying local perspectives are shaped by different priorities, fears, colonial and postcolonial histories, and histories of ethnic conflict.

These are the concerns that compelled me to rethink my previous approach to the Sarawak campaign. I have become increasingly convinced of the need to situate the campaign historically in order to highlight the dynamism that has characterized it. As I have suggested, if there is one thing that characterizes environmental discourses it is the rapidity with which they — and the counterdiscourses they provoke — evolve. Understanding something of the complexity and dynamism of a campaign such as this, wherein various agents are responding to the efforts of other agents, constantly reassessing the effectiveness of their efforts and those of others, and repositioning themselves or being repositioned, leads us toward a more nuanced perspective on the relationship between discursive production and agency than one premised on contestation alone.

THE CONTOURS OF A CAMPAIGN

One of the aspects of the Sarawak campaign that emerges most strongly in interviews with those involved, and is reflected in the pace of events, is the quality environmentalists refer to as momentum. The history of this campaign can in part be written as one of increasing and decreasing momentum. All those involved agree that there were periods when the possibility of success seemed certain, enthusiasm was high, and events followed one after the other. At some point in the early 1990s, this momentum began to dissipate. Different participants have varying interpretations of why this is so. Some are confused about where it went; others recognize, as author Wade Davis suggested, that "every campaign exists on a bell curve."

It was as a result of the attention brought by the 1987 blockades that a concerted international campaign began to be waged. The first Penan blockades were established at the same time that numerous rain forest groups in Europe, the United Kingdom, Australia, and Japan were in the process of forming. Many took up the Penan cause.

Two elements in particular—the activities of Sahabat Alam Malaysia and Bruno Manser—had a galvanizing effect on activists and the Euro-American public alike. A larger movement coalesced, and the campaign became increasingly internationalized. Increasingly, more and more Euro-American, Australian, and Japanese NGOs became involved in the Sarawak issue: Friends of the Earth, Greenpeace, Rettet den Regenwald, Pro-Regenwald, Urgewald, and Robin Wood in Germany; Global 2000 in Austria; Gesellschaft fur Bedrohte Volker in Switzerland, Austria, and Germany; Nepenthes in Denmark; Naturskydds Foreningen in Sweden; Steungroup voor Inheemse Volkeren and the European Alliance with Indigenous Peoples in Belgium; Werkgroep Inheemse Volken and European Youth Forest Action in the Netherlands; Survival International, the Singapore and Malaysia British Association, Earth Action Resource Centre, and the London Rainforest Action Group in the United Kingdom; Rainforest Information Centre and Sydney Rainforest Action Group in Australia; Japan Tropical Forest Action Network and Sarawak Campaign Committee in Japan; Western Canada Wildlife Committee, Sarawak People's Campaign and Environmental Youth Alliance in Canada; and Rainforest Action Network in the United States. Some of these groups organized campaigns focused specifically on the Penan and some on indigenous rights in Sarawak; others incorporated these into more inclusive rain forest campaigns.

As the Sarawak campaign gained momentum, numerous other events served to raise the profile of the Penan: films, documentaries by the BBC and *National Geographic,* and coverage on *Primetime Live.* Universal Studios began development of an action-adventure ecohorror script in which the forest wisdom of the Penan saves the world from catastrophe, and Warner Brothers began developing a script on the Bruno Manser story. The Penan received coverage in *Newsweek, Time,* the *New Yorker,* the *Wall Street Journal,* and *Rolling Stone;* they were featured on National Public Radio, the NBC *Evening News,* and CNN. Numerous politicians and celebrities were drawn into the campaign to make statements, serve as spokespersons, or otherwise raise the profile of the Penan. Among these were Prince Charles, Al Gore, Raffi, Danny Glover, and David Suzuki. Members of the Grateful Dead testified before the U.S. Congress on behalf of the Penan, and two Penan appeared onstage at a Grateful Dead concert at Wembley Stadium in the United Kingdom. In 1992, then senator Al Gore held a press conference on the Penan issue. Meanwhile, Penan were awarded the Reebok Human Rights Award and the Sierra Club's Chico Mendez Award, and SAM activist Harrisson Ngau was awarded the Goldman Prize for his work against logging in Sarawak.

In attempting to write the history of a campaign such as this, one must also foreground the role that various actions played in the way in which it unfolded. I must preface this by stressing the spectrum of diversity that exists among northern environmental NGOs with regard to their perspectives on the most effective ways to bring about change and hence their role in campaigns such as this. On one end of the spectrum are groups that focus their efforts on direct action. Such "grassroots" groups tend to be relatively nonhierarchical, stress the role of the committed individual in bringing about change, and focus on attracting media attention. They see their primary role as one of consciousness-raising. On the other end of the spectrum are mainstream groups such as the World Wide Fund for Nature, which place a much greater emphasis on long-term, cooperative institutional solutions to environmental problems and place more of a premium on establishing good working relationships with elites.

In any number of other environmental campaigns, there is a great deal of contact between groups along this spectrum. This can be problematic. Mainstream groups are considered by direct action groups to be overly accommodationist, hidebound, bloated, and more concerned about institutional survival than creating change. Direct action groups are considered by mainstream groups to have little appreciation for long-term goals and little understanding of the need to establish working relationships with opponents in order to create realistic change. They are thought to be short-term actors, as likely as not to disappear after stirring things up. In trying to understand the growth of the Sarawak campaign, it is necessary that we recognize the extent to which this dynamic played a role in how the campaign unfolded, gained momentum, and eventually began to diminish.

Where this dynamic most clearly manifested was in the process of implementation, or post facto evaluation, of a series of particular actions, activities, and encounters. The history of a campaign unfolds in part in the history of such specific events, events that certain individuals plan and attempt to garner support for and that others may distance themselves from or condemn. Environmental groups have staged protests in front of the offices of the Malaysian Airline System in London, blocked ships carrying timber from docking in Sydney and Rotterdam, walked in the streets of New York with a giant inflatable chainsaw, and confronted Malaysian trade delegations. Bruno Manser engaged in a sixty-day fast in front of the Swiss Parliament building in Bern, and he parachuted into a crowded stadium during the Rio Summit. Lobbying behind the scenes, environmentalists have persuaded the U.S. Congress and the European Parliament to pass resolutions condemning the use of Malaysian timber and, for a period at least, persuaded the Austrian Parliament to ban the importation of all tropical timber.

Two events in particular galvanized attention both in Malaysia and Europe/North America. The first event, which occurred just after Bruno Manser emerged from the forest in 1990, was the Voices for the Borneo Rainforest World Tour. Manser, Kelabit activist Anderson Mutang, and two Penan traveled from Australia to North America, Europe, and Japan. The second high-profile event was the SOS Sarawak action in July of 1991 described at the beginning of this essay. Both events were preceded by weeks of back-channel communication among NGOs, with the organizers attempting to garner support for these initiatives in the face of considerable opposition. In particular, both events were roundly condemned by SAM and many northern environmentalists. The World Tour was denounced for not being based on local consultation and SOS Sarawak for being a boldfaced example of northern environmental arrogance. Both events also attracted a great deal of negative attention in the Malaysian media.

It would be wrong to portray a campaign such as this as merely a series of planned events designed to raise the profile of an issue. It also can be seen in terms of a series of institutions and organizations that persist to a greater or lesser degree. Some were constituted not merely because of the Sarawak campaign but in response to a larger global interest in rain forest or indigenous rights issues. This campaign was in many ways interwoven with the founding and growth of such institutions. Some institutions were designed to facilitate communication among NGOs, for example, the World Rainforest Movement, the European Rainforest Movement, and the Third World Network. Others were designed (ostensibly at least) as forums in which NGOs could work together with governments and industry to find a middle ground; the Forest Stewardship Council is perhaps the best example of such a forum.

MALAYSIA RESPONDS

As noted, the attention that the Penan received in the international campaign was deeply resented by the Malaysian government, which mounted a vigorous and sustained response in the courts, in the Malaysian media, at international events such as the Rio Summit, and in trade delegations to northern countries designed to counter the efforts of environmentalists. In the speeches of politicians and senior civil servants, foreigners who criticized Malaysia were relentlessly condemned. Although the Malaysian government response to the Sarawak campaign has been directed not only at northern NGOs but at the Penan and Malaysian environmentalists as well, in the interest of brevity I want to concentrate my attention on its response to northern environmentalists.

One of the most prevalent points of attack was that directed at foreign "instigators." One official declared them to be "worse than communists." Another strategy employed in opposing northern environmentalists was to question the sincerity of their motives. It was at various times claimed that (1) environmentalists merely want to maintain the Penan as human museum specimens, (2) they are merely acting as a cover for temperate softwood logging interests, (3) northern NGOs have cynically used the Penan cause as a way to raise funds, (4) they use the Penan as a way to enrich themselves personally, (5) they are involved in the campaign because they like foreign travel, and (6) as one Malaysian official said to me in Kuala Lumpur, members of northern NGOs are interested in this issue only because it allows them to get close to celebrities like Olivia Newton-John. Yet another frequent point of attack, directed particularly at Americans and Australians, was that, given our own heritage of persecution of indigenous peoples, we are in no position to preach to Malaysians.

In addition to these critiques — rhetorical elements that environmentalists largely dismiss — three other, interlinked forms of rhetoric had particular resonance with northern NGOs. The first concerns the place of temperate forests in the global forest equation. Malaysia has asserted that before the North criticizes it for the destruction of Malaysian forests it should look at its own. Why, Malaysia asks, should it have to lock up its forests, while countries in the North continue to cut their own? Why should the North impose standards of sustainability for logging in tropical forests when no such efforts are made in their own countries? If the North wants Malaysia to preserve its forests, it should be willing to pay for this and put its own house in order.

Accompanying this was a compelling argument linking forest destruction in the South to northern consumption. Malaysian officials argued that the North places pressure on countries in the South to preserve their forests as a carbon sink. This is necessary only because of northern industrial production and consumption. The North, therefore, should consider its own patterns of consumption before it criticizes the South.

One of the most effective elements of Malaysian rhetoric was the linking of northern environmental activism to the legacy of colonialism — in fact, identifying it as nothing less than a latter-day form of colonialism. This refrain was repeated in any number of government press releases and speeches by government ministers. Malaysian prime minister Mahatir Mohamed referred to this campaign as a form of "eco-imperialism" and stated that "When we achieved independence we thought we would be free. But the North is still subjecting us to imperial pressures" (Mahatir bin Mohamed and Lutzenberger 1992).

Parts or all of these forms of rhetoric could be seen in Malaysia's response to the two events described above: the Voices for the Borneo Rainforest World Tour and the SOS Sarawak action at Kuala Baram. Both events prompted an aggressive response from Malaysia. Typical is an editorial that appeared in a Sarawak newspaper days after the SOS Sarawak action under the heading "Crude Interference."

A group of scruffy foreigners, including some grotesquely fat women, mindlessly chained themselves to metal structures belonging to a timber company in Kuala Baram. The bizarre behavior is their weird way of protesting against logging in Sarawak regardless [of] whether the extraction of timber is done on a sustainable yield basis or in conformity with the recommendations of the International Tropical Timber Organization. The self-proclaimed environmental pariahs are plain foreign political agitators who use the Penans and the environment as political issues against the State of Sarawak. They came from organizations and countries which had, decades ago, depleted their own forests. Those countries have emitted and will continue to emit prolific quantities of carbon dioxide into our atmosphere and destroy the ozone layer of the earth. Brushing aside their moral and environmental duties and responsibilities to afforest and reforest their flora and without casting a thought to abate the global pollution they are causing, they conveniently make the tropical rain forests countries as [sic] scapegoats. The Penans are [the] perfect smokescreen to camouflage double-standard[s] and double-talk. Aided by a powerful media network innocent Sarawak is portrayed as a land where minority natives are suppressed. . . . Is Sarawak expected to produce oxygen for the world when the supposedly responsible industrial world is out to deprive the earth of oxygen? Must we close down our factories and allow more than a hundred thousand workers to be idle when the industrial world goes full steam ahead with its millions [of] chimneys polluting the skies? . . . If the environment and ecology are indeed the issues, the foreign political agitators should do the battle in their own countries where forests have been long exhausted and the pollution is intolerable. . . . If the issue is one of suppression of the minorities, their protests are needed in North America for the Red Indians, in Australia for the Aborigines, in New Zealand for the Maoris, in Germany for the Turkish guest workers, in Switzerland for the Italians, and so forth. (*Sunday Tribune*, 14 July 1991)

Such elements of the Malaysian response had considerable resonance with northern NGOs, particularly later when the government began to find common cause with Malaysian NGOs in foregrounding northern consumption and increasingly defining itself not as one of the up and coming industrial tigers but as "the South."

SECOND THOUGHTS/REFORMULATIONS/RESPONSES

When they began the Sarawak campaign, northern NGOs, convinced that they held the moral high ground, never expected that their actions would be met with such a sustained, aggressive response from Malaysia. This was not a case in which landless peasants were forced to clear rain forest for the sake of survival. The line between good and bad seemed evident; a cadre of corrupt politicians was devouring Sarawak's forests for short-term profit at the expense of rural peoples. Even more compelling was the fact that these were *indigenous* peoples, bravely and unflinchingly staring into the face of power as they stood at their blockades. When Malaysia began to strike back at them, many northern environmentalists were surprised at the audacity of its response. For some time, it was easy to dismiss it as the defensiveness of corrupt politicians caught in the act. This was particularly easy to do because as the international Sarawak campaign began to accelerate in 1987 many of Malaysia's early responses were quite crude. Sarawak's minister of environment and public health, James Wong, for instance, became well known for such statements as, in response to concerns that deforestation may affect climate, "We get too much rain in Sarawak — it stops me playing golf." Claims such as those that environmentalists were a front for northern softwood interests or that they only wanted to hobnob with celebrities appeared to be deflections. With time, however, it became less easy to dismiss Malaysian responses. Two factors seem to have been key here.

First, the three above-mentioned elements of Malaysia's response — that temperate forests should also be an issue, that the problem was northern consumption, and that environmentalists were behaving like colonialists — were increasingly difficult for northern environmentalists to ignore. At a time when controversies about the logging of old growth forest were gaining greater prominence in Australia, the United States, Canada, and Scandanavia, northern environmentalists viewed Malaysia's criticism that more focus needed to be placed on temperate and boreal forests as essentially valid; indeed, many viewed it as a valuable tool for lobbying their governments to conserve old growth forests within their own countries. Further, Malaysia's argument that northern consumption was the real source of tropical forest destruction was consistent with critiques that northern environmentalists had themselves leveled for many years against industrial society. Northern environmentalists also recognized as a strategic matter that unless they were acknowledged and seriously engaged, Malaysia's arguments could be very effective in blunting much of the moral/political force of the arguments deployed in the campaign. They recognized that in order to retain any degree of moral authority in their encounter with Malaysia and avoid appearing hypocritical, arrogant, or heavy-handed, they had to be willing to position themselves as taking an evenhanded view of the problem of forest destruction on a global scale. This was particularly the case among environmentalists from mainstream organizations such as the World Wide Fund for Nature, who, because of their institutional affiliations, tended to take a longer-term, more global view as to what the most appropriate strategies might be for halting tropical forest destruction. Thus, while northern environmentalists had misgivings about the messenger, Malaysia, they could not ignore the message being conveyed.

Second, the power of these critiques was enhanced by the fact that as the campaign progressed Malaysian NGOs began to articulate a perspective increasingly distinct from that of many northern NGOs. To some extent, this was a strategic decision. If it were to have any influence within Malaysia, SAM realized that it had to counter the perception that it was merely doing the bidding of northern NGOs. The best way to do that was to distance itself from the northern campaign. It was given the opportunity to do this by events such as Voices of the Borneo Rainforest World Tour and the SOS Sarawak action.

At the same time that SAM was distancing itself from particular actions, its leaders, such as Martin Khor and Chee Yoke Ling, began to articulate a more resolutely southern perspective. This perspective, among other things, linked the fate of rain forests to northern consumption. This was precisely what the government needed to validate its own position. Thus, despite its history of criticism of the Malaysian government, SAM found itself increasingly courted by the authorities. After years as the target of government attacks, it came as a great relief to SAM members to finally feel that they were on the inside track within the government and were being heard.

Other developments were also occurring. Malaysia began to recognize the value of its participation in timber certification efforts and increasingly began to appropriate the discourse of sustainable forestry. Further, as rain forest campaigns in Europe began to have an effect on the market for Malaysian timber, Malaysia's hard-edged rhetoric was given a cosmetic makeover. Malaysia hired the public relations firms Burson-Marstellar and Hill and Knowlton to counter environmentalist rhetoric about the use of tropical timber. High-profile trade delegations visited northern countries in an effort to put a softer face on the Malaysian timber industry. Malaysia also became an active participant in pre- and post-UNCED negotiations, which, in part because of the vocal role Malaysia played, foregrounded northern forest management issues.

In time, northern environmentalists realized that they were no longer involved in a simple morality play. No longer was this merely an issue of stopping bulldozers or saving endangered forest dwellers. The "issue" *had* become more complex. In part, this was simply because northern environmentalists had come to be more aware of some complexities of the local situation in Malaysia that had previously eluded them. For instance, initially, few northern environmentalists appreciated how problematic the concept "indigenous" was in Malaysia or that the subject of ethnic difference was one of considerable sensitivity. Northern environmentalists only belatedly became aware of the complexity of the relationship between the state government of Sarawak and the Malaysian federal government.

With time, many northern environmentalists began to realize that some of their actions were actually complementing the agendas of the Malaysian officials they were criticizing. Particularly with events such as the SOS Sarawak campaign to refer to, Malaysian politicians had been given powerful symbols of northern neocolonialism in the face of which they could appear resolute.

It eventually became clear to many northern environmentalists that the contours of the campaign had shifted. Faced with the fact that this campaign had achieved none of its goals and with compelling arguments being made about northern consumption and neocolonialism, northern NGOs — accustomed to evaluating and reevaluating the success of their campaigns — were forced to determine what had gone wrong. By the early 1990s, the conventional strategy of demanding action could only be seen as neocolonial. Northern NGOs had to make a number of strategic decisions, but they had also become very aware that the moral and political contours of the campaign had changed and that they had to work in very different ways. As a result, a number of fundamental shifts occurred in the campaign. Such changes were not embraced by all groups; indeed, debate over this matter was one of the most important dynamics of the campaign.

One of the shifts that occurred early on was a move from an exclusive focus on Penan to a broader focus on indigenous peoples in Sarawak more generally. Northern NGOs increasingly recognized that logging was not an issue that affected only Penan. They continued to deploy images of the Penan but were increasingly self-conscious about the limitations of doing so. Associated with this was a shift from a focus only on logging to a broader focus on land rights.

An even more dramatic change, which occurred in direct response to Malaysian criticisms, was a shift in focus away from tropical forests to a broader emphasis on forests in general. Although initially this was a contentious issue, most northern NGOs recognized after the Rio Summit that it was necessary if they were to retain any degree of moral authority.

Another profound transformation was a change in emphasis from campaigning "there" to campaigning "here." Early in the campaign, many northern NGOs organized letter-writing campaigns directed at Malaysian officials, protests at Malaysian embassies, and the like. Whatever the form that such activities took, the focus was entirely on Malaysia's culpability in creating hardship for the Penan. Responding both to Malaysian criticisms about northern consumption and neocolonialism and to Malaysian NGO requests that they try to focus more on efforts in their own countries, northern NGOs began to place increased emphasis on the northern role in tropical deforestation and on what could be accomplished within their own countries.

As noted, one of the results of the campaign was that it produced not merely a set of events but a set of evolving institutions. As these institutions evolved, they increasingly privileged certain actors or organizations and marginalized others. Any campaign consists of a range of differently positioned actors: the changing contours of a campaign repositions them. At the center of the early Sarawak campaign were figures such as Bruno Manser: highly charismatic; able to move audiences with his words, his writings, and the image he projected; and speaking with directness, immediacy, and passion. However, as the campaign accelerated and NGOs began participating in ITTO meetings and other such institutional events, the role of such emblematic individuals was diminished. Manser had moral certitude and could convey it; he could put a human face on the issue. But he lacked what I heard many times referred to as an "analysis." There is little place for a figure such as Bruno Manser at a Forest Stewardship Council meeting in which criteria and indicators of sustainability are on the agenda. As the Sarawak campaign moved from consciousness-raising through direct action and letter writing to institution building and negotiation, a number of those who were active in the campaign early on were increasingly marginalized.

It is inevitable that this process of transformation would produce certain tensions among NGOs, both among those in the North and between those in the North and Malaysia. Most of these disagreements have been over the question of who should continue to work with whom or at what point should one engage, or disengage, with particular institutions. Environmentalists are well aware that institutions, whatever else they may do, inscribe certain discourses: they simultaneously create certain possibilities and preclude others. The NGOs are very aware that in the real world their goals are most realistically achieved when they can be incorporated into the workings of institutions. As such, they are concerned that they be given a voice in the development and operation of such institutions. At the same time, they are aware that one of the best ways to counter their efforts is to establish institutions that obstruct meaningful change through endless negotiation, legalistic evasion, and compromise. Many environmentalists are profoundly concerned that moral and political imperatives are excluded by techno-scientific forms of institutional intervention. They are also cognizant of the fact that NGO participation can give institutions a degree of legitimacy that they would otherwise lack and that their participation — or the appearance of it — may be sought for that purpose alone. The question that concerns them — and divides them — is at what point should they turn down a place at the table and the chance to get their issues on the agenda? At what point does participation become co-optation?

A second broad source of potential divisiveness concerns the issue of "local partners." That one's organization should take its lead from local partners is today a basic premise of northern environmental activism. Virtually all northern NGOs assert without qualification that any campaign, action, or project in the South must be undertaken in consultation with local NGOs and that they will act only when their participation is specifically requested. The point of contention lies in the question of where one finds a local voice. What does it mean to be "local"?[9] This is precisely the issue that emerged in the course of the Sarawak campaign. Penang-based SAM was involved in internationalizing the campaign from very early on. It was the Malaysian NGO with the greatest networking capacity; it had the highest profile and the most sophisticated analysis of the situation. For a time, most northern NGOs were content to work with SAM. However, as the campaign became increasingly internationalized, a number of grassroots northern environmentalists with little experience in Malaysia became involved. Several actions proposed by these individuals were not supported by SAM but were supported by certain Penan communities. Some northern environmentalists began to feel that SAM, operating from Penang and increasingly acting as naysayer, was trying to control the campaign, although there seemed to be voices that were *more* local. The question that arose, and subsequently divided northern NGOs, was whether they should listen to Penan or Penang. This disagreement over which "local" voice to heed was precisely the dynamic that occurred in the leadup to — and fallout from — the SOS Sarawak action and Voices of the Borneo Rainforest World Tour.

CONCLUSIONS

What I have attempted to show in my more recent work, particularly in an article published in the *American Anthropologist* (1999c) are some of the shifting historical, rhetorical, and institutional contours that have characterized this campaign as it evolved over time. Early in the campaign, much of the rhetoric, from northern NGOs in particular, centered around the imperative to "save" the Penan, initially portrayed as a matter of stopping bulldozers. This, it was believed, could be achieved by putting concerted international pressure on Malaysia. Direct action, aimed at raising the profile of the Penan, was the best way to achieve this end. But Malaysia talked back. In so doing, it fundamentally changed the terms under which environmental issues are debated between North and South. What was once a fairly simple issue — from the northern perspective a morality play — was transformed into something much more complex. As this occurred, northern NGOs could not decide among themselves what the central issue was: the Penan alone, indigenous rights in

342   J. Peter Brosius

Sarawak, Malaysia's forestry practices, the tropical timber trade, timber markets more broadly, northern consumption, or some other thing. Perceptions of the "issue" were fundamentally conditioned by each actor's position. It is with regard to these types of transformations, reevaluations, and repositionings — and the relations among them — that the story of the international Sarawak campaign raises a series of compelling issues with respect to how we might approach the study of environmental discourses.

The first issue concerns the question of how the terms of a debate change over time, particularly with respect to the way in which particularly positioned individuals or organizations respond to critiques, either internal or external. This occurs in any number of ways, but what is particularly significant is the question of the positioning of agents relative to each other. The Rainforest Action Network is likely to respond very differently to critiques from the Western Canada Wilderness Committee, WWF, SAM, or the prime minister of Malaysia. This foregrounds the need to look more closely at the discursive intersections that form the basis of critiques — for example, the ways in which environmentalism intersected the North-South debate in the 1990s. How such intersections occur is not only a function of abstracted, decontextualized discourses but of discourses subscribed to by particular political agents. One of the most critical dynamics of a campaign is not merely the existence of tensions or disagreements — points of contestation — but the shifting pattern of marginalization and privileging that occurs as the terms of a debate shift. Who is listened to or ignored and in which contexts? Who is it useful to engage and who should be kept at a distance? Such questions are at the center of any campaign and are a central element in its dynamics.

Another set of issues concerns the images and representations on which campaigns and countercampaigns are based. How are these images revised and reformulated as a result of a critique? For instance, the essentialized *Fern Gully* image of Penan as wide-eyed, forest-dwelling innocents in need of saving was the dominant image deployed in the initial stages of the Sarawak campaign. What became of that image as various critiques were directed at it (and its deployers) and as the center of gravity in the campaign shifted from the imperative to stop bulldozers to a campaign more mired in the complexities of transnational capitalism and postcolonial global politics?

Yet another set of issues concerns conceptions about the political and institutional space of environmental action. One of the results of the Sarawak campaign has been a much greater sense of awareness among northern NGOs concerning the appropriateness of acting in certain ways in certain spaces. Events such as the SOS Sarawak action at Kuala Baram initiated an extended discussion, borne of sharp criticism, of where and when northern "partners" should or should not act. Particularly in the later stages of the campaign, groups such as SAM encouraged northern NGOs to devote more attention to actions within their own borders, on the premise that it was more appropriate for them to campaign about tropical timber consumption in Belgium or Canada than to send letters to Malaysian officials demanding a moratorium on logging. One of the key sources of tension during the campaign has been the existence of fundamentally divergent conceptions of political space. Some northern environmentalists have been very explicit about defining themselves as global citizens, others have defined themselves with respect to their position in the North, while still others have defined themselves primarily with respect to traditional conceptions of the nation-state. In general, there is today a much more clearly articulated conception of hereness and thereness with respect to the geographical-political space of environmental action. When we speak today of political agency, we need to remember that agency exists in political space and that we need to be more explicit in defining where and under what circumstances environmental praxis is prescribed by differently positioned actors within that space.

Associated with this is the matter of the institutional/organizational space of environmental praxis. Institutions, be they NGOs, governments, or organizations such as ITTO, are both enabling and limiting. Defining themselves as filling particular spaces of discourse and praxis, institutions in effect redefine the space of action, privileging some forms of action (and actors) and limiting others.

ACKNOWLEDGMENTS

I wish to thank Anna Tsing and Paul Greenough for inviting me to participate in the 1995 conference Environmental Discourses and Human Welfare in South and Southeast Asia, out of which this essay emerged. Their close and perceptive reading of the original conference paper resulted in what I hope is a much clearer explication of the issues addressed here. The research on which this essay is based could never have been undertaken without the support and assistance of a great many people. I have drawn on interviews with dozens of individuals in North America, the United Kingdom, Europe, Australia, Japan, and Malaysia: environmentalists, government officials, and many others. The present discussion is a distillation of their insights, and I am grateful to them for sharing their views with me. I am particularly indebted to those Penan in both the Belaga and Baram Districts with whom I resided for most of my time in Sarawak. Finally, I must thank my wife Ellen Walker for the many insights she provided on the material presented here and for her superb editing. My research was supported by grants from the Social Science Research Council, the University of Georgia Research Foundation, the University of Georgia Center for Humanities and Arts, and the Body Shop Foundation (special thanks to Shane Kennedy for his efforts to help me secure the latter). Their support is gratefully acknowledged. All responsibility for statements here is expressly mine.

NOTES

1 For an account of the movement of Malaysian timber companies offshore, see World Rainforest Movement and Forests Monitor 1998. For more general accounts of logging and indigenous rights in Sarawak, see Bevis 1995; Colchester 1989; Hong 1987; Hurst 1990; Institute of Social Analysis 1989; Sesser 1991; and World Rainforest Movement and Sahabat Alam Malaysia 1990.

2 For more information on Penan in Sarawak, see Brosius 1986, 1988, 1991, 1993, 1995, 1995–96, 1997a, 1997b, 1999c, 2003; Harrisson 1949; Kedit 1982; Langub 1974, 1975, 1984, 1989, 1990; Needham 1954, 1965, 1972; Nicolaisen 1976; and Urquhart 1951. See King 1993; and Rousseau 1990 for more general overviews of the societies of Borneo.

3 For a history of international forest politics from a somewhat institutional perspective, see Humphreys 1996.

4 See Manser 1996; and Ritchie 1994.

5 "Negotiating Citizenship in a Commodified Landscape" was recently revised and will appear under the title "The Forest and the Nation: Negotiating Citizenship in Sarawak, East Malaysia" (Brosius 2003).

6 In referring to the government, it is important to keep in mind the distinction between the Sarawak state and the Malaysian federal governments. Sarawak agreed to join Malaysia in 1963, six years after Malaysia's independence in 1957. It was able to negotiate the terms of its entry into Malaysia and therefore has a considerable amount of control over its internal affairs. The policies of the state and federal governments are often at odds. In Sarawak, timber policy is established at the state level. Because of the negative attention that logging in Sarawak brought to Malaysia, the federal government has attempted to persuade the Sarawak state government to control logging. Despite the apparent differences between the state and federal governments, they have displayed a remarkably unified front in their responses to domestic and foreign critics of contemporary logging practices.

7 The emergence of the environmental justice movement exemplifies this process, whereby in response to a series of critiques a linkage developed between concerns about toxic waste and previously unassociated issues of poverty and racism.

Voices for the Borneo Rain Forest   345

8   For instance, environmental NGOs may recognize the representations they purvey to be overly romanticized or inaccurate yet deploy them nonetheless because they capture public attention.
9   See Peters 1996; and Forbes 1999 for discussions of the multiple meanings of the "local."

Susan M. Darlington

PRACTICAL SPIRITUALITY

AND COMMUNITY FORESTS

Monks, Ritual, and Radical

Conservatism in Thailand

In 1990, Phrakhru Pitak Nanthakhun, a well-known Buddhist monk, led the people of his home village in a tree ordination ritual to sanctify and formally constitute a community forest. The day before this ritual, the villagers held a ceremony to ask the village guardian spirit's permission to create a protected forest. The concept of establishing community forests to recognize and engender villagers' cooperation in preserving and managing local forests is part of a broader environmental discourse popular in Thailand today. This discourse of conservation, sustainable development, and local participation has been spearheaded by environmentalists, nongovernment organizations (NGOs), and a small number of socially active "ecology monks" concerned with alternatives to the government's engagement in economic development and industrialization.

While their application to the creation of community forests is new, tree ordinations themselves are not. Throughout Thailand, *bodhi* trees, the species under which the Buddha sat when he achieved enlightenment, are wrapped with robes to mark their sacredness. The ritual of a formal ordination "transforms trees from the untamed and uncivilized domain into sacred and venerated religious artifacts, a transformation which discourages people from cutting them down" (Taylor 1994, 19–20). The innovation in Phrakhru Pitak's village of Giew Muang, as in other communities in which tree ordinations are performed, is the rearticulation of the ritual's symbolic meanings to go beyond merely preventing individual people from harming a particular tree.

This use of ritual to invoke villagers' community, loyalty, and sensibility to the urgency of environmental protection is a good example of the "radical conservatism" of socially active monks across the nation.[1] They enact recognized symbols within Thai culture and religion, drawing on a "conservative" interpretation of them devoid of the elaboration that they feel much of contemporary Thai Buddhism has added to its practice. They invest these symbols with new meanings that are relevant to the immediate and long-term problems facing the villagers and the nation. The resulting interpretation and the practice based on it have the potential to move the Thai environmental movement beyond words and top-down, often locally inappropriate projects to greater efficiency in motivating local people to change their lifestyles and prevent further destruction to the natural environment. The involvement of Buddhist monks, the most highly respected category of person in Thai society, invests the environmental movement, and grassroots action specifically, with powerful legitimacy.

In Giew Muang, to understand the new meanings inherent in the rituals it is necessary to examine what makes "community" in the minds of the villagers: shared participation in rituals; the importance and definition of religion in their daily lives, incorporating folk Buddhism, Brahmanism and animism; and the respect they have for Pitak. We can see the process of defining community and engendering commitment to protecting the forest through the rearticulation of rituals that emerge from the history of the village: how it was settled, the degradation of the forest surrounding it, and Pitak's own history and relations with the villagers.

Giew Muang is not an isolated case. It highlights the need to understand and use local cultural and religious concepts of community in instituting grassroots environmental projects such as community forests. It also provides insight into the impact of the work of ecology monks (*phra nak-anuraksa*) within the broader environmental movement.

GIEW MUANG'S TREE ORDINATION

Holding a tree ordination, establishing a shrine for the guardian spirit, and placing a Buddha image as the "chief" of the forest to forbid cutting trees are all really clever schemes. It's not true Buddhism to conduct such rituals. But in the villagers' beliefs they respect the Buddha and fear some of his power. Thus, we can see that there is nothing as sacred or worthy of the villagers' respect as a Buddha image. Therefore, we brought a Buddha image and installed it under the tree that we believe is the king of the forest and ordained the tree. In general, villagers also still believe in spirits. Therefore, we set up a shrine for the guardian spirit together with the Buddha image. This led to the saying that "the good Buddha and the fierce spirits work together to take care of the forest." This means that the Buddha earns the villagers' respect. But they fear the spirits. If you have both, respect and fear, the villagers won't dare cut the trees. (Phrakhru Pitak Nanthakhun, quoted in Arawan 1993, 11; my translation)

In 1990, when Pitak conducted the ritual that formally marked Giew Muang's community forest, the village, similar to the rest of Nan Province and the nation as a whole, faced severe deforestation and water shortages. Much of the forest surrounding the village had been clear-cut to make way for fields in which cash crops were grown. Soil erosion was severe due to planting on the steep hillsides. Some forest did remain. It was to preserve these areas and institute new methods of agriculture that are less damaging that Pitak decided to help the villagers establish a community forest.

The village set up a conservation association in 1987 to begin this process (see below), but three years later it was still not particularly effective. Only a few villagers committed themselves to making the association work. Pitak therefore decided to hold a tree ordination and consecrate the protected forest in order to engender greater commitment and cooperation from the villagers and to make the project more their own through the use of Buddhist principles and symbolic meanings. The villagers took this notion further by first holding a ceremony asking the permission and assistance of the village guardian spirit to look after the forest.

The monk's decision to hold a tree ordination was the culmination of a series of actions aimed at protecting the forest through educating the villagers in the benefits and urgency of conservation. Pitak emphasized repeatedly that rituals were not the primary element in his conservationist activities. The larger issues of deforestation, the lack of sufficient and clean water for agriculture and personal use, the preservation of other species, and the suffering people face due to environmental destruction all claim the monk's attention. Invoking the sacred through ritual provided Pitak with greater social and religious authority in the village and Thai society, including the Sangha (the order of Buddhist monks) hierarchy and the government bureaucracy, strengthening his ability to carry out future actions. I argue that this ceremony was of even greater importance for the ritual construction of the community. A community forest is dependent on the strength of the local community, which is responsible for it. It is precisely because in Giew Muang community is ritually constructed that the tree ordination and the guardian spirit rite were such powerful acts.

The month prior to conducting the rituals, Pitak and some volunteers from local NGOs visited the village several times to educate the people about the community forest.[2] Pitak presented a slide show, which he has since shown many times in villages across the province, teaching both Buddhist *dhamma* (the moral teachings of the Buddha) and conservation. With every slide show, Pitak begins with cartoons illustrating *dhammic* stories. He engages the villagers with his humor and references to local people and events. He then moves into a dramatic set of images documenting the negative impact of deforestation, including scenes of severe drought and bodies drowned in the floods of 1988 in the south.[3] The combination of religious exegesis, personal humor, and shock grabs the villagers' attention and, he hopes, jolts them into action. The rituals that follow engender their moral commitment to putting the monk's ideas into practice.

For the ordination, Pitak chose the largest tree in the forest, which is seen as the "king" of the forest in northern Thai culture. It towered above the rest of the forest, although it stood only about one hundred yards off the main road through the village. A narrow dirt road led past a couple of small wooden houses, beyond this majestic tree, and farther into the woods. The people of Giew Muang frequently followed this trail on their way to collect mushrooms or gather other forest products. They recognized and respected the "king" as symbolic of their dependence on the forest.

The day before the ordination the villagers performed a ceremony for the village guardian spirit. They built a wooden shrine about two feet tall and set it on a pole a short distance from the tree to be ordained. Ui Mii, one of the oldest men in the village and a spirit ritual specialist (*mau phii*), officiated in a ceremony offering the guardian spirit food and whiskey.[4] As with all major changes in the village, the villagers informed the spirit of the tree ordination and the consecration of the forest and thanked him for looking after their well-being. Representatives from every household participated, demonstrating their recognition of the spirit's authority and the importance of the ritual as well as their membership in the community over which the spirit watched.

Buddhist monks conducted the tree ordination the following morning next to a large Buddha image Pitak had placed there earlier. Pitak had invited monks from neighboring villages and the provincial capital to participate, as they would in a monk's ordination. He also invited local government officials, environmentalists, and developmental NGO workers. Gathered around the tree, surrounded by the villagers sitting in the forest's shadows with hands held together in respect and faith, the more than ten monks performed a ceremony that was just short of a full monk's ordination.[5] Although orange robes were wrapped around the tree at the stage in the ritual when a monk would receive his own robes, no one believed the tree was now a monk, as only a human can officially be ordained. Nevertheless, the sanctity of the act was recognized by the villagers and monks alike, as it invoked both Buddhism and spirit beliefs.[6]

Together, the rituals of establishing the guardian shrine, requesting the spirit's protection for the forest, and ordaining the king of the trees both formally sanctified the forest and unified the community that regards it as its own. Combined with the slide shows, educational programs, and agricultural projects that the monk sponsored, the overall project had tremendous potential for preserving the forest around Giew Muang. None of the elements could work as effectively on its own. The depth of the multiple approaches provided the villagers with the knowledge, motivation, and commitment needed for the project to succeed. The key to pulling them together was the rituals, which most directly appealed to the people's faith and fostered the villagers' identification as a community that accepted the responsibility of managing and protecting its forest.

FROM FOREST TO VILLAGE

The earliest stories about Giew Muang are usually told by Ui Mii, one of the village elders. Ui Mii and two of his brothers, including Pitak's father, came to what is now Giew Muang in the 1930s. They came as hired laborers, working to clear fields in the forest, and as merchants, joining others who passed through on their way to sell forest products in the city. They also cleared dry rice fields for themselves and their families.

This is how Ui Mii described the forest of Giew Muang when he first arrived: "In the past, this was a deep, cool forest. There were many wild animals, not like today. There used to be teak forests, not like the forest now. At first, you could go to the forest to collect mushrooms, but you couldn't go far. The trunks of bamboo trees were as thick as your arm. Wherever anyone went [to live] they had to clear the forest, until it became what you see today" (interview, 3 April 1993).

The people came as immigrants from other areas, mostly in northern Laos. They arrived in search of land to farm and pushed higher into the mountains, as all the good rice paddy land had been claimed in the lowlands. The first settlers cleared the forest to grow food, using slash and burn techniques. A small field could easily support a family, producing enough rice to last until the next harvest. The soil was rich in nutrients, and no fertilizers or pesticides were needed. The villagers also earned a living from hunting or gathering forest products to sell in the city.

People continually migrated up into the forest in search of land. "This was a vast forest," one grandmother, who herself moved to Giew Muang in 1954, said. "Whoever cleared the land could claim it."

Today there is little room left for expansion. The village's seventy-six houses are crowded together in three groupings along the road and one just off the road. Few new families have migrated to the village since the mid-1970s. One woman commented that new people would not be welcome because the land could not support them.

Most of the people in Giew Muang earn a living by planting cash crops such as green beans and feed corn. They are heavily in debt and often have to buy rice to eat, as their rice fields have been converted to cash cropping. Every family raises chickens, and many also own a few head of cattle or a couple of pigs. The hillsides are too steep to allow large holdings of livestock or vast fields in any one place. The villagers live from the forest as well, collecting mushrooms and broom grasses and hunting animals to sell in the city. In the past, they ate what the forest offered; today they sell what they find and buy much of their food.

With competition over land, water, and forest resources, the potential for establishing a protected forest would seem insurmountable. Examining how the people of Giew Muang define their community provides the key to understanding how the village was able to overcome these obstacles. The local concept of community is crucial to implementing community forests across Thailand; in Giew Muang, we can see how the process of identifying and manipulating this concept through ritual action made the community forest viable.

THE CONCEPT OF COMMUNITY AND THE SACRED IN GIEW MUANG

The people of Giew Muang share a common identity and are proud of their village. Their sense of community most clearly takes shape through their shared participation in the rituals surrounding their spirit and Buddhist beliefs. Common history, ethnicity, language, social structure, and occupation contribute only minimally to uniting the village; religion is the critical factor. Their religious system consists of a union between Buddhism, Brahmanism, and animism. Their Buddhist practice is focused primarily on making religious merit through donating alms to monks. While it governs their sense of morality, the villagers see it as an individual practice. Brahmanism is incorporated with their Buddhist and animist beliefs through their cosmological conception of gods and demons. It is the ritual practices surrounding their spirit beliefs that most affect their daily lives and demarcate the boundaries of and membership in the community.

Spirits lived in the forest before the people came. Every aspect of the villagers' lives are intertwined with the spirits. Much of their indigenous knowledge of nature and the forest is encoded in and practiced through their spirit beliefs. Forest spirits, both malevolent and benevolent, live in the trees, waterways, and land. Children learn to respect the wilderness because of its embodiment in the spirits. Villagers hesitate before cutting a tree or killing an animal because of the spirits that reside within them. They therefore make offerings whenever they go to the forest to hunt, cut trees, or gather food and before clearing new fields, planting, and harvesting.

Although there are many spirits within their worldview, the most important one for the villagers as a community is the village guardian spirit, called in Northern Thai *phii chao luang*.[7] This spirit looks after the well-being of the entire community. He must be informed of any changes in the village, particularly if new people move in, people are married, or babies are born. He is the spirit the villagers informed of the creation of the community forest.

The villagers believe the guardian spirit protects them from problems and catastrophes. During the era in the 1960s, 1970s, and early 1980s, when communist insurgents roamed the forests of Nan, he kept peace and security for the people of Giew Muang. He also helps their crops to grow well and keeps people healthy.

In exchange for looking after them, the villagers make regular offerings to and rituals for the guardian spirit. In Giew Muang, the rituals surrounding the guardian spirit most clearly define the community. Members of the community and all long-term visitors are formally introduced to the spirit by a ritual specialist (usually Ui Mii). Every family joins in the semiannual feasting of the spirit, donating food and performing the ritual. For two years, he is fed chicken, with each family providing one bird. In the third year, he is fed pork, and every family contributes money to buy the pigs that are sacrificed. Through this participation, everyone knows who belongs to the community and shares responsibility for its well-being.

The villagers' participation in these rituals publicly demonstrates their acceptance of the social values encoded in the ceremony. Families are ritually recognized through their donations and participation. Cooperation among them is strengthened as they join together to make the ceremonies effective. Values of village harmony and loyalty are stressed, lessening the likelihood of conflict and hostility. When conflicts do arise, they are often explained as having been caused by a mistake or lack of participation in these rituals. The villagers then appeal to the guardian spirit to settle them and restore equanimity. Participants reaffirm the ritual's meaning to the group as a whole, giving the community definition and importance. The sanctity surrounding the ritual, through its unquestionable and unexplainable nature, grants even greater significance to the group and shared responsibility for its well-being.

Even those few villagers who openly deny a belief in spirits participate in the rituals for the guardian spirit. For example, two men told me they felt spirit beliefs were ignorant of the modern world. But they never failed to contribute their families' share of the food for the spirit, and usually one or the other of them represented his family at the ritual. Not to do so would be to act as if they were not part of the village community. The values of cooperation, recognition of the village as a community, and respect for their traditions and the elders meant more to these men than their personal beliefs.

In an example of radical conservatism, invoking the guardian spirit in establishing the community forest played on the importance of community within a new context. Never before had the entire village approached the spirit with regard to the forest; that had always been an individual act between a person and the forest spirits before he or she went to work in the forest or surrounding fields. The ceremony performed prior to the tree ordination redefined the forest and the villagers' relationship with it by extending the guardian spirit's authority over the people's use of the forest. The forest now clearly belonged to the community as a whole, and everyone accepted responsibility for its care. All residents of the village attended the community forest ritual, as they do all guardian spirit ceremonies. No one was excluded or excused from the creation of the protected forest, nor could any inhabitant deny his or her newly constituted relationship with it.

The sense of community created through the guardian spirit ritual was reinforced and strengthened by the villagers' Buddhist beliefs through the tree ordination as well. The villagers connected their animist practices to Pitak's teaching of a Buddhist ethic of responsibility and compassion in order to foster a lifestyle that could preserve the natural environment. Both the animist and Buddhist ceremonies served to pull the "wild" forest within the realm of the village community. The villagers no longer viewed the forest as an untamed territory to be claimed for per-

354   Susan M. Darlington

sonal benefits. But the radical application of these rituals would not have been as effective without the personal position of Pitak within the village, as both a monk and a villager, and his efforts as a self-defined ecology monk to promote an ecological ethic and practical action in the village.

PHRAKHRU PITAK

The case of Giew Muang's community forest does not stand in isolation. Pitak's project there is an example of the kind of work ecology monks are engaged in across Thailand. His history provides a link between the specifics of this case and the larger movement of ecology monks nationwide. Although they represent less than 2 percent of the total Sangha membership, ecology monks have a major impact on the legitimacy and the direction of the Thai environmental movement. These monks meet as many as ten times a year in seminars attended by twenty to two hundred monks to exchange experiences and the problems they face in their ecological work. Through their actions and these seminars, they define what being an ecology monk means and implement what I call a radical conservatist articulation of Buddhism. This process consists of applying a conservative interpretation of the Buddha's teachings, focusing on the basic teachings of the Buddha, to offer solutions to contemporary social problems, including poverty, economic development, and environmental degradation.

Pitak is a frequent speaker at the meetings of ecology monks, where he is asked to share his history as a model and motivation for other activist monks. The abstract principles underlying his work are integrated with his personal history and specific actions promoting ecological conservation. Through examining Pitak's history and connection with Giew Muang, the manner in which ecology monks apply their interpretations of Buddhism to environmentalism in Thailand can be seen.

Pitak was born in the village in 1958. His father made his living mostly from hunting, selling the meat to support his family. As a young boy, Pitak frequently accompanied his father on hunting trips. Some of his earliest memories and his motivations for both becoming a monk and engaging in environmental conservation come from experiences during these hunting trips. He witnessed the suffering animals endured at the hands of men in their own struggle for survival and vowed to seek a means of eliminating its root causes.

Pitak was sent away to school, as Giew Muang did not have its own at that time. He finished his formal schooling with the fourth grade and was ordained as a novice at a neighboring village temple. During his childhood, he often walked many hours through the forest to visit home. At this time, he witnessed the continual destruction of the forest as logging roads cut into the woods and people cleared more land for their fields.

At seventeen, the novice was invited by Giew Muang's headman to establish a village temple. The headman, originally from another province, donated the land, and the villagers began to cut wood for the building. Pitak realized that he had become a tool for the headman's greed when wood kept disappearing from the site and no temple was built. When he challenged the headman as to the whereabouts of the wood, the latter fled, and the young novice unofficially became both headman and abbot for the village.

The experience of the stolen wood, the greed behind it, and the ignorance of the villagers as to how to fight it, together with watching the forest, the people's source of livelihood, disappear, all influenced Pitak's interest in environmentalism and its effect on people. His sermons included teachings about man's responsibility toward nature. He promoted forest preservation and reforestation in denuded areas. Over the years, he also helped the village develop, constructing a short road to the new temple, a reservoir and wells, and a local cooperative store and introducing alternatives to cash cropping and logging as sources of income.

During this time, Pitak progressed rapidly through his religious education. In 1978, he was fully ordained as a monk. In the early 1980s, he became abbot of Wat Aranyaawaat in Nan city. He remained abbot of the village temple, too, as there were no other monks to take over. And he continued preaching an environmental ethic.

His first real struggle in the name of conservation came in 1986 when the provincial government, following a national tendency, began a program to make Nan Province "green." This entailed marshalling the province's resources to plant commercial forests, especially eucalyptus trees. The projected incomes led many local government representatives, particularly subdistrict chiefs and village headmen, to fell trees to make way for eucalyptus plantations. They had the idea that "the old forest cannot become money. We must cut it all down to plant economic forests" (Arawan 1993, 10). Pitak opposed the plan, seeing that eucalyptus would severely deplete the soil.[8] In his opinion, clearing primary forests to plant eucalyptus was not conservation but destruction. A letter he wrote to the governor of a nearby province who had himself done research on the negative impact of eucalyptus was published in a national newspaper. The Nan provincial authorities complained to the Sangha hierarchy that this was inappropriate behavior for a monk. In the end, Pitak convinced his superiors of the dangers of the plan. Finally, through his and other activists' efforts, the Green Nan Program was halted but not before many areas had been cleared.

Besides showing how the monk handled conflict through careful documentation, research, and convincing argument, this story illustrates how Pitak cultivated his relationships with his superiors in the Sangha hierarchy. The social and sometimes political actions of ecology monks tend to go beyond the practice of most Thai monks, often placing them in controversial situations with the hierarchy, which is traditionally supportive of the status quo. Yet Pitak won the provincial Sangha leadership over through his devotion to teaching the dhamma and working to relieve people's suffering. Ever aware of potential damage to the reputation of the Sangha as a whole through radical actions, he carefully grounded his practice in respect for his superiors and a solid knowledge and conservative interpretation of the dhamma. This balance between social action and religious exegesis, the essence of radical conservatism, is crucial to implementing social change based on Buddhism and helped Pitak avoid conflict with the Sangha hierarchy.[9]

In 1987, Giew Muang began to experience severe water shortages. The villagers had to ask the district government to send water in trucks for drinking and personal use. Through Pitak's teachings and their own experiences, the people began to understand the connection between deforestation and lack of water. The monk worked with the villagers to found the Giew Muang Conservation Association to protect the village's forests. This informal association aimed to conserve areas where the forest had not yet been drastically damaged. The monk asked the villagers not to clear new fields but to use more efficient methods of farming in order to keep the remaining trees standing.

The village households were divided into six groups (muat), the heads of which formed the association's committee. Each group was responsible for one of the protected areas of the forest. The committee's duties were to investigate complaints of violations and assess fines where they were deemed necessary. The sanctions were both social, as the entire village would know of violations, and legal, as the committee used the threat of bringing in the police if violators refused to pay. This was the first form of the village's community forest.

The project was both strengthened and threatened by the declaration in the same year of Giew Muang and its surrounds as part of a national forest reserve. At first, the declaration lent stronger legal sanctions to the association's informal regulations concerning the cutting of trees. Yet, because legally people are not allowed to live in forest reserves, the villagers were also afraid that the government would use the declaration as an excuse to take their land. They feared that they would be forced to move before they could benefit from any trees they planted, gardens they put in, or anything else done to improve the land (Arawan 1993, 9). Pitak similarly worried that, due to the legal definition of national reserve land, the Royal Forestry Department would grant permission to businessmen to plant commercial trees if it determined that the area was degraded. He used this argument to encourage the villagers to take care of their land and the forest.

Gradually the project began to show results. The areas that the villagers genuinely protected became more productive. Bamboo shoots, mushrooms, and various vegetables grew in greater amounts than there had been in recent years. Due to their actions or not, water began to flow again, enough that in following years the village did not have to request water from the district government. (Shortages of water for drinking and bathing remained an ongoing problem, however.)

Nevertheless, the community forest existed more in name than in reality as far as the whole village was concerned. Some people still secretly cut and sold trees. Pitak also wanted to preserve the whole environment, not just the trees, following the Buddhist concern for all sentient beings. Yet villagers continued to hunt animals within the protected areas.

In early 1990, Pitak visited other ecology monks across the nation. Having seen the impact of these monks' work, he returned to Nan inspired to increase his conservation activities from mostly preaching to a more active engagement in environmentalism. His first formal activity was the tree ordination in Giew Muang that same year. Since then, the monk has sponsored numerous other projects, including tree ordinations in other villages to mark new community forests, long-life ceremonies to conserve the Nan River, and numerous educational seminars for monks and laypeople. He also established Klum Hak Myuang Naan (We Love Nan Province Association), an NGO that acts as both a networking organization with other environmental NGOs in the province and its own association supporting Pitak's and other ecology monks' programs.

Pitak is part of a growing movement of activist ecology monks that uses basic Buddhist principles to deal with the current environmental crisis. His interpretation of Buddhism in ways that help build an ecological ethic is a clear example of the radical conservative philosophy on which the actions of ecology monks are based.

Conservation is not an end in itself for Pitak or other ecology monks. His primary motive is to promote spiritual well-being and religious practice. Central to his teaching is the Buddhist concept of the interconnectedness of all things. He tries to show the villagers how their actions affect nature, which in turn affects the quality of their lives. His slide shows include pictures of dead, bloated bodies after floods and the dry, blistered fields due to droughts. These tragedies are not natural, he says, but the results of human greed and ignorance, which lead to deforestation. He emphasizes the importance of the environment, natural and social, to the spiritual well-being of individuals and society. All this can be affected by changes in the villagers' lifestyles to build an attitude of responsibility that fosters conservation and self-reliance.

Traditional Buddhist practice focuses on the individual working through meditation and following the dhamma to achieve one's own spiritual enlightenment. While temples remain central to village life, Thai Buddhism has become increasingly ritualistic and conservative since the mid-1900s, when the government took over activities that formerly were centered in villages, including education, health care, and social welfare. The focus of religious practice became rituals, meditation, and individual spiritual development.

Pitak sees this individualistic approach to the religion as too narrow and ignorant of the root problems in society that prevent true spiritual development. He and other activist monks argue that social relations and economic circumstances must also be incorporated into Buddhist practice. A high-ranking, socially engaged monk in the north commented that if people's stomachs are empty they are not going to think seriously about meditation or religion.[10] Spiritual and material development, of the individual and of society, must go hand in hand.

While a few scholarly monks concentrate on interpreting the dhamma in light of social action, activist monks such as Pitak, who is closer to the villagers, are mostly concerned with applying the dhamma in tangible projects and dealing with the people's immediate and long-term problems. Pitak attempts to put abstract Buddhist principles into terms to which the villagers, who for the most part are untrained in religious philosophy, can more immediately relate. For example, in his sermons and slide shows, Pitak often describes the life of the Buddha in terms of conservation. The Buddha, he says, was the first environmentalist. From birth, through his search for truth, enlightenment, and teaching of the dhamma, until he passed away, the Buddha's life was closely intertwined with forests (see Chatsumarn 1998; Jaaruwannoo Bhikkhu 1992; Pipop 1993; and Sekhiyatham Group 1992, 2–3).

Still following the Buddhist goal of relieving suffering, Pitak, like other ecology monks, bases his work on Buddhist principles, which he frames to fit a changing world. This in itself is not unusual; throughout its history, Buddhism has always adapted to new cultures and situations. But the basic principles have always remained the same. The ways in which ecology monks express the ideals of the religion are what make the Buddhist educational approach distinctive.

Essential to Theravada Buddhism is understanding the root causes of suffering (the second Noble Truth), especially greed, ignorance, and hatred. Applying this principle to the environmental crisis in Thailand, the ecology monks began their interpretation of Buddhism by searching for the underlying social and spiritual causes of deforestation and environmental destruction. They generally agree that state economic development policies foster the situations that force local people to clear the forests to plant export and cash crops. The monks see these actions as symptoms rather than causes of deforestation and poverty. Luang Phau Khamkhian, an activist monk and meditation teacher in the northeast, "believes that the villagers have had a constant struggle with poverty and hunger because they have followed the mainstream, greed-motivated capitalist economy" (Taylor 1994, 42). He agrees with the government that ignorance of their needs and the full consequences of their actions lies behind villagers' cutting the forest. Khamkhian couples this ignorance with the greed emerging from a growing materialism in Thai society. Villagers are willing to switch to cash crops such as cassava, corn, and string beans because they desire televisions, refrigerators, and new pickup trucks. But, as one young activist monk in Nan told me, "you can't eat a pickup truck when it breaks down." Ecology monks such as Khamkhian and Pitak believe that the basic motivation behind the actions of both the government's capitalist development policies and the villagers' acquiescence to them needs to incorporate a greater spiritual base and understanding of the Buddha's teachings.

Pitak recognizes that economic problems and the struggle for survival are major factors behind people's cutting of the forest. Merely forbidding people to live in the forest or to use natural resources would not solve the environmental crisis. He frequently lists what he sees as the causes of deforestation in Nan (Thai Inter-religious Commission for Development n.d., 13). Each of these factors results from people's efforts to make money, including villagers growing cash crops or selling wood cut illegally to middlemen, logging and tobacco companies, and other outsiders who desire the wood for their own economic gain. The villagers' way of life, he says, must move away from materialism to effect a genuine solution to the problem. Similarly, the people in government and business who influence the broader policies that promote immediate economic benefits over long-term environmental and social well-being should base their goals and methods on Buddhist principles of generosity and simple living if Thailand is to avoid disaster.

Phra Somkit, another ecology monk in Nan, pointed out to me the cyclical effect of environmental destruction on people's lives. Social and economic problems and policies lead to deforestation. The resulting environmental problems themselves cause economic stress, as the land is worn out, crop production decreases, and people go into debt. This leads to social problems, as young people leave the villages to seek work in the cities, families break up, and people desire more and more material things. Communities eventually break down and people become increasingly selfish.

The Buddha taught a method for solving these problems, Somkit continued, noting that we should not be greedy for money and things but work towards having enough to eat and taking care of our families. As an example, Somkit compared the ills and debt ultimately resulting from growing corn as a cash crop to the benefits of growing rice for subsistence.

Establishing community forests is one of the activities in which many ecology monks are engaged across Thailand. These projects intersect with the broader environmental movement, as monks are not alone in promoting local management of forest land through the creation of community forests. A nationwide movement among environmentalists and academics to institute community forests and gain state recognition of their legitimacy and the local people's rights to live in and manage them has been gaining momentum since the early 1990s (see Local Development Institute 1992; and Saneh and Yos 1993).

The case of Giew Muang illustrates the importance of incorporating Buddhist principles as the basis of environmental projects with the elements of the local culture that give such projects greater meaning for the villagers. In this case, it was the integration of Pitak's Buddhist ecological practice with the villagers' spirit beliefs as the basis of their community that together made the community forest effective and increased its potential for success.[11]

The tree ordination in Giew Muang entailed the use of rituals and principles already familiar to the villagers that could be applied to their immediate situation. Pitak used the opportunity to teach concepts of environmentalism together with a radical conservatist interpretation of the religion. He drew on the concept of community through the guardian spirit ritual to engender greater commitment from all the villagers and to help them realize the importance of the forest to the entire village, not just individuals.

While the ceremony was conducted predominantly for the villagers, the monk involved NGOs and government officials who worked in the area as well. He recognized the importance of gaining their support for the project, as the village, especially since the declaration of its being within a national forest reserve, did not exist within a vacuum. Any activity the people undertook needed to be accepted by the state and the larger society around them to give it greater legitimacy and avoid its being countered by the state's policies. If the state formally recognized Giew Muang's community forest, it could not easily grant the land to businessmen for development of economic forests. Although the community forest has no legal status, the participation of government officials in the tree ordination and the continual attention the village gets from national and international environmentalists insure it against "encroachment" by the state or the business community.

The idea of the community forest was not introduced through the ceremony. The purpose of the Giew Muang Conservation Association, established earlier, was to protect the village's forest. Nevertheless, this project was not a "traditional" community forest protected through long-standing cultural practices. The villagers viewed the forest surrounding Giew Muang as an open resource there for individuals to take. Pitak worked over a long period of time to develop the concept of communal responsibility in the minds of the villagers. But asking them to protect the forest for its own sake or just teaching them about the ideas of conservation was not enough. Ultimately, the power of the sacred combined with the villagers' own concept of community worked to gain their commitment to the community forest.

Most residents of Giew Muang would agree with the assessment that since the tree ordination ritual there has been greater cooperation in protecting the forest and less encroachment within it. "Ordaining the tree and asking the spirits to help have equal success. The spirits and the

Buddha work together to protect the forest," Ui Mii observed. Fewer trees are cut, fewer animals killed. Some villagers even claim that the forest is more fertile and less dry. The ordination taught them awareness of the direct impact of their actions on the natural environment.

Some aspects of the project, however, are not without controversy and work in ways not expected or intended by Pitak. In particular, the spirits' influence in protecting the forest from encroachment through fear of retribution is thought by many of the villagers to be the primary reason for the community's success in conserving the forest (see Darlington b forthcoming).

One elder woman told me a story typical of how many villagers explain the four deaths and several illnesses that have occurred in relation to the protected forest since the rituals were performed. She said, "A lot has changed since then. Whoever comes to shoot animals has died because the spirits don't allow it. One man, Mr. Lun, from [a neighboring village], went at night last Phansaa [the Buddhist lenten season]. He died because he was hunting in the protected area, which is dangerous now. He didn't believe it, but we do. We said it wasn't good, but he said it was. Ordaining the tree has helped protect the forest" (interview, 3 April 1993).

Other stories were similar. Someone was accidentally shot in the forest because someone else thought he was an animal. The villagers believed the shooter was tricked by a spirit. Another person illegally cut wood in the forest. Shortly thereafter he got very ill. The spirit specialist (whom the villagers often consult concerning illnesses) determined that he had met a spirit in the forest, who afflicted him. Within days, he died. Others were more fortunate; they became very sick after encroaching on the community forest but did not die. Again the explanation the villagers provided was that these people had offended the spirits who had been asked to protect the forest.

A similar explanation existed in the villagers' understanding of Buddhism. In their concept of religious merit, one always experienced the consequences of one's actions. In a popular Thai phrase, this idea is summed up as "do good, receive good; do evil, receive evil." Hunting or cutting trees in the sanctified forest was clearly a case of bad behavior for the villagers, and the consequences were enacted by the spirits accordingly.

There is concern among environmentalists, academics, and many ecology monks about the use of spirit beliefs to promote conservation. Aacaan Phongsak Techathamamoo, a well-known former ecology monk in Chiang Mai, maintains that spirit beliefs control through fear, not understanding. People's harmony with nature, he argues, should be built on wisdom, compassion, generosity, and loving kindness, not fear (interview, 18 March 1993). Others claim that animism reflects the ignorance of the rural people and Buddhism represents enlightenment. This argument is put forth by some of the people who use Buddhism to promote development and social action.

Although Pitak was not directly responsible for the guardian spirit ceremony itself, he and many other monks and lay activists involved in the environmental and community forest movements disagree with these criticisms and recognize the value of using and adapting local culture and beliefs in conservation work. Each case is different, and the local people themselves will contribute their own ideas and cultural adaptations if they feel that the project belongs to them. The case of Giew Muang is a good example of how well different elements of local culture can be adapted and combined with practical development activities in order to gain the people's commitment to conservation projects and increase the degree to which the forest is preserved.

Sanctifying the forest creates a sense of awe, respect, and safety among the villagers, helping to connect them to the divine. Although this is not technically a part of the Buddha's teachings, the sacredness that is invoked is an important aspect of the villagers' worldview, fulfilling a need for belief in a superior force that can be called on to help in times of need (see Saeng 1991). Combined with indigenous spirit beliefs, the sanctification of the forest greatly strengthens the villagers' sense of community and commitment to conservation.

The adaptation of rituals and the positive reaction to them by the laity are a prime example of how most ecology monks negotiate tradition and use it to introduce new ideas into society. Ordinations and other rites are familiar and important rituals in the lives of Thai Buddhists. Participation earns merit while it signals acceptance and commitment to the religion and the community. Monks such as Pitak frame these rituals in a way that enables participants to gain religious merit while at the same time expanding the realm of commitments participation engenders. It is no longer limited to demonstrating commitment to local social and religious relations but now includes environmental relations with neighbors, wildlife, plants, and the entire ecosystem in which humans live. While the interdependence of all life is a basic Buddhist teaching, using traditional rituals to apply this principle to a contemporary, essentially political issue is a radical reworking of the concept.

The use of both animist and Buddhist beliefs through ritual enactment strengthens the villagers' perception of themselves as a community based

364   Susan M. Darlington

on sanctity and shared responsibility. The guardian spirit rite emphasized the villagers' preexisting identity as a community even as it channeled it in a new direction. The tree ordination and formal establishment and consecration of the community forest constructed the village as a community with a clear goal of taking control of and responsibility for its natural resources. Together the villagers' spirit beliefs and Buddhist practice promoted an alternative vision of environmentalism. The ceremonies extended the ritual domain and the authority of religion, which usually governed relations among people, to encompass the forest environment. Both the moral code established through Buddhism and the concept of community based on the guardian spirit rites were constituted in radically new ways that redefined how the villagers thought of and interacted with the forest, thus greatly strengthening the potential of the survival of both the people and the natural environment in which they live.

ACKNOWLEDGMENTS

This research was made possible by the Joint Committee on Southeast Asia of the Social Science Research Council and the American Council of Learned Societies with funds provided by the National Endowment for the Humanities and the Ford Foundation; the Association for Asian Studies, Southeast Asia Council, with funds from the Luce Foundation; and a travel grant from the Ford Foundation Comparative Scientific Traditions Program of Hampshire College. Thanks go to the National Research Council of Thailand for permission to conduct this research and to Marc Bermann for criticisms during the essay's revisions. I extend particular gratitude to Phrakhru Pitak and Giew Muang for welcoming and working with me.

NOTES

1   The term *radical conservatism* is borrowed from the title of a book published in honor of Buddhadasa Bhikkhu. The late Buddhadasa, who is recognized as the leading Thai Buddhist philosopher, advocated a return to the basic teachings of the Buddha in terms relevant to contemporary society (see Sulak 1990). I take the term further, using it here to describe the use of essential religious concepts, including elements of spirit beliefs as well as basic Buddhist principles, in new contexts and articulations in order to promote social change. This essay is based on twenty-one months of research conducted in Thailand from 1991 to 1994.

2   As I did not visit Giew Muang until one year after these events, these descriptions are based on what people who participated — villagers, NGO workers, and Pitak — told me about them and my observations and par-

ticipation in similar events performed in other villages in Nan Province. On tree ordinations in general, see Darlington 1998.

3 These floods provided the stimulus for the government to ban logging in January 1989. See Project for Ecological Recovery 1992, xi, 32.

4 *Ui* means "grandparent" in Northern Thai.

5 Recollections of the number of monks who attended this ceremony varied. All informants agreed, however, that there were at least the same number necessary to conduct an official monk's ordination.

6 Even the idea of wrapping monks' robes around some trees connects Buddhism and animism, as many Thais believe that spirits live within trees (Taylor 1994, 20).

7 This spirit has a royal name, but only the specialists in the village know it and they rarely refer to him by name.

8 On the ecological effects of eucalyptus plantations in Thailand, see Lohmann 1991; 1993, 211.

9 Not all ecology monks have been able to avoid conflicts with the hierarchy. Two famous activist monks, Phra Prajak Khuttajitto and Aacaan Phongsak Techathamamoo, were eventually derobed because of controversies surrounding their work (on Phra Prajak, see Taylor 1993).

10 This comment was made to me several times in personal communications with Phra Dhammathilok of Wat Pa Darabhirom, Chiang Mai, between 1986 and 1988.

11 The long-term impact of this project remains to be seen. In 2003, however, thirteen years after the tree ordination, the villagers were still maintaining their community forest.

Abraham, Itty. 1998. *The Making of the Indian Atomic Bomb: Science, Secrecy, and the Postcolonial State.* London: Zed.

Adas, Michael. 1990. *Machines as the Measure of Men: Science, Technology, and Ideologies of Western Dominance.* Delhi: Oxford University Press.

Adimihardja, Kusnaka. 1992. "The Traditional Agricultural Practices of the Kasepuhan Community of West Java." In *The Heritage of Traditional Agriculture among the Western Austronesians,* edited by James J. Fox, 33–46. Canberra: Department of Anthropology, Australian National University.

Agrawal, Arun. 1995. "Dismantling the Divide between Indigenous and Scientific Knowledge." *Development and Change* 26(3): 413–39.

Agarwal, Bina. 1991. *Engendering the Environment Debate: Lessons from the Indian Subcontinent.* CASID Distinguished Speaker Series, no. 8. East Lansing: Center for the Advanced Study of International Development, Michigan State University.

Ali, Salim. 1985. *The Fall of a Sparrow.* Delhi: Oxford University Press.

Allchin, Bridget, and Frank Raymond Allchin. 1988. *The Rise of Civilization in India and Pakistan.* Cambridge: Cambridge University Press.

Allchin, Frank Raymond. 1963. *Neolithic Cattle-Keepers of South India: A Study of the Deccan Ashmounds.* London: Cambridge University Press.

Anderson, Benedict. 1991. *Imagined Communities: Reflections on the Origin and Spread of Nationalism.* 2d ed. London. Verso.

Anderson, David. 1984. "Depression, Dust Bowl, Demography, and Drought: The Colonial State and Soil Conservation in East Africa during the 1930s." *African Affairs* 83:321–43.

Anderson, Warwick. 1992. "Climates of Opinion: Acclimatization in Nineteenth-Century France and England." *Victorian Studies* 35: 135–57.

———. [1994] 1995. "'Where Every Prospect Pleases and Only Man Is Vile': Laboratory Medicine as Colonial Discourse." In *Discrepant Histories: Translocal Essays on Filipino Cultures,* edited by Vicente Rafael. Philadelphia: Temple University Press.

———. 1995a. "Excremental Colonialism: Public Health and the Poetics of Pollution." *Critical Inquiry* 21 (spring): 640–69.

———. 1995b. "The Natures of Culture: Environment and Race in the Colonial Tropics." Paper presented at the conference Human Welfare and Environmental Discourses in Southeast Asia, Social Science Research Council, South and Southeast Asia Committees, Hilo, Hawaii, 27–29, December.

———. 1996. "Immunities of Empire: Race, Disease, and the New Tropical Medicine." *Bulletin of the History of Medicine* 70:94–118.

———. 1997. "The Trespass Speaks: White Masculinity and Colonial Breakdown." *American Historical Review* 102:1343–70.

———. 1998. "Leprosy and Citizenship." *positions: East Asia Cultures Critique* 6:707–30.

Anonymous. 1853. *Report on the Political States of Southwest Frontier Agency, Revenue Administration of Assam, and Wild Tribes Bordering Chittagong.* Selections from the Records of the Bengal Government 11. Calcutta: Bengal Secretariat Press.

———. 1871. *Papers Relating to East India Forest Conservancy.* Pt. 2: *Madras.* London: House of Commons.

———. 1934. "Proceedings of the All-India Sal Study Tour." *Indian Forestry Records,* 19(3).

———. 1992. "Logging Problems in Yandema Island (Maluku)." *Setiakawan* 7 (January–June): 102.

Appadurai, Arjun. 1988a. "Comments on 'The Jungle and the Aroma of Meats: An Ecological Theme in Hindu Medicine.'" *Social Science and Medicine* 27(3): 206–7.

———. 1988b. "Putting Hierarchy in Its Place." *Cultural Anthropology* 39(1): 36–49.

———. 1996a. "Disjuncture and Difference in the Global Cultural Economy." In *Modernity at Large: Cultural Dimensions of Globalization,* Minneapolis: University of Minnesota Press.

———. 1996b. "Global Ethnoscapes: Notes and Queries for a Transnational Anthropology." In *Modernity at Large: Cultural Dimensions of Globalization,* Minneapolis: University of Minnesota Press.

Appell, George. n.d. "Observational Procedures for Land Tenure and Kin Groupings in the Cognatic Societies of Borneo." Manuscript.

Appfel-Marglin, Frederique, and Stephen Marglin, eds. 1990. *Dominating Knowledge: Development, Culture, and Resolutionistance.* Oxford: Clarendon.

Arawan Karitbunyarit, ed. 1993. *Rak Nam Naan: Chiiwit lae Ngaan khaung Phrakhru Pitak Nanthakhun (Sanguan Jaaruwannoo)* [Love the Nan River: The Life and Work of Phrakhru Pitak Nanthakhun (Sanguan Jaaruwannoo)]. Nan: Sekiayatham. In Thai.

Arnold, David, ed. 1989. *Imperial Medicine and Indigenous Society.* Manchester: Manchester University Press.

Arora, D. 1994. "From State Regulation to People's Participation: Case of Forest Management in India." *Economic and Political Weekly* 29:691–98.

Arora, Hema, and Khare, Arvind. 1994. "Experience with the Recent Joint Forest Management Approach." Paper presented to the international workshop India's Forest Management, New Delhi, 10–12 February.

Atkinson, Fred W. 1905. *The Philippine Islands.* Boston: Ginn. Baden-Powell, B. H. [1892] 1972. *Land-Systems of British India.* Oxford: Clarendon.

Bailey, W. A. 1924. "Moribund Forests in United Provinces." *Indian Forester* 50:188–91.

Baker, D. 1984. "A Serious Time: Forest Satyagraha in Madhya Pradesh, 1930." *Indian Economic and Social History Review* 21:71–90.

Balfour, Edward. 1862. *The Timber Trees, Timber, and Fancy Woods as also the Forests of India and of Eastern and Southern Asia.* Madras: Union Press.

Balieo Maluku. 1995. "Profil Program Pengelolaan Sumberdaya Alam Secara

Terpadu Berbasis Adat Di Maur-Ohoiwut, Kei Besar, Maluku Tenggara"
[Program Profile of Integrated Natural Resources Management on Basis of
Custom in Maur-Ohoiwut, Ke Besar, Southeast Maluku]. Proposal.

Ball, Vincent. 1880. *Jungle Life in India, or the Journeys and Journals of an
Indian Geologist*. London: Thomas de la Rue.

Bancroft, H. H. [1899] 1912. *The New Pacific*. Rev. ed. New York: Bancroft.

Banuri, Tariq, and Frederique Apffel Marglin. 1993. "A Systems-of-Knowledge
Analysis of Deforestation." In *Who Will Save the Forests? Knowledge,
Power, and Environmental Destruction*, edited by Tariq Banuri and Fred-
erique Apffel Marglin, 1–23. London: Zed.

Barber, Charles. 1989. "State, People, and the Environment: The Case of Forests in Java." Ph.D. diss., University of California, Berkeley.

Bardhan, P. 1984. *The Political Economy of Indian Development*. Oxford:
Blackwell.

Barnes, B. 1977. *Interests and the Growth of Knowledge*. London: Routledge
and Kegan Paul.

Bartlett, Harley H. 1962. "Some Words Used in Connection with Primitive
Agriculture in Southeast Asia." *Proceedings of the Ninth Pacific Science
Congress* 4:274–75.

Basso, Keith. 1984. "Stalking with Stories: Names, Places, and Moral Narratives among the Western Apache." In *Text, Play, and Story*, edited by
E. Bruner, 19–55. Washington, D.C.: American Ethnological Society.

———. 1988. "Speaking with Names: Language and Landscape among the
Western Apache." *Cultural Anthropology* 3(2): 99–130.

Basu, R. N., Z. Jezek, and N. A. Ward. 1979. *The Eradication of Smallpox
from India*. New Delhi: WHO, South-East Asia Regional Office.

Battaglia, Debbora. 1995. "On Practical Nostalgia: Self-Prospecting among
Urban Trobrianders." In *Rhetorics of Self-Making*, edited by Debbora Battaglia, 77–96. Berkeley: University of California Press.

Baviskar, Amita. 1994. "Fate of the Forest: Conservation and Tribal Rights"
Economic and Political Weekly 29(38): 2493–2501.

———. 1995. *In The Belly of the River: Tribal Conflicts over Development in
the Narmada Valley*. Delhi: Oxford University Press.

———. 1997. "Who Speaks for the Victims of Development? The Problem of
Authenticity and Representation." *Seminar* 451:59–61.

Bayly, C. A. 1983. *Rulers, Townsmen, and Bazaars*. Cambridge: Cambridge
University Press.

———. 1988. *Indian Society and the Making of the British Empire*. Cambridge:
Cambridge University Press.

Bayly, Chris. 1993. "Knowing the Country: Empire and Information in India."
Modern Asian Studies 27(1): 3–43.

Beinart, William. 1984. "Soil Erosion, Conservationism, and Ideas about Development: A Southern African Exploration, 1900–1960." *Journal of Southern African Studies* 11(1): 52–83.

———. 1989. "The Politics of Colonial Conservation." *Journal of Southern
African Studies* 15(2): 143–62.

Bengal Forest Administration Report. 1875–76. *Reports*.

Bengal Forest Committee. 1939. *Report*. Calcutta: Government of Bengal.

Bennett, L., et al. 1991. *Gender and Poverty in India: World Bank Country Study.* Washington, D.C.: World Bank.

Benton, Lisa, and John Rennie Short. 1999. *Environmental Discourse and Practice.* Oxford: Blackwell.

———. 2000. *Environmental Discourses: A Reader.* Oxford: Blackwell.

Berwick, Stephen H., and V. B. Saharia, eds. 1995. *The Development of International Principles and Practices of Wildlife Management: Asian and American Approaches.* Delhi: Oxford University Press.

Best, J. W. 1935. *Forest Life in India.* London: John Murray.

Beveridge, Albert J. [1900] 1908. "The Star of Empire." In *Meaning of the Times.* Indianapolis: Bobbs-Merrill, 1908.

Bevis, William. 1995. *Borneo Log: The Struggle for Sarawak's Forests.* Seattle: University of Washington Press.

Bhandari, M. M. [1978] 1990. *Flora of the Indian Desert.* Jodhpur: MPS Repros.

Bird-David, Nurit. 1990. "The Giving Environment: Another Perspective on the Economic System of Gatherer-Hunters. *Current Anthropology* 31(2): 189–96.

Birdwood, H. M. 1910. *Indian Timbers: The Hill Forests of Western India.* London: Journal of Indian Arts and Industry.

Blaikie, Piers. 1985. *The Political Economy of Soil Erosion in Developing Countries.* New York: Longman.

Bloch, Maurice. 1995. "People into Places: Zafimaniry Concepts of Clarity." In *The Anthropology of Landscape: Perspectives on Place and Space,* edited by E. Hirsch and M. O'Hanlon, 63–77. Oxford: Clarendon.

Bloor, D. 1976. *Knowledge and Social Imagery.* Chicago: University of Chicago Press.

Blust, Robert. 1984. "Austronesian Culture History: Some Linguistic Inferences and Their Relations to the Archaeological Record." In *Prehistoric Indonesia: A Reader,* edited by Pieter van de Velde, 217–41. KITLV Verhandelingen, no. 104. Dordrecht: Foris.

———. 1987. "Lexical Reconstruction and Semantic Reconstruction: The Case of Austronesian 'House' Words." *Diachronica: International Journal for Historical Linguistics* 4 (1–2): 79–106.

Boeke, J. H. 1953. *Economics and Economic Policy of Dual Societies.* New York: Institute of Pacific Relations.

Boomgaard, Peter. 1989. *Between Sovereign Domain and Servile Tenure: The Development of Rights to Land in Java, 1780–1870.* Amsterdam: Free University Press.

Botkin, Daniel. 1990. *Discordant Harmonies: A New Ecology for the Twenty-first Century.* New York: Oxford University Press.

Bouchard, D. F., ed. 1977. *Michel Foucault: Language, Counter-memory, Practice: Selected Essays and Interviews.* New York: Cornell University Press.

Boucher, Douglas. 1996. "Islands in the Biosphere." Review of *Song of the Dodo: Island Biogeography in an Age of Extinctions. The Nation,* 26 May 1996: 30–32.

Bouquet, M. 1995. "Exhibiting Knowledge: The Trees of Dubois, Haeckel, Jesse, and Rivers at the *Pithecanthropus* Centennial exhibition." In *Shift-*

ing Contexts: Transformations in Anthropological Knowledge, edited by M. Strathern, 31–55. London: Routledge.

Bowring, J. 1859. *The Philippine Islands*. London: Smith, Elder.

Brandis, D. 1860. *Report on Teak Forests of Pegu*. London: HMSO.

———. 1884. "The Progress of Forestry in India." *Indian Forester* 10(9): 399–410; 10(10): 452–62; 10(11): 501–10.

Brara, Rita. 1992. "Are Grazing Lands 'Wastelands'? Some Evidence from Rajasthan." *Economic and Political Weekly*, 22 February, 411–18.

Braudel, Fernand. 1993. *A History of Civilizations*. Translated by Richard Mayne. New York: Penguin.

Breman, Jan. 1985. *Of Peasants, Migrants, and Paupers: Rural Labour Circulation and Capitalist Production in West India*. Delhi: Oxford University Press.

———. 1988. *The Shattered Image: Construction and Deconstruction of the Village in Colonial Asia*. Dodrect: Foris.

Brenneis, Donald. In press. "Sound Contracts, Performing Rights." In *Culture and the Question of Rights to Southeast Asian Environments: Forests, Coasts, and ·Seas*," edited by Charles Zerner. Durham: Duke University Press.

Brightman, Robert. 1993. *Grateful Prey: Rock Cree Human-Animal Relationships*. Berkeley: University of California Press.

Brilliant, Lawrence B., and Girija Brilliant. 1978. "Death for a Killer Disease." *Quest* (2)3: 1–10, 98.

Broad, Robin, with John Cavanagh. 1993. *Plundering Paradise: The Struggle for the Environment in the Philippines*. Berkeley: University of California Press.

Brody, Hugh. 1981. *Maps and Dreams*. New York: Pantheon.

Brosius, J. Peter. 1986. "River, Forest, and Mountain: The Penan Geng Landscape." *Sarawak Museum Journal*, n.s., 36(57): 173–84.

———. 1988. "A Separate Reality: Comments on Hoffman's *The Punan: Hunters and Gatherers of Borneo*." *Borneo Research Bulletin* 20(2): 81–106.

———. 1991. "Foraging in Tropical Rainforests: The Case of the Penan of Sarawak, East Malaysia (Borneo)." *Human Ecology* 19(2): 123–50.

———. 1993. "Contrasting Subsistence Ecologies of Eastern and Western Penan Foragers (Sarawak, East Malaysia)." In *Food and Nutrition in the Tropical Forest: Biocultural Interactions and Applications to Development*, edited by C. M. Hladik, A. Hladik, O. F. Linares, H. Pagezy, A. Semple and M. Hadley, 515–22. Paris: UNESCO.

———. 1995. "Signifying Bereavement: Form and Context in the Analysis of Penan Death-Names." *Oceania* 66(2): 119–46.

———. 1995–96. "Father Dead, Mother Dead: Bereavement and Fictive Death in Penan Geng Society." *Omega: Journal of Death and Dying* 32(3): 197–226.

———. 1997a. "Endangered Forest, Endangered People: Environmentalist Representations of Indigenous Knowledge." *Human Ecology* 25(1): 47–69.

———. 1997b. "Prior Transcripts, Divergent Paths: Resistance and Acquiescence to Logging in Sarawak, East Malaysia." *Comparative Studies in Society and History* 39(3): 468–510.

————. 1999a. "Analyses and Interventions: Anthropological Engagements with Environmentalism." *Current Anthropology* 40(3): 277–309.

————. 1999b. "Green Dots, Pink Hearts: Displacing Politics from the Malaysian Rainforest." *American Anthropologist* 101(1): 36–57.

————. 1999c. "The Western Penan of Borneo." In *The Cambridge Encyclopedia of Hunters and Gatherers,* edited by Richard B. Lee and Richard H. Daly, 312–16. Cambridge: Cambridge University Press.

————. 2001. "Local Knowledges, Global Claims: On the Significance of Indigenous Ecologies in Sarawak, East Malaysia." In *Indigenous Traditions and Ecology,* edited by J. Grimm and L. Sullivan, 125–57. Cambridge, Mass: Harvard University Press and Center for the Study of World Religions.

————. 2003 [in press]. "The Forest and the Nation: Negotiating Citizenship in Sarawak, East Malaysia." In *Cultural Citizenship in Southeast Asia: Nation and Belonging in the Hinterlands,* edited by Renato Rosaldo. Berkeley: University of California Press.

Brosius, J. Peter, Anna Tsing, and Charles Zerner. 1998. "Representing Communities: Histories and Politics of Community-Based Natural Resource Management." *Society and Natural Resources* 11:157–68.

Bryant, James. 1994. "From Laissez Faire to Scientific Forestry: Forest Management in Early Colonial Burma." *Forest and Conservation History* 38(4): 160–70.

Bryant, Raymond L. 1996. "Romancing Colonial Forestry: The Discourse of 'Forestry as Progress' in British Burma." *Geographical Journal* 162(2): 169–78.

Bryant, Raymond L., and Sinead Bailey. 1997. *Third World Political Ecology.* London: Routledge.

Bryant, Raymond L., Jonathan Rigg, and Philip Stott. 1993. "Forest Transformations and Political Ecology in Southeast Asia." *Global Ecology and Biogeography Letters* 3(4–6): 101–11.

Buch, M. N. 1991. *The Forests of Madhya Pradesh.* Bhopal: Madhya Pradesh Madhyam.

Buchori, Binny. 1996. " 'Sasi': Haruku's Style of Conservation Management." *Jakarta Post,* 21 January, 6.

Buhler, G. Tr. [1886] 1964. *The Laws of Manu.* Delhi: Motilal Banarsidass.

Burling, R. 1965. *Hill Farms and Padi Fields: Life in Mainland Southeast Asia.* Englewood Cliffs, N. J.: Prentice-Hall.

Burns, Peter. 1989. "The Myth of Adat." *Journal of Pluralism* 28:1–29.

Buttel, Frederick H. 1992. "Environmentalization: Origins, Processes, and Implications for Rural Social Change." *Rural Sociology* 57(1): 1–27.

Camerini, Jane R. 1994. "Evolution, Biogeography, and Maps: An Early History of Wallace's Line." In *Darwin's Laboratory: Evolutionary Theory and Natural History in the Pacific,* edited by Roy McLeod and Philip F. Rehbock, 70–109. Honolulu: University of Hawaii Press.

Cannon, Susan Faye. 1978. *Science in Culture: The Early Victorian Period.* New York: Dawson.

Carpenter, Carol. 1987. "Brides and Bride-Dressers in Contemporary Java." Ph.D. dissertation, Cornell University.

Carter, Paul. 1989. *The Road to Botany Bay: An Exploration in Landscape and History.* Chicago: University of Chicago Press.

Cell, John W. 1986. "Anglo-Indian Medical Theory and the Origins of Segregtion in West Africa." *American Historical Review* 91: 307–35.

Center for Science and the Environment. 1982. *The State of India's Environment, 1982: A Citizen's Report.* New Delhi: Center for Science and the Environment.

———. 1985. *The State of India's Environment, 1984–1985: The Second Citizens' Report.* New Delhi: Center for Science and the Environment.

———. 1996. *Protection of Nature Parks: Whose Business? Proceedings of a Debate.* New Delhi: Center for Science and the Environment.

Center for the Study of Developing Societies. 1995. Symposium on the Emergency, Recollecting, and Anxiety, 25 June, Delhi. (Ashish Nandy, Kuldip Nayar, Justice Sachi, Shumanta Banerjea).

Chakravarti, Sudeep. 1995. "Madhya Pradesh: Trying to Keep Up." *India Today,* 31 October.

Chambers, David Wade. 1987. "Period and Process in Colonial and National Science." In *Scientific Colonialism: A Cross-Cultural Comparison,* edited by R. Reingold and M. Rothenberg, 297–322. Washington, D.C.: Smithsonian Institution Press.

Chambers, Robert, N. C. Saxena, and Tushaar Shah. 1989. *To the Hands of the Poor: Water and Trees.* London: Intermediate Technology Publications.

Champion, Harry G., S. K. Seth, and G. M. Khattak. 1965. *Forest Types of Pakistan.* Peshawar: Pakistan Forest Institute.

Champion, Herbert. 1975. "Indian Silviculture and Research over the Century." *Indian Forester* 101(1): 3–8.

Chatrapati Singh, O. 1993. "Legal Aspects." Madhya Pradesh Integrated Forest Sector Project Preparation Working Paper 6, Bhopal.

Chatsumarn Kabilsingh. 1998. *Buddhism and Nature Conservation.* Bangkok: Thammasat University Press.

Chatterjee, Partha. 1993. *The Nation and its Fragments: Colonial and Postcolonial Histories.* Delhi: Oxford University Press.

Chaturvedi, M. D. 1931. "The Regeneration of Sal in United Provinces." *Indian Forester* 57(4): 157–66.

Chayanov, A. V. 1966. *On the Theory of the Peasant Economy.* Edited by Daniel Thorner, Baslie Kerblay, and R. E. F. Smith. Homewood, Ill.: R. D. Irwin.

Christie, Jan Wisseman. 1991. "States without Cities: Demographic Trends in Early Java." *Indonesia* 52: 23–40.

Christie, Nancy J. 1994. "Environment and Race: Geography's Search for a Darwinian Synthesis." In *Darwin's Laboratory: Evolutionary Theory and Natural History in the Pacific,* edited by Roy McLeod and Philip F. Rehbock, 426–73. Honolulu: University of Hawaii Press.

Cleghorn, Hugh. 1861. *The Forests and Gardens of South India.* London: W. H. Allen.

Cleghorn, Hugh, Forbes Royle, R. Baird Smith, and R. Strachey. 1852. "Report of the Committee Appointed by the Physical Point of View of the Destruction of Tropical Forests." *Journal of the Agricultural and Horticultural Society of India* 8:118–49.

Clements, Harry. 1983. *Alfred Russel Wallace: Biologist and Social Reformer.* London: Hutchinson.

Clifford, James. 1987. "Of Other Peoples: Beyond the Salvage Paradigm." In *Discussions in Contemporary Culture*, edited by Hal Foster. Dia Art Foundation no. 1. Seattle: Bay Press.

Clifford, James, and George Marcus. 1986. *Writing Culture: The Poetics and Politics of Ethnography.* Berkeley: University of California Press.

Clutterbuck, Peter. 1927. "Forestry and the Empire." *Empire Forestry Journal* 6:184–92.

Cohen, Jean, and Andrew Arato. 1992. *Civil Society and Political Theory.* Cambridge: MIT Press.

Cohn, Bernard S., and Nicholas Dirks. 1988. "Beyond the Fringe: The Nation-State, Colonialism, and the Technologies of Power." *Journal of Historical Sociology* 1(2): 224–29.

Colchester, Marcus. 1989. *Pirates, Squatters, and Poachers: The Political Ecology of Dispossession of the Native Peoples of Sarawak.* London: Survival International.

Coleman, William. 1966. "Science and Symbol in the Turner Frontier Hypothesis." *American Historical Review* 72:22–49.

Colfer, C. J. Pierce. 1987. "Change and Indigenous Agroforestry in East Kalimantan." In *Whose Trees?* edited by L. Fortmann and J. W. Bruce. Boulder: Westview.

Collins, H. M. 1992. *Changing Order: Replication and Induction in Scientific Practice.* Chicago: University of Chicago Press.

Compost, A. 1980. "Pilot Survey of Exploitation of Dugong and Sea Turtle in the Aru Islands." Yayasan Indonesia Hijau [Green Indonesia Foundation], Jakarta. Manuscript.

Conklin, Beth A., and Laura R. Graham. 1995. "The Shifting Middle Ground: Amazonian Indians and Eco-Politics." *American Anthropologist* 97(4): 695–710.

Cooper, Frederick. 1991. "Development and the Remaking of the Colonial World." Paper presented at the Social Science Research Council meeting on Social Science and Development, Berkeley, 15–16 November.

———. 1995. "Modernizing Bureaucrats, Backward Africans, and the Development Concept." Paper presented to the weekly colloquium, Program in Agrarian Studies, Yale University.

Coppola, Nancy W., and Karis, Bill, eds. 2000. *Technical Communication, Deliberative Rhetoric, and Environmental Discourse: Connections and Directions.* Westport, CT: Ablex.

Corry, Stephen. 1993. "The Rainforest Harvest: Who Reaps the Benefit?" *Ecologist* 23(4): 148–53.

Cosgrove, Denis. 1988. *The Iconography of Landscape: Essays on the Symbolic Representation, Design, and Use of Past Environments.* Cambridge: Cambridge University Press.

———. 1995. "Habitable Earth: Wilderness, Empire, and Race in America." In

Wild Ideas, edited by David Rothenberg, Minneapolis: University of Minnesota Press.

Coward, Walter. Forthcoming. "Building Models of Community-Based Natural Resource Management: A Personal Narrative." In *Representing Communities: Histories and Politics of Community-Based Natural Resource Management,* edited by J. Peter Brosius, Anna Tsing, and Charles Zerner.

Cowen, Michael, and Robert Shenton. 1995. "The Invention of Development." In *Power of Development,* edited by Jonathan Crush, London: Routledge.

Cranbrook, Earl of. [1885] 1989. Introduction to *A Naturalist's Wanderings in the Eastern Archipelago,* by Henry O. Forbes. Oxford: Oxford University Press.

Cronon, William. 1983. *Changes in the Land: Indians, Colonists, and the Ecology of New England.* New York: Hill and Wang.

——. 1990. "Modes of Prophecy and Production: Placing Nature in History." *Journal of American History* 76:1122–31.

——. 1991. *Nature's Metropolis: Chicago and the Great West.* New York: Norton.

——. 1995. "Getting Back to the Wrong Nature." In *Uncommon Ground: Toward Reinventing Nature,* edited by William Cronon, 69–90. New York: Norton.

Crosby, A. W. 1986. *Ecological Imperialism: The Biological Expansion of Europe, 900–1900.* New York: Cambridge University Press.

Crush, Jonathan. 1995a. "Introduction: Imagining Development." In *Power of Development,* edited by Jonathan Crush, London: Routledge.

——, ed. 1995b. *Power of Development.* London: Routledge.

Curtin, Philip. 1985. "Medical Knowledge and Urban Planning in Tropical Africa." *American Historical Review* 90 (1985): 584–613.

Dalton, George. 1972. "Peasantries in Anthropology and History." *Current Anthropology* 13(4): 385–415.

Darier, Eric, ed. 1999. *Discourses of the Environment.* Oxford: Blackwell.

Darlington, Susan M. 1998. "The Ordination of a Tree: The Buddhist Ecology Movement in Thailand." *Ethnology* 37(1): 1–15.

Darlington, Susan M. Forthcoming a. "Rethinking Buddhism and Development: The Emergence of Environmentalist Monks in Thailand." In *Socially Engaged Buddhism,* edited by Charles Prebish and Damian Keown. Richmond, Surrey: Curzon Press.

Darlington, Susan M. Forthcoming b. "The Spirit(s) of Conservation in Buddhist Thailand." In *Nature and Environment Across Cultures,* edited by Helaine Selin. Dordrecht, The Netherlands: Kluwer.

Davidson, Jamie and Douglas Kammen. 2002. "Indonesia's Forgotten War and the Lineages of Violence in West Kalimantan." *Indonesia* 73 (April 2002): 53–87.

Davis, D. 1931. "Sal Regeneration Fellings." *Indian Forester* 57(4): 153–57.

——. 1944. "Sal Natural Regeneration in United Provinces." *Indian Forester* 70(1): 1–5.

——. 1948. "Sal Natural Regeneration in United Provinces." *Indian Forester* 74(2): 50–56.

Davis, Wade, and Thom Henley. 1990. *Penan: Voice for the Borneo Rainforest*. Vancouver: Western Canada Wilderness Committee.

Davis, Wade, Ian McKenzie, and Shane Kennedy. 1995. *Nomads of the Dawn: The Penan of the Borneo Rain Forest*. San Francisco: Pomegranate Artbooks.

Day, Tony. 1994. " 'Landscape' in Early Java." In *Recovering the Orient: Artists, Scholars, Appropriations*, edited by Andrew Gerstle and Anthony Milner, 175–203. Singapore: Harwood Academic Publishers.

De, R. N. 1941. "Sal Regeneration de Novo." *Indian Forester* 67(6): 283–91.

de Bevoise, Ken. 1995. *Agents of Apocalypse: Epidemic Disease in the Colonial Philippines*. Princeton: Princeton University Press.

de Certeau, Michel. 1988. *The Practice of Everyday Life*. Translated by Steven Randall. Berkeley: University of California Press.

Deleuze, Gilles, and Félix Guattari. 1987. *A Thousand Plateaus: Capitalism and Schizophrenia*. Translated by Brian Massumi. Minneapolis: University of Minnesota Press. Originally published as *Mille Plateaux*, vol. 2 of *Capitalisme et Schizophrénie*. Paris: Les Editions de Minuit, 1980.

Demeritt, David. 1994. "The Nature of Metaphors in Cultural Geography and Environmental History." *Progress in Human Geography* 18:163–85.

Dempwolff, Otto. 1937. *Comparative Phonology of the Austronesian Word Lists*. 3 vols. Quezon City: Ateneo de Manila University. Translated from the German original published in 1938 in Berlin by Dietrich Reimer.

Departemen Kehutanan. 1989. *Laporan Survai Potensi Calon Taman Laut Aru* [Survey Report on the Potential of the Proposed Aru Marine Reserve]. Ambon: Departemen Kehutanan.

de Vries, Jan. 1974. *The Dutch Rural Economy in the Golden Age, 1500–1700*. New Haven: Yale University Press.

Dewald, Jonathan, and Liana Vardi. 1998. "The Peasantries of France, 1400–1789." In *The Peasantries of Europe from the Fourtheenth to the Eighteenth Centuries*, edited by Tom Scott, 21–47. London: Longman.

Diamond, Jared M. 1986. "The Environmentalist Myth." *Nature* 324(6): 19–20.

Dirks, Nicholas. 1990. "History as the Sign of the Modern." *Public Culture* 2:25–33.

———. 1992a. "Castes of the Mind." *Representations* 37:56–78.

———. 1992b. "From Little King to Landlord: Colonial Discourse and Colonial Rule." In *Colonialism and Culture*, edited by Nicholas Dirks, 175–208. Ann Arbor: University of Michigan Press.

Dixon, R. K., S. Brown, R. A. Houghton, A. M. Solomon, M. C. Trexler, and J. Wisniewski. 1994. "Carbon Pools and Flux of Global Forest Ecosystems." *Science* 263 (5144): 185–90.

District Rural Development Agency. 1993. *Jhabua: Handbook of Statistics*. Jhabua: District Rural Development Agency.

Djohani, R. 1989. *Marine Conservation Development in Indonesia, Coral Reef Policy: Recommendations and Project Concepts for the Implementation of Management of Marine Protected Areas in Indonesia*. Jakarta: World Wildlife Fund.

Doolittle, Amity A. 1999. "Controlling the Land: Property Rights and Power

Struggles in Sabah, Malaysia, 1881–1996." Ph.D. diss., School of Forestry and Environmental Studies, Yale University.

Douglas, Mary. [1966] 1976. *Purity and Danger: An Analysis of Concepts of Pollution and Taboo*. London: Routledge and Kegan Paul.

Dove, Michael. 1983. "Swidden Agriculture and the Political Economy of Ignorance." *Agroforestry Systems* 1:85–99.

———. 1985a. "The Agroecological Mythology of the Javanese and the Political-Economy of Indonesia." *Indonesia* 39:1–36.

———. 1985. *Swidden Agriculture in Indonesia: Subsistence Strategies of the Kalimantan Kantu'*. New York: Mouton.

———. 1986. "The Practical Reason of Weeds in Indonesia: Peasant vs. State Views of *Imperata* and *Chromolaena*." *Human Ecology* 14(2): 163–90.

———. 1992a. "The Dialectical History of 'Jungle' in Pakistan." *Journal of Anthropological Research* 48(3): 231–53.

———. 1992b. "Foresters' Beliefs about Farmers as a Priority for Social Science Research in Social Forestry." *Agroforestry Systems* 17:13–41.

———. 1993a. "A Revisionist View of Tropical Deforestation and Development." *Environmental Conservation* 20(1): 17–24.

———. 1993b. "Smallholder Rubber and Swidden Agriculture in Borneo as a Sustainable Adaptation to the Ecology and Economy of the Tropical Forest." *Economic Botany* 47(2): 136–47.

———. 1994. "Marketing the Rainforest: 'Green' Panacea or Red Herring?" *Asia Pacific Issues* 13:1–7.

———. 1998a. "Living Rubber, Dead Land, and Persisting Systems in Borneo: Indigenous Representations of Sustainability." *Bijdragen tot de Taal, Land- en Volkenkunde* 154(1): 20, 20–54.

———. 1998b. "Local Dimensions of 'Global' Environmental Debates." In *Environmental Movements in Asia*, edited by A. Kalland and G. Persoon, 44–64. Nordic Institute of Asian Studies, Man and Nature in Asia 4. Richmond, Surrey: Curzon.

Dove, Michael R., Marina Campos, Andrew Mathews, Anne Rademacher, Suk Bae Rhee, Danile Smith, and Laura Meitenur Yoder. 2003. "The Global Mobilization of Environmental Concepts: Re-Thinking the Western/Non-Western Divide." In *Nature Across Culture: Non-Western Views of the Environment and Nature*, edited by Helaine Selin, 19–46. Dordrecht: Kluwer.

Down to Earth. 1992. "Forest Reserves Opposed for Logging." *Down to Earth*, 17 June.

———. 1996. "Yamdema Loggers Move In." *Down to Earth*, 28 February.

Dreyfus, Hubert, and Paul Rabinow. 1983. *Michel Foucault: Beyond Structuralism and Hermeneutics*. Chicago: University of Chicago Press.

Drinnon, Richard. 1980. *Facing West: The Metaphysics of Indian-Hating and Empire-Building*. Minneapolis: University of Minnesota Press.

Dryzek, John S. 1997. *The Politics of the Earth: Environmental Discourses*. New York: Oxford University Press.

Dubois, Marc. 1991. "The Governance of the Third World: A Foucauldian Perspective on Power Relations in Development." *Alternatives* 16(1): 1–30.

Duncan, James, and David Ley, eds. 1993. *Place/Culture/Representation*. London: Routledge.

Dupuis, E. Melanie, and Peter Vandergeest, eds. 1995. *Creating the Countryside: The Politics of Rural and Environmental Discourse*. Philadelphia: Temple University Press.

Durning, Alan Thein. 1992. *Guardians of the Land: Indigenous Peoples and the Health of the Earth*. Worldwatch Paper 112. Washington: World Watch Institute.

Echols, John M., and Hassan Shadily. 1992. *Kamus Indonesia-Inggris: An Indonesian-English Dictionary*. 3d ed. Jakarta: PT Gramedia.

Ellen, Roy F. 1986. "What Black Elk Left Unsaid: On the Illusory Images of Green Primitivism." *Anthropology Today* 2(6): 8–12.

Elson, R. E. 1994. *Village Java under the Cultivation System, 1830–1970*. Sydney: Allen and Unwin.

Elwin, V. [1949] 1991. *Myths of Middle India*. Rpt. Delhi: Oxford University Press.

Escobar, Arturo. 1988. "Power and Visibility: Development and the Invention and Management of the Third World." *Cultural Anthropology* 3(4): 428–43.

———. 1995a. *Encountering Development: The Making and Unmaking of the Third World*. Princeton: Princeton University Press.

———. 1995b. "Imagining a Post-development Era." In *Power of Development*, edited by Jonathan Crush, 211–27. New York: Routledge.

———. 1995c. "Review of Mark Hobart (ed.), An Anthropological Critique of Development." *American Ethnologist* 22(3): 624.

Espiritu, Socorro C., and Chester L. Hunt. 1964. *Social Foundations of Community Development: Readings on the Philippines*. Manila: R. M. Garcia.

Esteva, Gustavo. 1992. "Development." In *The Development Dictionary*, edited by W. Sachs, London: Zed.

Estrella, Conrado. 1969. *The Democratic Answer to the Philippine Agrarian Problem*. Manila: Solidaridad.

Evans, Ivor H. N. [1923] 1970. *Studies in Religion, Folk-Lore, and Custom in British North-Borneo and the Malay Peninsula*. London: Frank Cass.

Fabian, Johannes. 1983. *Time and the Other: How Anthropology Makes Its Object*. New York: Columbia University Press.

Fairchild, David. 1945. *The World Was My Garden: Travels of a Plant Explorer*. New York: Scribners.

Fairhead, J., and M. Leach. 1994. "Contested Forests: Modern Conservation and Historical Land Use in Guinea's Ziama Reserve." *African Affairs* 93(373): 481–512.

———. 1995. "Reading Forest History Backwards: The Interaction of Policy and Local Land Use in Guinea's Forest-Savanna Mosaic, 1893–1993." *Environment and History* 1:55–91.

Falconer, H. 1852. *Selections from Records of Bengal Government, no. 9: Report on the Teak Forests of the Tenasserim Provinces with Other Papers on Teak of India*. Calcutta: Military Orphan Press.

Falkus, Malcolm. 1990. "Ecology and the Economic History of Asia (I): Economic History and Environment in Southeast Asia." *Asian Studies Review* 14(1): 65–79.

Fanon, Frantz. 1978. "Medicine and Colonialism." In *The Cultural Crisis of Modern Medicine*, edited by John Ehrenreich. New York: Monthly Review Press.

Farr, Ian. 1986. " 'Tradition' and the Peasantry: On the Modern Historiography of Rural Germany." In *The German Peasantry*, edited by Richard Evans and W. R. Lee, 1–36. London: Croom Helm.

Feld, Steven. 1982. *Sound and Sentiment: Birds, Weeping, Poetics, and Song in Kaluli Expression*. Philadelphia: University of Pennsylvania Press.

Fenner, F., D. A. Henderson, I. Arita, Z. Jezek, and I. D. Ladnyi. 1988. *Smallpox and Its Eradication*. Geneva: World Health Organization.

Fentress, James, and Chris Wickham. 1992. *Social Memory: New Perspectives on the Past*. Oxford: Blackwell.

Ferguson, James. 1994. *The Anti-politics Machine: "Development," Depoliticization, and Bureaucratic Power in Lesotho*. Minneapolis: University of Minnesota Press.

Fernow, Bernhard. 1907. *A Brief History of Forestry in Europe, the United States, and Other Countries*. Toronto: University of Toronto Press.

Fitzpatrick, Daniel. 1997. "Disputes and Legal Pluralism in Modern Indonesian Land Law." *Yale Journal of International Law* 22 (winter): 172–212.

Foley, Kathy. 1987. "The Tree of Life in Transition: Images of Resource Management in Indonesian Theatre," *Crossroads* 3:66–77.

Forbes, Ann. 1999. "The Importance of Being Local: Villagers, NGOs, and the World Bank in the Arun Valley, Nepal." In *Ethnographic Presence: Environmentalism, Indigenous Rights, and Transnational Cultural Critique*. Special issue of *Identities: Global Studies in Culture and Power* 6(2–3): 319–44.

Forbes, Henry O. 1885. *A Naturalist's Wanderings in the Eastern Archipelago: A Narrative of Travel and Exploration from 1878 to 1883*. New York: Harper and Brothers.

Ford-Robertson, F. C. 1927. "The Problems of Sal Regeneration with Special Reference to the 'Moist' Forests of the United Provinces." *Indian Forester* 53(9): 500–11.

Forest Research Institute. 1953a. *Proceedings of the All-India Sal Study Tour and Symposium*. Dehradoon: Forest Research Institute.

———. 1953b. *Proceedings of the All-India Teak Study Tour and Symposium*. Dehradoon: Forest Research Institute.

Forsyth, J. 1889. *The Highlands of Central India: Notes on Their Forests and Wild Tribes, Natural History, and Sports*. London: Chapman and Hall.

Foucault, Michel. 1973. *The Order of Things*. New York: Vintage.

———. 1979. *Discipline and Punish: The Birth of the Prison*. Translated by Alan Sheridan. New York: Vintage.

Fox, James J. 1973. "On Bad Death and the Left Hand: A Study of Rotinese Symbolic Inversions." In *Right and Left: Essays on Dual Symbolic Classification*, edited by Rodney Needham, 342–68. Chicago: University of Chicago Press.

Fredrickson, George M. 1987. *The Black Image in the White Mind: The Debate on Afro-American Character and Destiny, 1817–1914*. Hanover, NH: Wesleyan University Press.

Freer, Paul C. 1909. "Address at the Commencement Exercises of the Philippine Medical School." *Philippine Journal of Science* (4B):71–75.

Gaboude, Louis. 1990. "Thai Society and Buddhadasa: Structural Difficulties." In *Radical Conservatism: Buddhism in the Contemporary World,* edited by Sulak Sivaraksa, 211–29. Bangkok: Sathirakoses-Nagapradipa Foundation.

Gadgil, Madhau, and Ramachandra Guha. 1992. *This Fissured Land: An Ecological History of India.* Delhi: Oxford University Press.

———. 1995. *Ecology and Equity: The Use and Abuse of Nature in Contemporary India.* London: Routledge.

Gandhi, Indira. 1975. "The Ecological Crisis." In *The Years of Endeavour: Selected Speeches of India Gandhi, August 1969–August 1972,* 443–47. New Delhi: Publications Division, Ministry of Information and Broadcasting. Speech delivered before the National Committee on Environmental Planning and Coordination, New Delhi, 12 April 1972.

———. 1982. "Man and His World." In *Peoples and Problems,* 60–67. London: Hodder and Stoughton. Address delivered to the United Nations Conference on Human Environment, Stockholm, 14 June 1972.

———. 1984a. "Defend Democracy." In *Selected Speeches and Writings, 1972–1977.* New Delhi: Publications Division, Ministry of Information and Broadcasting.

———. 1984b. "Meeting Demands—Made Peacefully" In *Selected Speeches and Writings, 1972–1977.* New Delhi: Publications Division, Ministry of Information and Broadcasting. Parliamentary Speech on no confidence motion.

———. 1986a. "Environmental Education." In *Selected Speeches and Writings of Indira Gandhi.* Vol. 5: *January 1, 1982–October 30, 1984,* 215–16. Inaugural address delivered at the First National Conference for Legislators on Environment, New Delhi, 30 April 1982. N.p.

———. 1986b. "Conservation and Economic Development." In *Selected Speeches and Writings of Indira Gandhi.* Vol. 5: *January 1, 1982–October 30, 1984,* 217–18. Speech delivered on receiving the Order of the Golden Ark from Prince Bernhard of the Netherlands, President of the World Wildlife Fund and Grand Master of the Order, New Delhi, 18 May 1982. N.p.

———. 1986c. "Enriching the Sylvan Heritage." In *Selected Speeches and Writings of Indira Gandhi.* Vol. 5: *January 1, 1982–October 30, 1984,* 218–23. Inaugural address delivered at the State Forest Minister's Conference, New Delhi, 18 October 1982. N.p.

———. 1986d. "Coexisting with Nature." In *Selected Speeches and Writings of Indira Gandhi.* Vol. 5: *January 1, 1982–October 30, 1984.* 223–26. Address delivered at the centenary celebrations of the Bombay Natural History Society, Bombay, 15 September 1983. N.p.

———. 1986e. "Wildlife Conservation." In *Selected Speeches and Writings of Indira Gandhi.* Vol. 5: *January 1, 1982–October 30, 1984,* 226. Foreword to *Indian Wildlife,* text by Romesh Bedi, pictures by Rajesh Bedi, New Delhi, 1984.

Geertz, C. 1963. *Agricultural Involution: The Processes of Ecological Change in Indonesia.* Berkeley: University of California Press.

Ghoshal, U. N. [1929] 1973. *The Agrarian System in Ancient India.* Calcutta: Saraswat Library.

Glacken, C. J. 1967. *Traces on the Rhodian Shore: Nature, Culture, and Western Thought from Ancient Times to the End of the Eighteenth Century.* Berkeley: University of California Press.

Godlewska, Anne, and Neil Smith, eds. 1995. *Geography and Empire.* London: Blackwell.

Gogate, Neel, and R. S. Chundawat. 1997. "Ecology to Tiger: To Enable a Realistic Projection of the Requirements Needed to Maintain a Demographically Viable Population of Tigers in India." Second Progress Report on the Fieldwork Carried out during the Period September 1996 to July 1997, Panna tiger reserve. Posted to the Tiger Information Web site, 1999: ⟨http://www.5tigers.org/indprog1.htm⟩.

GOI, Departemen Kehutanan. 1986. *Sejarah Kehutanan Indonesia Buku II.* Vol. 1. Jakarta: Departemen Kehutanan.

Gold, Ann Grodzins. 1988. *Fruitful Journeys: The Ways of Rajasthani Pilgrims.* Berkeley: University of California Press.

——. 1992b. *A Carnival of Parting.* Berkeley: University of California Press.

——. 1998. "Sin and Rain: Moral Ecology in Rural North India." In *Ecological Concern in South Asian Religion,* edited by Lance Nelson, 165–95. Albany: State University of New York Press.

——. 1999a. "Abandoned Rituals: Knowledge, Time, and Rhetorics of Modernity in Rural India." In *Religion, Ritual, and Royalty,* edited by N. K. Singhi and Rajendra Joshi, 262–75. Jaipur: Rawat.

——. 1999b. "From Wild Pigs to Foreign Trees: Oral Histories of Environmental Change in Rajasthan." In *State, Society, and Environment in South Asia,* edited by S. T. Madsen. London: Curzon.

Gold, Ann Grodzins, and Bhoju Ram Gujar. 1994. "Drawing Pictures in the Dust: Rajasthani Children's Landscapes." *Childhood* 2:73–91.

Gold, Ann Grodzins, with Bhoju Ram Gujar. 1997. "Wild Pigs and Kings: Remembered Landscapes in Rajasthan." *American Anthropologist* 99(1): 70–84.

——. 2002. *In the Time of Trees and Sorrows.* Durham: Duke University Press.

Gooding, D. 1990. *Experiment and the Making of Meaning.* Dordrecht: Kluwer Academic.

Goodman, Doug, and Daniel McCool. 1999. *Contested Landscape: The Politics of Wilderness in Utah and the West.* Salt Lake City: University of Utah Press.

Gore, Al. 1992. *Earth in the Balance: Ecology and the Human Spirit.* New York: Plume/Penguin.

Gouda, Frances. 1995. *Poverty and Political Culture: The Rhetoric of Social Welfare in the Netherlands and France, 1815–1854.* Landham, Md.: Rowman and Littlefield.

Gouldsbury, Charles E. 1909. *Dulall the Forest Guard: A Tale of Sport and Adventure in the Forests of Bengal.* London: Gibbings.

Government of Bengal. 1935. *The Forests of Bengal.* Calcutta: Superintendent of Government Printing.

Government of India. 1978. *Provisions in the Constitution of India for Scheduled Tribes.* New Delhi: Ministry of Home Affairs.

————. 1981. *Village and Town-Wise Primary Census Abstract.* Jhabua District Census Handbook, Pt. XIII–B. Series 11. Madhya Pradesh: Census of India.

Government of Indonesia, Departemen Kehutanan. 1986. *Sejarah Kehutanan Indonesia, Buku II.* Vol. 1. Republik of Indonesia: Departemen Kehutanan.

Gramsci, Antonio. 1968. *The Modern Prince and Other Writings.* 3d ed. New York: International Publishers.

Greenough, Paul. 1995. "Intimidation, Coercion, and Resistance in the Final Phase of the Smallpox Eradication Programme, South Asia, 1975–77." *Social Science and Medicine* 41(5): 633–45.

————. 2001. "*Naturae Ferae:* Wild Animals in South Asia and the Standard Environmental Narrative." In *Agrarian Studies: Synthetic Work at the Cutting Edge,* edited by James C. Scott. New Haven: Yale University Press.

————. 2002. "The Social and Cultural Background to Disease and Health in India." In *Encyclopedia of the Social Sciences in South Asia,* edited by Veena Das, Delhi: Oxford University Press.

————. 2003. "Bio-ironies of the Fractured Forest: India's Tiger Reserves." In *Rainforests Then and Now,* edited by Candace Slater, Berkeley: University of California Press. Forthcoming.

Greenough, Paul, and Anna Tsing. 1994. "Environmental Discourses and Human Welfare in South and Southeast Asia." *Items* 48(4): 95–99.

Griffith, A. L., and R. S. Gupta. 1948. "The Determination of the Characteristics of Soil Suitable for Sal." *Indian Forestry Bulletin,* n.s., Silviculture, no. 138.

Griffith, Ralph T. H., trans. 1973. *The Hymns of the Rgveda.* Delhi: Motilal Banarsidass.

Grigson, E. A. [1944] 1993. *The Aboriginal Problem in the Central Provinces and Berar.* Nagpur: Government Printer.

Grove, Richard. 1989. "Early Themes in African Conservation: The Cape in the Nineteenth Century." In *Conservation in Africa: People, Policies and Practice,* edited by David Anderson and Richard Grove, Cambridge: Cambridge University Press.

————. 1993. "Conserving Eden: The (European) East India Companies and Their Environmental Policies on St. Helena, Mauritius, and in Western India, 1660 to 1854." *Comparative Studies in Society and History* 35:318–51.

————. 1995. *Green Imperialism: Colonial Expansion, Tropical Island Edens, and the Origins of Environmentalism, 1600–1860.* Cambridge: Cambridge University Press.

Grove, Richard, Vinita Damodaran, and Satpal Sangwan. 1998a. Introduction to *Nature and the Orient: The Environmental History of South and Southeast Asia,* edited by Richard Grove, Vinita Damodaran, and Satpal Sangwan, 1–26. Delhi: Oxford University Press.

Grove, Richard, Vinita Damodaran, and Satpal Sangwan, eds. 1998b. *Nature and the Orient: Essays on the Environmental History of South and Southeast Asia.* Delhi: Oxford University Press.

————. 1988. "Ideological Trends in Indian Environmentalism." *Economic and Political Weekly* 23(49): 2578–81.

Guha, Ramachandra. 1983. "Forestry in British and Post-British India: An Historical Analysis." *Economic and Political Weekly* 17:1882–96.

———. 1989. "Radical American Environmentalism and Wilderness Preservation: A Third World Critique." *Environmental Ethics* 11(1): 71–83.

———. 1993. "The Malign Encounter: The Chipko Movement and Competing Visions of Nature." In *Who Will Save the Forests?* edited by T. Banuri and F. Marglin. London: Zed.

———. 1997. "The Authoritarian Biologist and the Arrogance of Anti-humanism: Wildlife Conservation in the Third World." *Ecologist* 27(1): 14–20.

Guha, Ramachandra, ed. 1994. *Social Ecology.* Delhi: Oxford University Press.

———. 2000. *The Unquiet Woods: Ecological Change and Peasant Resistance in the Himalaya.* Berkeley: University of California Press.

Guha, Ramachandra, and Madhav Gadgil. 1995. *Ecology and Equity.* London: Routledge.

Guha, Ranajit. 1993. "The Malign Encounter: The Chipko Movement and Competing Visions of Nature." In *Who Will Save the Forests?* edited by T. Banuri and F. Marglin, 80–113. London: Zed.

Guha, Sumit. 1995a. "Kings of the Forest versus Lords of the Land: Conflict and Collaboration in Peninsular India." Paper presented at the weekly colloquium, Program in Agrarian Studies, Yale University.

———. 1995b. "People and Landscape under the Maratha Regime: Ideologies, Practices, and Consequences for the Land." Manuscript.

———. 1999a. "Communities, Kings, and Woodlands: Historical Reflections on Joint Forest Management." In *A New Moral Economy for India's Forests?* edited by R. Jeffery and N. Sundar, 55–70. New Delhi: Sage.

———. 1999b. *Environment and Ethnicity in India, 1200–1991.* Cambridge: Cambridge University Press.

Gujar, Bhoju Ram, and Ann Grodzins Gold. 1992. "From the Research Assistant's Point of View." *Anthropology and Humanism Quarterly* 17(3): 72–84.

Gupta, Akhil. 1995. "Blurred Boundaries: The Discourse of Corruption, the Culture of Politics, and the Imagined State." *American Ethnologist* 22(2): 375–402.

———. 1998. *Postcolonial Developments: Agriculture in the Making of Modern India.* Durham: Duke University Press.

Gupta, Akhil, and James Ferguson. 1997. *Culture, Power, Place: Explorations in Critical Anthropology.* Durham: Duke University Press.

Gupte, Pranay. 1992. *Mother India: A Political Biography of Indira Gandhi.* New York: Scribner's.

Guthman, Julie. 1997. "Representing Crisis: The Theory of Himalayan Environmental Degradation and the Project of Development in Post-Rana Nepal." *Development and Change* 28:45–69.

Hacking, Ian. 1983. *Representing and Intervening.* Cambridge: Cambridge University Press.

———. 1992. "The Self-Vindication of the Laboratory Sciences." In *Science as Practice and Culture,* edited by Andrew Pickering, 29–64. Chicago: University of Chicago Press.

Haines, H. H. 1905. *Working Plan for Reserved Forests of Singhbhum, 1903–1918.* Calcutta; Bengal Secretariat Press.

Hajer, Maarten A. 1995. *The Politics of Environmental Discourse*. New York: Oxford University Press.

Hall, Stuart. 1996. "On Postmodernism and Articulation: An Interview with Stuart Hall." In *Stuart Hall: Critical Dialogues in Cultural Studies*, edited by D. Morley and K. Chen, 131–50. London: Routledge.

Haraway, Donna. 1988. "Situated Knowledges: The Science Question in Feminism and the Privilege of Partial Perspective." *Feminist Studies* 14(3): 575–99.

———. 1992. "The Promises of Monsters: A Regenerative Politics for Inappropriate/d Others." In *Cultural Studies*, edited by Lawrence Grossberg, Cary Nelson, and Paula Treichler, 295–337. New York: Routledge.

Hardiman, D. 1985. "The Politics of Drinking in South Gujarat." In *Subaltern Studies IV*, edited by R. Guha, 165–228. Delhi: Oxford University Press.

———. 1987. *The Coming of the Devi: Adivasi Assertion in Western India*. Delhi: Oxford University Press.

———. 1994. "Power in the Forests: The Dangs, 1820–1940." In *Subaltern Studies VIII: Essays in Honor of Ranajit Guha*, edited by Gyanendra Pandey and Partha Chatterjee, Delhi: Oxford University Press.

Harding, Sandra. 1986. *The Science Question in Feminism*. Ithaca: Cornell University Press.

Harley, J. B. 1988. "Maps, Knowledge, and Power." In *The Iconography of Landscape*, edited by D. Cosgrove and S. Daniels, 277–312. New York: Cambridge University Press.

———. 1989. "Deconstructing the Map." *Cartographica* 26:1–20.

Harre, Ron, Peter Muhlhausler, and Jens Brockmeier. 1998. *Greenspeak: A Study of Environmental Discourse*. London: Sage.

Harrison, Robert P. 1992. *Forests: The Shadow of Civilization*. Chicago: University of Chicago Press.

Harrisson, Tom. 1949. "Notes on Some Nomadic Punans." *Sarawak Museum Journal*, n.s., 5(1): 130–46.

———. 1970. *The Malays of South-West Sarawak before Malaysia: A Socio-economic Survey*. East Lansing: Michigan State University Press.

Hart, Gillian. 1986. *Power, Labor, and Livelihood: Processes of Change in Rural Java*. Berkeley: University of California Press.

———. 1991. "Engendering Everyday Resistance: Gender, Politics, Patronage, and Production in Rural Malaysia." *Journal of Peasant Studies* 19(1): 93–121.

———. 1992. "Household Production Reconsidered: Gender, Labor Conflict, and Technological Change in Malaysia's Muda Region." *World Development* 20(6): 809–24.

Hart, Gillian, Andrew Turton, and Benjamin White, eds. 1989. *Agrarian Transformations: Local Processes and the State in Southeast Asia*. Berkeley: University of California Press.

Harvey, David. 1989. *The Condition of Postmodernity: An Enquiry into the Origin of Cultural Change*. Oxford: Blackwell.

Hatt, C. C. 1905. *Working Plan for the Reserved Forests of Buxa Division*. Calcutta: Bengal Secretariat Book Depot.

Hawes, Gary. 1987. *The Philippine State and the Marcos Regime: The Politics of Export.* Ithaca: Cornell University Press.

Haynes, Edward S. 1998. "The Natural and the Raj: Customary State Systems and Environmental Management in Pre-integration Rajasthan and Gujarat." In *Nature and the Orient,* edited by Richard H. Grove, Vinita Damodaran, and Satpal Sangwan, 734–92. Delhi: Oxford University Press.

———. 1999. "Land Use, Natural Resources, and the Rajput State, 1780–1980." In *Desert, Drought, and Development: Studies in Resource Management and Sustainability,* edited by Rakesh Hooja and Rajendra Joshi, 53–119. Jaipur: Rawat.

Hays, Samuel P. 1959. *Conservation and the Gospel of Efficiency: The Progressive Conservation Movement, 1890–1920.* Cambridge: Harvard University Press.

Heiser, Victor G. 1906. "The Progress of Medicine in the Philippine Islands." *Journal of the American Medical Association* 57:245–47.

Herring, R. J. 1983. *Land to the Tiller: The Political Economy of Agrarian Reform in South Asia.* New Haven: Yale University Press.

Hettne, Bjorn. 1990. *Development Theory and the Three Worlds.* London: Methuen.

Hill, Leonard, O. W. Griffith, and M. Flack. 1916. "Measurement of the Rate of Heat Loss at Body Temperature by Convection, Radiation, and Evaporation." *Philosophical Transactions of the Royal Society of London,* B ser. 207:183.

Hirsh, Philip, and Carol Warren, eds. 1998. *The Politics of Environment in Southeast Asia.* London: Routledge.

Hitipeuw, C., Caroline Raymakers, Victor S. Ruhunlela, Ketut Sarjana Putra, John Lefmanut, and Mark van der Wal. 1994. "Awareness and Education Programme for a Community Based Management of the Marine Resources in Southeast Aru Strict Nature Reserve, Ambon." Universitas Pattimura, WWF, Jakarta and Aid Environment, Amsterdam.

Hobart, Mark, ed. 1993. *An Anthropological Critique of Development: The Growth of Ignorance?* London: Routledge.

Hobley, Mary, and Eva Wollenberg. 1996. "A New Pragmatic Forestry or Another Development Bandwagon?" In *Participatory Forestry: The Process of Change in India and Nepal,* edited by M. Hobley. Rural Development Forestry Study Guide 3. London: ODI.

Hobsbawm, Eric J. 1973. "Peasants and Politics." *Journal of Peasant Studies* 1(1): 3–22.

Hole, R. S. 1919. "Regeneration of Sal Forests." *Indian Forester* 45:119–32.

Holston, James. 1989. *The Modernist City: An Anthropological Critique of Brasilia.* Chicago: University of Chicago Press.

Homfray, C. K. 1936. *Notes on Thinnings in Plantations.* Alipore: Bengal Government Press. Bengal Forest Bulletin 1, Silviculture ser.

Hong, Evelyne. 1987. *Natives of Sarawak: Survival in Borneo's Vanishing Forests.* Penang: Institute Masyarakat.

Hooker, J. D. 1854. *Himalayan Journals: In Bengal, the Sikkim, and Nepal Himalayas and the Khasia Mountains.* London: Ward, Lock, and Bowden.

Horigan, Stephen. 1988. *Nature and Culture in Western Discourses*. New York: Routledge.

Horne, Elinor Clark. 1974. *Javanese-English Dictionary*. New Haven: Yale University Press.

Horsman, Reginald. 1981. *Race and Manifest Destiny: The Origins of American Racial Anglo-Saxonism*. Cambridge: Harvard University Press.

Houghten, F. C., and C. P. Yagloglou. 1923. "Determining Lines of Equal Comfort." *Transactions of the American Society of Heat and Vent Engineers* 29.

Houghton, R. A., and D. L. Skole. 1990. "Carbon." In *The Earth as Transformed by Human Action*, edited by B. L. Turner, B. L. Turner II, William C. Clark, Robert W. Kates, John F. Richards, Jessica T. Mathews, and William B. Meyer, 393–408. New York: Cambridge University Press.

Hughes, J. 1987. "The Languages of Kei, Tanimbar, and Aru: A Lexico-Statistic Classification." *Nusa* 27:71–110.

Humboldt, Alexander von. 1850–58. *Cosmos: Sketch of a Physical Description of the Universe*. Translated by Edward Sabine. 4 vols. London: Longman, Brown, Green, and Longman's.

Humphreys, David. 1996. *Forest Politics: The Evolution of International Cooperation*. London: Earthscan.

Hunter, W. W. 1868. *The Annals of Rural Bengal*. New York: Leypoldt and Holt.

Huntington, Ellsworth. 1915. *Civilization and Climate*. New Haven: Yale University Press.

———. 1924. *Character of Races as Influenced by Physical Environment, Natural Selection, and Historical Development*. New York: Charles Scribner's Sons.

Hurst, Philip. 1990. *Rainforest Politics: Ecological Destruction in South-East Asia*. London: Zed.

Hutterer, Karl L. 1985. "People and Nature in the Tropics: Remarks concerning Ecological Relationships." In *Cultural Values and Human Ecology in Southeast Asia*, edited by Karl L. Hutterer, A. Terry Rambo, and George Lovelace, 55–75. Ann Arbor: Center for South and Southeast Asian Studies, University of Michigan.

Hutton, Patrick H. 1993. *History as an Art of Memory*. Hanover: University of Vermont.

Huxley, T. H. 1894. *Aphorisms and Reflections from the Works of T. H. Huxley*. Selected by Henrietta A. Huxley. London: Macmillan.

Hvalkof, Søren. 2000. "Outrage in Rubber and Oil: Extractivism, Indigenous Peoples, and Justice in the Upper Amazon." pp. 83–116. In *People, Plants, and Justice: Resource Extraction and Conservation in Tropical Developing Countries*, edited by Charles Zerner. New York: Columbia University Press.

Imperial Gazetteer of India. [1908] 1989. *Rajputana*. New Delhi: Usha Rani Jain.

India. 1979a. "International Symposium on Tiger, 1979, Discussions and Resolutions." Forestry Division, Ministry of Agriculture and Irrigation, New Delhi, 22–24 February.

———. 1979b. "International Symposium on the Tiger 1979, Abstracts of Papers." Project Tiger, Ministry of Environment and Forests, New Delhi, 22–24 February.

———. 1990. *India 1990: A Reference Manual*. New Delhi: Ministry of Information of Broadcasting and Information.

———. 1993a. "Critical Review of Project Tiger." Ministry of Environments and Forests, New Delhi.

———. 1993b. "International Symposium on the Tiger, Proceedings and Resolutions." Project Tiger, Ministry of Environment and Forests, New Delhi, 22–24 February.

Indian Board for Wildlife. 1972. "Task Force, Project Tiger: A Planning Proposal for Preservation of Tiger (*Panthera tigris Linn.*) in India." Ministry of Agriculture, New Delhi.

Ingold, Tim. 1993. "Globes and Spheres: The Topology of Environmentalism." In *Environmentalism: The View from Anthropology,* edited by Kay Milton, 31–42. ASA Monograph 33. London: Routledge.

IIPA (Indian Institute of Public Administration). 1994. "Biodiversity Conservation through Ecodevelopment: An Indicative Plan." UNDP and Ministry of Forests and Environment, October.

Institute of Social Analysis. 1989. *Logging against the Natives of Sarawak.* Petaling Jaya: INSAN.

International Union for the Conservation of Nature and Natural Resources. 1976. "Conservation of the Tiger in India: A Report to the Chairman of the Tiger Steering Committee on a Mid-term Study of Project Tiger, March/April 1976," by Colin W. Holloway, Paul Leyhausen, and M. K. Ranjitsinh, Morges, Switzerland, November.

Isaacman, Allen F. 1993. "Peasants and Rural Social Protest in Africa." In *Confronting Historical Paradigms,* edited by Fred Cooper, 205–317. Madison: University of Wisconsin.

Ives, J., and B. Messerli. 1989. *The Himalayan Dilemma: Reconciling Development and Conservation.* London and New York: Routledge and the United Nations University.

Jaaruwannoo Bhikkhu (Phrakhru Pitak Nanthakhun). 1992. "Phudthasaadsanaa kap Singwaedlaum" [Buddhism and the Environment]. *Muubaan* 4(46): 16. In Thai.

Jackson, Jean. 1995. "Culture, Genuine, and Spurious: The Politics of Indianness in the Vaupes, Columbia." *American Ethnologist* 22(1): 3–27.

Jackson, Peter. 1985. "Man-Eaters!" *International Wildlife,* November, 4–11.

Jackson, W. B. 1854. *Report on Darjeeling.* Selected Records of the Bengal Government 17. Calcutta: N.p.

Jackson, W. B., and H. Ricketts. 1854. *General Report of a Tour of Inspection by W. B. Jackson and Report on the District of Singhbhum by H. Ricketts.* Selected Records of the Bengal Government 16. Calcutta: N.p.

Jagor, Fedor. [1873] 1965. *Travels in the Philippines.* Translator unknown. Manila: Filipiniana Book Guild.

Jakarta Post. 1992. "Forest Concession in Yamdena Stands Despite Bloody Clash." *Jakarta Post,* 24 September.

Jansonius, Herman. 1950. *Groot Nederlands-Engels Woordenboek Voor Studie en Practijk.* Vol. 2. Leiden: Nederlandsche Uitgeversmaatschappij N.V.

Jayakar, Pupul. 1992. *Indira Gandhi, a Biography.* New York: Viking.

Joarder, A. A., D. Tarantola, and J. Tulloch, eds. 1980. *The Eradication of Smallpox from Bangladesh.* New Delhi: WHO South-East Asia Regional Office.

Jodha, N. S. 1985. "Population Growth and the Decline of Common Property Resources in Rajasthan, India." *Population and Development Review* 11(2): 247–64.

John, D., and J. Jackson. 1973. "The Tobacco Industry of North Borneo: A Distinctive Form of Plantation Agriculture," *Journal of Southeast Asian Studies* 4:88–106.

———. 1990. "Rural Common Property Resources: Contributions and Crisis." *Economic and Political Weekly,* 30 June. A65–78.

Kachhawaha, O. P. 1985. *Famines in Rajasthan, 1900 A.D.–1947 A.D.* Jodhpur: Hindi Sahitya Mandir.

Kahn, Joel S. 1980. *Minangkabau Social Formations: Indonesian Peasants and the World Economy.* Cambridge: Cambridge University Press.

Kain, Roger J. P., and Elizabeth Baigent. 1992. *The Cadastral Map in the Service of the State: A History of Property Mapping.* Chicago: University of Chicago Press.

Kamath, H. S. 1941. *Grazing and Nistar in the Central Provinces Estates: The Report of an Enquiry.* Bhopal: Government of the Central Provinces.

Kane, P. V. 1974. *History of Dharmasastra.* 2d ed. Poona: Bhandarkar Oriental Research Institute.

Kangle, R. P. [1969] 1988. *The Kautilya Arthasastra.* 3 vols. 2d ed. Delhi: Motilal Banarsidass.

Karanth, K. Ullas. 1987. "Tigers in India: A Critical Review of Field Censuses." In *Tigers of the World,* edited by R. L. Tilson and U. S. Seal. Park Ridge, N. J.: Noyes.

Karliner, Josh. 1997. *The Corporate Planet: Ecology and Politics in the Age of Globalization.* San Francisco: Sierra Club.

Kartodirdjo, Sartono. 1973. *Protest Movements in Rural Java: A Study of Agrarian Unrest in the Nineteenth and Early Twentieth Centuries.* Singapore: Oxford University Press.

Kearney, Michael. 1996. *Reconceptualizing the Peasantry: Anthropology in Global Perspective.* Boulder: Westview.

Keck, Margaret. 1995. Social Equity and Environmental Politics in Brazil: Lessons from the Rubber Tappers of Acre." *Comparative Politics* (27) 4: 409–24.

Keck, Miriam, and K. Sikkink. 1998. *Activists without Borders.* Ithaca: Cornell University Press.

Kedit, Peter M. 1982. "An Ecological Survey of the Penan." *Sarawak Museum Journal,* n.s., special issue no. 2, 30(51): 225–79.

Kemp, Jeremy. 1988. *Seductive Mirror: The Search for the Village Community in Southeast Asia.* Dordrect: Foris.

Khare, A. K. 1993. "Forest Products Marketing." Madhya Pradesh Integrated Forestry Sector Project Preparation Working Paper 4, Bhopal.

Kidd, Benjamin. 1898. *The Control of the Tropics.* London: Macmillan.

King, Victor T. 1993. *The Peoples of Borneo.* Oxford: Blackwell.

Kirch, Patrick Vinton. 1994. *The Wet and the Dry: Irrigation and Agricultural Intensification in Polynesia.* Chicago: University of Chicago Press.

Kirkvliet, Benedict J. Tria. 1990. *Everyday Politics in the Philippines: Class and Status Relations in a Central Luzon Village.* Berkeley: University of California Press.

Kloppenburg, Jack. 1991. "Social Theory and the De/Reconstruction of Agricultural Science: Local Knowledge for an Alternative Agriculture." *Rural Sociology* 56(4): 519–48.

Kolff, D. H. 1840. *Voyages of the Dutch Brig of War DOURGA, through the Southern and Little-Known Parts of the Moluccan Archipelago and along the Previously Unknown Southern Coast of New Guinea.* London: James Madden.

Koloniaal Verslaag. 1893. *Handelingen der Staten-Generaal.* Bijlagen: 1893–1894.

Kothari, Smitu, and Pramod Parajuli. 1993. "No Nature without Social Justice: A Plea for Cultural and Ecological Pluralism in India." *Global Ecology: A New Arena of Political Conflict,* edited by Wolfgang Sachs, 224–41. London: Zed.

Lalas, Sitaram. 1962–78. *Rajasthani Sabad Kos.* 9 vols. Jodhpur: Rajasthani Shodh Sansthan.

Langton, John. 1998. "Conclusion: The Historical Geography of European Peasantries, 1400–1800." In *The Peasantries of Europe from the Fourtheenth to the Eighteenth Centuries,* edited by Tom Scott, 372–400. London: Longman.

Langub, Jayl. 1974. "Adaptation to a Settled Life by the Punan of the Belaga Sub-district." *Sarawak Museum Journal* 22(43): 295–301.

———. 1975. "Distribution of Penan and Punan in the Belaga District." *Borneo Research Bulletin* 7(2): 45–48.

———. 1984. "Tamu: Barter Trade between Penan and Their Neighbors." *Sarawak Gazette* 110(1485): 11–15.

———. 1989. "Some Aspects of Life of the Penan." *Sarawak Museum Journal,* n.s., special issue no. 4, pt. 3, 40(61): 169–84.

———. 1990. "A Journey through the Nomadic Penan Country." *Sarawak Gazette* 117(1514): 5–27.

Leach, Edmund. 1960. "The Frontiers of 'Burma'." *Comparative Studies in Society and History* 3: 49–73.

Leavitt, Judith Wolzer. 1996. *Typhoid Mary: Captive to the Public's Health.* Boston: Beacon.

Lefebvre, Henri. 1979. *The Production of Space.* Translated by Donald Nicholson-Smith. Cambridge: Blackwell.

Lehning, James R. 1995. *Peasant and French: Cultural Contact in Rural France during the Nineteenth Century.* Cambridge: Cambridge University Press.

Lev, Daniel. 1985. "Colonial Law and the Genesis of the Indonesian State." *Indonesia* 40 (Oct.): 57–74.

Lewin, T. H. 1869. *The Hill Tracts of Chittagong and the Dwellers Therein.* Selected Reports of the Bengal Government 43A. Calcutta: n.p.

Lewis, Michael L. 2003. *Inventing Global Ecology: Tracking the Biodiversity Ideal in India.* Hyderabad: Orient Longman.

Li, Tania. 1999. *Transforming the Indonesian Uplands*. London: Harwood Academic Press.

———. 2000. "Articulating Indigenous Identity in Indonesia: Resource Politics and the Tribal Slot." *Comparative Studies in Society and History* 42(1): 149–78.

Lim Teck Ghee. 1977. *Peasants and Their Agricultural Economy in Colonial Malaya, 1874–1941*. Kuala Lumpur: Oxford University Press.

Limerick, Patricia Nelson. 1987. *The Legacy of Conquest: The Unbroken Past of the American West*. New York: Norton.

Linden, Eugene. 1991. "Lost Tribes, Lost Knowledge." *Time*, 23 September, 46–56.

Litfin, Karen T. 1994. *Ozone Discourses: Science and Politics in Global Environmental Cooperation*. New York: Columbia University Press.

Livingstone, David N. 1994. "Climate's Moral Economy: Science, Race, and Place in post-Darwinian British and American Geography." In *Geography and Empire*, edited by Anne Godlewska and Neil Smith. Oxford: Blackwell.

Local Development Institute. 1992. *Community Forestry: Declaration of the Customary Rights of Local Communities — Thai Democracy at the Grassroots*. Bangkok: Local Development Institute.

Lohmann, Larry. 1991. "Peasants, Plantations, and Pulp: The Politics of Eucalyptus in Thailand." *Bulletin of Concerned Asian Scholars* 23(4): 3–17.

———. 1993. "Thailand: Land, Power, and Forest Colonization." In *The Struggle for Land and the Fate of the Forests*, edited by Marcus Colchester and Larry Lohmann, 198–227. London: Zed.

Lombard, D. 1974. "La vision de la forêt a Java (Indonesie)." *Etudes Rurales* 53–56: 473–85.

Lowe, Celia. 2000. "Global Markets, Local Injustice in Southeast Asian Seas." In *People, Plants, and Justice: The Politics of Nature Conservation*, edited by Charles Zerner. New York: Columbia University Press.

Lowood, Henry E. 1990. "Calculating Forester: Quantification, Cameral Science, and the Emergence of Scientific Forestry Management in Germany." In *The Quantifying Spirit in the Eighteenth Century*, edited by Tore Frangsmyr, J. L. Heilbron, and Robin E. Rider, Berkeley: University of California Press.

Ludden, David. 1984. "Productive Power in Agriculture: A Survey of Work on the Local History of British India." In *Agrarian Power and Agricultural Productivity in South Asia*, edited by M. Desai, S. H. Rudolph, and A. Rudra, 51–99. Delhi: Oxford University Press.

———. 1989. *Peasant History in South India*. Delhi: Oxford University Press.

———. 1992a. "Anglo-Indian Empire." In *The Making of Agrarian Policy in British India, 1770–1990*, edited by Burton Stein. New Delhi: Oxford University Press.

———. 1992b. "India's Development Regime." In *Colonialism and Culture*, edited by Nicholas Dirks. Ann Arbor: University of Michigan Press.

———. 1996. "Archaic Formations of Agricultural Knowledge in South India. In *Meanings of Agriculture in South Asia: Essays in South Asian History and Economics*, edited by Peter Robb, 35–70. Cambridge: Cambridge University Press.

Luke, Timothy. 1997. *Ecocritique: Contesting the Politics of Nature, Economy, and Culture.* Minneapolis: University of Minnesota Press.

Lynch, Owen, and Kirk Talbott. 1995. *Balancing Acts: Community-Based Forest Management and National Law in Asia and the Pacific.* Washington, D.C.: World Resources Institute.

MacAndrews, Colin. 1977. *Mobility and Modernization: The Federal Land Development Authority and Its Role in Modernising the Rural Malay.* Yogyakarta: Gadjah Mada University Press.

Mackenzie, J. W. 1988. *The Empire of the Nature: Hunting, Conservation, and British Imperialism.* Manchester: Manchester University Press.

Mackenzie, J. W., ed. 1990. *Imperialism and the Natural World.* Manchester: Manchester University Press.

Mackie, J. A. C. 1974. *Konfrontasi: The Indonesian-Malaysia Dispute, 1963–1974.* Kuala Lumpur; New York: Australian Institute of International Affairs [by] Oxford University Press.

MacLeod, Roy, and Milton Lewis, eds. 1988. *Disease, Medicine, and Empire: Perspectives on Western Medicine and the Experience of European Expansion.* London: Routledge.

MacMicking, Robert. 1967. *Recollections of Manila and the Philippines during 1848, 1849, and 1850,* edited and annotated by Morton J. Netzorg. Manila: Filipiniana Book Guild.

Madhya Pradesh Forest Department. 1981. *Annual Administrative Report for 1979–80.* Bhopal: Government of Madhya Pradesh.

Madhya Pradesh Forest and Nistar Committee. 1959. *Report.* Bhopal: Government of Madhya Pradesh.

Mahatir bin Mohamed and José Lutzenberger. 1992. "Eco-imperialism and Bio-monopoly at the Earth Summit." *New Perspectives Quarterly* 9(3): 56–58.

Maheshwari, P., and Umrao Singh. 1965. *Dictionary of Economic Plants in India.* New Delhi: Indian Council of Agricultural Research.

Maithani, G. P. 1994. "Management Perspective of Minor Forest Produce." *MFP News* 4(4).

Makins, F. K. 1920. "Natural Regeneration of Sal in Singhbhum." *Indian Forester* 46:292–96.

Malhotra K. C. 1993. "People, Biodiversity, and Regenerating Tropical Sal (*Shorea robusta*) Forests in West Bengal." In *Tropical Forests, People, and Food,* edited by C. M. Hladik, A. Hladik, O. F. Linares, H. Pagezy, and A. Semple, 745–52. Man and Biosphere, 13. Paris: Carnforth.

Malkki, Lisa. 1992. "National Geographic: The Rooting of Peoples and the Territorialization of National Identity among Scholars and Refugess." *Cultural Anthropology* 7(1): 24–44.

Mann, Michael. 1993. *The Sources of Social Power, volume 2: The Rise of Classes and Nation-States, 1760–1914.* Cambridge: Cambridge University Press.

Manning, Chris. 1971. "The Timber Boom: with Special Reference to East Kalimantan." *Bulletin of Indonesian Economic Studies* 7, 3 (November): 30–61.

Manser, Bruno. 1996. *Voices from the Rainforest: Testimonies of a Threatened People.* Basel and Petaling Jaya: Bruno Manser Foundation and INSAN (Institute of Social Analysis).

Marchant, James. 1916. *Alfred Russel Wallace: Letters and Reminiscences.* New York: Harper and Brothers.

Marlessy, Cliff. 1991. "Nasib Lautan Kita [The Fate of Our Seas]" and "Masalah Lautan Kita [The Problems of Our Oceans]," *Kabar Dari Kampung* [News from the Village] 9(48): 8–20.

Martinez de Zuñiga, Joaquin. [1893] 1973. *Status of the Philippines in 1800.* Translated by Vicente del Carmen. Manila: Filipiniana Book Guild.

Marx, Karl. 1972. *The Eighteenth Brumaire of Louis Bonaparte.* New York: International Publishers.

Mason, R. 1992. *Contested Lands: Conflict and Compromise in New Jersey's Pine Barrens.* Philadelphia: Temple University Press.

Massey, Doreen B. 1994. *Space, Place and Gender.* Minneapolis, University of Minnesota Press.

Mathers, A. S. 1992. "The Forest Transition." *Area* 24(4): 367–79.

Mathur, Jivanlal. 1977. *Brj-Bavani.* Sawar: Mani Raj Singh.

Mathur, V. P. 1968. *Forest Management for Forest Colleges and Working Plan Officers.* Dehra Dun: Jugal Kishore.

Mayer, Judith. 1996. "Environmental Organizing in Indonesia: The Search for a New Order." In *Global Civil Society and Global Environmental Governance,* edited by Ronnie Lipshutz, 167–213. Albany: State University of New York Press.

McAfee, Katherine. 1997. "Selling Nature to Save It? Biodiversity and the Rise of Green Developmentalism." Paper presented at the inaugural International Conference of Critical Geographers, Vancouver, B.C., 13 August.

McCann, James C. 1997. "The Plow and the Forest: Narratives of Deforestation in Ethiopia." *Environmental History* 2(1): 138–59.

McIntire, A. L. 1909. "Notes on Sal in Bengal." *Forest Pamphlet,* no. 5. Calcutta: Superintendent of Government Printing.

McIntosh, Alistair. 1994. "Reclaiming the Scottish Highlands: Clearance, Conflict, and Crofting." *Ecologist* 24(2): 64–70.

McKinney, H. L. 1972. *Wallace and Natural Selection.* New Haven: Yale University Press.

Menzies, Nicholas K. 1994. *Forest and Land Management in Imperial China.* New York: St. Martin's.

Metz J. J. 1989. "Himalayan Political Economy: More Myths in the Closet?" *Mountain Research and Development* 9(2): 175–86.

Miller, James. 1993. *The Passion of Michel Foucault.* New York: Simon and Schuster.

Milton, Kay. 1996. *Environmentalism and Cultural Theory: Exploring the Role of Anthropology in Environmental Discourse.* New York: Routledge.

Ministry of Primary Industries. 1992. *Forever Green: Malaysia and Sustainable Forest Management.* Kuala Lumpur: Ministry of Primary Industries.

Mitchell, Timothy. 1988. *Colonising Egypt.* Cambridge: Cambridge University Press.

———. 1991. "America's Egypt: Discourse of the Development Industry." *Middle East Report* 169 (March–April): 18–34.

———. 1995. "The Object of Development: America's Egypt." In *The Power of Development*, edited by Jonathan Crush, 129–57. London: Routledge.

Moertono, Soemarsaid. 1981. *State and Statecraft in Old Java: A Study of the Later Mataram Period, Sixteenth to Nineteenth Century*. Rev. ed. Modern Indonesia Project Monographs 43. Ithaca: Southeast Asia Program, Cornell University.

Moniaga, S. 1993. "Toward Community-Based Forestry and Recognition of Adat Property Rights in the Outer Islands of Indonesia." In *Legal Frameworks for Forest Management in Asia: Case Studies of Community/State Relations*, edited by J. Fox. Honolulu: East-West Center.

Monier-Williams, Monier. 1899. *A Sanskrit-English Dictionary*. Oxford: Clarendon.

Monk, Paul. M. 1996. *Truth and Power: Robert S. Hardie and Land Reform Debates in the Philippines, 1950–1987*. Rev. ed. Quezon City: New Day.

Moore, Sally Falk. 1986. *Social Facts and Fabrications: "Customary" Law on Kilimanjaro, 1880–1980*. New York: Cambridge University Press.

Mosko, Mark S. 1987. "The Symbols of 'Fruit': A Structural Analysis of Mbuti Culture and Social Organization." *American Anthropologist* 89(4): 896–913.

Mukarji, Nirmal. 1989. "Decentralization below the State Level: Need for a New System of Governance." *Economic and Political Weekly,* 4 March, 467–72.

Murali, Atluri. 1995. "Whose Trees? Forest Practices and Local Communities in Andhra, 1600–1922." In *Nature, Culture, Imperialism: Essays on the Environmental History of South Asia*, edited by David Arnold and Ramachandra Guha, 86–122. Delhi: Oxford University Press.

Music, Stanley I. 1976. "Smallpox Eradication in Bangladesh: Reflections of an Epidemiologist." D.T.P.H. diss., London School of Hygiene and Tropical Medicine.

Myers, Fred. 1986. *Pintupi Country, Pintupi Self: Sentiment, Place, and Politics among Western Desert Aborigines*. Washington, D.C.: Smithsonian Institution Press.

Nanda, B. R. 1974. *The Nehrus: Motilal and Jawaharlal*. London: Allen and Unwin.

Nash, Roderick. 1982. *Wilderness and the American Mind*. 3d ed. New York: Yale University Press.

Nath, Kamal. 1993. *A Critical Review of Project Tiger*. Delhi: Ministry of Environment and Forests.

Needham, R. 1954. "The System of Teknonyms and Death-Names of the Penan." *Southwestern Journal of Anthropology* 10:416–31.

———. 1965. "Death-Names and Solidarity in Penan Society." *Bijdragen tot de Taal-, Land- en Volkenkunde* 121:58–76.

———. 1972. "Penan-Punan." In *Ethnic Groups of Insular Southeast Asia*, Vol. 1: *Indonesia, Andaman Islands, and Madagascar,* edited by F. M. Lebar, 176–80. New Haven: Human Relations Area Files Press.

Nehru, Jawaharlal. 1942. *Jawaharlal Nehru, an Autobiography*. New Edition. London: Bodley Head.

Neumann, Roderick P. 1992. "Political Ecology of Wildlife Conservation in the Mt. Meru Area of Northern Tanzania." *Land Degradation and Rehabilitation* 3(3): 87–98.

Ngo, Merring. 1995. "Kayan Property Rights." In *Borneo in Transition: People, Forests, Conservation, and Development*, edited by C. Padoch and N. L. Peluso. Kuala Lumpur: Oxford University Press.

Nicolaisen, J. 1976. "The Penan of the Seventh Division of Sarawak: Past, Present, and Future." *Sarawak Museum Journal*, n.s., 24(45): 35–61.

Nye, David E. 1994. *American Technological Sublime*. Cambridge: MIT Press.

Nyerges, A. Endre. 1994. "Deforestation History and the Ecology of Swidden Fallows in Sierra Leone." *Culture and Agriculture* 49:6–11.

Obidzinsky, Krystof. 2003. "Logging in East Kalimantan, Indonesia: Historical Experience of Illegality." Ph.D. diss., Universiteit von Amsterdam.

O'Connor, Richard. 1995. "Agricultural Changes and Ethnic Succession in Southeast Asian States." *The Journal of Asian Studies* 54(4): 968–96.

Ogden, Horace. 1987. *CDC and the Smallpox Crusade*. Centers for Disease Control, U.S. Department of Health and Human Services, Publication no. (CDC) 87–8400. Washington, D.C.: Government Printing Office.

Olson, Gary L. 1974. *U.S. Foreign Policy and the Third World Peasant: Land Reform in Asia and Latin America*. New York: Praeger.

Ong, Aihwa. 1987. *Spirits of Resistance and Capitalist Discipline: Factory Women in Malaysia*. Albany: State University of New York Press.

———. 1990. "State versus Islam: Malay Families, Women's Bodies, and the Body Politic in Malaysia." *American Ethnologist* 17(2): 258–77.

Orissa Forest Enquiry Committee. 1959. *Report*. Bhubaneswar: Government of Orissa.

Ortner, Sherry. 1989. *High Religion: A Cultural and Political History of Sherpa Buddhism*. Princeton: Princeton University Press.

Osmaston, F. C. 1929. "Sal and Its Regeneration." *Indian Forester* 54(12): 639–55.

Paasi, Anssi. 1996. *Territories, Boundaries, and Consciousness: The Changing Geographies of the Finnish-Russian Border*. New York: Wiley.

Padoch, Christine. 1994. "The Woodlands of Tae: Traditional Forest Management in Kalimantan." In *Forest Resources and Wood-Based Biomass Energy as Rural Development Assets*, edited by William R. Bentley and Marcia M. Gowen, 307–414. New Delhi: Oxford University Press.

Padoch, Christine, and Nancy Lee Peluso, eds. 1996. *Borneo in Transition: People, Forests, Conservation, and Development*. Kuala Lumpur: Oxford University Press.

Padoch, Christine, Emily Harwell, and A. Susanto. 1998. "Swidden, Sawah, and In-between: Agricultural Transformation in Borneo." *Human Ecology* 26(1): 3–20.

Padoch, Christine, and Charles Peters. 1993. "Managed Forests of West Kalimantan, Indonesia," In *Perspectives on Biodiversity: Case Studies of Genetic Resources for Conservation and Development*, edited by C. S. Polter et al,

167–76. Washington, D.C.: American Association for the Advancement of Science.

Panayotou, Theodore. 1994. "Empirical Tests and Policy Analysis of Environmental Degradation at Different States of Economic Development." *Pacific and Asian Journal of Energy* 4(1): 23–42.

Pangare, Ganesh, and Vasudha Pangare. 1992. *From Poverty to Plenty: The Story of Ralegan Siddhi.* New Delhi: INTACH.

Parajuli, Pramod. 1991. "Power and Knowledge in Development Discourse." *International Social Science Journal* 127:173–90.

Pathak, A. 1999. "Law, Strategies, Ideologies: Legislating Forests in Colonial India, 1792–1882." Ph.D. diss., University of Edinburgh.

Pearson, Charles H. 1893. *National Life and Character: A Forecast.* London: Macmillan.

Peet, Richard, and Michael Watts. 1993. "Development Theory and Environment in an Age of Market Triumphalism." *Economic Geography* 69(3): 227–53.

———. 1996. *Liberation Ecologies: Environment, Development, Social Movements.* London: Routledge.

Peluso, Nancy Lee. 1992. *Rich Forests, Poor People.* Berkeley: University of California Press.

———. 1993. "Coercing Conservation: The Politics of State Resource Control." In *The State and Social Power in Global Environmental Politics,* edited by R. Lipschutz and K. Conca. New York: Columbia University Press.

———. 1995. "Whose Woods Are These? The Politics of Counter-mapping in Kalimantan Indonesia." *Antipode* 27(4): 383–406.

———. 1996a. "Fruit Trees and Family Trees in an Indonesian Rainforest: Ethics of Access, Property Zones, and Environmental Change." *Comparative Studies in Society and History* 38(3): 510–48.

———. 1996b. "Personal comments on 'Custom, Property, and Forestry in Southeast Asia.'" Paper presented at the conference Voices from the Commons, International Association for the Study of Common Property, 5–8 June, Berkeley, California.

Peluso, Nancy Lee, and Christine Padoch. 1996. "Changing Resource Rights in Managed Forests of West Kalimantan." In *Borneo in Transition: People, Forests, Conservation, and Development,* edited by Christine Padoch and Nancy Lee Peluso, Singapore: Oxford University Press.

Peluso, Nancy Lee, and Emily Harwell. 2001. "Territory, Custom, and the Cultural Politics of Ethnic War in West Kalimantan, Indonesia." In *Violent Environments,* edited by Nancy Lee Peluso and Michael Watts, 83–116. Ithaca: Cornell University Press.

Peluso, Nancy Lee, and Peter Vandergeest. 2001. "Genealogies of the Political Forest and Customary Rights in Indonesia, Malaysia, and Thailand." *Journal of Asian Studies* 60(3).

Peluso, Nancy Lee, Peter Vandergeest, and Lesley Potter. 1995. "Social Aspects of Forestry in Southeast Asia: A Review of Trends in the Scholarly Literature." *Journal of Southeast Asian Studies* 26(1): 196–218.

Pelzer, Karl. 1945. *Pioneer Settlement in the Asiatic Tropics.* New York: American Geographical Society.

———. 1957. "The Agrarian Conflict in East Sumatra." *Pacific Affairs* 30: 151–59.

Pemberton, John. 1994. *On the Subject of "Java."* Ithaca: Cornell University Press.

Peritore, N. Patrick. 1993. "Environmental Attitudes of Indian Elites." *Asian Survey* 33(8): 804–18.

Persoon, G. A., H. H. de Longh, and B. Wenno. 1996. "Exploitation, Management, and Conservation of Marine Resources: The Context of the Aru Tenggara Marine Reserve (Moluccas, Indonesia)." *Ocean and Coastal Management* 32(2): 97–122.

Peters, Pauline. 1994. *Dividing the Commons: Politics, Policy, and Culture in Botswana*. Charlottesville: University of Virginia Press.

———. 1996. "Who's Local Here? The Politics of Participation in Development." *Cultural Survival Quarterly* 20(3): 22–25.

Phillips, P. J. 1924. *Revised Working Plan for the Reserved Forests of the Saranda and Kolhan Division in the Singhbhum District, Bihar and Orissa Circle*. Patna: Superintendent of Government Printing.

Pickering, Andrew. 1992. "From Science as Knowledge to Science as Practice." In *Science as Practice and Culture*, edited by Andrew Pickering, Chicago: University of Chicago Press.

———. 1995. *The Mangle of Practice: Time, Agency, and Science*. Chicago: University of Chicago Press.

Pieterse, Jan Nederveen, and Bhikhu Parekh. 1995. *The Decolonization of Imagination: Culture, Knowledge, and Power*. London: Zed.

Pigg, Stacy Leigh. 1992. "Constructing Social Categories through Place: Social Representations and Development in Nepal." *Comparative Studies in Society and History* 34(3): 491–513.

———. 1993. "Unintended Consequences: The Ideological Impact of Development in Nepal." *South Asia Bulletin* 13(1–2): 45–58.

Pipop, Udomittipong. 1993. "Why Should Buddhist Monks Be Involved in Conservation?" *Seeds of Peace* 9(1): 6–7.

———. 1994. "Buddhist Natural Conservation in Thailand." Paper presented at the third annual meeting of the Network for Multidisciplinary Exchange for Environment and Development, Montreal, 5–9 September.

Poffenberger, Mark. 1994. "The Resurgence of Community Forest Management in Eastern India." In *Natural Connections: Perspectives in Community-Based Conservation*, edited by David Western and R. Michael Wright, 53–79. Washington, D.C.: Island Press.

Poffenberger, Mark, ed. 1990. *Forest Management Partnerships: Regenerating India's Forests*. New Delhi: Ford Foundation.

Poffenberger, Mark, and B. McGean, eds. 1996. *Village Voices, Forest Choices*. Delhi: Oxford University Press.

Popkin, Samuel. 1979. *The Rational Peasant: The Political Economy of Rural Society in Vietnam*. Berkeley: University of California Press.

Posey, Darrell. 1985. "Indigenous Management of Tropical Forest Ecosystems: The Case of the Kayapo Indians of the Brazilian Amazon." *Agroforestry Systems* 3:139–58.

Potter, Leslie. 1987. "Case Study of Banjarese Swiddeners in South Kalimantan." In *Land Degradation and Society,* edited by P. Blaikie and H. Brookfield. London: Methuen.

Potter, Lesley, ed. 1988. "Indigenes and Colonizers: Dutch Forest Policy in South and East Borneo (Kalimantan), 1900 to 1950." In *Changes in Tropical Forests: Historical Perspectives on Today's Challenges in Asia, Australia, and Oceania,* edited by J. Dargavel, Sydney: N.p.

Potter, Leslie, H. Brookfield, and Y. Byron, eds. 1995. *In Place of the Forest: Environmental and Socioeconomic Transformation in Borneo and the Eastern Malay Peninsula.* Tokyo: United Nations University Press.

Poulgrain, Greg. 1998. *The Genesis of Konfrontasi: Malaysia Brunei Indonesia 1945–1965.* Bathhurst, London: Crawford House Publishing.

Prakash, Gyan. 1990. "Writing Post-orientalist Histories of the Third World: Perspectives from Indian Historiography." *Comparative Studies in Society and History* 32(2): 383–408.

Prasad, Archana. 1994. "Forests and Subsistence in Colonial India: A Study of the Central Provinces." Ph.D. thesis, Jawaharlal Nehru University, New Delhi.

Pratt, Mary Louise. 1992. *Imperial Eyes: Travel Writing and Transculturation.* New York: Routledge.

Prawiroatmodjo. [1957] 1981. *Bausastra Jawa-Indonesia.* Jakarta: Gunung Agung.

Project for Ecological Recovery. 1992. *The Future of People and Forests in Thailand after the Logging Ban.* Bangkok: Project for Ecological Recovery.

Project Tiger. 1993. "Proceedings and Resolutions." International Symposium on the Tiger, New Delhi, India, 22–24 February, Ministry of Environment and Forests, New Delhi.

———. 1994. "National Tiger Action Plan." Ministry of Environment and Forests, New Delhi.

Putra, Ktut Sarjana. 1994. "Buklet Informasi Cagar Alam Laut Aru, Program Kesadartahuan Konservasi Kelautan Di Pulau-Pulau Aru Maluku Tenggara" [Marine Nature Reserve Information Booklet for Aru, Yearly Conservation Awareness Program on Aru Island, Southeast Maluku]. WWF Indonesia Program, Directorat General PHPA, Directorat of Forestry. Manuscript.

Putzel, James. 1992. *A Captive Land: The Politics of Agrarian Reform in the Philippines.* New York: Monthly Review Press.

Quammen, David. 1995. *The Song of the Dodo: Island Biogeography in an Age of Extinctions.* New York: Scribners.

Rahail, J. P. 1993. *Larwul Ngabal: Hukum Adat Kei Bertahan Menghadapi Arus Perubahan* [Larwul Ngabal: Kei Customary Law Survives Changing Currents]. Seri Pustaka Khasana Budya Lokal [Library Series on Special Local Cultures] 1. Jakarta: Yayasan Sejati Institute.

———. 1995. *Bat Batang Fitroa Fitnangan: Tata Guna Tanah and Laut Tradisional Kei* [Traditional Land and Ocean Management Systems in Kei]. Seri Pustaka Khasanah Budaya Lokal [Document Treasures of Local Cultures] 4. Jakarta: Yayasan Sejati Institute.

Rajan, B. K. C. 1994. *Ten Forest Products.* New Delhi: Jaya Publications.

Rajendran, S. 1995. "Plant Prospects." *Down to Earth,* 31 December, 20.

Ramadhiyani, K. K. 1941. *Report on Land Tenures and the Revenue System of the Orissa and Chattisgarh States.* Berhampur: Indian Law Publication Press.

Ramakrishna, Kilaparti. 1985. "The Emergence of Environmental Law in the Developing Countries: A Case Study of India." *Ecology Law Quarterly* 12(4): 907–35.

Rangan, Haripriya. 1992. "Romancing the Environment: Popular Environmental Action in the Garhwal Himalayas." In *In Defense of Livelihoods: Comparative Studies in Environmental Action,* edited by J. Friedmann and H. Rangan. West Hartford: Kumarian.

———. 1995. "Contested Boundaries: State Policies, Forest Classifications, and Deforestation in the Garhwal Himalayas." *Antipode* 27(4): 343–62.

Rangarajan, Mahesh. 1992. "Forest Policy in the Central Provinces, 1860–1914." Ph.D. thesis, Oxford University.

———. 1994. "Imperial Agendas and India's Forests: The Early History of Indian Forestry, 1800–1878." *Indian Economic and Social History Review* 31(2): 147–67.

———. 1996. *Fencing the Forest: Conservation and Ecological Change in India's Central Provinces, 1860–1914.* Delhi: Oxford University Press.

———. 1998. "Production, Dessiccation, and Forest Management in the Central Provinces." In *Nature and the Orient: The Environmental History of South and Southeast Asia,* edited by Richard Grove, Vinita Damodaran, and Satpal Sangwan. Delhi: Oxford University Press.

Raynor, E. W. 1940. "Sal Regeneration de novo." *Indian Forester* 66(9): 525–29.

Redford, K. 1990. "The Ecologically Noble Savage." In *Romanticizing the Stone Age: Special Report on the Tasaday, Cultural Survival Quarterly* 15:46–48.

Reid, Anthony. 1997. "Inside Out: The Colonial Displacement of Sumatra's Population." In *Paper Landscapes: Explorations in the Environmental History of Indonesia,* edited by P. Boomgaard, F. Colombijn, and D. Henley, 61–89. Leiden: KITLV Press.

Reingold, R., and M. Rothenberg, eds. 1987. *Scientific Colonialism: A Cross-Cultural Comparison.* Washington, D.C.: Smithsonian Institution Press.

Renn, Ortwin, Thomas Webler, and Peter Wiedemann, eds. 1995. *Fairness and Competence in Citizen Participation: Evaluating Models for Environmental Discourse.* Dordrecht: Kluwer Academic.

RePPProT (Regional Physical Planning Programme for Transmigration). 1990. *Review of Phase 1 Results, West Kalimantan.* Jakarta: ODA Land Resources Department and Direktorat Bina Program.

Retraubun, Alex S. W. 1996. "Sasi: Konservasi Tradisional Ala Maluku" [Sasi: Traditional Moluccan Conservation à la Maluku y Kompas], On-line, 22 February.

Reyes Lala, Ramon. 1898. *The Philippine Islands.* New York: Continental.

Reynolds, Craig. 1995. "A New Look at Old Southeast Asia." *Journal of Asian Studies* 54(2): 419–46.

———. n.d. "The State in Southeast Asian History: Its Representations and Rivals." Unpublished essay.

Ribbentrop, Berhtold. 1900. Forestry in British India. Calcutta: Superintendent of Government Printing.

Ribot, Jesse, and Nancy Lee Peluso. 2003. "Theorizing Access." Rural Sociology (in press).

Richards, Anthony. 1981. An Iban-English Dictionary. Oxford: Clarendon.

Richards, John F., Edward S. Haynes, and James R. Hagen. 1985. "Changes in the Land and Human Productivity in Northern India, 1870–1970." Agricultural History 59(4): 523–48.

Richards, Paul. 1992. "Saving the Rain Forest? Contested Futures in Conservation." In Contemporary Futures: Perspectives from Social Anthropology, edited by Sandra Wallman, 138–53. ASA Monographs 30. London: Routledge.

Ricketts, H. 1855. Papers Relating to the Southwest Frontier Comprising Reports on Purulia or Manbhum and Chota Nagpur. Selected Reports of the Bengal Government 20. Calcutta: N.p.

Ritchie, James. 1994. Bruno Manser: The Inside Story. Singapore: Summer Times.

Rival, Laura. 1993. "The Growth of Family Trees: Understanding Huaorani Perceptions of the Forest." Man 28(4): 635–52.

Rival, Laura, ed. 1998. The Social Life of Trees: Anthropological Perspectives on Tree Symbolism. Oxford: Berg.

Robbins, Paul. 1998. "Paper Forests: Imagining and Deploying Exogenous Ecologies in Arid India." Geoforum 29(1): 69–86.

Rodger, A. 1925. "Research in Forestry in India." European Forestry Journal 14:45–53.

Rosaldo, Renato. 1980. Ilongot Head–hunting, 1883–1974: A Study in Society and History. Stanford: Stanford University Press.

Rose, Carol. 1994. Property and Persuasion: Essays on the History, Theory, and Rhetoric of Ownership. Boulder: Westview.

Rose, Gillian. 1993. Feminism and Geography: The Limits of Geographical Knowledge. Cambridge: Polity Press.

Roseberry, William. 1993. "Beyond the Agrarian Question in Latin America." In Confronting Historical Paradigms, edited by Fred Cooper, 318–68. Madison: University of Wisconsin Press.

Roseman, Marina. 1991. Healing Sounds from the Malaysian Rainforest: Temiar Music and Medicine. Berkeley: University of California Press.

Rosener, Werner. 1994. The Peasantry of Europe. Translated by Thomas Barker. Oxford: Blackwell.

Rosin, R. Thomas. 1987. Land Reform and Agrarian Change. Jaipur: Rawat.

Rousseau, Jérôme. 1990. Central Borneo: Ethnic Identity and Social Life in a Stratified Society. Oxford: Clarendon.

Rushdie, Salman. 1991. Imaginary Homelands. London: Granta.

Saberwal, Vasant, Mahesh Rangarajan, and Ashish Kothari. 2001. People, Parks, and Wildlife: Towards Coexistence. Hyderabad: Orient Longman.

Sachs, Wolfgang. 1994. "The Blue Planet: An Ambiguous Modern Icon." Ecologist 24(5): 170–75.

Sachs, Wolfgang, ed. 1992. The Development Dictionary. London: Zed.

Sack, Robert David. 1986. *Human Territoriality: Its Theory and History.* Cambridge: Cambridge University Press.

Saeng Chandra-ngam. 1991. *Sasanasart* [The Science of Religion]. Bangkok: Thai Watthana Phanich. In Thai.

Sahabat Alam Malaysia. 1987. *Forest Resources Crisis in the Third World.* Penang: Sahabat Alam Malaysia.

Sahlins, Peter. 1994. *Forest Rites: The War of the Demoiselles in Nineteenth Century France.* Cambridge: Harvard University Press.

Said, Edward. 1978. *Orientalism.* London: Routledge and Kegan Paul.

Saigal, S., C. Agarwal, and J. Y. Campbell. 1996. "Sustaining Joint Forest Management: The Role of Non Timber Forest Products." Society for the Promotion of Wasteland Development. Mimeo.

Sanderson, M. 1988. *Griffith Taylor: Antarctic Scientist and Pioneer Geographer.* Ottawa: Carleton University Press.

Saneh Chamrik and Yos Santasombat, eds. 1993. *Community Forests in Thailand: The Direction for Development.* 3 vols. Bangkok: Local Development Institute.

SAPROF Team for the Overseas Economic Cooperation Fund, Japan. 1991. Final Report on Afforestation Project in Aravalli-Hills State of Rajasthan, India, March 1991.

Sarin, M. 1996a. "From Conflict to Collaboration: Institutional Issues in Community Management." In *Village Voices, Forest Choices: Joint Forest Management in India,* edited by Mark Poffenberger and B. McGean, 165–209. Delhi: Oxford University Press.

———. 1996b. *Who Is Gaining? Who Is Losing? Gender and Equity Concerns in Joint Forest Management.* New Delhi: Society for Promotion of Wastelands Development.

Sather, Clifford. 1990. "Trees and Tree Tenure in Paku Iban Society: The Management of Secondary Forest Resources in a Long-Established Iban Community." *Borneo Review* 1: 16–40.

Savyasaachi. 1994. "The Tiger and the Honey-bee." *Seminar* 423: 30–35.

Saxena, N. C. 1993. *Policy Issues.* Madhya Pradesh Integrated Forestry Sector Project.

Schlich, W. 1876. "Notes on Preliminary Working Plans." In *Report of the Proceedings of the Forest Conference Held at Simla October 1875,* edited by D. Brandis and A. Smythies. Calcutta: Superintendent of Government Printing.

Schmink, M., and C. Wood. 1992. *Contested Frontiers in Amazonia.* New York: Columbia University Press.

Schroeder, Richard A. 1997. "Community, Forestry, and Conditionality in the Gambia." Paper presented at the conference Representing Communities: Histories and Politics of Community-Based Resource Management," Helen, Georgia, 1–3 June.

Schroeder, Richard, and Roderick P. Neumann. 1995. "Manifest Ecological Destinies: Local Rights and Global Environmental Agendas." *Antipode* 27(4): 321–24. Introduction to special issue "Manifest Ecological Destinies."

Schulte, R. 1994. *The Village in Court: Arson, Infanticide, and Poaching in the*

Court Records of Upper Bavaria, 1848–1910. Translated by Barrie Selman. Cambridge: Cambridge University Press.

Scott, James C. 1976. *The Moral Economy of the Peasant*. New Haven: Yale University Press.

———. 1977. "Protest and Profanation: Agrarian Revolt and the Little Tradition." *Theory and Society* 4(1): 1–38; 4(2): 211–46.

———. 1985. *Weapons of the Weak: Everyday Forms of Peasant Resistance*. New Haven: Yale University Press.

———. 1998. *Seeing Like a State: How Certain Schemes to Improve the Human Condition Have Failed*. New Haven: Yale University Press.

Scott, James, and Benedict J. Tria Kirkvliet, eds. 1986. *Everyday Forms of Peasant Resistance in South-East Asia*. Totowa, N.J.: Frank Cass.

Seidensticker, John, Sarah Christie, and Peter Jackson, eds. 1999. *Riding the Tiger: Tiger Conservation in Human-Dominated Landscapes*. Cambridge: Cambridge University Press.

Sekhiyatham Group. 1992. *Phra kap Paa: Khwaamcing thii Haaj Paj* [Monks and the Forest: The Truth Which Has Disappeared]. Bangkok: Thai Interreligious Commission on Development. Summary of the seminar The Sangha and Agreement between the Vinaya and the Law. In Thai.

Sekretariat Kerjasama Pelestarian Hutan Indonesia [Indonesian Collaborative Secretariat for Forest Conservation]. 1992. *To Sink the Island: Logging Problems in Yamdena Island*. Jakarta: SKEPHI.

Sen, Geeti, ed. 1992. *Indigenous Vision*. New Delhi: Sage.

Sen, J. N. and T. P. Ghose. 1925. "Soil Conditions under Sal." *Indian Forester* 51(6): 243–53.

Sesser, Stan. 1991. "Logging the Rain Forest." *New Yorker*, 17 May, 42–67.

Shah, Ghanshyam. 1991. "Tribal Identity and Class Differentiation: The Chaudhri Tribe" In *Social Stratification*, edited by Dipankar Gupta, Delhi: Oxford University Press.

Shamsul, A. B. 1986. *From British to Bumiputera Rule: Local Politics and Rural Development in Peninsular Malaysia*. Singapore: Institute of Southeast Asian Studies.

Shanin, Teodor. 1990. *Defining Peasants*. Oxford: Blackwell.

Sharma, B. D. 1995. *Whither Tribal Areas? Constitutional Amendments and After*. New Delhi: Sahyog Pustak Kutir.

Sharma, S., and B. Tiagi, 1979. *Flora of North-East Rajasthan*. New Delhi: Kalyani Publishers.

Shetty, B. V., and V. Singh, ed. 1987. *Flora of Rajasthan*. Calcutta: Botanical Survey of India.

Shiva, M. P. 1993. "Determinants of the Key Elements of Demand and Supply of Non-timber Forest Products." Mimeo.

Shiva, V. 1989. *Staying Alive: Women, Ecology, and Development in India*. London: Zed.

———. 1991. *Ecology and the Politics of Survival: Conflicts over Natural Resources in India*. New Delhi: Sage.

Shiva, V., and J. Bandhyopadhyaya. 1986. *Chipko: India's Civilisation Response to the Forest Crisis*. New Delhi: Indian National Trust for Art and Cultural Heritage.

Short, John R. 1991. *Imagined Country: Society, Culture, and Environment.* London: Routledge.

Silverman, Sydel. 1979. "The Peasant Concept in Anthropology." *Journal of Peasant Studies* 7(1): 49–69.

Singh, C. 1995. "Forests, Pastoralists, and Agrarian Society in Mughal India." In *Nature, Culture, Imperialism,* edted by D. Arnold and R. Guha. Delhi: Oxford University Press.

Singh, C. 1993. *Legal Aspects.* Working Paper 6. Bhopal: Madhya Pradesh Integrated Forest Sector Project Preparation.

Singh, Dool. 1964. *Land Reforms in Rajasthan.* Alwar, Rajasthan: Sharma Brothers.

Sinha, J. N. 1962. *Working Plan for the Reserved, Protected, and Private Protected Forests of Manbhum Division.* Patna: Superintendent of Government Printing.

Sinha, Subir, Brian Greenberg, and Shubhra Gururani. 1997. "'The New Traditionalist' Discourse of Indian Enviornmentalism." *Journal of Peasant Studies* 24:65–99.

Sivaramakrishnan, K. 1995. "Imagining the Past in Present Politics: Colonialism and Forestry in India." *Comparative Studies in Society and History* 37(1): 3–40.

———. 1996a. "Forests, Politics, and Governance in Bengal, 1794–1994." Ph.D. diss., Yale University.

———. 1996b. "Joint Forest Management: The Politics of Representation in West Bengal." Paper presented at the workshop participation and the Micropolitics of Development Encounters, Harvard University, May.

———. 1997. "A Limited Forest Conservancy in Southwest Bengal, 1864–1912." *Journal of Asian Studies* 56(1): 75–112.

———. 1998. "Co-managed Forests in West Bengal: Historical Perspectives on Community and Control." *Journal of Sustainable Forestry* 7(3–4): 23–51.

———. 1999. *Modern Forests.* Stanford: Stanford University Press.

———. 2000. "State Sciences and Development Histories: Encoding Local Forestry Knowledge in Bengal." *Development and Change* 31:61–89.

Skaria, Ajay. 1992. "A Forest Polity: The Dangs, 1800s–1920s." Ph.D. thesis, Cambridge University.

———. 1998. "Timber Conservancy, Dessicationism, and Scientific Forestry: The Dangs, 1840s–1920s." In *Nature and the Orient: Essays in Environmental History of South and Southeast Asia,* edited by Richard Grove, Vinita Damodaran, and Satpal Sangwan, New Delhi: Oxford University Press.

Smith, Dorothy. 1987. *The Everyday World as Problematic: A Feminist Sociology.* Boston: Northeastern University Press.

Smith, Eric Alden, and Joan McCarter, eds. 1997. *Contested Arctic: Indigenous Peoples, Industrial States, and the Circumpolar Environment.* Seattle: University of Washington Press.

Smith, Neil. 1984. *Uneven Development: Nature, Capital, and the Production of Space.* Oxford: Blackwell.

Smith, V. 1986. *The Practice of Silviculture.* New York: Wiley.

Smythies, E. A. 1920. "Silvicultural Systems for Sal." *Indian Forester* 46(8): 381–91.

———. 1929. "Sal and Its Regeneration." *Indian Forester* 55(9): 510–17.

———. 1940. "Sal Regeneration de Novo." *Indian Forester* 66(4): 193–99.

Soja, Edward. 1971. *The Political Organization of Space.* Resource Paper 8. Washington, D.C.: Association of American Geographers.

———. 1985. "The Spatiality of Social Life: Towards a Transformative Retheorization." In *Social Relations and Spatial Structures,* edited by D. G. A. J. Urry. New York: St. Martin's.

———. 1989. *Postmodern Geographies: The Reassertion of Space in Critical Social Theory.* London: Verso.

Spate, O. H. K., and A. T. A. Learmonth. 1967. *India and Pakistan: A General and Regional Geography.* 3d ed. London: Methuen.

Spyer, Patricia. 1998. "The Tooth of Time, or Taking a 'Look' at the Clothing in Late-Nineteenth Century Aru." In *Border Fetishisms: Material Objects in Unstable Spaces,* edited by Patricia Spyer, 150–83. New York: Routledge.

———. 1992. "The Memory of Trade: Circulation, Autochthony, and the Past in the Aru Islands (Eastern Indonesia)." Ph.D. diss., University of Chicago.

———. 1995a. "Diversity with a Difference: Adat and the New Order in Aru (Eastern Indonesia)." *Cultural Anthropology* 11(1): 25–50.

———. 1995b. "The Eroticism of Debt: Pearldivers, Traders, and Sea Wives in the Aru Islands, Eastern Indonesia." *American Ethnologist* 24(3): 515–38.

———. 1995c. "Fetishes after Fashion: Fragments for a History of Clothing in Aru, Eastern Indonesia." Manuscript.

Stallybrass, Peter, and Allon White. 1986. *The Politics and Poetics of Transgression.* Ithaca: Cornell University Press.

Stebbing, E. P. 1920. *The Diary of a Sportsman Naturalist.* London: John Lane.

———. 1922–62. *The Forests of India.* 4 vols. London: John Lane.

Stepan, Nancy. 1982. *The Idea of Race in Science: Great Britain, 1800–1960.* London: Archon.

Stivens, Maila. 1983. "Sexual Politics in Rembau: Female Autonomy, Matriliny, and Agrarian Change in Negeri Sembilan, Malaysia." Occasional Paper 5, University of Kent at Canterbury, Centre of South-East Asian Studies.

Stoler, Ann. Forthcoming. "Development Historical Negatives: Race and the Disquieting Visions of a Colonial State." In *Along the Archival Grain: Colonial Cultures and Their Affective States.* Princeton: Princeton University Press.

Stracey, P. D. 1931. "A Short Note on Uncovering Sal Regeneration in Grass in the Goalpara Forest Division, Assam." *Indian Forester* 57(10): 513–15.

Subrahmanyam, Sanjay. 1992. "The Mughal State: Structure or Process? Reflections on Some Recent Western Historiography." *Indian Economic and Social History Review* 29(3): 291–322.

Sulak Sivaraksa, ed. 1990. *Radical Conservatism: Buddhism in the Contemporary World.* Bangkok: Sathirakoses-Nagapradipa Foundation.

Sundar, Nandini. 1997. *Subalterns and Sovereigns: An Anthropological History of Bastar, 1854–1996.* Delhi: Oxford University Press.

———. 2001. "Beyond the Bounds? Violence at the Margins of New Legal Geographies." In *Violent Environments,* edited by Nancy Lee Peluso and A. Michael Watts. Ithaca: Cornell University Press.

Sundar, N., R. Jeffery, et al. 2001. *Branching Out: A Comparative Study of*

Joint Forest Management in Four Indian States. Delhi: Oxford University Press.

Surat Keputusan Menteri Kehutanan Republik Indonesia. 1991. Decision Letter of Minister of Forests, Republic of Indonesia/No. 72/Kpts-II/1991.

Svensson, Thommy. 1990. "Bureaucracies and Agrarian Change: A Southeast Asian Case." In *Agrarian Society in History*, edited by Mats Lundahl and Thommy Svensson, 282–317. London: Routledge.

Swanson, Maynard. 1977. "The Sanitation Syndrome: Bubonic Plague and Urban Native Policy in the Cape Colony, 1900–1909." *Journal African History* 18:387–410.

Swearer, Donald K. 1989. Introduction to *Me and Mine: Selected Essays of Bhikkhu Buddhadasa*, edited by Donald K. Swearer, 1–12. Albany: State University of New York Press. •

Taft, W. H. 1902. *Hearings before the Senate Committee on the Philippine Islands*, 57th Cong., 1st sess., S. Doc. 331, pt. 1, 329.

Takahashi, Akira. 1972. "The Peasantization of Kasama Tenants." *Philippine Sociological Review* 20(1–2): 129–33.

Talbott, K., and O. J. Lynch. 1995. *Balancing Acts: Community-Based Forest Management and National Law in Asia and the Pacific*. Washington, D.C.: World Resources Institute.

Taylor, Griffith. 1916. *The Control of Settlement by Humidity and Temperature*. Melbourne: Bureau of Meteorology.

———. 1918. "Geographical Factors Controlling the Settlement of Tropical Australia." *Queensland Geographical Journal* 32–33:1–67.

———. 1923. *Environment and Race*. London: Oxford University Press.

Taylor, Jean. 1983. *The Social World of Batavia: European and Eurasian in Dutch Asia*. Madison: University of Wisconsin Press.

Taylor, Jim. 1993. "Social Activism and Resistance on the Thai Frontier: The Case of Phra Prajak Khuttajitto." *Bulletin of Concerned Asian Scholars* 25(2): 3–16.

———. 1994. *A Social, Political, and Ethnoecological Study of Community Forests and Rural Leadership in Northeastern Thailand*. IOCPS Occasional Paper 36. Nedlands, Western Australia: Indian Ocean Centre for Peace Studies.

Taylor, Peter, and Frederick Buttel. 1992. "How Do We Know We Have Global Environmental Problems? Science and the Globalization of Environmental Discourse." *Geoforum* 23(3): 405–16.

Temple, Sir Richard. 1880. "Forest Conservancy in Bombay." *Indian Forester* 5(3): 335–67.

Thai Inter-religious Commission for Development. [1993]. "Phrasong kap kaananurak singwaetlaum: Karanii suksaa Phra Palad Sanguan Jaaruwannoo, Wat Aranyaawaat, T. Naiwiang, J. Naan" [Monks and Environmental Conservation: Case Study of Phra Palad Sanguan Jaaruwannoo, Wat Aranyaawaat, Nan Province.] N.p. In Thai.

Thompson, E. P. 1975. *Whigs and Hunters: The Origins of the Black Act*. New York: Pantheon.

Thompson, Herb. 1993. "Malaysian Forestry Policy in Borneo." *Journal of Contemporary Asia* 23(4): 503–14.

Thompson, M., M. Warburton, and T. Hatley. 1986. *Uncertainty on a Hima-*

layan Scale: An Institutional Theory of Environmental Perception and a Strategic Framework for the Sustainable Development of the Himalaya. London: Ethnographica.

Thorburn, Craig. 2000. "Sasi Lola in the Kei Islands, Indonesia: An Endangered Marine Resource Management Tradition." *World Development* 28(8): 1461–80.

———. 2001. "The House That Poison Built: Marine Property Rights and the Live Food Fish Trade in Kei Islands, Indonesia" *Development and Change* 32(1): 151–80.

Tolba, Mostafa K., and Osama A. El-Kholy, eds. 1992. "Loss of Biological Diversity." In United Nations Environment Program, *The World Environment, 1972–1992.* London: Chapman and Hall.

Tsing, Anna L. 1993. *In the Realm of the Diamond Queen: Marginality in an Out-of-the-Way Place.* Princeton: Princeton University Press.

———. 1999. "Becoming a Tribal Elder and Other Green Development Fantasies." In *Transforming the Indonesian Uplands: Marginality, Power, and Production,* edited by Tania Murray Li, 159–202. Amsterdam: Harwood Academic Publishers.

———. 2003. "Cultivating the Wild: Honey Hunting and Forest Management in Southeast Kalimantan." In *Culture and the Question of Rights to Southeast Asian Environments: Forests, Coasts, and Seas,* edited by Charles Zerner. Durham: Duke University Press.

Tucker, Richard P. 1989. "The Depletion of India's Forests under British Imperialism: Planters, Foresters, and Peasants in Assam and Kerala." In *The Ends of the Earth: Perspectives on Modern Environmental History,* edited by D. Worster, Cambridge: Cambridge University Press.

Turner, Frederick Jackson. [1924] 1932. *The Significance of Sections in American History.* New York: Holt.

Turner, Terence. 1991. "Representing, Resisting, Rethinking." In *Colonial Situations: Essays on the Contextualization of Ethnographic Knowledge,* edited by George W. Stocking, 285–313. Madison: University of Wisconsin Press.

Turner, Victor. 1967. *The Forest of Symbols.* Ithaca: Cornell University Press.

Ukru, Yunus, Soeleman Ubro, Robby Teniwut, Pieter Elmas, Minggus Umbu Saza, Dudit Widodo, Erwin Panjaitan, and Roem Topatimasang. 1993. *Portret Orang Orang Kalah: Kumpulan Kasus Penyingkiran — Orang-Orang Asli Kepulauan Maluku* [Portrait of Defeated Peoples: Cases of Marginalization of the Indigenous Inhabitants of the Maluku Islands]. Jakarta: Yayasan Sejati Institute.

UNDP (United Nations Development Program). 1995. "Regional Tiger Conservation Initiative." Global Environment Facility Document, 15 March, New Delhi.

Urdu-English Dictionary. 1977. Rev. ed. Lahore: Ferozsons.

Urquhart, Ian A. N. 1951. "Some Notes on Jungle Punans in Kapit District." *Sarawak Museum Journal* 5 (13 new series): 113–16.

Vanak, A. T. F. 1997. "Movement Patterns of Radio-Tagged Tigers in Panna National Park, Madhya Pradesh." M.Sc. diss., Saurashtra University.

van Beek, Walter E. A., and Pieteke M. Banga. 1992. "The Dogon and Their

Trees." In *Bush Base, Forest Farm: Culture, Environment and Development,* edited by Elisabeth Croll and David Parkin, 57–75. London: Routledge.

van den Muijenberg, Otto, and Willem Wolters. 1988. *Conceptualizing Development: The Historical-Sociological Tradition in Dutch Non-Western Sociology.* Dordrecht: Foris.

Vandergeest, Peter. 1996. "Territorialization of Forest Rights in Indonesia." *Society and Natural Resources* (9): 159–75.

Vandergeest, Peter, and Nancy Peluso. 1995. "Territorialization and State Power in Thailand." *Theory and Society* 24:385–426.

van der Wal, Mark. 1994. "EC Helps Improve Environmental Centre in Moluccas." *European Union Newsletter,* April.

van Zanden, J. L. 1994. *The Transformation of European Agriculture in the Nineteenth Century: The Case of the Netherlands.* Amsterdam: VU University Press.

Vasavi, A. R. 1994. " 'Hybrid Times, Hybrid People': Culture and Agriculture in South India." *Man* 29(2): 283–300.

Venkataramiah, E. S. 1988. "Citizenship: Rights and Duties." R. K. Tankha Memorial Lecture. N.p.

Vernon, H. M. 1926. "Is Effective Temperature or Cooling Power the Better Index of Comfort?" *Journal of Industrial Hygiene* 8:392.

Vickers, Adrian. 1986. "History and Social Structure in Ancient Java: A Review Article." *Review of Indonesian and Malayan Affairs* 20(2): 156–85.

Vidal de la Blache, P. 1926. *Principles of Human Geography,* edited by Emmanuel de Martonne, translated by Millicent T. Bingham. New York: Henry Holt.

von Benda-Beckmann, Franz, Keebet von Benda-Beckmann, and Arie Brouwer. 1992. "Changing 'Indigenous Environmental Law' in the Central Moluccas: Communal Regulation and Privatization of Sasi." Paper presented to the Congress of the Commission on Folk Law and Legal Pluralism, Victoria University, Wellington, New Zealand.

Waddell, L. A. 1899. *Among the Himalayas.* London: Constable.

Wadley, Susan S. 1994. *Struggling with Destiny in Karimpur, 1925–1984.* Berkeley: University of California Press.

Wallace, Alfred Russel. [1869] 1983. *The Malay Archipelago, the Land of the Orang-Utan, and the Bird of Paradise: A Narrative of Travel with Studies of Man and Nature.* Singapore: Graham Brash.

———. [1878] 1891. *Natural Selection and Tropical Nature: Essays on Descriptive and Theoretical Biology.* London: McMinn.

Ward, Geoffrey C. 1987. "India's Intensifying Dilemma: Can Tigers and People Coexist?" *Smithsonian,* November, 53–65.

———. 1992. "India's Wildlife Dilemma." *National Geographic,* 1, May: 22–28.

Warner, John Harley. 1991. "Ideals of Science and Their Discontents in Late-Nineteenth-Century American Medicine." *Isis* 82(313): 454–78.

Warren, W. D. M. 1940. "Sal Regeneration de Novo." *Indian Forester* 66(6): 334–40.

———. 1941. "Sal Regeneration de Novo in B–3 Sal." *Indian Forester* 67(3): 116–23.

Washbrook, D. 1981. "Law, State, and Agrarian Society in Colonial India." *Modern Asian Studies* 15:3.

Washburn, William S. 1905. "The Relation between Climate and Health with Special Reference to American Occupation of the Philippine Islands." *American Journal of Medical Science* 130:497–517.

Watts, Michael. 1991. "Visions of Excess: African Development in an Age of Market Idolatry." *Transition* 51:126–41.

———. 1995. "A New Deal in Emotions: Theory and Practice and the Crisis of Development." In *Power of Development,* edited by Jonathan Crush, London: Routledge.

———. 2000. "Contested Communities, Malignant Markets, and Gilded Governance: Justice, Resource Extraction, and Conservation in the Tropics." In *People, Plants, and Justice: The Politics of Nature Conservation,* edited by Charles Zerner, New York: Columbia University Press.

WCED [World Commission on Environment and Development]. 1987. *Our Common Future.* New Delhi: Oxford University Press.

Weightman, Simon, and S. M. Pandey. 1978. "The Semantic Field of Dharm and Kartavy in Modern Hindi." In *The Concept of Duty in South Asia,* edited by W. D. O'Flaherty and J. D. M. Derrett. New Delhi: South Asia Books.

Wessing, Robert. 1992. "A Tiger in the Heart: The Javanese Rampok Macan." *Bijdragen* 148(2): 287–308.

Whitmore, T. C. 1975. *Tropical Rain Forests of the Far East.* Oxford: Clarendon.

Whyte, R. O. 1968. *Grasslands of the Monsoon.* London: Faber and Faber.

Wilkinson, R. J. 1959. *A Malay-English Dictionary.* 2 vols. London: Macmillan.

Williams, Raymond. 1980. "Ideas of Nature." In *Problems in Materialism and Culture,* 67–85. London: Verso.

Wilmot, S. Eardley. 1910. *Forest Life and Sport in India.* Oxford University Press.

Wilson, Rob. 1991. *American Sublime: The Genealogy of a Poetic Genre.* Madison: University of Wisconsin Press.

———. 1992. "Techno-Euphoria and the Discourse of the American Sublime." *boundary* 2 19:205–29.

Winichakul, Thongchai. 1994. *Siam Mapped.* Honolulu: University of Hawaii Press.

Wolf, Eric R. 1966. *Peasants.* Engelwood Cliffs, N.J.: Prentice-Hall.

Wong, Diana. 1987. *Peasants in the Making: Malaysia's Green Revolution.* Singapore: Institute of Southeast Asian Studies.

Wood, Denis. 1992. *The Power of Maps.* New York: Guilford.

Woodruff, Charles E. 1909. *Expansion of Races.* New York: Rebman.

Woost, Michael. 1993. "Nationalising the Local Past in Sri Lanka: Histories of Nation and Development in a Sinhalese Village." *American Ethnologist* 20(3): 502–21.

World Commission on Environment and Development. 1987. *Our Common Future.* New Delhi: Oxford University Press.

Worcester, Dean C. 1914. "Philippine Forests." In *The Philippines Past and Present,* 2 vols. London: Mills and Boon.

World Rainforest Movement and Forests Monitor. 1998. *High Stakes: The Need to Control Transnational Logging Companies—A Malaysian Case Study.* Montevideo: World Rainforest Movement and Forests Monitor.

World Rainforest Movement and Sahabat Alam Malaysia. 1990. *The Battle for Sarawak's Forests.* Penang: World Rainforest Movement and Sahabat Alam Malaysia.

World Wildlife Fund. 1971. "World Wildlife, India: The Tiger Must Be Saved." *Indian National Appeal* (Bombay), newsletter no. 4, July.

World Wildlife Fund Indonesia Program. 1994. *Forest Support and Nature Conservation.* N.p.

World Wildlife Fund Indonesia Program/Direktoral Jendral PHPA, Departmen Kehutanan. 1994. *Program Kesadartahuan Konservasi Kelautan di Pulau-pulau Aru Bagian Tenggara Maluku* [Marine Conservation Awareness Program in the Aru Islands, Southeast Maluku]. N.p.

Worster, Donald. 1994. *Nature's Economy: A History of Ecological Ideas.* 2d ed. New York: Cambridge University Press.

Wright, Gwendolyn. 1987. "Tradition in the Service of Modernity: Architecture and Urbanism in French Colonial Policy, 1900–1930." *Journal of Modern History* 59:291–316.

Yayasan HUALOPU. 1996. "Community-based Resource Management in Central Moluccas." Proposal submitted to the Biodiversity Support Programme (BSP), unpublished manuscript.

Yule, Henry, and A. C. Burnell. [1886] 1903. *Hobson-Jobson: A Glossary of Colloquial Anglo-Indian Words and Phrases and of Kindred Terms, Etymological, Historical, Geographical, and Discursive.* 2d ed. London: John Murray.

Zerner, Charles. 1994a. "Through a Green Lens: Constructing Customary Environmental Law and Community in Indonesia's Maluku Islands." *Law and Society Review* 28(5): 1079–1122. Special symposium issue, "Law and the Definition of Individual and Collective Selves: Community and Identity in Sociological Studies."

———. 1994b. "Transforming Customary Law and Coastal Management Practices in the Maluku Islands, Indonesia, 1870–1992." In *Natural Connections: Perspectives in Community-Based Conservation,* edited by David Western and R. Michael Wright, 80–112. Washington, D.C.: Island Press.

———. 1995. "Telling Stories about Biological Diversity." In *Intellectual Property Rights and Indigenous Peoples,* edited by Steven Brush and Doreen Stabinsky. Washington, D.C.: Island Press.

———. 1998. "Of Men and Mollusks and the Marine Environment in the Maluku Islands: Imaging Customary Law and Institutions in Eastern Indonesia." In *Nature and the Orient: Essays on the Environmental History of South and Southeast Asia,* edited by Richard Grove, Vaneeta Damodaran, and Satpal Sangwen, New Delhi: Oxford University Press.

———. 2000. "Toward a Broader Vision of Justice and Conservation." In *People, Plants, and Justice: The Politics of Nature Conservation,* edited by Charles Zerner, New York: Columbia University Press.

———. 2003a. "Moving Translations: Poetics, Performance, and Property in Indonesia and Malaysia." In *Culture and the Question of Rights: Forests,*

Coasts, and Seas in Southeast Asia, edited by Charles Zerner, Durham: Duke University Press.

———. 2003b. "Sounding the Makassar Strait: Poetics and Politics in an Indonesian Marine Environment." In *Culture and the Question of Rights to Southeast Asian Environments: Forests, Coasts, and Seas,* edited by Charles Zerner. Durham: Duke University Press.

Zimmerer, Karl. 1994. "Human Geography and the 'New Ecology': The Prospect and Promise of Integration." *Annals of the Association of American Geographers* 84(1): 108–25.

Zimmerer, Karl, and Kenneth R. Young, eds. 1998. *Nature's Geography: New Lessons of Conservation in Developing Countries:* Madison: University of Wisconsin Press.

Zimmermann, Francis. 1987. *The Jungle and the Aroma of Meats: An Ecological Theme in Hindu Medicine.* Berkeley: University of California Press.

Zimmerman, Michael E. 1994. *Contesting Earth's Future: Radical Ecology and Postmodernity.* Berkeley: University of California Press.

CONTRIBUTORS

WARWICK ANDERSON is Associate Professor in the Department of Anthropology, History, and Social Medicine and Director of the History of Health Sciences Program at the University of California, San Francisco.

AMITA BAVISKAR is Reader in the Department of Sociology at the University of Delhi in India.

J. PETER BROSIUS is Associate Professor of Anthropology at the University of Georgia, Athens.

SUSAN M. DARLINGTON is Associate Professor of Anthropology and Asian Studies in the School of Social Science at Hampshire College.

MICHAEL R. DOVE is Margaret K. Musser Professor of Social Ecology at the Yale School of Forestry and Environmental Studies at Yale University.

ANN GRODZINS GOLD is Professor of Anthropology and Religion at Syracuse University.

PAUL GREENOUGH is Professor in the Department of History and Director of the Global Health Studies and Crossing Borders Programs at the University of Iowa.

ROGER JEFFERY is Professor of Sociology of South Asia in the School of Social and Political Science at the University of Edinburgh in Scotland.

ABHA MISHRA is a freelance researcher in Orissa, India.

NANCY LEE PELUSO is Professor in the Division of Resource Institutions, Policy, and Management and Director of the Berkeley Workshop on Environmental Politics at the University of California, Berkeley.

ʀ works for Winrock International in New Delhi, India.

ᴀMAKRISHNAN is Assistant Professor in the Anthropology De-
ᴨent at the University of Washington, Seattle.

ᴀNDINI SUNDAR is Reader in the Sociology Unit of the Institute of
Economic Growth in Delhi, India.

PRADEEP J. THARAKAN is a doctoral candidate in the College of Environmental Science and Forestry at the State University of New York,
Syracuse.

ANNA LOWENHAUPT TSING is Professor in the Department of Anthropology at the University of California, Santa Cruz.

CHARLES ZERNER is Barbara B. and Bertram Cohn Professor of Environmental Studies at Sarah Lawrence College.

Note: page numbers followed by a t indicate a table or, if followed by an f, a figure.

Ethnography: and cultural ecology, 105, 106; ethnographic writing, 322–23; forest discourses, 19, 107–14, 185–87; misuse of, 105, 191

Eucalyptus, 356–57

Euroimperialism, 327

Europe: idea of nature in, 220; peasant images, 133–37, 138, 140–41, 153, 167 nn.9, 11, 13; perception of tropics in, 32–34, 73 n.11; Sarawak Campaign, 332–35, 339; scientific forestry, 280 n.25

European Parliament, 322, 334

European Union, 58

Evav (Kei), 52, 68

Everyman, concept of, 148, 155

Evolution, 35, 36

Fabrics, 189–90, 192, 196 n.40

Fairhead, J., 123 n.31

Families/family units, 155–56, 159–60

Famine, 181, 195 n.24

Famine Commission (India), 257

FAO. *See* United Nations Food and Agriculture Organization

Farmers, 147–53, 157

Fasts, 322, 334

Feasts, 353

Federal Land Development Authority (FELDA; Malaysia), 147

Ferguson, James, 276

Fern Gully: The Last Rainforest (1997), 329, 343

Fertilizer, 173, 186–87, 192, 195–96 n.31

Feudalism, 137, 139, 150

Field-forest dialectic, 110–14

Fire, anthropogenesis of, 108

Firewood, 181–83

Floods, 350, 359, 366 n.3

Flour mills, 185, 187–88, 189

Foege, William, 227–28 n.4

Foley, Kathy, 122 n.24

Folklore, 260

Forbes, Henry, 72 n.2

Forbes, W. Cameron, 42, 44

Ford Foundation, 163

Foreign Investment Act (Indonesia; 1967), 239

Forest Act (India; 1878), 87

Forest Act (India; 1927), 95

Forest agent (India), 178, 180–81, 195 nn.17, 20, 274, 284 n.75, 295

Forest Conservation Act (India; 1980), 222

Forest fundamentalism, 104

Forestry Act (Indonesia; 1967), 239, 240–41, 242

Forests: alien species in, 20, 170–92; community forests, 23, 347–65, 366 n.11; and ethnography, 107–14; forest law origins, 261, 280 n.28; as global environmental focus, 103–5, 340; improvement felling, 269–70, 284 nn.65, 69, 70; mythologies of, 113, 122 nn.18, 21; old growth, 338; peasant access to, 11, 223, 241, 242, 244; place of temperate forests, 335–36, 338

Forests (India): colonial era, 11, 19, 21, 85–91, 95, 254–63, 275–77, 279–80 nn.21, 28, 285 n.78; conservation policy, 222–23, 257, 262, 276, 279 n.15; defined, 193 n.3; kham system (forest leasing), 87; local knowledge of, 257, 258, 265, 278 n.9, 279 n.18, 284 n.69, 301–2; management policy, 82–91, 93–98, 118, 122–23 nn.29, 32, 175, 190, 223, 258; and nation-building, 275, 285 n.81; nevad clearings, 294–96, 298, 314; Project Tiger, 216, 218, 230 n.23; regeneration systems, 270–73, 284 n.72; territorialization, 261; timber harvest permit system, 266, 282 n.52; trees/rulers relationship, 179–80, 195 n.19. *See also* Nistār; Scientific forestry

Forests (Indonesia): colonial era, 238–39, 241, 247–49, 251 n.7; forest cover, 106; legal claims to, 240–42; management policy, 116–17, 141, 237; Population Resettle-

Forests (Indonesia) (*cont.*)
ment program, 116. *See also* Rain
forests
Forests (Malaysia), 119–20
Forests (Pakistan), 106–9, 116
Forests (Thailand), 351; community
forests, 23, 347–65, 366 n.11; na-
tional forest reserves, 357–58,
362; tree ordination, 23, 347,
348–51, 354, 358, 362–64, 366
n.11
Forest Stewardship Council, 341
Foster-Quirino Agreement (Philip-
pines), 150
Foucault, Michel, 13, 105–6, 253,
278 n.3
Fourth Five Year Plan (India), 222
Fourth World Forestry Congress
(1954), 82
Fox, James J., 111
Fox, Jeff, 242
France, 134–35, 284 n.69
Freer, Paul C., 43
Friends of the Earth, 324, 332
Frontier, notions of, 39, 43, 46 n.26,
149, 168 n.21
Fruit trees, 244, 246

Gadchiroli District, Maharashtra
Province, 97
Gadgil, Madhav, 87, 191
Gandhi, Indira, 202, 210, 212, 213,
220, 221–26, 229–30 n.22
Gandhi, Mahatma, 194 n.14, 225–
26, 227 n.2, 305
Gandhi Peace Foundation, 307
Gandhi, Rajiv, 219, 220
Garcia, Jerry, 319
Gardens/gardening practices, 186–
87, 248
Geertz, Clifford, 141, 142–43
Gender roles, 150, 156, 158–59,
160, 169 nn.28, 29
General Agreement on Tariffs and
Trade (GATT), 329
Geography, study of, 6–7
Germany, 135–36, 167 n.9, 261
Ghatiyali, India, 170–92

Ghosh, Arin, 215, 219
Global environmental activism, 20,
162, 165, 202, 219–20; in India, 5,
7, 315; in Indonesia, 242, 249. *See
also* Campaigns; Environmental
movements; Transnationalism
Global lungs image, 103–4, 119
Global Positioning System (GPS),
242, 250
Gore, Al, 319, 333
Gouda, Frances, 137, 167 n.11
Gouldsbury, Charles E., 284 n.69
GPS. *See* Global Positioning System
Gramsci, Antonio, 124
Grateful Dead, 319, 333
Green consumerism, 318 n.17
Green Imperialism (Grove), 276
Green Nan Program (Thailand),
356–57
Greenough, Paul, 115
Greenpeace, 324, 332
Green Revolution, 8; in Indonesia,
116; in Malaysia, 156, 159; in
Thailand, 356–57
Grove, Richard, 30–31
Guattari, Felix, 104
Guha, Ramachandra, 87, 191
Gujarat, 301, 308, 311, 312, 317
n.10
Gujar, Bhoju Ram, 171, 179, 193
n.1, 318 n.15

Hacking, Ian, 256
Halai, 300
Hall, Stuart, 77–78 n.39
Hardiman, D., 98 n.2
Harra, 92–93
Harrison, Robert P., 328
Harrisson, Tom, 142
Hart, Gillian, 143, 156, 169 nn.28,
29
Harvey, David, 280 n.26
Hill, Leonard, 36–37, 42, 45 n.21
Hinduism, 303–4, 313
"Hippocratic agenda," 30, 44 n.1
Hitipeuw, C., 59
Holt, R. S., 284 n.72
Homesites, exchange of, 244

Homesteaders, 149
Homfray, C. K., 270, 284 n.69
Honey, 84
Hookworm, 39
Houghten, F. C., 37
Households. *See* Families/family
   units
HTI. *See* Hutan tanaman industri
Hukbalahap movement, 149
Huk peoples, 149, 150–51
Humboldt, Alexander von, 33
Hume, A. O., 223
Hunt, Chester, 144
Huntington, Ellsworth, 37–38, 41
Hutan tanaman industri (HTI; Indo-
   nesia), 116–17
Hutterer, Karl L., 31, 122 n.21
Huxley, T. H., 29

Ibanic dialect, 110, 122 n.15
Ideology, and agendas, 13–14
Imperata cylindrica (sword grass),
   117
Improvement felling, 269–70, 284
   nn.65, 69, 70
India, 79–98; antidam campaign
   (Andolan movement), 10, 22, 290,
   301, 305–6, 309–10; big game
   tourism, 211, 219; caste system,
   173, 285 n.82, 292, 293, 303, 318
   n.11; conservation legislation, 95,
   210, 222–23; currency, 195 n.18;
   definitions of land types, 88; Department of the Environment, 222,
   230 n.26; Emergency Act, 212,
   224, 228–29 n.18, 229–30 n.22;
   Forest Department, 295–96, 298,
   305, 317 n.7; government corruption, 180, 195 n.21; industrialization, 301–2; international
   relations, 202, 205; land reform,
   172; Non-resident Indians (NRIs),
   176; population economic classification, 88–90, 96–97; precolonial economy, 86, 98–99 n.15;
   smallpox eradication programs,
   201–9, 219–20, 227–28 nn.4, 6,
   8, 11; timber industry, 81, 82, 84,

87; trees/rulers relationship, 179–
   80, 195 n.19. *See also* Bengal; Forests (India); Rajasthan; Tigers; Villages
Indian National Congress, 223
Indigenization rebellion (Aru Islands), 55, 72–73 n.9
Indigenous agency, and environmental change, 116–18, 120, 122 n.28,
   166–67 n.8
Indigenous rights movements: global
   nature of, 5, 324, 331, 332, 334,
   337; in India, 291–92, 296–302;
   in Indonesia, 69–70, 77 n.35, 243,
   249; in Malaysia, 161, 320, 323,
   340, 347; in the Philippines, 125,
   161
Indonesia, 231–50; colonial era, 19,
   113–14, 139–41, 238–39, 241,
   247–49, 251 n.7; cultural ecology,
   49, 64–70, 71, 106, 123 n.34;
   customary law, 69–70, 74–75
   n.20, 76 n.32, 77 nn.35, 36, 232,
   236, 238, 239, 241, 251; environmental awareness programs, 59,
   125–26; ethnography of, 21, 105,
   107, 110–14; fisheries operations,
   59, 74 n.16; homesite transfer,
   244–45; hutan tanaman industri
   (HTI), 116–17; indigenous rights
   movement in, 69–70, 77 n.35;
   Konfrontasi, 239, 252 n.9; land
   use policy, 68, 238–42; nature reserves, 55–61, 74–75 n.20; resource management policy, 232–
   37, 245–49; spice trade, 65; timber industry, 65–66, 77 n.37, 117;
   transmigration policy, 116, 246.
   See also Aru Islands; Forests (Indonesia); Java
Indonesian Department of Nature
   Conservation (PHPA), 56, 57
Indonesian/Malay languages, 110
Industrialization, 224–25, 301–2
Indus Valley, 108
Integrated Tribal Development Pro-
   gram, 292
Internal colonization, 68

Monks. *See* Ecology monks

Moral ecology, 191–92

Mother-of-pearl. *See* Pearl cultivation

Mountfort, Guy, 210

MP. *See* Madhya Pradesh Province

Muda Irrigation Scheme, 159

Mughal empire, 86, 261

Multinational corporations, 223–24

Museums, 73 n.11, 335

Mushrooms, 350, 351, 352, 358

Mutang, Anderson, 334

Myers, Fred, 326

Myths: Bhilala myth of creation, 294; forest mythologies, 113, 122 nn.18, 21; "lost" Chinese cargo ship myth, 67–68, 76 n.31; national environmental ideologies as, 328

Napolean (humphead) wrasse, 74 n.16

Narmada Bachao Andolan. *See* Andolan movement

Nationalism, and environmental movements, 125–26, 222–23

Nationalist movements, 85

National Wildlife Action Plan (India; 1983), 222

Nation-building, 144–53, 254, 260–61, 275–77, 278 n.5, 285 n.81

Nature: colonial mindset, 29, 39, 220, 225; as factory, 52; fragmentation of, 62–63, 75 nn.25, 26; policing of, 55–61, 73 n.13, 225; quest for, 61–64, 74 n.18, 75 n.14; remaking of, 226; romanticizing of, 329–30, 346 n.8; scientific concept of, 203; as sublime, 42, 45 nn.20, 21; and tribalism, 289; zoning of, 58, 60

Nature-culture dialectic, 49, 64–70, 71, 109, 115–16

Nature-culture zones, 49, 64–70, 71

Nature reserves: in Bangladesh, 228 n.14; in Bengal, 264; in Indonesia, 55–61, 74–75 n.20; Project Tiger, 84, 209, 218, 228 nn.12, 14, 16; in Thailand, 357–58, 362

Naxalite groups, 297, 302, 305, 317 n.8

Nehru, Jawaharlal, 210, 220–21

Neocolonialism, 323, 339, 340

Nepal, 210, 228 n.12

Netherlands, 136–37, 167 nn.11–13

Netherlands East Indies, 11–12, 238, 251–52 n.8

Nevad clearings, 294–96, 297, 314

New Economic Policy (Malaysia), 158

New York Botanical Garden, 244

New Zealand, 38

Nistār (India), 81, 85–98, 98 n.10

Nongovernmental organizations (NGOs): ecology monks, 10–11, 22–23, 347–50, 355–64, 366 n.7; in Malaysia, 324, 332, 338–39, 338–40, 342; motives of, 7, 335, 337–41, 342–43; nature-culture dialectic, 49; North-South debate, 4–5, 321, 323, 329, 335–43; property rights, 232, 242–43, 250–51; role of, 341–42, 344; Sangath, 290–91, 295, 296–302, 304–6, 309–14, 316, 317 n.7; Sarawak Campaign, 321, 332–35, 337–41

Non-resident Indians (NRIs; India), 176

Nontimber forest products (NTFP), 79–80, 95; harvesting of, 11–12, 95, 96–97, 293, 350–52; income generation from, 19, 82–85, 98 n.3, 264, 282 n.45, 352; marketing of, 85, 92–93. *See also* Nistār

North, Shambhu, 184

North-South debate, 4–5, 321, 323, 329, 335–43

NRIs. *See* Non-resident Indians

NTFP. *See* Nontimber forest products

Nutmeg, 65

Old growth forests, 338

Ong, Aihwa, 158

Oral history, 170–72, 194 nn.6, 7, 246

Orissa Forest Enquiry Committee (1959), 95

Orissa Province (India), 79, 81, 84, 85, 93–98
Osmaston, F. C., 267, 273
Outer Islands, Indonesia, 240, 241, 251–52 n.8

Padoch, Christine, 244
Pakistan, 202; cultural ecology of, 106; ethnography of, 105; Northwest Frontier Province, 116; social outcasts in, 116. *See also* Forests (Pakistan)
Pakistan Forest Service, 109
Panchayati raj (local government), 311
Papuans, 52–53
Partai Islam SeMalaysia (PAS), 158
Paternalism, 307, 318 n.13
Pearl cultivation, 55, 57–59, 68, 72 n.7, 74 n.19, 77 n.36
Peasant life (Volkskunde), 135–36
Peasants, 130–61, 163–65; and allegory, 20, 124–25, 166 n.6; colonial administration of, 138, 143–44, 167 n.14; core peasant models, 128–29, 130, 137–44; defined, 124, 163–64, 165; European images of, 133–37, 138, 140–41, 153, 167 nn.9, 11, 13; forest access, 11, 223, 241, 242, 244; as homesteaders, 149; and local land use, 128–29, 166 n.6; national environmental movements, 125–26; politicization of, 143–54, 157–61, 169 n.28, 194 n.14; population control policies, 146, 168 n.20. *See also* Tribes/tribalism
Peasant studies, 126–33, 146–47, 153–55, 166 nn.3–5, 7, 168 nn.25, 26
Peluso, Nancy Lee, 280 n.27
Pelzer, Karl, 141–42, 168 n.21
Pemberton, John, 137
Penang, Malaysia, 324
Penan peoples, 22, 319–27; international profile of, 322, 326–27, 332–33, 335, 342, 343; Malay government profile of, 327–28

Permit system, 266, 282 n.52
Persoon, G. A., 74 n.15
Petuanan (managed territories), 58
Philippines: environmental movement in, 125–26; Foster-Quirino Agreement, 150; Hukbalahap movement, 149; land reform policies, 150–51, 168 n.24; medical study in, 43; national administration, 149–51; nineteenth-century encounters with, 18–19, 33–35, 42–43; Poverty Alleviation Program, 163; Spanish administration of, 136; tenant farmers, 147, 148–49, 151, 152; U.S. administration of, 37, 38–39, 41–42, 45 n.14, 147–50
PHPA. *See* Indonesian Department of Nature Conservation
Phrakhru Pitak Nanthakhun. *See* Pitak
Phra Somkit, 361
Physiology, colonial theories on, 37–38
Pigg, Stacy Leigh, 285 n.81
Pitak, 22, 347, 349–50, 355–64
Plantation schemes. *See* Afforestation
Plekhanov, Georgy Valentinovich, 135
Political agency, 329, 330, 344
Pond field system, 111–13, 118, 120, 122 nn.19, 20
Population classification (India), 88–90, 96–97. *See also* Caste system
Population control policies, 146, 168 n.20
Population Resettlement program (Indonesia), 116
Poverty Alleviation Program (Philippines), 163
Prasad, Archana, 93, 98 n.13, 282 n.45
Pratt, Mary Louise, 327
Projects, 15–17; Marine Turtle Project (IUCN; Indonesia), 58; Project Tiger, 20–21, 201–3, 209–20, 225, 228 n.12, 14–16, 229–30 nn.22, 23; World Bank Forestry

Stebbing, E. P., 280 n.22, 284 n.69
Suharto, 71, 236, 239, 240
Sukarno, 239, 240
Sumatra, 113–14, 122 n.25, 251–52
n.8
Sustainable development, 3–4, 74
n.19, 289–90, 300–302, 304–5,
309, 312, 316
Sustainable forestry, 339
Svensson, Thommy, 141
Swidden systems: Indonesia, 236,
240, 244–49; Malaysia, 119, 142–
43; Southeast Asia, 111–13, 120,
122 nn.18–21, 25
Sword grass (*Imperata cylindrica*),
117
swrc. *See* Social Work and Research
Center

Theravada Buddhism, 360
Taft, W. H., 39
Tagalog peoples, 148
Tanimbar Kei, 52, 68–69
Taungya system, 267, 270, 272
Taylor, J. C., 230 n.24
Taylor, Jean, 137
Tea cultivation, 264
Teak forests, 81, 82, 239, 262, 269,
279–80 n.21, 291, 351
Tembawang (fruit forests; Indo-
nesia), 244–46, 249
Temperate forests, place of, 335–36,
338
Temperature, measurement of, 36–
37
Temple, Richard, 281 n.31
Tenant farmers, 147–53, 157
Ternate, Indonesia, 65
Territorialization (Indonesia): prop-
erty rights, 231–35, 251 n.1; and
resource management policy, 21,
235–38
Thailand, 22, 347–65; conservation
associations, 349, 357–58, 362;
ecology monks, 10–11, 22–23,
347–50, 355–64, 366 n.7; flood-
ing in, 350, 359, 366 n.3; national
forest reserves, 357–58, 362; radi-

cal conservatism, 10–11, 347, 354,
355, 358, 365 n.1; Royal Forestry
Department, 358; tree ordination,
23, 347, 348–51, 354, 358, 362–
64, 366 n.11
Thaluas (landless tenants; India), 91
Third World, 153–54
Thompson, E. P., 280 n.28
Tiagi, B., 175
Tiger Information Center Web site,
228 nn.12, 15
Tigers: killing of, 216, 230 nn.23, 24;
population counts, 202, 209–11,
212–13, 219, 227 n.3, 228 n.15,
229–30 nn.19, 22, 25, 230 n.25;
Project Tiger, 20–21, 201–3, 209–
20, 225, 228 nn.12, 14–16, 229–
30 nn.22, 23; symbolism of, 113
"Tiger Tales" (*Times of India*), 213–
14, 215
Timber industry: Bengal, 262, 265–
66, 282 n.52; India, 81, 82, 84, 87,
256; Indonesia, 65–66, 77 n.37,
117, 239, 240, 252 n.10; ITTO,
321, 336, 341, 344; Malaysia,
320–21, 323, 339
Times of India, Project Tiger coverage, 213–14, 216–17, 218, 229
n.20
Tobacco, 113–14, 122 n.25, 361
Torrid Zone, 29
Tourism, 125, 211, 219, 228 n.14
Trade unions. *See* Sangath
Tradition: interpretation of, 60, 74
n.18, 75 nn.21, 22, 105, 191; and
peasants, 140–41; role of, 133–34,
166 n.7
Traditional use zones, 60–61
Transmigration, 141–42, 147, 149,
168 n.21, 246
Transnationalism, 5, 21–22, 320,
329, 330–31, 343
Tree plantations. *See* Afforestation
Trees: ordination of, 23, 347, 348–
51, 354, 358, 362–64, 366 n.11;
Western symbolism of, 104. *See
also* Forests
Tribes/tribalism, 161–65; and alle-

Library of Congress Cataloging-in-Publication Data

Nature in the global south : environmental projects in South and Southeast Asia / Paul Greenough and Anna Lowenhaupt Tsing, editors.

p. cm.

Includes bibliographical references and index.

ISBN 0-8223-3150-0 (cloth: acid-free paper)

ISBN 0-8223-3149-7 (pbk.: acid-free paper)

1. Environmental management — South Asia. 2. Sustainable development — South Asia. 3. Environmental management — Asia, Southeastern. 4. Sustainable development — Asia, Southeastern. I. Greenough, Paul. II. Tsing, Anna Lowenhaupt.

GE320.S64N37 2003

333.7′2′0954 — dc21   2003004909